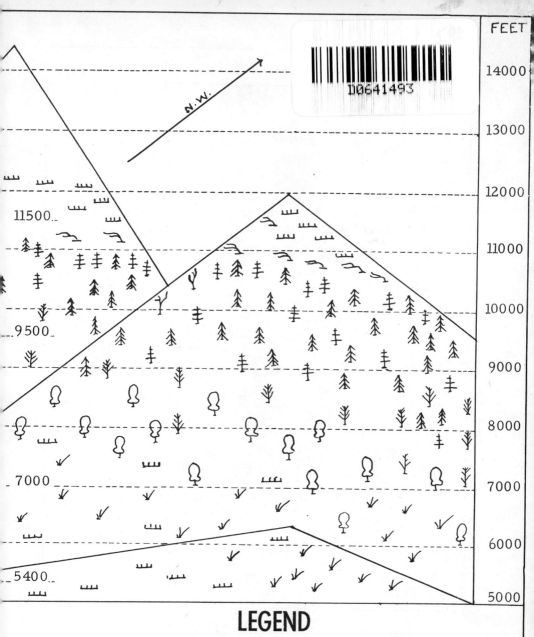

FEET

14000

N.W.

13000

12000

11500

11000

10000

9500

9000

8000

7000

7000

6000

5400

5000

LEGEND

(Life zone equals vegetation zone.)

The chart shows a simplified diagram of the life zones as they appear along the east face of the Front Range in Colorado.

Corresponding plant communities are at higher elevations at the southern end and on the south-facing slopes than they are on the north-facing slopes, with some "inter-fingering."

(See chapter on life zones, p. 27.)

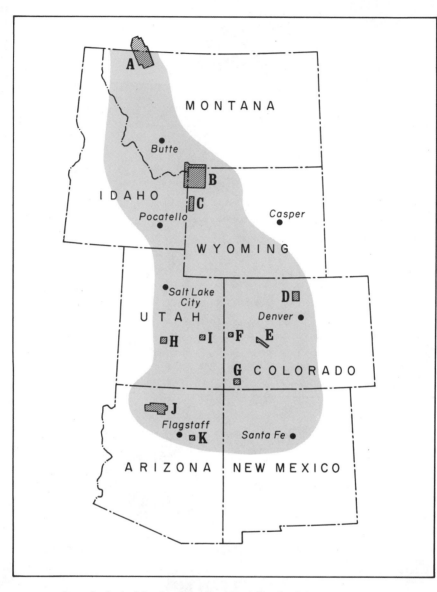

Area included in the *Handbook of Rocky Mountain Plants*
National Parks and Monuments in the Area:

 A. Glacier National Park
 B. Yellowstone National Park
 C. Grand Teton National Park
 D. Rocky Mountain National Park
 E. Black Canyon of the Gunnison National Monument
 F. Colorado National Monument
 G. Mesa Verde National Park
 H. Cedar Breaks National Monument
  I. Canyon Lands National Park
 J. Grand Canyon National Park
 K. Walnut Canyon National Monument

handbook of
Rocky Mountain Plants

by Ruth Ashton Nelson

drawings by
Dorothy V. Leake

Skyland Publishers
Box 1258, Estes Park, Colorado 80517

Library of Congress Catalog Card No. 75-82307
ISBN No. 0-912762-08-x paperbound
ISBN No. 0-912762-09-8 clothbound

Copyright 1969
Second edition, 1977
Third edition, 1979
by
Ruth Ashton Nelson

Skyland Publishers
Box 1258, Estes Park, Colorado 80517

PRINTERS & LITHOGRAPHERS
ESTES PARK.   COLORADO

Manufactured in the United States of America

This book is presented to
plant lovers of the Rocky Mountain region
as a memorial to

AVEN NELSON

Inspiring Teacher
Faithful Friend
Beloved Companion

Contents

Preface

This book is written for outdoor people who are neither botanists nor even natural scientists, but who would like to be able to identify the wildflowers they see on their mountain excursions, and who might, along the way, be encouraged to acquire some interesting, non-technical information about plants in general and the places where plants live. Some of this background information is drawn from historical, ecological, geological, ethnobotanical, economic and conservation sources. Much of it is based on personal observation and experience.

The main purpose of the book is to give residents and visitors to the region the means of identifying plants on a simplified botanical basis. In addition it is my desire to suggest some of the many fascinating fields which are open for exploration, in the hope that some readers may be inclined to venture farther, but it is not within the scope of this work to go deeply into the many phases of botany and geology touched upon.

In treating a scientific subject in a "popular" manner an author always encounters pitfalls. Generalizations are dangerous, but more meaningful to the uninitiated than elaborately detailed explanations. It is in the nature of living organisms to vary, and thus they never perfectly fit man's attempts to classify them. Instead of citing exceptions which, it is felt, would only confuse most users of this book, a liberal use is made of qualifying adjectives.

Keys, based whenever possible on the most obvious characteristics, are drawn to fit the conspicuous plants and those important from the wildflower lovers' point of view. To provide for all of the rarely seen or inconspicuous species which are mentioned in the text would have made the keys too cumbersone to serve their purpose. The using of keys is a valuable exercise in observation. They are supplied because many users of my earlier publication, *Plants of Rocky Mountain National Park,* which contains similar keys, have found them helpful

Where no key to a large group is given it is because the botanical details that differentiate the individuals are too technical to permit a popular treatment.

For serious students and trained botanists there are many other more valuable volumes. But if those who drive the highways, ride the horse trails, walk the paths, roam the canyons, and climb the heights, find herein something to enrich their experiences, this book will have fulfilled its purpose.

The following explanations may be of interest to professional botanists. Authors' names, which in technical publications follow the plant's specific name, are omitted because it it believed that they are of no interest to the majority of those who will use the book. If desired they can easily be found by reference to one of the floras listed in the Useful References, p 312.

Due to the extensive area covered which has never been treated as a whole by any authoritative botanical work it has not been possible consistently to follow any one author in choosing names. In general, Latin names have been used in accordance with the most recent works on the individual regions, but in some instances when it seemed this would result in confusion for the users of this book, an older or more widely known name has been retained. In the use of common names I have, in the main followed the same proceedure, but occasionally it has been necessary to choose from several names or to use the generic name where there is no appropriate or generally accepted common name.

Some supplementary Latin names are included. These follow the accepted names in parentheses. In some cases they are synonyms in the strict botanical sense. In other cases they are names which in one way or another—sometimes erroneously—have come into use for the plant under consideration and have been so generally known that some readers are familiar with them. They are included as a convenience to those who may be looking for a familiar name.

No one could write a book such as this without making extensive use of the work of other authors. Two volumes have been my almost constant companions during the years this work has been in progress. First: the *Manual of Plants of Colorado* by H. D. Harrington, professor of botany and curator of the herbarium, Colorado State University. Dr. Harrington's painstaking labor in assembling· detailed information on all flowering plants known to grow in Colorado, together with their geographic ranges, has supplied me with an invaluable foundation on which to base my own work.

Second: *Rocky Mountain Flora,* and its predecessor, *Handbook of Plants of the Colorado Front Range,* by Wm. A. Weber, professor of natural history and curator of the herbarium, University of Colorado Museum. Dr. Weber has been most generous of his time and helpful with his knowledge, besides graciously allowing use of the Museum herbarium.

The other state and regional floras, the texts dealing with ecology and geology and the popular handbooks cited in the Useful References, as well as many publications not mentioned, have all been much used and appreciated sources from which important material has been obtained.

The privilege of using the herbaria of the region has been of equal importance with books in determining the identity of plants and their relationships, and in making the decisions as to which species should be included and which excluded. My gratitude goes to Dr. C. L. Porter, curator of the Rocky Mountain Herbarium, University of Wyoming, for permission to use the specimens under his care and for his kind assistance; also to Dr. C. Wm. T. Penland, professor of botany at Colorado College, and to Dr. George J. Goodman, of the University of Oklahoma, for reading parts of the manuscript and giving valuable suggestions; and to Dr. Chas. T. Mason, Jr., of the University of Arizona Herbarium for his helpful reading of the entire text.

I wish also to express appreciation to the following ecologists who have read and given useful suggestions on Part I which deals with the environment: the late Dr. Herbert C. Hanson, formerly with the University of Notre Dame; Dr. Elroy Rice, Plant Science Department, University of Oklahoma; Dr. Beatrice Willard, University of Colorado Institute of Arctic and Alpine Research. To Dr. Willard, and to other personal friends, go special appreciation for encouragement and for help in field work. Finally, I would express much gratitude to Dr. Dorothy Van Dyke Leake, who has expertly and patiently—sometimes under trying circumstances—made the numerous line drawings without which the text would be of little value.

Illustrations

COLOR PICTURES

There are 72 in the center section of the book. They are arranged in the same numerical order as used in the text.

Pl. 1a-ALPINE LADY FERN, *Athyrium alpestre* var. *americanum* (7), p. 57.

Pl. 1b-WHITE FIR, *Abies concolor*, p. 65.

Pl. 1c-ENGELMANN SPRUCE, *Picea engelmanni* (16), p. 66, and BIG SAGE, *Artemisia tridentata*, p. 306.

Pl. 1d-CREEPING JUNIPER, *Juniper horizontalis*, p. 67.

Pl. 1e-WESTERN SPIDERWORT, *Tradescantia occidentalis* (25), p. 78.

Pl. 1f-WOODLILY, *Lilium philadelphicum* (33), p. 82.

Pl. 2a-YELLOWBELLS, *Fritillaria pudica* (35), p. 82.

Pl. 2b-SANDLILY, *Leucocrinum montanum* (36), p. 84.

Pl. 2c-MARIPOSA LILY, *Calochortus gunnisonii* (42), p. 87.

Pl. 2d-ALPLILY, *Lloydia serotina* (43), p. 88.

Pl. 2e-WESTERN TRILLIUM, *Trillium ovatum*, p. 88.

Pl. 2f-YELLOW LADY SLIPPER, *Cypripedium calceolus* (46) p. 90.

Pl. 3a-FAIRY SLIPPER, *Calypso bulbosa* (48), p. 91.

Pl. 3b-Leaves of W. RED BIRCH, *Betula occidentalis*, in autumn, p. 102.

Pl. 3c-BITTER ROOT, *Lewisia rediviva* (76), p. 115.

Pl. 3d-MOSS CAMPION, *Silene acaulis*, (79), p. 117.

Pl. 3e-ARCTIC SANDWORT, *Arenaria obtusaloba* (83), p. 120.

Pl. 3f-YELLOW PONDLILY, *Nuphar luteum* var. *polysepalum* (85), p. 121.

Pl. 4a-SUBALPINE CLEMATIS, *Clematis pseudoalpina*, p. 124.

Pl. 4b-COLORADO COLUMBINE, *Aquilegia caerulea* (88), p. 125.

Pl. 4c-W. RED COLUMBINE, *Aquilegia elegantula* (90), p. 126.

Pl. 4d-SUBALPINE BUTTERCUP, *Ranunculus eschscholtzia*, p. 129.

Pl. 4e-WHITE MARSH-MARIGOLD, *Caltha leptosepala* (97), p. 130.

Pl. 4f-NELSON LARKSPUR, *Delphinium nelsonii* (104), p. 135.

Pl. 5a-GOLDEN DRABA, *Draba aurea* (113), p. 143.

Pl. 5b-ROSECROWN, *Sedum rhodanthum* (121), p. 148.

Pl. 5c-FENDLERBUSH, *Fendler rupicola* (122), p. 149.

Pl. 5d-JAMESIA, *Jamesia americana*, in autumn (124), p. 150.

Pl. 5e-APACHE PLUME, *Fallugia paradoxa* (141), p. 161.

Pl. 5f-CLIFF ROSE, *Cowania mexicana*, p. 162.

Pl. 6a-DWARF or DEER CLOVER, *Trifolium nanum* (164), p. 177.

Pl. 6b-NEW MEXICAN LOCUST, *Robinia neomexicana* (169), p. 179.

Pl. 6c-LAMBERT LOCO-WEED, *Oxytropis lambertii* (176), p. 184.

Cover color pictures: *top*, aspen in autumn; *middle*, field of Beargrass in Glacier National Park; *bottom*, Indian Paintbrush in Colorado.

PHOTOGRAPHIC PLATES

LINE DRAWINGS AND DIAGRAMS
ILLUSTRATING CHARACTERISTICS
OF PLANT AND FLOWER

LINE DRAWINGS OF INDIVIDUAL PLANTS

Introduction

Plants are friends to man and very interesting ones when man takes the trouble to become acquainted with them. Outdoor activities become more meaningful when we recognize kinds of plants by their individual characteristics, learn something about the relationships between them, and understand the part they play in making our earth a livable place.

The Rocky Mountain region provides a distinct set of living conditions for plants. These are different from those of other geographic regions such as New England, the Mississippi Valley, the Pacific Coast or the semi-desert Southwest.

Because this region is so different its plants are worthy of special attention. In the montane regions at least 75% of the species belong exclusively to the mountains. For the subalpine regions the figure is even higher. The mountains have such a great variety of subsidiary climatic conditions that the number of kinds of plants found here is very great. More than 900 are described in this book but that is only a portion of the whole number.

When one starts learning about plants he soon finds that environment, that is, living conditions, has much to do in determining where certain kinds of plants grow. The study of living organisms (plants or animals) in relation to their environment is called *ecology*. There are several factors which determine environment. The most important of them are climate, soil structure and, in our region, the effects of altitude.

To understand why and how certain kinds of plants live where they do one must learn something about plant ecology, so the first part of this book will take up environmental conditions in the Rocky Mountains and the second part will name and describe plants that grow in this environment.

Part I: The Environment

CLIMATE AND ADAPTATIONS

The Rocky Mountain climate is characterized by dryness, abundant sunlight, and rapid temperature changes. There is a great difference between day and night temperatures. During the growing season the difference between the extremes of day and night averages nearly 30 degrees. There is also a wide difference between temperatures in sun and shade because the air, becoming thinner as the altitude increases, loses its heat-holding capacity proportionately. Precipitation is low and evaporation is high.

Because the elevation of this entire area is above 5,000 feet the atmosphere is clear; humidity is normally low and light is intense. Our weather produces occasional periods of high winds especially in winter, and sometimes local cloudbursts, when torrents of rain wash away soil uprooting plants in the process. At high altitudes the drying and scouring effect of wind· is severe. Spring comes late and autumn early.

These conditions eliminate most lush-looking, tender-foliaged plants and those dependent on mild temperatures and high humidity. We have hardy, needle-leaved evergreen trees, a few of the most hardy deciduous trees, many drouth-resistant shrubs and numerous smaller plants which are especially adapted to resist loss of moisture from their foliage. These give the mountains a distinctive type of vegetation which is of great beauty and interest.

Annual precipitation, including rain and snow, at the base of the mountains between 5,000 and 6,000 feet is somewhere between 11 and 14 inches. It increases with an increase in altitude. Estes Park, at 7,500 feet, receives about 18 inches. At 9,000 feet on Longs Peak it averages 21½ inches and in some places at timberline, which is between 11,000 and 12,000 feet in central Colorado, it may be 30 inches or more. As a comparison, the normal annual amount of water available to plants in the Mississippi Valley varies from 30 to 60 inches.

The small amount of rainfall is not the only condition which affects a plant's moisture supply here. The high rate of evaporation is also important. Some of the snow evaporates (scientists say *sublimates*) without melting. Dry air, especially when in motion as wind, constantly removes moisture from plant tissues and unless this can be replaced from the soil through the root system, the plant will wilt and perhaps die. Another factor is soil texture. Much mountain soil is made up of coarse particles which have very little water-holding capacity, so that rainfall and melted snow drain away rapidly.

18

With the foregoing conditions in mind we should not be surprised that many mountain plants are equipped by nature to survive adverse conditions, and that few of them have the bright green appearance of plants which grow in more humid climates. However, there are exceptions. In the varied conditions presented by this mountain environment there are certain areas where local conditions are very favorable for plants requiring abundant moisture and sheltered situations. These climates within climates are called micro-climates.

Exposure has much to do with the micro-climates. Mountainsides which face the sun are warmer and dry out more quickly than those which are turned away from its direct rays. On slopes facing south and southwest snow melts and evaporates quickly. On those facing north and northeast it persists and accumulates. This in part accounts for the fact that ridges are often forested on one side and grass or shrub-covered on the other. It explains why streams are most abundant on the northern sides of our mountain ranges.

Still another influence which affects plant life in mountainous regions is the length of the growing season. Partly because mountain masses tend to cool the atmosphere surrounding them and partly because an increase in elevation is somewhat similar in effect on climate to an increase in latitude, the growing season is shortened as the altitude is increased. Frosts occur late in spring and come early in the fall. This means that the plants here ordinarily make less growth in a single season than those which live where the season is longer. Cool nights also tend to limit the rate of growth. It takes more years for trees to attain a size comparable to that of trees growing under more favorable conditions. Often plant growth is retarded as the result of a late freeze coming after the buds have unfolded in spring; sometimes a freeze in late summer or early autumn destroys the seed crop.

Because of the severe conditions of this mountain environment many of the plants which grow here show more or less conspicuous adaptations to these conditions. It seems evident that the native vegetation of any region has been formed during periods of geologic time, as the region developed, by the process of evolution. By careful observation anyone can see that the offspring of a particular pair of parents show some slight variations, whether the parents are people, dogs or Ponderosa Pine trees. In very simple terms evolution means that those individuals which have characteristics that make them better adapted to their environment are the ones which survive and perpetuate these characteristics in their descendents. This process, carried on over millions of years, results in a population of plants that have become adapted to their environment.

The adaptations shown by Rocky Mountain plants are mainly those which reduce evaporation from plant tissues, which make possible the storage of water and which give the ability to produce and mature seed in a short season. Loss of water is reduced by firm waxy surfaces as on yucca or kinnikinnik leaves and by reduction of surface area as in pine and spruce tree needles. Another device which helps to reduce evaporation, often seen especially in grasses and in ferns, is the inrolling of the margins of leaves. The presence of coatings of hairs, as on sagebrush foliage, protects plant tissues from intense light and heat. Plants which store water in their stems or leaves are called succulents. Some examples found here are several kinds of cactus plants, stonecrops, and saxifrages.

Mountain vegetation includes a large proportion of perennial plants as compared to annuals and this proportion increases as altitude increases. In the alpine regions there are only two or three annual species. Perennials have an advantage in a short-season climate because they are ready to start flowering immediately when spring arrives. Many mountain plants bloom before their leaves unfold, or as they are unfolding. The climax of all flowering plant activity is seed production. Plants that bloom early and so assure ample time for the seeds to mature have an advantage in a short-season climate. This is increasingly important at the higher elevations where the growing season may not be much over a month long.

SOIL BUILDING

There are some stream-watered valleys between the mountains where fields of wildflowers and lush hay meadows flourish on deep, fine-grained soil. There are also great areas of hillside where the slope varies from gentle to very steep and the soil is thin and gravelly. Here we find dry land plants. The aspects of the two types are very different. A little study of the forces which bring about these results will help us to understand why this is so. A comparison of soil samples from two such areas is interesting. In the well-watered valley we find the soil is fine grained and dark in color. If we take a handful of this soil when it is moist and squeeze it, it will stick together. The soil from the dry hillside is light colored, coarse grained and the particles will not adhere to each other even when wet. The reason for the difference is that the first contains humus and the second lacks it. Humus is the dark colored, fibrous substance which results from the decomposition of vegetable matter.

With the low annual rainfall and frequent long periods of drouth which are characteristic of this region the plant growth of each year is much less than in more humid regions and the decomposition takes place more slowly. The result is that at the end of each growing season the amount of decayed vegetable matter added to the soil is relatively small. In many places, especially at the higher elevations, there is no soil cover—the bare rock is exposed. Sometimes this is because there has not yet been an opportunity for soil formation and sometimes it is because what soil was formed has been carried away by glaciers, blown away by wind, or washed away by running water.

Right here in our own area we have the opportunity to see how the original bedrock of our earth is transformed into soil. Plants play an important part in it, but first the process is started by physical forces: the sun's heat, frost, water and wind.

Many of our rocks are granular, composed of hard grains held together by softer substances. Rain, as it falls, absorbs carbon dioxide from the air and so by the time it reaches the earth's surface it has become slightly acid. Thus as rain water runs down periodically and streams run continuously during long periods of time, the softer parts of granite or sandstone and other rocks are partially or completely dissolved.

Changes in temperature, from extreme cold to extreme heat and the reverse, result in alternate expanding and contracting of minerals. This further weakens the rock structure.

By the dissolving action of water and the expanding-contracting effect of changing temperature small cracks or pockets are formed in the rock. When water fills these openings and freezes, it expands. Thus frost puts pressure on the rock and forces cracks to widen or pieces to break off.

Then the wind enters into this story by blowing away loosened pieces and dropping them in other places.

On boulders, cliffs and rock walls of canyons there are patches which are different from the basic color of the rock itself. They show their colors of gray, pale grayish-green, soft dull yellow, black, and sometimes orange, most plainly when wet. In one place the patterns are definitely circular, in another the colors and patterns are less definitely defined, blending into each other. Scratch off a bit of the colored matter and you discover that you have in your hand not rock but a soft material which feels a little like wet leather, though not so tough. Probably some gritty bits of rock will be sticking to it.

What you are holding is a very important plant called a *lichen*. It is interesting to see that plants actually help to break down the rocks and build up the soil. Lichens and certain mosses are the first plants to gain footholds on rocks.

Plate I — *Soil building. Plant succession on a rock surface. Southwest-facing rock, montane zone, moderately dry. Shows lichens (note circular patch at right), mosses (small dark cushions), and various pioneer seed plants in pockets and crevices. Photo by author.*

The lichens stick very tightly to the surface and when they dry out they curl up or shrink together. In doing this they pull very strongly on the bits of which rocks are made and some particles may come away as grains of sand.

Mosses are usually small, cushion-like plants which are able to absorb and hold moisture. They become established in pockets or crevices of rocks where a few mineral particles have accumulated.

As water collects in these depressions the dead particles of plant bodies slowly decay. As they decay they become humus and so both the lichens and the mosses help to start the gradual process of soil building. As soon as organic life is present in any form, no matter how small, organic acids are present and both the lichens and mosses secrete small amounts of acid which, becoming dissolved in water, add to its ability to break down rocks—to loosen the particles of which the rocks are made.

Eventually the wind brings some seeds which drop into the crevices. When spring comes with melting snow and rain a moss bed makes a perfect nursery for the seeds and they soon absorb enough moisture to cause them to sprout. Before long seed plants, perhaps grasses or shrubs, send roots into the litter in the crevice and by dropping leaves year after year add their contribution to the developing soil of a slowly growing island of vegetation. All this time the weather has been causing a slow disintegration of the rock surface and particles of it have dropped off now and then. Also, leaves and

Plate II — *Soil building. Plant succession on a rock surface. Northwest-facing rock, montane zone, shows mosses and lichens, and, in addition, mats of* LITTLE CLUB MOSS *and conspicious* ALUMROOT *and* BRITTLE FERN *in crevices. Photo by author.*

perhaps pine needles carried by the wind from other places pile up around it. In this way bedrock is gradually buried in soil.

Around pools of water plant succession follows a different pattern. Here small plants called *algae*, which belong to the large group including the seaweeds and pond scums, are the first living plants to become established. Some of these float in the water, others adhere to wet rocks at the margins. There are also water-loving mosses and their relatives, the liverworts, which become established among rocks at the water's edge and help to build up pockets of soil.

But the most numerous in this succession are certain seed plants which become established, some on the wet mud of the shore, others in shallow water, others in deeper water. Some of these are rooted in the mud at the bottom in water several feet deep and are completely submersed; others grow in less deep water with their leaves floating; others stand in shallow water with their stems and leaves erect, extending above the water. There are also free-floating species which form masses of tangled vegetation. So there develop around these ponds visible, concentric zones of differing vegetation. In the Rocky Mountains the floating-leaf zone is often composed of pond-lilies (85), water buckwheat (67) and buckbean (250). The shallow water zone is occupied by species of sedge, rushes, and water grasses. Back of these there may be willows and other shrubs and still farther back, dryland grasses.

Gradually the accumulation of decaying vegetable matter builds up a type of soil called peat which is composed mostly of humus. This lowers the water level and consequently plants which require a drier habitat take root and by competition the wetland plants are pushed towards the water which is gradually becoming shallower as the pond fills up with this peat and the sand and other particles carried into it by water flowing down from higher ground. So, by degrees, the outer zone changes from a water habitat to a meadow and in time the pond will disappear.

Plant succession usually proceeds more rapidly around water than on dry rocks but around the very high altitude lakes which occupy glacial rock basins there is little opportunity for this sequence to take place. The very low temperatures and short ice-free season do not permit much annual growth, so there is little accumulation of soil.

Often soil is found in little pockets and on shelves and crevices of the walls of the canyons and cliffs throughout the Rocky Mountain area. In these places hardy plants, shrubs, and small trees grow singly or in small groups for a time. But another step in soil building may occur when increased amounts of running water flowing over the rocks down steep slopes catch up some of these little islands and accumulations, and carry all along to nearly level ground. Here as its pace is slowed it begins to let go of its load. First the heavier rocks and larger pieces drop out, and then the smaller ones.

As floods succeed each other, each adding a layer of soil through ages of time, what is called a "flood plain" is built up. This happens in mountain valleys and where valleys open out onto the plains. In these places the soil may be deep and fertile. The dead and rotting lichen, moss, leaves, roots of grass plants and sedges, all contribute to this fertility by helping soil to retain moisture; and also, as their particles are broken down, they release chemical substances which provide elements necessary for plant life. In brief and very much simplified, that is the story of soil formation. As it proceeds, plant communities change from pioneer communities to more complex and highly developed ones.

SHAPING THE LANDSCAPE

From individual drops of rain, each one contributing to the dissolution of a piece of granite, to mighty rivers carving out beds for themselves such as the Grand Canyon, the Black Canyon of the Gunnison, or the Columbia River Valley, water is one of the most powerful influences which has been and is at work in shaping our landscape. It transports the material which its force has removed thousands of miles to build up deltas of fertile soil.

As we have seen, rivers rushing down from high land to the plains cut themselves valleys. Waters originating in high, rocky regions follow cracks or weak places in the rocks, enlarging these by the grinding effect of the debris which they carry. Waters falling on less rugged ground accumulate in the depressions and flow away more gently in the direction of the main slope of the land. But they also produce some erosion. In both cases the valleys which these streams cut for themselves are V-shaped. In some instances where streams follow joints in the rock itself this is not always evident—but in general their side walls slope away from the river bed and contributing streams cut their beds at the same rate as the main stream so their beds open into the larger valley on a level with its bed. A magnificent example of a V-shaped valley is the Grand Canyon of the Yellowstone River in Yellowstone National Park.

But there is a different type of valley often seen in high mountains. The old V-shaped valleys were originally formed after the first great ice age, about one million years ago. Since that time there have been alternating periods of warm-and-dry and cold-and-wet climates in earth's history.

During the cold-wet times so much snow fell every winter that it never completely melted away during the short cool summers. Instead it accumulated until great ice fields were built up on the shoulders of our mountain ranges. This resulted in glaciers that deepened and widened the the higher river valleys giving them a U-shape.

During these periods each winter added a new layer of snow and the weight and extreme cold transformed the lower layers into solid ice. Under such conditions ice moves. It actually flows much as very cold molasses or tar flows—very slowly. So these great rivers of ice, called *glaciers*, started creeping down from the high peaks.

They were thousands of feet thick and they ground the rock beneath them into powder. This powder, which is called "rock flour," and rocks of all sizes, from pebbles to boulders as big as houses, became embedded in the ice. Those rocks which eventually got into the bottom layer became tools similar to plows and scrapers under the tremendous weight of thousands of tons of ice above them. So as they were forced down the mountain sides they literally plowed out the beds of the valleys. They cut off protruding points and smoothed, even polished, the surfaces. This greatly deepened and widened the valleys leaving them with a U shape instead of a V shape.

All this loosened rock embedded in the ice was carried along by it. If these pieces were carried for a long time or a great distance their corners and edges were broken off in the grinding process and so now glacial boulders may be recognized by their smooth surfaces.

Later when the ice melted it sometimes left boulders which had been carried from a distance, perched on the surface of an entirely different kind of bedrock. These are called "erratics" and their presence is one evidence of glaciation.

Finally the fronts of the glaciers came to the drier and warmer regions in a period when the annual snowfall was less than the amount annually melted. Here the ice began turning to water and great streams gushed from it. With this melting the load of rock carried in the ice was released. But the smaller particles were carried along for a time by the water.

The big rocks were dumped in a heap across the path of the glaciei. Today we call these ridges of boulders *terminal moraines. Lateral moraines* were formed at the sides of a glacier. Sometimes terminal moraines became dams and later when the ice had melted still farther back the morainal dam held the waters flowing from the front of the glacier in a lake.

Then, plant succession began the slow process of building up soil around the lake, and the stream flowing into it from the melting ice of the retreating glacier carried gravel and silt, rock flour, into it until it was gradually filled and became first a marsh and then a meadow. This accounts for the origin of those mountain valleys which have a perfectly level floor, such as Horseshoe and Moraine Parks in Rocky Mountain National Park.

Plate III — *Landscape carved by ice: a U-shaped valley left by a mountain glacier. Photo courtesy National Park Service.*

At the close of one of the earlier glacial periods the stony "mesas" at the border between the mountains and the plains were formed by the outwash from melting ice.

During the ice ages main valleys were filled by glaciers to depths of hundreds of feet and the grinding out of the bed took place beneath that moving mass of ice, much beneath the level of the tributary valleys, so when the climate changed and the ice finally melted, the tributary valleys were left at a higher level than the main valley. The streams which now flow in these hanging valleys drop over the steep sides of the main valley in cascades and waterfalls. Beautiful examples of such valleys (Plate III) exist in our national parks. Magnificent views of U-shaped, glacier-cut gorges in the Teton Range may be seen from the highway along the eastern side of Grand Teton National Park. Roaring River tumbles out of a hanging valley near the entrance to Fall River Canyon in Rocky Mountain National Park, and several of the falls of Yosemite and Glacier are from hanging valleys.

Geologists believe that during the period from 25,000 to 8,000 years ago the ice advanced and retreated several times. The latest cold period is called the "little ice age" and lasted until about 1,300 years ago. The few small glaciers which now exist in the central and southern Rocky Mountains are considered to be remnants of this period. The glaciers of this "little ice age" put the main finishing touches on the high mountain scenery of our area. The occurrence of tundra in the Rockies, the distribution of our alpine plants, and the presence of glacial lakes are some of the effects of mountain glaciation.

The scenery of our Rocky Mountains is the result of rock, water, frost, organic life, and physical forces acting and reacting between and upon each other over long periods of time. Some understanding of this background will help one to enjoy both the majesty of these mountains and the exquisite beauty of an Alpine Forget-me-not growing in its thin layer of soil which took such a long time to accumulate.

PLANT SUCCESSION

We have seen that lichens and mosses start the vegetation cycle in dry areas, and that water plants start it in and around ponds. They are called the first plant *pioneers*. When they have prepared the way, some pioneer species of flowering plants follow them. These are plants which are adaptable to severe conditions. Ecologists learn to look for certain kinds of plants which form groups or *communities* in certain types of environment They also find that a certain sequence of communities exists which they call *plant succession*. As succession proceeds, the pioneer plants are crowded out by invading species which are able to maintain themselves on the improved conditions established by the pioneers.

Plant succession develops from one stage to another as soil is built up by the continuing process of disintegration of the bedrock and the accumulation of plant debris. Even the environment itself is improved by growing plants. Each stage is characterized by a community which is adapted to the soil and climatic conditions of that stage, and the final or mature community is called a *climax*. The climax is thought to be the most complex development of vegetation which a particular environment can support. Climax communities are usually either grasslands or forest-lands.

The large communities always include smaller less complex communities which develop under local conditions. An example is a pioneer community on a bare rock outcropping within a large forest, or a marsh community surrounded by dry grassland.

In the montane zone dryland succession proceeds from pioneer communities of lichens and mosses to sedum or grasses and other hardy herbaceous seed plants such as Geranium (180), Penstemon (281 ff.), Leafy Potentilla (155), and Alumroot (128). With these are several woody species: Kinnikinnik (234), Jamesia (124), Nine-bark (144), and Squaw Currant (135). Among them seedlings of Ponderosa Pine (13) become established on the dry, south-facing slopes, and of Douglas-fir (15) on the more moist, north-facing slopes, with some intermixture of both. Eventually an open pine forest including a scattering of Douglas-firs develops on the dry south-facing slopes and a more dense Douglas-fir forest, with scattered pines included, develops on the north-facing ones.

On the moist soil of ravines, around meadows and on stream borders, groves and sometimes forests of Aspen (53) will be found. And on the east and west slopes various combinations of all these species occur. The Ponderosa and Douglas-fir forests are considered to be climax communities under the conditions of the montane region and will perpetuate themselves, unless disturbed by some outside influence.

When this succession pattern is disturbed by fire, insect infestation, plowing, or other cause, different results usually follow which are called secondary succession. When the open Ponderosa Pine forest is destroyed by fire it usually reestablishes itself in due course of time. When montane grassland has been plowed and then abandoned, a crop of vigorous ponderosa seedlings frequently appears within a few years. When Douglas-fir stands are burned they are often replaced by a very dense growth of Lodgepole Pine.

In the subalpine region the early stages of succession are usually followed by meadow or willow thickets which will be invaded by Engelmann Spruce, and this by Subalpine Fir. The climax here is the beautiful Engelmann Spruce-Subalpine Fir forest, A fire in such a forest becomes so hot that the humus in the soil is burned to such an extent that the succession cycle is et back to pioneer conditions and usually the secondary stage is a Lodgepole Pine forest. In some cases spruce-fir reestablishes itself but very, very slowly and sparsely as has been the case around Bear Lake in Rocky Mountain National Park where the subalpine Engelmann Spruce forest was destroyed by fire about 1900.

CLIMATE AND VEGETATION ZONES

Climbing a mountain is a little like travelling northwards. Students of geography and plant and animal life have recognized on continents distinct latitudinal zones of climate, each characterized by its own type of vegetation and animal life.

In western North America from south to north we find the Sonoran (Mexican), Transition (central United States), Canadian (northern United

States and southern Canada), Hudsonian (Hudson Bay Region), and the Arctic Zones. On high mountains there are regions which in certain respects correspond to these zones. Because they do not agree exactly, ecologists use a different set of names for mountain zones, but in some books these terms are still used.

In central Colorado they recognize the Plains Zone, below 5,400 feet; Foothill Zone, 5,400 to 7,000 feet; Montane Zone, 7,000 to 9,500 feet; Subalpine Zone, 9,500 to 11,500 feet; and Alpine Zone, above 11,500 feet.

But because of the great extent of the area covered by this book, these elevations can only be used to give an approximate idea of the altitudes as they apply in the central part of our region. The end papers of this book show a diagrammatic illustration of plant zones.

A climb of 1,000 feet is roughly equal to a trip of 600 miles northward. Average temperature is decreased approximately 3° F. for every 1,000 feet of altitude. Within our range the elevation of timberline decreases northward at the rate of about 360 feet per degree of latitude. In New Mexico the corresponding plant zones will be at a higher elevation—in Montana they will be considerably lower. To a certain extent blooming seasons are correlated with altitude or latitude. It is said, "To find the season just past go either up a mountain or up north." That statement is true of the three lower zones but does not apply to the Alpine and Arctic zones partly because these are more directly affected by light intensity and day length, and partly because there is a greater accumulation of snow below timberline. Summer comes in the Alpine earlier than in the next lower zone.

The corresponding plant communities in different areas may contain different species but the appearance of the vegetation will be similar. The boundaries of these zones are not marked by continuous, definite lines. They vary up and down with the topography, soil and exposure. There is much overlapping and interfingering. Along water courses and on north-facing slopes there is always a downward extension of the next higher zone; on dry, sunny slopes an upward extension of the lower zone. Often there are, for some reason not easily understood, islands of shrub or tree communities surrounded by grassland. The best way to recognize the zones is by the plant communities which are typical of each.

Foothills or Shrub Zone

This region extends from where the plains break at the foot of the mountains up to the region where large trees are dominant. Here the grassland which is typical of the plains begins to give way to a shrub-type vegetation. At first the grassland continues up the south-facing slopes in fingerlike extensions, and shrubs appear only in the breaks and on the north sides of mesas and ridges. A little higher, shrubs become more conspicuous and appear on the northwest and northeast slopes. Fingers of grassland run up between them on the south- and southwest-facing slopes. Still higher, a few small trees begin to appear in the ravines and on the north exposures. Gradually as we proceed upwards the trees become more

Plate IV — *Looking east to foothills, showing interfingering of grass-land and shrubs, foothill zone. Note extensions of forest downward along north-facing slopes. Photo by author.*

numerous until we pass from the shrub zone into the montane zone which is characterized by forest.

In as large an area as this we find considerable variation in the composition of the shrub belt. But brushland of some kind exists as a transition between the grassland and forest belts throughout this great region.

Along the east face of the Rockies there is a division point in central Colorado which is formed by a ridge of hills extending roughly eastward from the "Front Range." This is the divide between the basins of the Arkansas and the Platte rivers and is sometimes referred to as the Palmer Lake Divide and on the highway is called "Monument Hill." It is located about 20 miles north of Pikes Peak, and seems to constitute a natural barrier to weather conditions as well as to plants. Several species have their northern or southern limits in this vicinity, and the aspect of the foothill slopes south and north of this dividing place is distinctly different. The intermountain valleys have their own type of shrub formation and the western border of our region has a still different and complex form of brushland which consists of semi-desert species in the southwest and includes species with high moisture requirements in the northwest.

Probably the most common and widely distributed shrubs throughout all of the Rocky Mountain foothill regions are species of juniper, sage-brush, and mountain mahogany. There is more than one species of each, and in the main each species occupies its own portion of the whole area, with some overlapping. But the species of each are similar in general appearance and occupy corresponding habitats. One exception is that in the northeastern section the upright juniper is replaced by a creeping form.

29

Plate V. — *Looking north at timberline, showing extensions of tree growth upward along protected slopes. Photo courtesy of National Park Service.*

In northern New Mexico and Arizona and southern Colorado and Utah much of the foothill region is covered by an open, shrubby forest of piñon, p. 64, and juniper, p. 67, interrupted here and there by deciduous shrub communities. Scrub-oak, p. 103-4, also occurs, usually at a higher level than the piñon-juniper, and interspersed with groups of other shrubs. In extreme northern New Mexico Apache Plume (141) is characteristic of the transition from shrub land to Ponderosa Pine forest, while farther south it is much more widely distributed. In central Colorado piñon and scrub oak disappear, the piñon at the Arkansas-Platte Divide and the oak just north of Denver and Boulder, and farther north the Mountain Mahogany (146), Antelopebrush (142), Buckbrush (301), and sagebrush (354), with others, cover the foothill slopes and merge into the lower edge of the montane forest. Along the east side north of that divide the foothill slopes are clothed with small- and medium-sized shrubs. Their appearance tells the story of a dry and barren habitat. At the lower edge of this zone they are small and widely scattered. Slightly higher where moisture is a little more abundant they are larger and grow closer together. Many of them have small, grayish leaves.

The intermountain valleys are ringed about with sagebrush and the small hills included within them are usually covered with it. On the slightly higher slopes are thickets of tall shrubs largely made up of Chokecherry (151) and serviceberry (140), which often extend projections upward into the montane forest. In western Colorado and Utah the lower part of this foothill shrub zone consists of almost pure stands of sagebrush with thickets of taller shrubs such as scrub oak, serviceberry, and Chokecherry above. In the mountains of north central Utah and occasionally northwards through Idaho into Montana, some moist canyon sides are covered with thickets of

30

the Wasatch Maple (190). On drier areas scrub oak is abundant but only as far north as Idaho.

From whatever side you approach the mountains as you ascend the foothills you will pass from grassland, or at least what was once grassland but may now be farmland, through a zone of brushland into a zone of forest. This may consist of small, gray-leaved shrubs, of piñon-juniper scrub forest, of scrub oak or maple thickets, or of other medium or tall shrubs, but your approach to the true forest will always cross this vegetation zone of brushland.

Montane or Ponderosa Pine—Douglas-fir Zone

The montane zone is a forested region but it has as much variation in kinds of trees and types of forest as we find in the foothills zone. In northern Montana it begins almost at the edge of the plains at an altitude of about 4,000 feet. In New Mexico and Arizona it is above the piñon-juniper belt and is almost entirely above 8,000 feet.

From northern New Mexico into southern Wyoming along the east side of the mountains, across southern Colorado and from northern Arizona into Utah and southwestern Colorado, Ponderosa Pine (13) is the dominant and characteristic tree of this zone. At the lower edge of its altitudinal range it may appear stunted, deformed, often shrubby, but at about 8,000 feet it becomes a tall, spreading dignified tree with a beautiful orange-brown trunk. It grows scatteringly in open formation so that plenty

Plate VI—*Open, park-like landscape in* Ponderosa Pine *stand of montane zone.*

of light reaches the ground permitting the growth of grasses and many wild flowers beneath it.

In this same area on north-facing slopes, in ravines, and elsewhere in the upper portion of the zone, the Douglas-fir (15) occurs intermingled with Ponderosa. On the western side of the Continental Divide in northern Colorado, Utah and Wyoming, Douglas-fir is the tree characteristic of the region and the pine is rarely seen.

Occasionally throughout the montane zone on barren ridges and rock outcrops we find the Limber Pine (14). The early stage of succession on rock usually includes seedlings of hardy grasses, several different kinds of perennial wildflowers such as sedums, saxifrages, geraniums, cinquefoils, and penstemons besides shrubs and limber pines which often find footholds in rock crevices.

This may be followed by either one or both of two trees which cover large areas in this region and often extend into the subalpine region: Lodgepole Pine and Aspen. Lodgepole does not occur south of Colorado. Often Lodgepole Pine and Aspen forests occupy areas where the natural plant succession has been interrupted so that a climax type of vegetation, which in this case would be the Ponderosa and Douglas-fir forest, could not develop. Fire is the usual cause of such a change, but other influences such as logging or excessive erosion have the same effect.

Aspen usually appears on moist soil and Lodgepole on drier areas. The lodgepoles grow in such dense stands that practically nothing can live beneath them, but aspens are more open, permitting enough light to reach the ground so that lovely flower gardens are found among them and in the small meadow openings between groves.

In the northwestern and northern parts of our range the montane forests are almost entirely of Lodgepole Pine. This is especially true in Yellowstone and Glacier National Parks.

This zone includes many open valleys where mountain streams flow between flowery meadows and beautiful trees are arranged in natural groupings. Because of this planted appearance they were called by the early settlers "parks," so today there are many place names which include the word "park," such as Sandia Park in New Mexico, and South Park, Estes Park and others in Colorado. Here we find a greater number of different kinds of trees and shrubs than in any other part of the mountain region. Along the streams are narrowleaf and balsam poplars, alders (58), and water birch.

Two of the most beautiful evergreens of North America are found in the protected canyons of this region. In our southern section, that is from northern New Mexico as far north as Pikes Peak and westward, is found the White Fir. In favorable situations this devolps into a tall, handsome, silver-green, conical tree. It is confined to stream banks and the lower canyon slopes where it is found in groves or as scattered individuals. In the canyons west of Denver and northward into southern Wyoming, the Colorado Blue Spruce (16) occupies the same sort of habitat and is equally beautiful. It is more rigid and emphatic in pattern than the fir, and many individual trees, though not all, are very distinctly blue in color. In the Pikes Peak region this spruce forms a poor-looking forest at middle elevations where it never seems to attain the symmetry of those trees in the

Plate VII — *Streamside community of willows and blue spruce, with aspen on higher slopes. Montane zone. Photo by author.*

stream-side groves. Farther north it seems to occur only in such groves.

Along its upper edge the montane forest becomes more dense, and with its overlapping areas of aspen and lodgepole, merges into the subalpine forest.

Subalpine or Engelmann Spruce—Subalpine Fir Zone

This region has a more homogeneous type of tree growth than the zone below it. It begins in the south between 11,000 and 11,500 feet and in the north at about 6,500 feet and is composed of an almost continuous forest of Engelmann Spruce, with some mixture of Subalpine Fir. This spruce-fir forest covers the whole area, north, south, and west except as it is sometimes interrupted by lodgepole pine and aspen intrusions. But these are not nearly as conspicuous as in the montane zone.

When you look out over miles and miles of dense, unbroken, deep green conifer-covered mountainside you are almost certainly looking at the subalpine forest. The only breaks in this are made by steep water courses, rock outcrops, or fire scars. The water courses are usually marked by the lighter green of aspens and at close range show bordering, flower-filled meadows.

The rock outcrops are places where rough, often gnarled five-needled pines find footholds in crevices. There are three of these pines which are found on wind-swept slopes and crags. The Limber Pine (14) is the most widely distributed. The Bristlecone Pine, also called "Foxtail Pine," is found on Mount Evans and south and westward into the mountains of Arizona, Nevada, and California. From northern Wyoming north and westwards in similar situations there is the White-barked Pine. All three of

Plate VIII — ENGLEMANN SPRUCE forest and flowery meadow, sub-
alpine zone. Photo by author.

these are very rugged. They are often twisted and distorted by the constant
winds into interesting and picturesque shapes. Many of them are several
hundreds of years old.

The ground under the spruce forest is brown and soft with accumulations of rotting needles and the rotted wood of long-fallen tree trunks.
This is the part of the mountains where moisture is most abundant. Much
snow falls here, accumulating all winter and remaining late into the summer
because the trees protect it from melting and from blowing away. So here
we find an environment in which moisture-loving plants can thrive. Many
dainty woodland plants grow and bloom here such as Fairy Slipper (48),
Woodnymph (230); Twin Flower (296), and Dotted Saxifrage (131).

At the upper edge of this zone we come to the timberline region. This
is, to many people, the most interesting and delightful part of the whole
mountain territory. Here there is sufficient moisture to supply a luxuriant
growth of wildflowers. The season is short and the nights cold but the
days are long in June and July and the sunlight brilliant. Because of the
severe winter winds and the weight of snow, the trees here are twisted and
become shorter and shorter until they finally spread out over the ground
or form little canopies 3 or 4 feet high and closed on the windy side by a
dense growth of twigs and needles.

This timberline forest, called "elfin timber" or *Krummholz,* seems to
send out bands of scouts which advance a short distance beyond the main
frontier and stand as isolated wind-beaten sentinels. Timberline varies up
and down with the topography. On southeast and southwest slopes and
in sheltered draws the tree line extends higher; on north and northwest
exposures and wind-swept ridges it is lower.

34

All along in the little protected meadows formed by this irregular line and watered by slowly melting snowdrifts there are luxuriant flower gardens. Here we begin to find some of the many species that are common at much lower altitudes in northern latitudes. The white-flowered Marsh Marigold (97) is one of these, Rose Crown (121) is another. Great beds of the yellow-flowered Snow-lily (41) spring into bloom almost before the snow is gone and follow as it retreats up the open slopes. Always under the "elfin timber" there are the dainty leaves and pale sky-blue flowers of Jacobs Ladder (259). Parry Primrose (239) with clusters of brilliant rose flowers stands with its roots in the icy water of little streams. Many more are here to delight the adventurous nature lover.

Alpine Zone or Tundra

Above timberline we find a region of grassland and rock fields. This is called *tundra* because it is very similar to the great treeless regions of the Arctic which are known by that term. Spring comes earlier in this very high region than it does in the sub-alpine zone because the snow disappears more rapidly from the exposed alpine slopes than it does in the tree-shaded areas below. Much of the alpine region is so windswept that it is bare of snow most of the winter. But there are great permanent snow banks where the drifting snow is trapped in draws and depressions. Around the melting edges of these perpetual drifts flowers bloom throughout the short summer season.

But the great alpine flower display of the mountain tops comes in late June and early July, and it is at about the same date whether you visit it in northern New Mexico, in Utah or in Montana. Its date is influenced more by the snow accumulation of the previous winter in different areas than by the relative distance north. The alpine flowers must bloom during the longest days in order to mature seed before winter-like storms bring sustained subfreezing temperatures to these heights.

Most of the alpine plants are able to withstand considerable frost. If they were not so hardy they would have disappeared from such a stormy habitat long ago.

The climax vegetation of arctic regions and of mountain tundra is a tight, short, sedge turf. When well established this formation excludes other plants but on gravel and rock chip pavements, around rock outcrops, and wherever the soil is more or less disturbed by frost or other action, there are pioneer communities, natural gardens of flowering plants.

Most of these are short-stemmed; many of them grow in a cushion or carpet form. Most of them have brilliant and comparatively large blossoms. The rose, mustard, saxifrage and aster families are each represented by several species. All colors are in evidence. A few of the commonest and most conspicuous species in order of their blooming times are: Fairy Primrose (238), Alpine Forget-me-not (267), Moss Campion (79), Alpine Sandwort (83), Alpine Avens (156), Rydbergia (329), and Arctic Gentian (249). Dozens more are there tucked in among the rocks or decorating the bare gravel fields.

Flowering plants disappear completely somewhere between 12,000 and 14,000 feet and the only evident plant life on the very highest moun-

Plate IX — *Alpine zone from timberline, showing in foreground deformed, wind-shaped trees, and in the distance tundra and perpetual snow. Photo by author.*

tain tops are members of that pioneer group of lichens about which we wrote in an earlier chapter.

Part II: Rocky Mountain Plants

PLANT NAMES AND CLASSIFICATION

All plants have Latin names. In this respect Latin is a universal language. Its use makes it possible for two botanists of different countries who speak different languages to communicate with each other about plants and know that they are talking about the same kind of plant.

Each language has its own common names for plants. Very often the same plant has several different names in different parts of our own country. Also the same common name is frequently applied to different kinds of plants in different regions. This would make for endless confusion if botanists who were doing scientific work on plants had to depend on the common, or vernacular, plant names. But by using the universally accepted Latin names they are able to be exact in their work.

Even travelers within the Rocky Mountain region are apt to find that the common names in general use in one part for a given plant are not always the same as those used in another part for the same plant.

Most plant names whether Latin or English are intended to be descriptive. In Latin each *genus* is given a name which is a Latin noun. Then each *species* is given an additional descriptive name which is usually a Latin adjective. For instance, *Rosa* is the name for a genus which includes all the different kinds of true roses. Included in the genus is *Rosa acicularis* which in English means the "rose with needlelike prickles." There is also *Rosa woodsii* which was named in honor of a man whose name is Joseph Wood, and *Rosa arkansana* is the "rose which grows near the Arkansas River." Other descriptive names are *Fragaria americana,* "American wild strawberry" and *Saxifraga chrysantha,* the "yellow-flowered saxifrage."

An international group of botanists has set up a system of rules for botanical nomenclature. It sometimes happens that a name has come into general use for a certain plant and later after more research it is found that this generally accepted name is not in accord with these rules. In that case this name has to be superseded by the correct one.

Also botanical research sometimes reveals that a plant which has been going under a distinct name is the same as one of another region which has a much older name. In that case the older name must be accepted. These two provisions account for many of the recent apparent name changes of Rocky Mountain plants.

During recent years extensive botanical study in our area has revealed that some of our plants, at first believed to be distinct species, are actually the same as species of the arctic or European mountains. Consequently the names by which we have known our plants become *synonyms* and the older names take their places. This causes some confusion but not nearly as much as would be involved if we used only common names. In some instances botanical specialists consider the related Rocky Mountain form of a northern or European species to be sufficiently distinct to warrant designation as a *variety* or *subspecies.* Such plants are indicated in this book by the abbreviation var. or ssp., whichever form was used by the botanist who described it.

Another problem connected with the use of common names in this area is that because the region has been comparatively recently settled and because of the great number of plants which are different from those of older parts of the country, many of our plants do not have common names. Actually it is not nearly as difficult to learn the Latin names as most people think. Many of them are already in general use, such as *Geranium, Yucca, Viburnum, Phacelia* and *Phlox.*

In this book common names are given first, followed by the Latin name in italics. Then, usually there is a number in parenthesis which designates the illustration of this particular plant. The same number appears with the illustration and in the text of Part I if reference is made to this plant.

An attempt has been made to include the most widely used and most appropriate names. In some cases where there is no well-known common name in use the generic name is used as a common name. Readers are encouraged to learn and use the generic name.

[The editor apologizes for this book's inconsistency in capitalizing common names, a problem always irritating to botanical editors. In later chapters the exact use of the preferred common name is set in capitals and small capitals. To have done so in introductory chapters would have resulted in a confusing hodgepodge.]

Plants are classified by *species, genus,* and *family.* The unit of classification is the species. All the plants of one kind belong to one *species.* Another way of putting it is that all individual plants which appear more like each other than like other individuals are of one species.

A group of closely related species constitutes a *genus.* The plural of this Latin word is *genera.*

Closely related *genera* are grouped into plant families. The members of a particular plant family have certain fundamental distinguishing features in common. For instance, flowers of plants in the Mustard Family have four separate petals and a two-celled seed pod whereas flowers of the Lily Family have six petals and a three-celled seed pod, and flowers of the Figwort Family have petals united into an irregular five-lobed corolla and a two-celled seed pod.

All the plants of one genus have some characteristics in common. All violets have five separate petals forming an irregular flower and all maples have opposite leaves. These family and generic characters are used in the keys for identification but it must be borne in mind that plants are variable and there are exceptions to all rules.

Certain statements can be made which are true in general in regard to the plants which make up a family, genus, or species. But all the individuals vary to some extent and occasionally one varies beyond the limits of a general description, so the author hopes that the users of this book will be patient with the seemingly excessive use of qualifying adjectives such as "usually" and "generally." In botany one can never safely make unqualified statements.

THE FIRST THING TO LEARN ABOUT PLANTS

Characteristics of the Plant and Flower Described and Illustrated

The Plant

The flowering plants comprise only one of several large groups which make up the plant kingdom. They are sometimes referred to as *seed plants.* Other groups are: mosses, ferns, mushrooms and seaweeds. But the flowering plants are the most conspicuous in our environment and the ones with which this book is mainly concerned. Many of the descriptive terms used in the text are briefly explained in the next few pages and illustrated on *Plates A* through *G.* There is also a glossary giving definitions. Much botanical information may be found in a good dictionary.

Plants are *annual* if they complete their life cycle of growth and fruition within one year. They are *perennial* if they live for an indefinite number of years. Plants are *herbs* if their leaves and stems die back to the ground at the end of each growing season. They are *woody* if their stems above ground remain alive through the winter sending out new growth in the spring. The woodiness of a stem is usually obvious. Woody plants are either *vines, shrubs* or *trees.* There are very few woody vines in the Rocky Mountains because vines in general are not adapted to severe climates.

Shrubs may be anywhere from a few inches to 15 feet tall; they are bushy in habit with several main stems.

Trees are usually 15 feet or more tall with one main stem, called a *trunk,* which is 3 inches or more in diameter. In the Rocky Mountains several woody species are on the borderline between shrubs and trees. Sometimes in favorable locations they grow to 15 feet or more in height but have several trunks and a bushy habit. In other places the same species will be only a few feet tall. Western Red Birch, alder (58), and Rocky Mountain Maple (189) fall into this class. Trees and shrubs are *deciduous* or *evergreen* according to whether they drop their leaves in the fall or hold them through the winter. Leaves which are evergreen are more firm and tough than those which are deciduous.

A typical flowering plant consists of *stem, roots, leaves, flowers* and *fruit.*

Stems (Plate A)

The stem is the axis of the plant. All the other parts arise from it. A stem may be long and intricately branched as in tall trees or it may be short and compact as the base of an onion bulb. It may even be green and take over the food-making process as in the cacti. Buds and roots originate in the stem.

The Latin term *acaulescent,* meaning "stemless," which is inaccurate but commonly used, applies to plants which have only short stems at ground level, *Plate A2.* In such cases leaves and flower stalks arise directly from this consolidated stem which is often called a crown or *caudex.* These plants may appear tufted or if the caudex is branched the plants are said to be *caespitose* and appear mat-like or cushion-like, as the Moss Campion (79), and several other alpine species. Stems may rise strictly *erect* from the crown or they may lean outward and be described as *ascending.* If they are horizontal they are said to be *decumbent* and if they start out horizontally and then bend so as to become more or less erect they are described as "decumbent at base." A spreading underground stem is called a *rootstock* or *rhizome.* In a strict botanical sense a leafless stalk of a flower is not a stem. Stems bear leaves and buds. This distinction is important in using the keys in this book.

Stems have joints which are called *nodes, Plate A7.* The spaces between the nodes are the *internodes, (A7).* Leaves and branches grow from buds at the nodes, and in some cases roots also grow from nodes. If there is only one leaf at each node the *leaf arrangement* is *alternate, (A3).* If there are two leaves at each node it is *opposite, (A4).* If there are more than 2 leaves at each node the leaves are in *whorls, (A6).* The angle formed by the stem and the leaf is the *axil, (A3).* Buds formed in the axils are called *axillary buds, (A3).* The bud at the tip of a stem is called a *terminal* bud, *(A7).* If leaves are alternate these axillary buds produce an *alternate branching* pattern, *(A3);* if they are opposite the buds produce an *opposite branching* pattern, *(A4).* Sometimes flowers are axillary.

Roots

The roots of plants serve to anchor them to the ground and are organs through which water and nutrient materials in solution are absorbed. The scientific botanist needs to learn the type of root when classifying an unknown plant, but in this book root characters will be seldom used and

The Plant

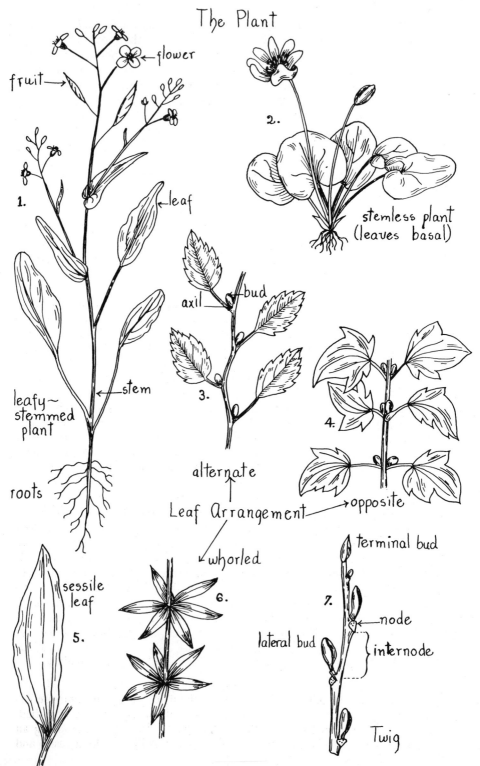

1. leafy-stemmed plant
   - flower
   - fruit
   - leaf
   - stem
   - roots

2. stemless plant (leaves basal)

3. alternate
   - axil
   - bud

4. opposite

Leaf Arrangement

5. sessile leaf

6. whorled

7. Twig
   - terminal bud
   - node
   - lateral bud
   - internode

Plate A

Leaves

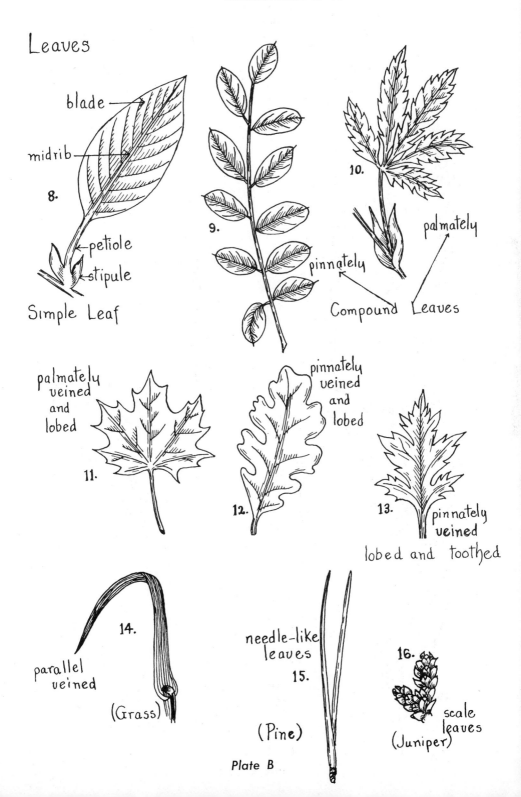

blade

midrib

8.

petiole

stipule

Simple Leaf

9.

10.

pinnately

palmately

Compound Leaves

palmately
veined
and
lobed

11.

pinnately
veined
and
lobed

12.

13.

pinnately
veined

lobed and toothed

14.

parallel
veined

(Grass)

needle-like
leaves

15.

(Pine)

16.

scale
leaves
(Juniper)

Plate B

Leaf Forms

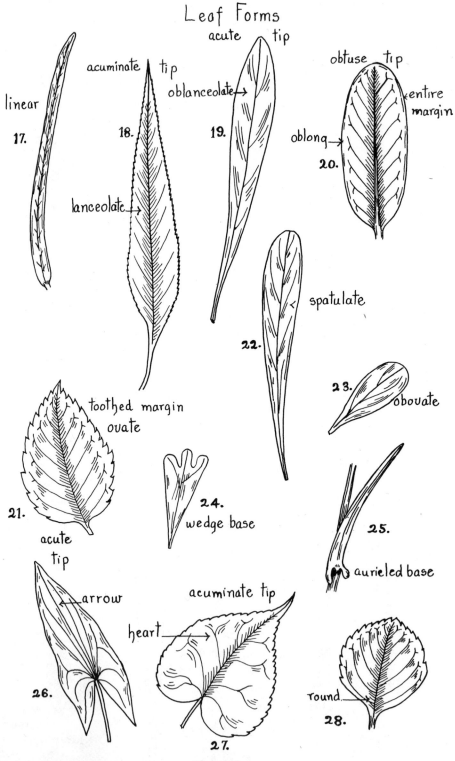

linear

17.

acuminate tip

18.

lanceolate →

acute tip

oblanceolate →

19.

obtuse tip

← entire margin

oblong →

20.

spatulate

22.

23. obovate

toothed margin
ovate

21.

acute tip

24.
wedge base

25.

aurieled base

arrow

acuminate tip

heart →

26.

27.

round

28.

Plate C

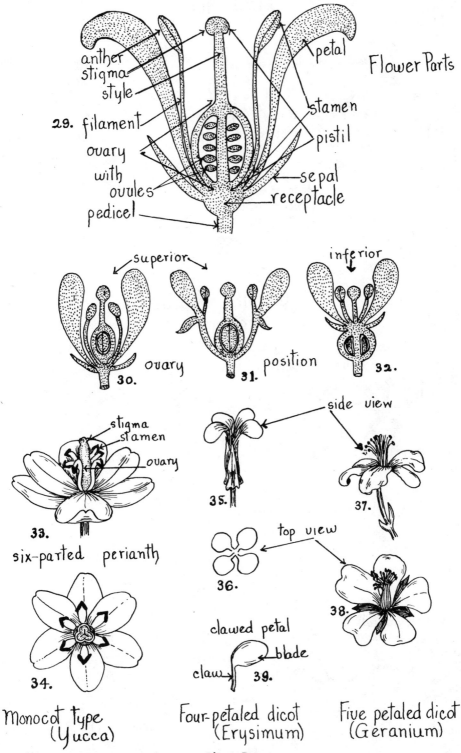

Flower Parts

anther
stigma
style
29. filament
ovary
with
ovules
pedicel

petal

stamen

pistil

sepal
receptacle

superior

inferior

ovary   position

30.   **31.**   **32.**

stigma
stamen
ovary

side view

35.   **37.**

33.

six-parted   perianth

top view

36.

38.

clawed petal

blade

claw   **39.**

34.

Monocot type
(Yucca)

Four-petaled dicot
(Erysimum)

Five petaled dicot
(Geranium)

Plate D

Calyx Types

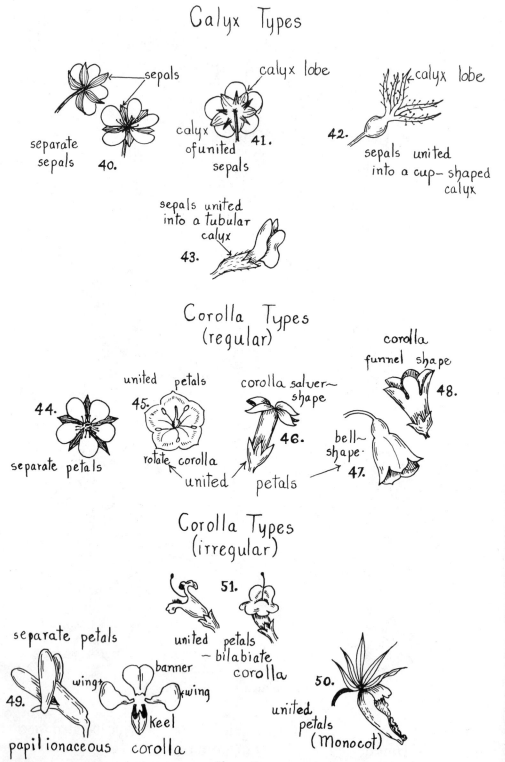

sepals

calyx lobe

calyx lobe

separate sepals   40.

calyx of united sepals   41.

42.

sepals united into a cup-shaped calyx

sepals united into a tubular calyx

43.

Corolla Types (regular)

corolla funnel shape

united petals

corolla salver-shape

44.

45.

46.

48.

separate petals

rotate corolla

united petals

bell-shape

47.

Corolla Types (irregular)

51.

separate petals

united petals — bilabiate corolla

banner

wings

wing

49.

keel

50.

united petals (Monocot)

papilionaceous corolla

Plate E

Inflorescences

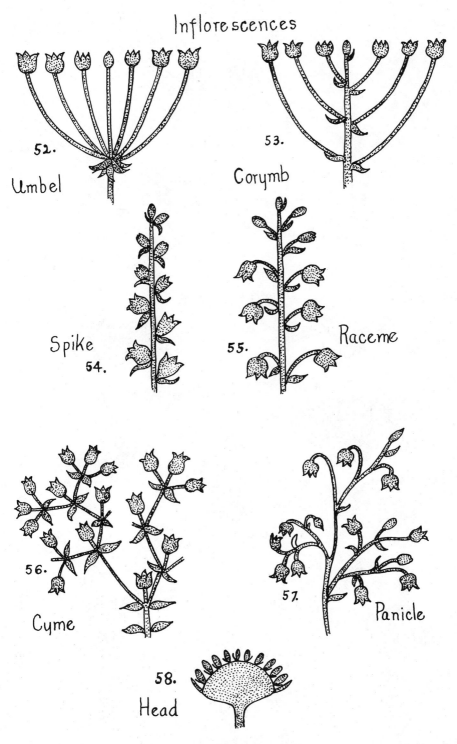

52. Umbel

53. Corymb

Spike 54.

55. Raceme

56. Cyme

57. Panicle

58. Head

Plate F

Composites

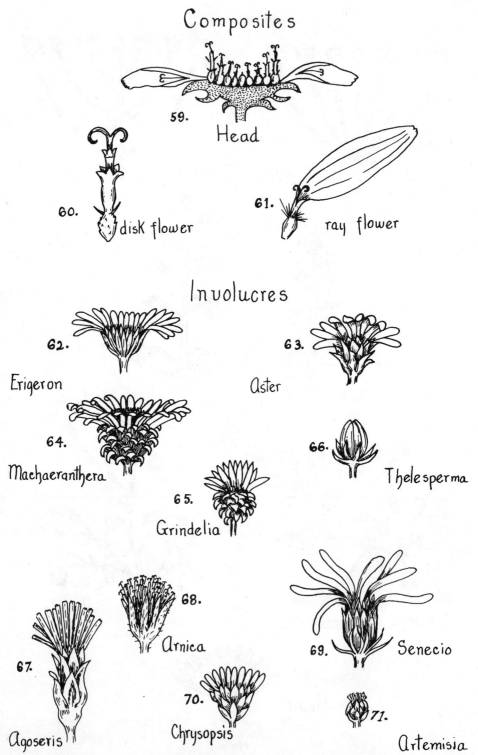

59.
Head

60.
disk flower

61.
ray flower

Involucres

62.
Erigeron

63.
Aster

64.
Machaeranthera

66.
Thelesperma

65.
Grindelia

68.
Arnica

69.
Senecio

67.
Agoseris

70.
Chrysopsis

71.
Artemisia

Plate G

so there will be only a brief statement in regard to them.

Tap roots are those which have a main axis extending downward with smaller side branches. This main axis is sometimes thickened by the storage of food as in the carrot and several related wild plants. Many annuals and biennials and some perennials have this type.

Other plants have an irregularly branched root system which is said to be *fibrous*. Stems may give rise to roots. This is particularly true of underground stems. Such roots usually appear at the nodes. When this happens the plant spreads out in a mat or carpet form, or trails along the ground, and is described as "rooting at the nodes."

Annual plants usually have less extensive root systems than perennials.

Leaves (Plates B and C)

A typical leaf consists of *blade, petiole* and *stipules, (B8)*. Often stipules are absent, or very tiny, or they soon drop off. Sometimes the petiole is absent and then the leaf is *sessile*. Leaves are *simple* if the blade consists of a single piece. *Compound* leaves are made up of *leaflets, (B9, 10)*. Simple leaves may be distinguished from the leaflets of compound leaves by the presence of axillary buds. Leaflets never have axillary buds but there is always a bud at the base of a compound leaf. Simple leaves and leaflets of compound leaves may be variously *toothed* or *lobed, (B11, 12)*. Compound leaves may be *palmate* or *pinnate (B11, 12)*. Pinnate leaves may have an even or odd number of leaflets. Leaf forms *(Plate C)* may be *linear, lanceolate, oblanceolate, ovate, obovate, oblong, spatulate, heart-shaped, arrow-shaped* or *round*. Leaf tips may be *acute, acuminate* or *obtuse*. The bases may be *heart-shaped, arrow-shaped, wedge-shaped* or *auricled*. Leaf margins may be *entire, toothed* or *scalloped*. Leaves at ground level are called basal leaves. These often form what is referred to as a *rosette*.

Leaves have distinctive *venation*. If a leaf has a midrib running from the base to the apex with lateral veins extending from this towards the margin, it is said to be feather-veined or *pinnately-veined*. If it has more than one main vein and all originate at the base and spread as a fan, or as the fingers of a hand spread from the palm it is said to be *palmately-veined*. Both of these types of leaves occur on plants which belong to the group of Dicots. Their veins branch and the veinlets form a netted pattern with the branches ending at the leaf margin. Such leaves are said to be *netted-veined*. (Monocots, see p. 68; Dicots, p. 93.)

If the leaf has several veins extending the length of the leaf parallel to each other and parallel to the margins it is *parallel-veined, (B14)*. Parallel-veined leaves are usually long and narrow as are grass leaves but they may be broad as are the leaves of Solomonplume (31). Leaves of Monocot plants are always parallel-veined even though this is not always evident, and leaves of dicot plants are always netted-veined though occasionally their principal veins may appear parallel.

Flowers and Inflorescences (Plates D, E, F)

The flowering part of a plant is called the *inflorescence*. Some plants have *solitary* flowers, or flower clusters, on unbranched stalks which rise from the caudex. Such a stalk is called a *scape* and the plant is said to be *scapose, (A 2)*. If the plant has a branched stem and the flower stalks rise from the axils the inflorescence is *axillary* and the main stalk of the flower cluster is a *peduncle*. The stalk of an individual flower in a cluster is a *pedicel, (D 29)*. If the inflorescence is branched it follows a pattern which will usually agree with one of the patterns illustrated on *Plate F*. If the axis is unbranched and the individual flowers are without pedicels it is a *spike*. If the axis is unbranched and the individual flowers are pediceled it is a *raceme* which is one of the most common types of inflorescence. If it is alternately and irregularly branched it is a *panicle*. If it is oppositely and regularly branched with the terminal flower blooming first, it is a *cyme*. If all the pedicels arise from one point and are of equal length as the rays of an umbrella it is an *umbel, (F 52)*. Umbels may be compounded as in Cow Parsnip (224), or Sulphur Flower (68). If the pedicels arise from different positions on the axis and are of different lengths but come to one level, the inflorescence is a *corymb, (F 53)*. A spike may be modified into a *catkin,* as in the aspen (53), or it may be compacted into a *head, (F 58),* as in Parry Clover (165).

The essential parts of a flower are the *pistil* and the *stamen*. A flower is functional and is called *perfect* if it contains only these two parts because by their cooperation it is able to reproduce itself by seed. There are flowers which consist of pistils only or stamens only. Such flowers are *unisexual* and are either *pistillate* or *staminate* and are said to be *imperfect*. The two kinds may both be on the same plant or on different plants.

Most flowers which depend on insects for pollination secrete nectar and advertise its presence by scent or showy structures attached to the flower, such as brightly colored petals, sepals, or petal-like bracts. The different parts of the flower 'are in series and they are attached to the enlarged top of a stalk called the *receptacle* in a definite arrangement.

The easiest part of this arrangement to recognize is the numerical pattern. These patterns are guides to family relationships. For instance, the Lily Family has a pattern based on the numbers 3 and 6, the Mustard Family has its flower parts based on the number 4, most members of the Rose Family have 5 petals. The numbers of pistils and stamens are not always the same as those of petals but they are usually constant for the group. (See definition of *-merous,* Glossary p. 317.)

Diagrams showing some of these patterns are given in *Plate D*. Learning these patterns helps one to recognize at first sight the family to which a plant belongs.

A *complete* flower consists of *sepals, petals, stamens* and *pistil*. The outermost series is formed by the sepals, the next by the petals, the next by the stamens and the innermost by one or more pistils. The parts may be all separate as in a buttercup, *(Plate E 40, 44),* or they may be joined to each other or to parts of a different series. The sepals collectively constitute the *calyx* and the petals collectively constitute the *corolla*. These terms are generally used when the sepals or petals are *united, (Plate E 46, 47)*. When sepals and petals are similar, as is the case with many species of the monocot group, the whole is referred to as a *perianth*.

In the dicot group if there is only one series outside the stamens it is said to be made up of sepals even though they are petal-like and brightly colored. An example is the Pasque Flower (99). Sepals may be entirely separate and early deciduous as in the Buttercup *(E 40)*, or they may be united at base as in the Potentilla, *(E 41)*, or they may be united into a cup as in the rose *(E 42)*, or a tube as in the milkvetches, *(E 43)*.

Flowers may be *regular* or *irregular*. If a flower is regular it is radially symmetrical as is the case in potentilla *(E 44)*, and phlox *(E 46)*. If it is irregular it is bilaterally symmetrical as is the case in the pea flower *(E 49)*, and the penstemon *(E 51)*. *Papilionaceous* is a term used to describe irregular, separate-petal corollas such as those of the legume family *(E 49)*. United corollas are of many forms. Some of these forms are illustrated in *Plate E.*

Corollas of regular flowers may be *rotate (E 45), bell-shaped (campanulate) (E 47), funnel-shaped (E 48),* or *salver-shaped (E 46).* Corollas of irregular flowers are usually 2-lipped *(bi-labiate) (E 51).* When corollas are united the stamens are often inserted on the inside of the corolla tube.

The stamen is composed of *anther* and *filament (D 29).* Anthers contain *pollen.* The pistil may be simple or compound and is composed of *stigma, style* and *ovary (D 29).* The stigma is the surface which receives the pollen. The ovary·contains the *ovules* which, when fertilized, develop into seeds. The *style* which connects stigma and ovary may be short or long; sometimes it is absent and the stigma is *sessile* on the top of the ovary. A *carpel* is the unit of structure of the pistil. If the pistil is compound the ovary is composed of two or more united *carpels.*

The ovary is *superior* if the stamens, petals, and sepals are attached to the receptacle at its base, as in *Caltha* (97), or if the petals and stamens are inserted on the calyx cup as in the plum *(D 31).*

It is *inferior* if the calyx cup is joined to it and the other parts are attached above it *(D 32)* as in the gooseberry (173) and the harebell (306). There are intermediat stages where the lower part of the ovary is embedded in the receptacle as in some saxifrages.

Fruits

After fertilization takes place the ovary and whatever parts are closely associated with it ripen into a *fruit* Fruits are of many kinds. They may be one-seeded and enclosed in a hard covering as the grains of grasses or the *achenes* of composites. They may be dry *capsules* as in the seed-pods of poppies, or follicles as those of columbines, or they may be fleshy.

The fleshy parts of fruits are derived from various structures which are associated with the flower. Some examples are: serviceberries which are like apples where the calyx enlarges and encloses the ovary; strawberries where the receptacle enlarges and each individual ovary becomes an achene attached to it; plums and cherries which are technically called *drupes,* where the outer seed coat becomes thick and juicy; raspberries and blackberries which are really clusters of small drupes called *drupelets,* attached to a receptacle from which the whole cluster separates when ripe; or true *berries,* such as huckleberries, which are soft fruits with seeds embedded in a juicy pulp. These developments help to insure wide distribution of seeds.

HOW TO USE THE KEYS

There are more than 970 different kinds of plants described in this book. Over one-third of them are illustrated by line drawings. These drawings will be useful in identifying species of plants which are closely related to the species shown, because plants of a given family or genus have characteristics in common.

The author has used easily recognized characters in the keys, such as: habit of branching, types of leaf and inflorescence, color of flowers, numerical patterns and, sometimes, habitat or distribution. An effort has been made to keep the use of technical terms to a minimum, but in order to provide an accurate and useful treatment of our mountain vegetation certain technical words are necessary. Most of those used are explained. and many are illustrated in the section entitled *The First Things To Learn About Plants,* p. 38, and *Plates A* through *G.* Others may be found in the glossary or a good dictionary.

There is a series of keys. First, a short key on p. 52, to the four large groups included.

Next there are keys to the plant families included in each group.

Then, in many cases, there are family keys which lead to a genus or directly to a species.

Finally, in most cases where a genus has several species, there are generic keys which lead to the individual species.

There are group, family and generic descriptions and all the information in these preliminary descriptions, besides that given in the key, pertains to each species.

So to be sure you have the correct determination of a plant you should, at first, begin at the beginning and then learn to keep all this information in mind as you go and check each character against the specimen you wish to identify. To repeat all this information in every plant description would require a book much too large and cumbersome to be useful.

With a little practice one can soon learn to use the keys to identify unknown plants. These keys are made so that the reader always has a choice between two contrasted groups of characters. Usually the unknown plant will fit into one or the other of these groups. By making a choice in accord with the characteristics of your plant at each successive pair of statements you will eventually come to the name of a plant, followed by a page number. This name will appear further on in the text followed by a brief description and a statement as to where the plant occurs and under what sort of environmental conditions it grows.

If the description or notes on distribution and habitat do not fit the plant you are trying to identify you must go back to the key and reconsider each point carefully; possibly you made an incorrect choice or missed a point and followed the wrong path, so try another one.

Because all living organisms vary, it is difficult to construct a key, or even to write a description which will always fit every individual of a species. Excessive moisture or lack of it can change the size and appearance of plants or a cow may bite the top off a plant which normally has an erect, unbranched stem, causing it to send out branches lower down.

All such things have to be taken into consideration. By practice you will gradually learn the range of permissible variation. As you come to know more plants intimately you will have a better understanding of the terms used and a basis for comparison. Following is an example showing how to use the keys.

Suppose you find a plant with a cluster of 4-petaled, yellow flowers growing on an open, sunny field at an altitude of about 8,000 feet in Colorado. If you would like to find out the name of it proceed as follows: Turn to page 52. Read the statements under both "a" and "aa." Your plant does not fit under "a" because it is not woody, that is, it is neither a tree nor a shrub.

The next category "aa" includes both woody and herbaceous plants. So your plant fits here because it is herbaceous, and so you now must choose between "b" and "bb". Your plant has flowers so you choose "bb." Following on under "c" you find "flower arrangement on the plan of 3" which excludes your plant. Since your plant has 4 petals you choose "cc," and under that, since the petals are separate, you choose "d," "Flowers without petals or with petals separate."

If you are not sure that you understand the difference between a corolla of separate petals and a united corolla look up the diagrams on *Plate E*. Your plant has 4 separate petals so you come to the group Free Petal Dicots, p. 94

When you turn to p. 94, you will find a key to the families included in this group. By following the process outlined above through this key you will discover that your plant belongs to the Mustard Family.

Then you turn to p. 139. Here you should read the family description carefully and check the characters of your plant against it. Then repeat the process through the key to this family. A 6-inch ruler and a good hand-lens are a great help. If you are accurate in your observations you will find that your plant is a wallflower, of the genus *Erysimum,* so turn to p. 143. Here you will find four kinds, species, of wallflower described. By reading the descriptions you will find that one species has a number.

If you look up this number among the illustrations, you will find a sketch of this species with which you can compare your specimen. You will also be able to decide from the description which species of wallflower you have and you will find some interesting information about the plant and where it grows.

After you have followed this whole process through for several times you will begin to recognize the groups and families to which plants belong and then you will be able to save time by going directly to the family or genus key to identify your species.

If you need help in finding the name of some particular plant, the staffs of state experiment stations and the herbaria of state universities will usually report on dry, pressed specimens sent to them for identification. Senders should always enclose a self-addressed postcard or envelope and send ample material. Each specimen should have a number and be accompanied by information as to locality and date of collection. The sender should retain a specimen of each number for his own reference, as the identifier will send back only the name with the number.

KEYS AND DESCRIPTIONS

The first step in identifying an unknown plant by this book is to look down the following key and decide which one of these groups it fits into. It helps to read both of the coordinate statements in the key before making the choice. For instance, read both "a" and "aa" or "c" and "cc" and compare the two statements, then turn to the page of the group which best fits your plant.

a. Woody plants, trees, or shrubs, with needle-like or awl-shaped evergreen leaves

PINE FAMILY. p. 60.

aa. Plants either woody or herbaceous, but never with evergreen, needle-like, or awl-shaped leaves.

  b. Plants never bearing flowers; reproduction is by spores

FERNS, HORSETAILS, CLUB-
MOSSES, p. 52.

  bb. Plants bearing flowers and reproducing by seeds.

    c. Flower arrangement on a plan of 3, or flowers inconspicuous and leaves grass-like

MONOCOTS, p.68.

    cc. Flower arrangement on a plan of 4 or 5; leaves not grass-like (DICOTS).

      d. Flowers without petals or with petals separate

FREE PETAL DICOTS, p. 94.

      dd. Flowers with petals united into a regular or irregular corolla

UNITED PETAL DICOTS, p. 212.

Ferns, Horsetails and Clubmosses

These plants are included in the large group called the Pteridophytes, or "Fern-plants." In addition to the true ferns, *Polypodiaceae,* it includes the HORSETAILS or SCOURING RUSHES, *Equisetaceae,* the CLUBMOSSES or GROUND-PINE, *Lycopodiaceae,* and the SELAGINELLAS or LITTLE CLUB-MOSSES, *Selaginellaceae,* and other small families not described here. The group is placed below the seed plants in the evolutionary system because in it reproduction is carried on by spores which are simpler structures than seeds.

Spores, being much smaller and lighter even than seeds, are capable of being carried by wind or water over great distances. Perhaps this partly explains why many fern species are very widely distributed over the world. This is especially true of those species which are adapted to growing in moist habitats. All of our large species and several of the smaller ones belong in this group.

In the comparatively arid areas of the American west a group of dry-land ferns has evolved. These are able to live under minimum moisture conditions by special morphological adaptations. All these are small plants and that in itself is an advantage because of the reduced evaporating surface of the leaves. Most of them are dull green in color, showing that there is a tough, thick covering over the upper surface. In addition, on some there are devices which cause in-rolling of the margins during particularly dry periods; in other species one or both surfaces are covered by scales or hairs. In these and other ways evolution has made it possible for some ferns to grow in desert habitats.

During the geologic period called the Carboniferous Age ferns and their relatives had attained dominance and they provided the vegetative material which produced our great coal beds. But, through evolution, seed plants have superseded them and become the most conspicuous part of our present vegetation.

FERN FAMILY, *Polypodiaceae*

The leaf of a fern plant is called a *frond* and usually consists of a stalk, called the *stipe,* and a leafy part called the *blade.* The main extension of the stipe through the blade is the *rachis.* The blade is usually divided one or more times. The first division is a *pinna* (plural *pinnae*). Pinnae may be divided into *pinnules* and these are sometimes further divided or variously lobed or toothed. Fronds arise from an underground stem or rootstock. If this stem is short the fronds form a tuft or rounded clump. If the stem is creeping the fronds may form a large, dense, irregular clump or bed, or they may occur scatteringly, sometimes, as with Bracken, over a large area. Some species often grow in rock crevices. This habit may result in a line of fronds following the crevice, as is seen in Polypody.

The reproductive body which contains the spore cases, *sporangia,* is called a *sorus* (plural, *sori*). Sori occur on the undersides of the *fertile* fronds. They are often very numerous, but some fronds, usually the earlier ones, lack them altogether and are referred to as *sterile* fronds. The shapes and positions of sori are distinctive and useful in identification. Certain species have a very small membranous cover over the sorus called an *indusium* (plural, *indusia*), which sometimes withers and disappears as the frond ages. The presence or absence of this and its shape is also important in determining species.

a. Fronds of 2 kinds; fertile ones taller and with narrower divisions
than the sterile ones
ROCK-BRAKE, p. 54.
aa. Fronds all similar in appearance, usually at least some bearing
sori on their under surfaces.
b. Fronds with conspicuously zigzag branching; pinnae small, firm,
powdery white beneath
ZIGZAG CLOAK FERN, p. 54.
bb. Fronds lacking both conspicuously zigzag branching and white
powdery undersurface.
c. Fronds narrow, elongate, evergreen, 1-pinnate.
d. Sori round; fronds leathery.
e. Plants of rock crevices, growing from creeping rootstocks;

sori without indusia
                    COMMON POLYPODY, p. 55
  ee. Plants tufted, round indusia present on young sori
                    MOUNTAIN HOLLY FERN, p. 55
  dd. Sori elongated; plants of rock crevices.
    e. Blades appearing grass-like, usually with 1 or few narrow
       lobes
                    GRASS-LEAVED SPLEENWORT, p. 55
    ee. Blades 1-pinnate with roundish pinnae; rachises dark, shining
                    MAIDENHAIR SPLEENWORT, p. 56
cc. Blades of fronds narrow or triangular but more than 1-pinnate.
  d. Fronds triangular, that is, with the 2 basal divisions elon-
     gated.
    e. Fronds stout and firm-textured, 1 to 4 feet tall
                    BRACKEN, p. 56.
    ee. Fronds delicate, usually less than 10 inches tall
                    OAK FERN, p. 57.
  dd. Fronds elongated with 1 main axis.
    e. Fronds usually more than 12 inches long..
      f. Sori dot-like, without evident indusia
                    ALPINE LADY FERN, p. 57.
      ff. Sori with evident indusia.
        g. Sori elongated; indusia attached at one side.
                    COMMON LADY FERN, p. 57.
        gg. Sori round; indusia attached at center.
          h. Fronds 2-pinnate
                    MALE FERN, p. 57.
          hh. Fronds 3-pinnate
                    MOUNTAIN WOODFERN, p.58.
    ee. Fronds usually less than 12 inches tall.
      f. Fronds smooth; indusia hood-like when young
                    BRITTLE FERN, p. 58.
      ff. Fronds usually with scales or hairs, at least on lower
         surfaces.
        g. Indusia formed by the inrolled margins of the segments
                    LIPFERN, p. 58.
        gg. Indusia attached beneath the sori and appearing as slen-
           der filaments; often concealed as the sori mature. (Use
           a lens.)   WOODSIA, p. 58.

ROCK-BRAKE or PARSLEY FERN, *Cryptogramma crispa* ssp. *acrosticoides,* fig. 1, is a tufted plant 6 to 10 inches tall, conspicuous because the fertile fronds with their slender, pod-like pinnules, overtop the sterile ones. In the northern Colorado and Wyoming mountains it is most commonly found above 9,000 feet on dry, rocky slopes, often in crevices, but may occur from the foothills to the alpine zone. Its range is from Quebec across Canada, in northern Michigan, Nebraska, in the western states and north to Alaska.

ZIG-ZAG CLOAK FERN, *Notholaena fendleri,* fig. 2, is sometimes found in rock crevices or on ledges of dry cliffs in the foothills. Its brittle stipe and rachis are dark brown with scattered small oval or irregularly shaped pinnules. These are dull green above and covered on their undersides with whitish powder. It occurs from southeastern

Wyoming to southern New Mexico.

COMMON POLYPODY, *Polypodium vulgare,* fig. 3, has a creeping rootstock and may be found along shaded crevices of granite rocks, usually on north exposures, in the montane zone. The fronds vary with the amount of moisture available and may be between 4 and 8 inches in length. The round sori are conspicuous on the backs of the upper portion of the fronds. When young they are well separated and pale green, becoming golden and finally orange-brown and confluent. It occurs from Newfoundland to Alaska and southward in the mountains to Mexico, also in Eurasia.

MOUNTAIN HOLLY FERN, *Polystichum lonchitis,* fig. 4, with dark green, tough, 1-pinnate fronds having pinnae enlarged at base on their upper edges and with sharp, bristle-tipped teeth, occurs occasionally in shaded locations on cliffs and rock slides of the subalpine zone from Newfoundland to Alaska and south in the mountains to New Mexico, Arizona and California.

GRASS-LEAVED SPLEENWORT, *Asplenium septentrionale,* fig. 5. This is a curious looking plant for a fern as it hangs in tufts and fringes from crevices of dry granitic rocks. Its evergreen fronds are slender and grass-like with one to three main divisions and are usually mixed with rust-colored dry leaves of previous seasons. In the Rockies it is found in the foothill and montane zones and occurs from South Dakota and southeastern Wyoming southward through Colorado to western Oklahoma, New Mexico, Arizona and Mexico; also in Eurasia.

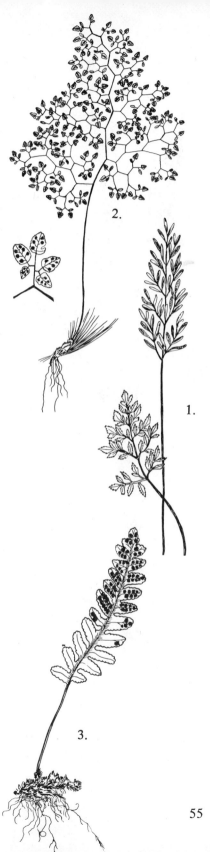

2. ZIGZAG CLOAK FERN, ½ ×

1. ROCK-BRAKE, ½ ×

3. COMMON POLYPODY, ½ ×

6. OAK FERN, ½ ×

MAIDENHAIR SPLEENWORT, *Asplenium trichomanes,* a small and rare fern with narrow, dainty fronds composed of roundish pinnules along a shining, dark rachis, is sometimes found in crevices of granitic rocks, especially in moist situations, in the montane zone.

BRACKEN, *Pteridium aquilinum,* is a coarse, stout fern with triangular-shaped fronds up to 4 feet tall which occurs throughout our range and is widely distributed in the world. Sori marginal but rarely seen. It grows in open areas on either moist or dry ground. Its stout rootstock is widely creeping so the plant usually appears in large patches. It sometimes becomes established on burned-over areas. When killed by frost the fronds turn a bright rusty color which makes patches of it conspicuous in autumn.

OAK FERN, *Gymnocarpium dryopteris,* fig. 6, is a delicate, sweet-scented fern of moist woods or shaded seepage areas, where its slender, creeping rootstocks send up scattered, triangular, smooth fronds. It has had several different names, among them *Dryopteris disjuncta* and *Phegopteris dryopteris.* It occurs from Newfoundland to

4. MOUNTAIN HOLLY FERN, ½ ×

5. GRASS-LEAVED SPLEENWORT, ½ ×

7. Alpine Lady-fern, ½ ×   8. Brittle Fern, ½ ×

Alaska and south into the northern United States and in mountainous areas as far as Virginia, New Mexico and Arizona.

Common Lady-fern, *Athyrium felix-femina.* A fern of moist ravines, woods, and stream banks with fronds up to 3 or 4 feet tall, growing in clumps. It may be distinguished from Bracken by its unbranched main rachis, the stalk of the leaf continuing through to its apex. This plant is very widely distributed throughout the world in the cooler parts of both hemispheres. In our mountains it occurs from the upper foothills to the subalpine regions. Alpine Lady-fern, *A. alpestre,* var. *americanum,* fig. 7, is a delicate, fragrant fern with fronds from 8 to 40 inches tall which grows in large clumps or

beds in crevices or among rocks in the timberline region and lower part of the alpine zone in Wyoming and Colorado. It also occurs in Newfoundland, Quebec, and from Alaska southward to Colorado, Nevada and California; also in the mountains of Europe. [Color Pl. 1a].

Male-fern, *Dryopteris felix-mas* is a large, coarse fern which grows in clumps with fronds from 15 to 40 inches tall. The stipes bear numerous thin, brown scales, especially near the base; blades are 2-pinnately divided; the pinnae have toothed margins; sori are round with kidney-shaped indusia attached at the sinus. This fern grows in many localities around the world in the northern hemisphere, and in our mountains is found in moist situations from the upper foothills to the

57

subalpine zone. MOUNTAIN WOOD FERN, *D. spinulosa,* is a rare plant occurring in a few moist, shaded situations in Rocky Mountain National Park and northward. It is similar to but more delicate than the Male Fern, having a scaly stipe but the tips of the leaf divisions are bristle-tipped.

BRITTLE FERN, *Cystopteris fragilis,* fig. 8. This is probably the most commonly seen fern in our range and one of the most common throughout the world. The fronds, 6 to 8 inches long, are delicate with brittle stipes which break off easily so that one does not find many of last season's stipes still persisting on the rootstocks. It grows in most moist situations from the foothills to timberline, on stream banks, under ledges, between rocks. It appears quickly in spring and often withers early as the season advances and soil dries out, but sometimes sends up fresh fronds during a later, moist period. It is usually not so definitely tufted as the Woodsias and is inclined to be less rigid and stiffly erect than OREGON WOOD-

9. FENDLER LIP FERN, ½ ×

SIA; differs from ROCKY MOUNTAIN WOODSIA in lacking hairs. NORTHERN BRITTLE FERN, *C. montana,* which is circumboreal, extends into Colorado where it is found in only a few localities. It differs from the common BRITTLE FERN in having the two lower pinnae considerably larger than the others. This gives a triangular effect to the frond.

FENDLER LIP-FERN, *Cheilanthes fendleri,* fig. 9, is a small fern growing in dense clumps or beds among shaded rocks, sometimes in crevices or at the foot of dry cliffs. Its fronds are 3 to 10 inches tall with small, roundish segments covered on their backs with thin, tapering, transparent scales. Foothills and lower montane zone from western Texas to Colorado and Arizona. SLENDER LIP-FERN, *C. feei,* is similar except that the lower surfaces of the fronds are covered with reddish-brown hairs instead of scales. This occurs on dry cliffs on the plains and foothills.

WOODSIA, *Woodsia.* Two species occur in our area. To distinguish these ferns from some of our other small species it is helpful to have a good hand lens. The important character for identification is the indusium which consists of small filaments attached beneath the sorus. To see this plainly the specimen should be in good condition, neither too young nor too old. ROCKY MOUNTAIN WOODSIA, *W. scopulina,* is a small fern usually found in tufts in rather dry, rocky situations of the upper montane and subalpine zones. Its fronds are 5 to 9 inches tall with hairs on their under surfaces which sometimes give a glistening appearance. The filaments of the indusia are often concealed by the spreading brown sporangia. OREGON WOODSIA, *W. oregona,* fig. 10, is similar but lacks the hairs on the under surfaces, stands more stiffly erect, and usually has a bright brownish stipe and rachis. It grows most commonly in foothill and lower montane regions. Both occur throughout our range.

HORSETAIL FAMILY,
Equisetaceae

These plants have hollow, green, striate, jointed stems which are either unbranched or have whorls of branches. The plant tissue contains minute bits of silica which make it unpalatable and detrimental to animals if eaten and give it an abrasive quality. The leaves are very small, like pointed teeth which form a short crown around each joint.

Our commonest species is the COMMON HORSETAIL, *Equisetum arvense,* a plant 6 to 20 inches tall in which the sterile stems bear whorls of slender branches at each joint. Its fertile stems appear earlier and soon wither. The fertile stems are pale brown, 2 to 10 inches tall and each bears one pale, brown, cone-like structure which contains the sporangia. It is often found on moist, sandy soil and especially along railroad embankments. Two similar species with much stouter and unbranched stems 2 to 4 feet tall may be found. Both occur on moist ground, along ditches or streams, and along railroads. The KANSAS SCOURING RUSH, *E. laevigatum,* has annual aerial stems and the TALL SCOURING RUSH, *E. hyemale,* has perennial stems which remain green all winter. The stems of these plants, as their name implies, were used for scouring purposes.

CLUBMOSS FAMILY,
Lycopodiaceae

This is a small family of low,

10. OREGON WOODSIA, ½ ×

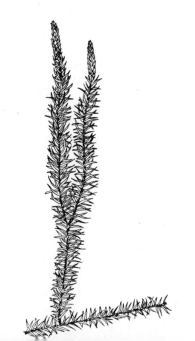

11. MOUNTAIN CLUB MOSS, ½ ×

12. SELAGINELLA, ½ ×

creeping plants having narrow, pointed leaves about one-half inch long, arranged in whorls which entirely clothe the stems. Only two species are found in our range but in the northeast and northwest states several other species occur which are often called GROUND-PINE or GROUND-CEDAR.

MOUNTAIN CLUBMOSS, *Lycopodium annotinum,* fig. 11, is our most common species. But even it is rarely seen. It grows under spruce forest or in sphagnum moss at the edge of subalpine ponds. The sporangia are in cone-like structures at the tips of upright branches. Each "leaf" of the "cone" bears one round sporangium filled with tiny spores. It occurs from Labrador to Alaska and south to Pennsylvania, Michigan, Colorado and Oregon;

also in Greenland and Eurasia.

SELAGINELLA FAMILY, *Selaginellaceae*

This is a small family of moss-like plants which includes important natural ground covers on rocky or gravelly soil. They are sometimes called "LITTLE CLUBMOSSES" because they are similar to those of the last family but smaller in every way and usually more compact, and are much more appropriately called "moss-like." Our commonest SELAGINELLA is *Selaginella densa,* fig. 12, with stems that are much branched, densely tufted and never more than 2 inches high. The closely appressed leaves are pointed, bristle-tipped, and less than ¼-inch long. The fruiting branches are strongly 4-sided. In dry weather the plants are dull or grayish but when moist they show a more lively green. This species and a few other similar ones are very abundant, especially on dry slopes among grasses or rocks from the foothills to the alpine zone. From Alberta south to South Dakota, New Mexico, Utah and Washington.

Pine Family (Pinaceae)

PINE FAMILY includes all of the evergreen trees and some evergreen shrubs of this region. Their leaves are always very narrow. This reduction in leaf surface keeps evaporation at a minimum and permits these trees to grow under very severe climatic conditions. Their "flowers" are small and simple and are found attached to scales which form a cone. They are unisexual, but in all genera except the junipers both kinds may occur on the same plant.

The junipers which many authors place in the Cypress Family, differ from other members of the Pine Family by having small, juicy, berry-like cones. The members of the Pine Family may be recognized and distinguished by use of the following key.

a. Leaves needle-like; fruits are dry cones
  b. Needles attached to twig in bundles of 2 (rarely 1) to 5 (the PINES).
    c. Needles in bundles of 5,
      d. Needles marked by white granules, central Colorado and south
BRISTLECONE PINE, p. 64

dd. Needles lacking white granules.
    e. Cones 1 1/2- to 3 inches long, remaining closed
                  WHITEBARK PINE, p. 64.
    ee. Cones 5 to 10 inches long, opening at maturity.
      f. Cones with stalks 1/2- to 2/3-inches long; southern
                    SOUTHWESTERN WHITE PINE, p. 63.
      ff. Cone stalks less than 1/2-inch long, entire region
                    LIMBER PINE, p. 63
cc. Needles in bundles of 2 (rarely 1) to 3.
    d. Trees usually shrub-like; seeds nut-like, without wings;
    needles 1 or 2
                  PIÑON or NUT PINE, p. 64.
    dd. Trees usually with single erect trunk; seeds with wings
    (Hard Pines).
      e. Needles 4 to 7 inches long; cones opening and falling
                  PONDEROSA PINE, p. 62.
      ee. Needles 1 to 3 inches long; cones remaining closed and
        persistent
                  LODGEPOLE PINE, p. 62.
bb. Needles attached to twig singly.
    c. Needles soft and flat.
      d. Needles attached by a small stem; buds sharp-pointed
                  DOUGLAS-FIR, p. 65.
      dd. Needles attached by a disk; buds blunt and pitch-covered
                  the TRUE FIRS, p. 64.
    cc. Needles rigid, 4-angled, sharp-pointed
                  the SPRUCES, p. 66.
aa. Leaves scale-like or awl-shaped; fruits are berry-like (the
JUNIPERS).
    b. Leaves all needle-like or awl-shaped, 1/4- to 3/4-inches long
                  COMMON JUNIPER, p. 67.

    bb. Leaves on mature branches scale-like, not over 1/8-inch long.
      c. A creeping shrub, northern Wyoming and northward
                  CREEPING JUNIPER, p. 67.
      cc. Small bushy trees or large, upright shrubs.
        d. Trunk bark thick, broken into squares; berries usually
        4-seeded
                  ALLIGATOR, JUNIPER, p. 67.
        dd. Trunk bark shredding, fibrous; berries usually 1- to 3-seeded.
          e. Berry red-brown, seed 1
                  UTAH JUNIPER, p. 67.
          ee. Berry bluish,
            f. Leaf margin smooth; seeds 1 to 3
                  ROCKY MOUNTAIN JUNIPER, p. 68
            ff. Leaf margin seen under a lens toothed; seed usually 1
                  ONE-SEED JUNIPER, p. 67-68.

    The PINES, *Pinus.* The members of this genus are easily distinguished from their relatives, the spruces and firs, because pine needles, which are leaves, are always bound together by a membranous sheath, in bundles of from two to five (rarely the PIÑON PINE is found with only 1 needle).

The male and female flowers are in separate cones.

The male cones are small, about an inch long, and papery in texture. They are sometimes reddish before they ripen but at the time the pollen is being shed, which is often dispersed in great clouds of yellow powder, they are usually bright orange. They will be found clustered around the base of the terminal shoots.

The carpellate, or female, cones are fewer in number and appear first as small, purple knobs near the ends of the young shoot, or "candle," just before the needles break out. At the time of fertilization the scales of the infant cone separate so that windblown pollen can reach the ovules. After fertilization takes place the cone scales close and will remain tightly closed over the developing ovules for about 18 months. In most pines, when these ovules have matured at the end of the second growing season, the scales separate and release the seeds.

After that, except in the case of the Whitebark and Lodgepole Pine, the cones drop off. When we learn how long it takes for pine ovules to ripen into seeds we understand why pine cones are such sturdy, protective structures.

Our pines are divided into three groups, the White or Soft Pines, the Yellow or Hard Pines and the Nut Pines. These are distinguished by the number of needles in the bundle, and by characters of the cones and of the bark.

PONDEROSA PINE, *P. ponderosa* (13). This becomes the largest of all trees in the Rocky Mountain region. In favorable locations it grows to 150 feet in height and 3 to 4 feet in diameter with straight trunk and few, large, horizontally spreading branches which form at maturity an open, rounded or flat-topped crown. The young trees are often branched to the ground and usually have black bark which later becomes a beautiful orange-brown. Needles are 2 or 3 in a bundle, 5-7 inches long.

This is the most widely distributed of the western pines. Its eastern outposts are in the Black Hills of South Dakota, in eastern Wyoming, western Nebraska, the hills of northeastern New Mexico, and the mountains of West Texas. It is an important forest tree and is cut for lumber in Colorado, New Mexico, Arizona, eastern Utah, northern Idaho and western Montana. It skips the Great Basin but extends through the mountains of the Pacific states into British Columbia.

LODGEPOLE PINE, *P. contorta,* var. *latifolia*. This tree is most commonly noticed when it grows in close, dense stands as it does on the western slope in Colorado, and in Yellowstone and Glacier National Parks. Under such conditions the

13. PONDEROSA PINE, 2/5 ×

trunks are slender, straight, and gray and the lower branches die off. The needles are in bundles of 2 and usually about 2 inches long, yellowish green; the lopsided cones remain closed and attached to the branches for many years.

The bark is thin and scaly, usually gray on trees in dense stands but often partly orange-brown on isolated individuals. The slender trunks were used by the Indians for teepee poles. This is a pioneer tree of the montane and subalpine zones.

Lodgepole forests grow on dry slopes and because of the dry situations, the closeness of the stands, and the pitchiness of their wood and bark they are very susceptible to fire. The heat of a forest fire opens the long-closed cones so that seeds are released. Partly on this account and partly because these seedlings thrive in full sunshine and on very poor soil, Lodgepole forests often succeed themselves following repeated fires. Also, because of their tolerance of sun they usually succeed spruce-fir forest when that is destroyed by fire.

LIMBER PINE, *P. flexilis* (14). This tree received its Latin name because its branches are very flexible. Its bark is light gray on young trunks and branches, and dark, almost black, on old trunks. The needles, in bundles of 5, are dark green, more bluish than those of the Ponderosa Pine. The cones are cylindrical, 4-10 inches long with a short stalk and often very pitchy. Each scale is rounded with a pale border.

LIMBER PINE is found from the foothills to timberline throughout our region, most commonly on windy ridges and rock outcrops. It is scattered among Ponderosa Pine and Engelmann Spruce where the situation is too rugged for those species.

Sometimes looking over a mountainside of dense spruce forest one will notice a variation in the texture of the dark green surface and on close observation will discover a rocky ridge cutting across the slope, covered with these pines. This situation may be seen from the Trail Ridge Road in Rocky Mountain National Park, as one approaches the forest.

Occasionally Limber Pines attain large size. Near South Pass, Wyoming, there are several of these big, old trees growing from an almost solid rock pavement. At timberline and at other windy sites they become gnarled and twisted. Sometimes the trunk separates into several main, upward-reaching branches.

Always these trees are interesting because of their distinctive shapes. They become mature at about 300 years and some are definitely known to have lived to an age of 1300 years in Utah, Idaho and California.

SOUTHWESTERN WHITE PINE, *P. reflexa, (P. strobiformis)*, is found in the mountains of New Mexico. It resembles the Limber Pine when it grows in exposed situations but in congenial surroundings it develops a tall, straight trunk and appears more like the eastern white pine. Its

14. LIMBER PINE, 2/5 ×

needles are longer and more slender than those of the Limber Pine and its cone has a stalk ½- to ⅔-inch long. On very old trees the bark becomes red-brown, resembling that of the mature Ponderosa Pines.

BRISTLECONE PINE, *P. aristata.* This is another 5-needled pine. It may be easily recognized by the white specks of pitch on the needles which remain on the tree for 10 or 15 years so that young branches are completely covered with them and have a brush-like appearance. Because of this characteristic the tree is sometimes called "Foxtail Pine." In our area this species is restricted to higher altitudes of the mountains from north central Colorado southward and westward. It grows in high, windy places and old trees are often twisted into very picturesque shapes. They attain ages of 300 to 400 years and perhaps become much older in the Rocky Mountains. In the White Mountains of eastern California and Nevada there are some ancients which are believed to be even older than the Sequoias.

WHITEBARK PINE, *P. albicaulis.* This tree is hard to distinguish from the Limber Pine except by its cones which are short and roundish. The scales do not separate, but after several years the whole cone disintegrates and in that way the large seeds are released. It seems to replace the Bristlecone Pine in the northern part of the Rocky Mountains. It grows in rocky places and particularly near timberline where it often sprawls on the ground in typical "wind timber" formation. It occurs in northwestern Wyoming, central and northern Idaho, western Montana and northwards, and is also found in the mountains of central and northern California.

PINON or NUT PINE, *P. edulis.* This is the bushy pine of the southern and southwestern foothills. It grows in an open formation intermingled with junipers, giving a spotted appearance to the slopes. The common form in our area normally has two needles in a bundle but throughout much of the Great Basin there is a one-needle form which is similar in appearance. Its cones are short with a few thick scales which open in August or September, releasing the large edible seeds. Shells of seeds of *Pinus edulis* are soft enough to be easily cracked with the teeth. These trees are very important to the Indians of Arizona and New Mexico. Some of their fuel is wood from this pine. It also provides posts and material for furniture. "Piñon nuts" are an important staple food for Navajo and Pueblo Indians and are available in the markets of the Southwest.

FIR, *Abies.* The trees of this genus have whorled, horizontal branches and soft, flat needles. Their cones are held upright on the topmost branches. These cones mature at the end of the first growing season and instead of dropping off they disintegrate where they are, so that the winged seeds are released at some distance above the ground. Thus they are assured of wide dispersal by the wind. After the cone scales and the seeds have fallen, the slender spike-like axis to which they were attached persists on the branch. One can frequently see the two- or three-year-old spikes stiffly erect on the upper branches of a fir tree. This character is helpful in recognizing trees of this genus during fall and winter when no full cones are in evidence. True firs may be distinguished from the

DOUGLAS-FIR by their blunt, resin-covered buds.

WHITE FIR, *A. concolor*. When well grown this is one of the most beautiful trees of North America. It produces a dense, silver-green conical crown, 80-100 feet tall, densely clothed with branches to the ground. Its needles are from 1 to 3 inches long, the longer ones on lower branches and the shorter on the upper or fruiting branches. The cones are 3 to 5 inches long and sometimes brightly colored from yellow to purple. White firs are found in the canyons of southern Colorado and northern New Mexico, mountains of Arizona, and westwards to California. [Color Pl. 1b].

SUBALPINE FIR, *A. lasiocarpa*. In the moist shade of the subalpine forests this tree develops a slender, spire-like crown 60 to 100 feet tall with short, horizontal branches which often have a shelf-like appearance. At timberline it takes various forms, frequently becoming a prostrate, matted shrub. Sometimes one sees a slender trunk standing erect in the midst of a cluster of low branches like a mother with several small children hanging onto her skirts. The "flag trees" at timberline are frequently of this species. They are the ones which have only a line of branches on the lee side of the trunk, all the others having been shorn off by the severe winds. Often it forms "hedges" or "windrows" shaped by the wind.

The bark on young wood is light gray, thin and smooth except for resin blisters, but on old trunks it becomes thick and rough. The needles are about an inch long and dark green. Cones are 2-4 inches long, dark blue or purple and often decorated with crystalline drops of pitch. This tree is found in all the high parts of the Rocky Mountains. It provides the best firewood available at high altitudes.

A variety of it called the CORKBARK FIR, *A. lasiocarpa* var. *arizonica,* grows in the southern part of our area. It may be distinguished by its soft, corky, yellow-white or ash-gray trunk bark and by its longer, narrower cones.

DOUGLAS-FIR, *Pseudostuga menziesii (P. taxifolia),* (15). In our area this tree seldom grows more than 100 feet tall but may be 3 feet in diameter with a pyramidal, irregularly much-branched crown. On young trees its bark is smooth and gray, with resin blisters somewhat similar to those on the true firs, but on old trunks it becomes very thick, patterned in dark and light brown, and deeply furrowed.

The soft, flat needles are bright green and the sharply-pointed, scaly buds are shiny brown. The cones hang down and may be distinguished from those of the spruce by the 3-parted bracts which protrude from between the scales.

This tree has almost as wide a distribution in the Rockies as does the PONDEROSA PINE and is usually found in association with it. The DOUGLAS-FIR is more abundant on north-facing slopes and in ravines than the pine and is the dominant tree of the montane zone in the

15. DOUGLAS FIR, 2/5 ×

parks and valleys of Colorado's western slope where this pine is seldom seen. The common name of this tree commemorates David Douglas, a Scottish botanist and horticulturist, who explored and collected plants in northwest America early in the 19th century.

SPRUCE, *Picea*. These trees may be distinguished from their Rocky Mountain neighbors by their 4-angled, sharp-pointed needles, and by the fact that their cones hang down and lack the fringed appearance of the Douglas-fir cones.

COLORADO BLUE SPRUCE, *P. pungens* (16), is a conical, handsome tree sometimes 100 feet tall and 2 feet in diameter. It is often a beautiful silver blue color but there are also many fine green specimens.

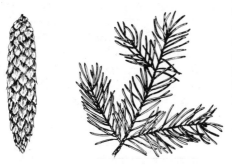

16. COLORADO BLUE SPRUCE, 2/5×

This species may be distinguished from other spruces of our area by the excessively sharp-pointed needles and by the larger size of the cones which are usually about 3½-inches long. The bark is gray and scaly.

It is at its best in the montane canyons of central and northern Colorado, although its range extends from the Mexican border into western and central Montana. It occurs in small groves along streams and occasionally in mixed forests.

ENGELMANN SPRUCE, *P. engelmannii,* is the tree which forms great, unbroken forests in the upper montane and subalpine areas of the Rockies. Its needles are 4-angled and pointed but not as sharp as those of the blue spruce. Its cones are similar but smaller, usually less than 2½-inches long. It is an important lumber tree of this region. The bark on old trunks is in thin, reddish plates. [Color Pl. 1c].

Named in honor of Dr. George Engelmann, who lived for a long time in St. Louis, Mo., where he had an active medical practice and also carried on botanical work. He traveled widely in the western U.S. to study particular plant groups, especially the cone-bearing trees. Although he did not collect extensively himself, he acquired plant collections of others and his personal herbarium became the basis of the now world-famous Missouri Botanical Garden Herbarium.

JUNIPER or ROCKY MOUNTAIN CEDAR, *Juniperus*. These are shrubs or small trees of bushy habit. Except for one species the leaves of mature individuals are very short, scale-like, and closely appressed (pressed close together for the whole length). Their "berries" are really much-modified cones in which the few small, soft scales enclose one to a few seeds in a berry-like structure. If you look closely at a juniper "berry" (cone) you will be able to see on its surface two or more little points which correspond to the tips of pine cone scales. Some books include this genus in the Cypress Family.

Plants of this genus show the

interesting characteristic of two types of leaves. They have *juvenile* and *mature* foliage.

The common JUNIPER is the exception. It has only the juvenile type of leaf, a very sharp pointed, awl-shaped needle, ¼- to ¾-inch long. All of the other species have similar awl-shaped leaves when they are young and often older plants will show this type of leaf on young shoots near the base of the main trunk, but when seedlings of these other species are several years old they begin to develop their adult foliage, the short scale-like type of leaf.

If you look near the base of an old juniper tree, especially if it has been injured there, you are quite likely to find some sprouts with awl-shaped leaves. This is not an abnormal condition but a normal one. Because of this habit, botanists who study plant evolution have decided that the common juniper is close to the original juniper species from which these other different, but evidently related, species have evolved.

The wood of the upright junipers is very durable. It furnishes excellent fence posts and is sometimes used for furniture.

COMMON JUNIPER, *J. communis* ssp. *nana,* a shrub from 1 to 3 feet tall, sometimes forming large clumps, found on north slopes and under open forest from the foothills to timberline. The very sharp-pointed leaves are green with a white line on the upper surface, and the round berries are blue when ripe. This species is very widely distributed and forms of it are found in all the northern lands of the northern hemisphere.

CREEPING JUNIPER, *J. horizontalis.* This plant varies from a very low creeper with trailing, rooting stems only a few inches high which sometimes carpet the ground, to low spreading shrubs which may be as much as a foot tall. There are both green and silver forms. When exposed to winter sun the foliage often turns purplish. It is found on open dry slopes in Wyoming and Montana, and across the northern United States. Its "berries" (cones) are dark blue with a silvery bloom and are always borne on short, curved stalks. [Color Pl. 1d].

ALLIGATOR JUNIPER, *J. deppeana (J. pachyphloea),* may be as much as 50 feet tall and 2 feet in diameter. More often it is a smaller, compact tree or large spreading shrub. It takes its name from the thick, brown or grayish bark which breaks into square plates on the trunks of old trees. Its foliage is blue-green and its berries dark red-brown. This is found in the mountains of southern New Mexico and Arizona.

UTAH JUNIPER, *J. osteosperma (J. utahensis),* and ONE-SEED JUNIPER, *J. monosperma,* are the common junipers of the foothills of the southern and western parts of our region. They are not easily distinguished. Both have, in general, a yellowish-green foliage color. Both usually have several main stems from the ground. Both usually have one-seeded berries.

The berries of the Utah juniper are usually larger than the others and its range is farther west.

Along the eastern side of the mountains in southern Colorado and New Mexico only the ONE-SEED occurs. In the western third of both states the two species are intermingled. In Wyoming only the UTAH JUNIPER is found.

The shreddy bark of both these trees makes excellent kindling for camp fires. They often grow inter-mingled with Piñon Pines.

ROCKY MOUNTAIN JUNIPER, *J. scopulorum.* This juniper, some-times called "WESTERN RED CE-DAR," usually has a silvery or gray-ish color, but sometimes it is green. Its berry-like fruits are light blue when mature and usually have 2 or 3 seeds.

On the eastern side of the Conti-nental Divide from Palmer Lake, Colorado, northward it is the only upright juniper, and is frequently the first tree form found as one ascends the dry foothill slopes. At higher elevations on south and southwest slopes it is intermixed with PONDEROSA PINE, the juniper being found on the driest and most rocky sites.

Throughout the rest of our area it occurs intermingled with piñon and oak. In general where its geo-graphic range overlaps that of the ONE-SEED and UTAH JUNIPERS it is found at a higher elevation than those species.

Monocotyledonous Plants (Monocots)

Plants which have only one seed-leaf (cotyledon) are called *Mono-cotyledons,* or *Monocots* for short. They have other characters in common which help us to recognize the plants that belong to this group. Those having conspicuous flowers have their flower parts in threes. Those having small, chaffy flowers have long, narrow leaves and all our species have leaves with entire margins. All the grass-like plants belong in this group.

If the plant you are trying to identify has flowers and leaves which both agree with these characters you will find it in this section. It may have broad leaves but if the other characters agree it will be found here.

However, even if it has narrow leaves and apparently parallel veins, but the flower parts are in fours or fives, look for it under the heading Dicots, p. 93.

KEY TO MONOCOT FAMILIES

a. Plants with conspicuous petals or sepals (perianth segments).
  b. Flowers regular (radially symmetrical).
    c. Pistils numerous, in a head or ring
        WATERPLANTAIN FAMILY
        Alismaceae, p. 71.
  cc. Pistils 1, usually 3-celled.
    d. Perianth segments 6, all petal-like.
      e. Ovary superior
        LILY FAMILY
        Liliaceae, p. 80.
      ee. Ovary inferior
        IRIS FAMILY
        Iridaceae, p. 88.
    dd. Perianth of 3 sepals and 3 petals.
      e. Petals blue, upper leaf spathe-like

SPIDERWORT FAMILY
Commelinaceae, p. 78
 ee. Petals not blue.
  f. Leaves 3, broad, just below flower
   Trillium, p. 88.
   in LILY FAMILY
  ff. Leaves narrow, tapering
   MARIPOSA-LILY, p. 87
 bb. Flowers irregular (not radically symmetrical)
  ORCHID FAMILY
  Orchidaceae, p. 89.
aa. Plants without conspicuous petals.
 b. Plants aquatic, completely submersed or free floating.
  c. Plants minute; not differentiated into stems and leaves
   DUCKWEED FAMILY
   Lemnaceae, p. 77.
  cc. Plants with distinct stems and leaves.
   d. Leaves usually alternate, not in 3's
    PONDWEED FAMILY
    Najadaceae, p. 71.
   dd. Leaves opposite below, in 3's above
    FROGBIT FAMILY
    Hydrocharitaceae, p. 72
 bb. Plants terrestial or more or less aquatic, but not free floating nor completely submerged.
  c. Plants aquatic with zigzag stems and floating leaves
   BUR-REED FAMILY
   Sparganiaceae, p. 71.
  cc. Plants with straight stems and erect leaves.
   d. Stems round, circular in cross-section.
    e. Stems without joints.
     f. Flowers in erect, dense, terminal spikes.
      g. Plants 3 to 5 feet tall; spikes ½ to 1 inch thick
       CAT-TAIL FAMILY
       Typhaceae, p. 70.
      gg. Plants less than 2 feet tall; spikes less than ½ inch thick
       ARROWGRASS FAMILY
       Juncaginaceae, p. 71.
     ff. Flowers in clusters, panicles, or heads
      RUSH FAMILY
      Juncaceae, p. 78.
    ee. Stems jointed, hollow
     GRASS FAMILY
     Gramineae, p. 72.
   dd. Stems 3-angled, triangular in cross section
    SEDGE FAMILY
    Cyperaceae, p. 75.

CATTAIL FAMILY,
Typhaceae

The cattails are tall plants of marshes and ditch borders with long strap-like leaves and cylindrical spikes of tiny, crowded flowers which are of two kinds. The straw-colored staminate ones are above the dark brown pistillate ones. The former soon wither and fall away leaving the long, bare axis exposed. In the two following species at flowering time, the staminate portion appears larger than the pistillate.

BROAD-LEAVED CATTAIL, *Typha latifolia* (17), is the most conspicuous and the commonest in most places. Its stalks are 3 to 5 feet tall, not quite as tall as the leaves. In this species the staminate flowers

are directly above the pistillate ones.

NARROW-LEAVED CATTAIL, *T. angustifolia* (18), is usually a smaller plant with a more slender spike on which the pistillate flowers are separated from the staminate ones by 1 or 2 inches of bare stalk. The two often grow together in wet places of the foothills and mountain valleys. This genus is worldwide in its distribution in temperate and tropical regions.

18. NARROW-LEAVED   CATTAIL, ½ ×

17. BROAD-LEAVED   CATTAIL, ½ ×

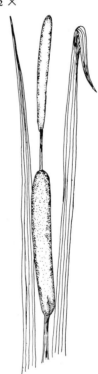

Cattails have been valuable to man in several ways. Indians obtained a starch from the root, peeled and roasted the lower part of the stem and the young flower spikes for food, used the down from the ripened spikes for padding cradle boards and dressing wounds, and the yellow pollen is used as a sacred offering by the Apaches.

The long flat leaves were woven into mats by the American pioneers and used to make seats for the old-fashioned rush-bottomed chairs. A cattail marsh is a good place for wildlife, especially muskrats, geese, red-wing blackbirds, and marsh wrens.

BUR-REED FAMILY,
Sparganiaceae

BUR-REED, *Sparganium angustifolium*. This water plant has zigzag stems and long, narrow leaves arising from the mud at the bottom. Most of the leaves bend and become floating at the surface of the water. There are round clusters of tiny flowers which ripen into bur-like heads of seeds. Two or three additional species may be found. All provide good food for muskrats, water birds and deer. They are found in shallow water around the margins of many ponds and lakes.

PONDWEED FAMILY,
Najadaceae

PONDWEED, *Potamogeton*. This is a group of water plants having some submersed leaves and some floating ones. Often there are two kinds on the same plant. The submersed ones are very thin, narrow and fragile, the floating ones are broader and tougher in texture. Their flowers are very small and after blooming are withdrawn under water where the seeds ripen.

About 20 species are known from the waters of the Rocky Mountain region. One of the commonest is *Potamogeton gramineus;* others are *P. natans, P. alpinus,* and *P. nodosus.* This family is one of the most valuable we have as a

source of food for ducks and other wildlife.

ARROWGRASS FAMILY,
Juncaginaceae

ARROWGRASS, *Triglochin*. These plants have slender, fleshy basal leaves, and leafless, erect stalks thickly set along the upper portions with tiny green flowers.

SHORE ARROWGRASS, *T. maritima,* is a stout plant with stems up to 3 feet tall, found on alkaline soil around ponds and in marshes of the high plains and foothills.

SWAMP ARROWGRASS, *T. palustris,* is a smaller plant, occurring in mountain swamps and around lakes. The seeds of both kinds are valuable food for small mammals and birds. In Yellowstone National Park they grow on the geyser and hot spring formations.

WATERPLANTAIN FAMILY,
Alismaceae

WATERPLANTAIN, *Alisma plantago-aquatica,* is a plant of marshes and ponds with basal, sheathing leaves and upright stalks bearing whorls of many, small, white or pinkish flowers.

Another plant of the same family is ARROWHEAD or DUCK-POTATO, *Sagittaria latifolia,* (26), which varies according to its situation. When completely submersed its leaves are long and ribbon-like; when protruding from the water it develops broad, arrowhead-shaped leaves and sends up stalks bearing pretty 3-petalled, white flowers.

This plant furnishes food for water birds and muskrats. Its roots produce starchy tubers which were used for food by the early settlers as well as by Indians.

FROGBIT FAMILY, *Hydro-charitaceae*

WATERWEED, *Elodea canadensis (Anacheris canadensis),* grows submersed in ponds and slow streams. Its leaves are one-nerved, transparent, and arranged oppositely on the lower parts of the stem and in threes on the upper parts. Its flowers are inconspicuous and it seldom produces seeds but it grows so rapidly that it sometimes fills ponds and ditches in the foothills. Small fish like to nibble on its leaves, so it is often used in aquaria.

26. ARROWHEAD, ½ ×

GRASS FAMILY, *Gramineae*

When looked at closely, grasses in bloom are found to be very beautiful, but many people pass by without seeing them and few think of them as wild flowers. These plants lack showy flower parts or attractive scents because they do not depend on insects but are wind pollinated.

This is one of the very large plant families and one of the most important to man. Grasses provide much of the pasture, hay, and grain which support domestic animals, so, indirectly, they are the source of our meat. In addition, our cereals and flour are derived from the seeds of grasses.

Some grasses grow in wet situations but in general the plants of this family are adapted to regions of low rainfall. In dry areas of the West such as our high plains and foothill slopes where the annual precipitation is only 8 to 15 inches plant communities made up predominantly of several kinds of grasses form the natural vegetative cover. Here there is not sufficient moisture to support the growth of trees.

The grass cover is very important in soil conservation. Grass roots penetrate deeply into the ground. They not only help keep the soil from washing away but as they die and are renewed they add humus to the soil.

Most grasses are perennial but much of their root system and all of the leaves and stalks die and are replaced annually. This process alone adds a great amount of organic material to the soil every season. If grass land is moderately grazed it is constantly being improved by the growth of the grass.

There is a direct relationship between the amount of leaf growth and the amount of root growth. If more than half of the bulk of the grass plant is eaten by stock or game on a pasture the plants cannot make enough roots to support a vigorous growth. Consequently both the pasturage and the soil become poorer each year. But if grazing is carefully regulated so that at least half of the leaves and stems of each plant are left, the forage value improves each year.

The plants of this family are characterized by having round, jointed stems which are usually hollow except at the joints, called *nodes,* and flat, narrow leaves which are jointed to a sheath-like base which surrounds the stalk. The inflorescence may be a spike, raceme or panicle.

The fruit is one seed tightly enclosed in the hardened ovary wall. Technically it is called a *caryopsis* but in agriculture it is called a grain. Corn and wheat grains are examples.

In most grass genera the individual flowers, which are called *florets,* are perfect, but in some cases the pistillate and staminate ones are separate on the same plant or on different plants. Each perfect floret consists of a group of chaffy scales which represent petals and sepals arranged around one pistil and from 1 to 6 stamens. The florets with the chaffy scales surrounding them are grouped into *spikelets.*

Classified according to their habit of growth, grasses are of two types. They may be *sod formers* or *bunch grasses.* In the first group the stems spread horizontally either underground or at the surface sending leaves up and roots down from the nodes. Thus they form a continuous, interwoven, sod groundcover. Bunch grasses grow singly in tufts and so never form a tight sod.

Only a few of the best known and most easily recognized species of this large family will be described here. (For more about grasses see *First Book of Grasses* by Agnes Chase and other publications listed in Useful References, p. 312).

BUFFALO GRASS, *Buchlöe dactyloides.* A short grass of the high plains and mesas. It never grows more than 3 or 4 inches tall. Its stems spread on the surface of the ground, rooting at the nodes and forming a dense, tough sod. This has two kinds of flowers. The staminate ones are held above the leaves but those which form the seeds will be found tucked down close to the ground.

PARRY OATGRASS, *Danthonia parryi* (22), is strictly a mountain grass 8 inches to 2 feet tall with few large, sometimes drooping heads. Its slender, tufted leaves are 4 to 9 inches long. Each spikelet is enclosed in one-inch long, papery *glumes.* A few bent and twisted *awns* stick out from between these glumes. Each awn is attached to one

22. PARRY OATGRASS, ½ ×

of the *lemmas* of the enclosed spike-let. This is found in open woods or on rocky hillsides through the mountains from Alberta to New Mexico, and in Colorado it occurs at altitudes between 6-10,000 feet. C. C. Parry, for whom it is named, was one of the important of the early botanical explorers in Colorado.

SWEETGRASS, *Hierochloe odorata,* is common in swampy mountain meadows. It grows about a foot to 18 inches tall and the ripe spikelets are a rich golden-brown. This is also common in the eastern United States where its sweet-scented stems were used by Indians in making baskets.

BLUE GRAMMA, *Bouteloua gracilis* (20). A grass of medium height, sometimes only 6 inches and rarely more than a foot tall. The spikelets are arranged along one side of the rachis and the inch-long spikes, 1 to 3 to a stalk, are set at an angle so they look like purple flags. This is common in the foothills and on open mountain slopes up to 8,500 feet. SIDE OATS GRAMMA, *B. curtipendula,* is taller and has many short spikes along one side of the erect, slender stalk.

TIMOTHY, *Phleum pratence,* is a tall, introduced grass with a compact, cylindrical spike 2 to 4 inches long, sometimes found on good moist soil in meadows and along roads or trails where hay has been carried. The native ALPINE TIMOTHY, *P. alpina* (19), is similar but not so tall and with a shorter, usually dark purplish spike. It grows in subalpine meadows.

BLUEGRASS, *Poa.* Several species occur naturally in our area and some European species have become established here. There are both sod-forming grasses and bunch grasses in this genus. The common KENTUCKY BLUEGRASS used in lawns is a sod-forming kind. Some of the little tufted grasses found above timberline are bunch grass Poas. Most kinds provide good forage and some are called "MUTTON GRASS."

SPIKE FESCUE, *Leucopoa kingii (Hesperochloa kingii),* is a stout, conspicuous bunch grass of the pine forests with stalks 15 to 30 inches tall and dence panicles 3 to 7 inches long. Its bluish-green leaves are flate, tough, striated and about ¼-inch wide. It was named for the geologist and explorer, Clarence King.

SQUIRREL-TAIL, *Sitanion longifolium (S. hystrix* (21). The bristly, brush-like inflorence of SQUIRREL-TAIL is made up of groups of florets which have long spreading awns. When these florets ripen, the central axis of the spike disarticulates so that the seeds with their attached awns are free to be moved about by wind or other agencies. These long, sharp awns catch in the hair of animals or the clothing of people. Thus wide distribution of the seeds is assured. The axis of the more compact head of FOXTAIL BARLEY, *Hordeum jubatum,* breaks up in much the same way. Its florets also have sharp, rigid but more slender awns about 2 inches long so its inflorescence is very bristly.

NEEDLE-AND-THREAD, *Stipa comata.* This grass has a slender stem about 2 or 3 feet tall with a narrow, sparse and drooping inflorescence. Each floret has an awn which is sometimes more than 6 inches long. It is twisted and bent. This long awn is the "thread" and the opposite end of the grain which is very sharp is the "needle." There are

20. Blue Gramma, ½ ×

19. Alpine Timothy, ½ ×

21. Squirrel-tail, ½ ×

several other species of NEEDLE GRASS found in our area which are similar but do not have quite such long awns.

COMMON REED, *Phragmites communis.* This is the largest grass in our region, sometimes reaching 12 feet in height with leaves half an inch to about 1 inch in width. It grows in very wet places on the plains and lower foothills. The inflorescence is a large, fluffy panicle. It is worldwide in distribution and has been useful to man in many ways. In Mexico and in our Southwest it was used for thatching, for arrow shafts, weaving rods, mats, cords and nets.

SEDGE FAMILY, *Cyperaceae*

The Sedges constitute a family of grass-like plants which by many people are not distinguished from the true grasses. Most of them grow in cold, wet places and especially in arctic and alpine regions. They make up a large proportion of the plants found above timberline.

With careful observation anyone can easily learn to distinguish members of this family from the grasses. Most of them have 3-cornered stalks which are solid and without joints (compare description of a grass, p. 73); their leaves are usually in 3 ranks, each folded and its base enclosing the stalk. In most cases all of the leaves rise from the rootstock.

Sedges may be tufted or have creeping underground stems which sometimes form tubers called "ground nuts." These are hunted by animals, waterfowl, and sometimes people, for food.

The seeds are achenes. They depend on the wind for pollination and their small flowers are arranged in spikes, sometimes referred to as spike-lets. Some species are very tall with drooping heads, others stiffly erect, still others only a few inches high. In the small species the leaves often tend to curl.

BULRUSH, *Scirpus*. Some members of this genus are giants. They grow in water around the edges of ponds and reservoirs or in marshes and are sometimes, but not always, as much as 12 feet tall. But the one most likely to be found in the mountains, *S. paludosus,* rarely reaches more than 5 feet and may be much less. The flowers are in clusters of several fat spikes at the top of the main stalk with 2 long, unequal leaves extending above them.

COTTONSEDGE, *Eriophorum*. This is a conspicuous plant in swamps and along borders of ponds in the high mountains during late summer because its flower heads become tufts of white or tawny, silky bristles. It is sometimes called COTTON-GRASS or "HARE'S TAIL." The NAR-ROW-LEAVED COTTONSEDGE, *E. angustifolium,* is the most common kind in the central Rockies. Several other species are very common farther north, especially in Canada and Alaska. *E. chamissonis* has tawny "cotton" and occurs from Yellowstone Park northward into Alaska.

SEDGE, *Carex*. This is a very large genus and its members are difficult to distinguish. In general their inflorescence is made up of a few compact spikes which may be

from about ¼-inch to 2 inches long. In several of the high-altitude species they are quite conspicuous because they are black or very dark brown. These plants often make a lush-looking growth along subalpine streams and in meadows near timberline. MERTENS SEDGE (24), *C. mertensii,* has light-colored heads which are usually drooping and its leaf blades are often more than ¼-inch wide. It grows from 1 to 3 feet tall and is found in Montana, especially in Glacier National Park. FISH-SCALE SEDGE, *C. chalciolepis* (23), is a plant 8 inches to 2 feet tall, which holds its heavy inch-long, black heads erect or drooping. Common in wet places of the subalpine zone but occurs from 8,000 to 13,000 feet and grows from Wyoming through Colorado into Arizona and Utah.

ROCKY MOUNTAIN SEDGE, *C. scopulorum,* is one of the most abundant sedges of the subalpine and alpine zones. It grows 10 to 15 inches tall and the new leaves come up through tufts of coarse, old, dry ones but it shows· up in wet places as patches of bright green in the otherwise brownish landscape. Much dry tundra is covered with the short, curly leaves of *C. rupestris.* A very common sedge of the mesas and foothills is SUN SEDGE, *C. heliophila,* which grows in small clumps, is from 4 to 10 inches tall and has noticeable, yellowish blooms in very early spring. Its yellowish-green leaves are somewhat curved. This is similar and closely related to C. *pennsylvanica,* which is very common throughout the eastern United States.

KOBRESIA, *Kobresia myosuroides,* a close relative of the sedges, is a densely-tufted plant with very slender stalks and almost thread-like leaves. It grows in the arctic and on high ridges and peaks of the Rockies in snow-free areas and is the dominant plant on mature alpine tundra. Its uniform stands of short, close, grass-like growth may be recognized in late summer and fall by their lovely orange-gold color.

FEW-FLOWERED SPIKERUSH, *Eleocharis pauciflora,* is another member of this family which is found on margins of ponds and in bogs of the subalpine zone. It grows from slender underground stems and has no obvious leaves. Its green stalks, 4 to 8 inches tall, are tipped by small compact flower spikes.

DUCKWEED FAMILY,
Lemnaceae

DUCKWEED, *Lemna trisulca,* is a tiny green plant body not differentiated into stem and leaf but bearing a very simple flower and a thread-like root. The individuals are from ¼- to ½-inch long and are frequently joined together in short chains. They are usually found submersed in the water of ponds and slow streams, at altitudes up to 10,000 feet. A still smaller species, *L. minor,* with separate floating disks not over ¼-inch long is much

23. FISH-SCALE SEDGE, ½ ×

24. MERTENS SEDGE, ½ ×

25. WESTERN SPIDERWORT, ½ ×

more abundant than the first and grows in similar places but is most commonly found below 8,500 feet.

These midget plants occur in great numbers, often forming large floating colonies. In late summer they are an important duck food as their name implies. They are perennial plants but they seldom produce seed and survive cold weather by sinking into the mud at the bottom of the pond or stream. These species of duckweed are found throughout North America and almost throughout the world.

SPIDERWORT FAMILY,
Commelinaceae

The plants of this family are somewhat succulent and have a slimy juice. The leaves have sheathing bases and long, tapering blades. The flowers have three petals, usually blue or purplish, which last only one day.

WESTERN SPIDERWORT, *Tradescantia occidentalis* (25). This very fragile and lovely blossom grows on a coarse plant. The flower has three similar blue or purplish petals, and six stamens. The filaments are hairy and this character is said to be the reason for the name SPIDERWORT. The long leaves have sheathing bases and stick out at awkward angles to the stem so that as the plant ages it begins to appear very weedy. It grows commonly along the base of the foothills from Arizona to Montana, also in Zion Canyon and several of the southwestern National Monuments. In the mornings in June and early July the plants are showy and attractive, covered with bright blue flowers. [Color Pl. 1e].

A closely related species found in Arizona is *T. pinetorum*. It has tubers on the roots which were used by the Indians for food. DAYFLOWER, *Commelina dianthifolia,* has an irregular flower which is borne in a green, funnel-shaped spathe. It occurs in the foothills and occasionally in the montane regions from Mexico as far north as central Colorado.

RUSH FAMILY,
Juncaceae

This group of plants is very closely related to the Lily Family. Its flower pattern is the same as that of the lilies, but its sepals and petals have in most cases become reduced to small brownish scales. As in the grasses and sedges, its members depend on wind-pollination. Its leaves, when present, are long and slender. For these reasons it is often "lumped" with the "grass-like" plants. It may be distinguished from sedges by its round stem, from grasses by its stem without joints, and from both by the pattern of the brown flowers which have 6 similar perianth segments, representing calyx and corolla, 3 or 6 stamens and 1 pistil with 3 stigmas which ripens into a capsule containing 3 or many seeds. Two genera of this family are commonly found in our area.

RUSH, *Juncus*. These plants have stiff, pithy, green stems which occur in clumps. Their leaves are often reduced to mere sheaths. They can be recognized among other vegetation because they are a much darker green than most plants. They grow in moist or wet places.

ARCTIC RUSH, *J. arcticus* ssp. *ater (J. balticus)*, (29), is one of the commonest. It will be seen forming clumps or zones of very dark green around seepage spots, from the plains to timberline. SUBALPINE RUSH, *J. mertensianus* (27), forms clumps of smooth stems 6 to 15 inches tall, each topped by a round head of small dark flowers. Each flower has 6 sharply pointed perianth segments. At flowering time the pink stigmas show up against the brownish black perianth. There are no leaves in evidence.

This is found in moist places of the subalpine zone throughout our range.

WOODRUSH, *Luzula*. These plants have flat, soft, grass-like leaves, hollow stems and capsules containing only three seeds. The COMMON WOODRUSH, *L. parviflora* (28), usually grows in a tuft 1 to 2 feet tall with a drooping, open and many-flowered inflorescence. It is found widely distributed over northern North America and in our mountains from 8,000 feet to timberline.

SPIKED WOODRUSH, *L. spicata,* is a smaller, more compact plant of mountainous regions and occurs in our subalpine and alpine zones. It

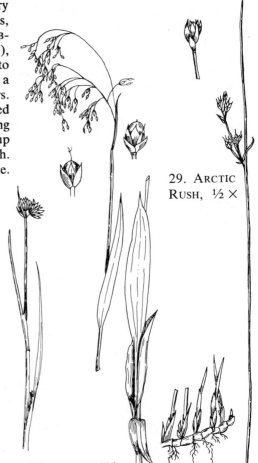

29. ARCTIC RUSH, ½ ×

27. SUBALPINE RUSH, ½ ×

28. COMMON WOODRUSH, ½ ×

rootstock of Arctic rush

has small nodding clusters of spikes. There are thin, chaffy bractlets between them which give a frosted appearance to the inflorescence.

LILY FAMILY, *Liliaceae*

All the plants in this family have their flowers built on the numerical plan of 3 and 6. In our species the sepals and petals are alike or almost alike, except in Calochortus and Trillium; leaves are mostly linear, usually not differentiated into distinct blade and petiole; leaf margins are entire; the root is often a bulb, corm, or a fleshy rootstock. In some genera the bulbs are edible and were used by Indians and pioneers as food; in some others they are poisonous.

a. Sepals and petals alike forming a 6-parted perianth.
  b. Plants coarse; flower stalks stout, 2 to 6 feet tall
    c. Leaves along the stem, large and pleated
                      CORN-LILY, FALSE HELLEBORE, p. 81.
    cc. Leaves mostly basal, in large tufts.
      d. Leaves stiff, very sharp-pointed, flowers about 2 inches long
                  YUCCA, SOAPWEED, p. 83.
      dd. Leaves flexible, reduced in size upwards, flowers small
                  NORTHERN BEAR-GRASS, p. 82.
  bb. Plants usually less than 2 feet tall, leaves smooth and soft textured.
    c. Stems leafy, basal leaves few or absent.
      d. Plants with some leaves whorled, that is, more then 2 at a node.
        e. Flower erect, 2 to 4 inches long, orange-red
                  WOOD LILY, p. 82.
        ee. Flowers pendant, not over 1 inch long
                  FRITILLARY, p. 82.
      dd. Leaves always alternate, never more than 1 at a node.
        e. Flowers or red berries pendant from underside of stem
                  TWISTED STALK p. 81.
        ee. Flowers at end of leafy stem.
          f. Flowers usually 1, berry 3-lobed, red
                  FAIRYBELLS, p. 81
          ff. Flowers several or many; berries round, greenish
                  SOLOMONPLUME, p. 81.
    cc. Leaves all, or mostly, at or near ground level.
      d. Flowers 1 inch or more broad, not taller than the leaves.
        e. Leaves 2 to 5, at least 1/3 as broad as long.
          f. Flowers white, leaves usually 5
                  BEADLILY, p. 87.
          ff. Flowers yellow, leaves 2
                  SNOW-LILY, p. 86
        ee. Leaves many, grass-like, flowers pure white, stemless
                  SAND-LILY, p. 84.
      dd. Flowers colored or creamy; if pure white, over 1/2-inch broad.
        e. Flowers solitary or in umbels.
          f. Flowers blue or purplish; leaves without onion odor

WILD HYACINTH, p. 85.
 ff. Flowers not blue·
  g. Flowers pink, rose, or whitish; leaves with onion odor
   WILD ONION, p. 84.
  gg. Flowers creamy white with dark veins, usually solitary
   ALP-LILY, p. 88.
 ee. Flowers in racemes.
  f. Flowers blue or purplish
   CAMAS, p.85.
  ff. Flowers creamy with greenish markings
   WAND-LILY, DEATH CAMAS, p. 85.
aa. Sepals and petals distinct, each 3; sepals narrow and green.
 b. Leaves broadly ovate, in a whorl of 3
  WESTERN TRILLIUM, p. 88.
 bb. Leaves few, alternate, long and narrow
  MARIPOSA-LILY, p. 87

CORN-LILY, *Veratrum californicum*. This plant, because of its large coarse, pleated and strongly-veined leaves, is sometimes called "skunk cabbage" in our area where the true skunk cabbage does not grow. On marshy ground of the aspen and spruce belts its stout shoots push up soon after the snow disappears. In Colorado it is found much more commonly on the western than on the eastern slope. Wherever it grows it is usually abundant. The tall, much-branched inflorescence is composed of many small white or greenish flowers.

SOLOMONPLUME, *Smilacina*. These plants have terminal clusters of small white flowers which produce berries. The STAR SOLOMONPLUME, *S. stellata* (32), has flowers like 6-pointed stars and is found in many kinds of habitats. In the foothills it is one of the very early spring flowers in canyons and along streams. Later it blooms at higher elevations on open slopes, meadows, and sometimes on dry banks.

The CLASPLEAF SOLOMONPLUME, *S. racemosa* (31), is less common and occurs in shady, moist locations. Its flowers are smaller and more crowded.

Two closely related plants with rather similar leaves found along streams and in moist woods are: FAIRYBELLS, *Disporum trachycarpum,* and TWISTED STALK, *Streptopus amplexifolius* (30); both have

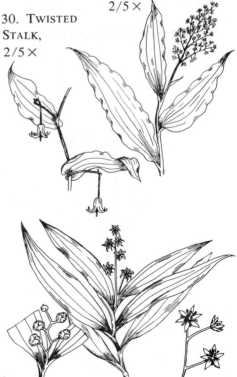

31. CLASPLEAF SOLOMONPLUME, 2/5×

30. TWISTED STALK, 2/5×

32. STAR SOLOMONPLUME, 2/5×

33. WESTERN WOOD LILY, ½ ×

35. YELLOWBELLS, ½ ×

greenish or yellowish-white flowers and bright red berries. FAIRYBELLS, which is quite rare, has flowers and berries at the ends of the stem. TWISTED STALK has long arching branches with its flowers and berries hanging from their undersides. All these are found in the spruce and aspen zones from New Mexico to Montana.

NORTHERN BEAR-GRASS, *Zerophyllum tenax,* is very conspicuous when in bloom with its tall clusters of creamy white flowers. They stand 3 to 6 feet high like a host of white banners on the hillsides of Glacier National Park, in other areas of Montana, Idaho, and into northern California. The tough grass-like leaves grow in dense tufts at the base and extend up the stalks becoming smaller towards the flowering portion. (See color illustration on cover). (In the Southwest the name "beargrass" is used for plants of the genus *Nolina,* which is quite different.)

WESTERN WOOD LILY, *Lilium philadelphicum* var. *andinum* (33), is one of the most brilliant and most rare of our mountain wild flowers. Its large, orange-red blossom with dark purple anthers is unmistakable. There is nothing else like it in the wild. Once it was frequently seen in mountain meadows and open woods from New Mexico northward into Canada but picking has reduced its numbers until now it is nearly extinct in many places. So, please, protect it carefully. [Color Pl. 1f]

FRITILLARY, *Fritillaria.* There are two species of this genus in the western mountains. One is called YELLOWBELLS, *F. pudica* (35), which grows 4 to 12 inches tall with a hanging bloom which turns from green to yellow to orange-brown. It grows on grassy plains, mesas and hillsides of Montana, Wyoming and northwestern Colorado. It is common in Yellowstone National Park. [Color Pl. 2a]

PURPLE FRITILLARY, *F. atropurpurea,* is taller and has 1 to 4 hanging flowers of a mottled purplish color. Its range is about the same as that of YELLOWBELLS.

YUCCA or SOAPWEED , *Yucca glauca* (34). This is one of the most conspicuous and interesting plants of the foothills of eastern Colorado and New Mexico. Its tufts of dagger-like, evergreen leaves give a light green color to many otherwise barren slopes. In May or June each clump may send up flower spikes 2 to 5 feet tall bearing numerous creamy-white blossoms. The flowers hang down and during daylight hours they are partially closed. In darkness the 6 thick petals open.

Inside there is a stout, greenish pistil with 6 white stamens standing around it. The pollen in the anthers of these stamens is very heavy and sticky—not at all powdery. Because of this sticky nature it cannot be scattered about by wind or wandering insects. But a little white moth of the genus *Pronuba,* less than an inch long, which flies at night, brings about pollination by the following method.

It is called the Yucca Moth because its whole life history is intertwined with the life of this plant. The mother moth flies to a Yucca flower and takes from one of its anthers a ball of pollen which she carries to another flower. There she pierces the ovary wall and deposits an egg inside an ovule, then she crawls up onto the pistil and forces the little ball of pollen into the depression in the top of the stigma. This effects pollination. She repeats the process several times.

By placing the pollen on the stigma she assures fertilization of the Yucca ovules and development of the seeds. When the tiny grubs hatch they find themselves surrounded with food in the form of developing seeds and they literally eat their way out of the Yucca seed pod. If you look closely at almost any ripened pod you will be able to discover the tiny hole where the grub came out. Without the help of *Pronuba* there would be no seeds

34. YUCCA, 1/5 ×

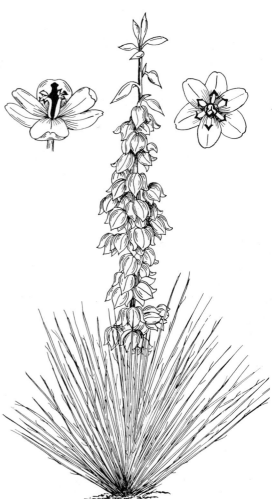

to carry on the generations of Yucca plants.

SPANISH BAYONET is another name for our Yucca. Its roots were used by Indians and pioneers in place of soap and the fibers of the leaves were used by the Indians to make a coarse rope. These coarse fibers can often be seen fraying out along the leaf edges. This is especially true in the DATIL, *Y. baccata,* a species of southern Colorado, New Mexico and Arizona, where they form decorative curls along the leaf margins. The leaves of this are broader and thicker than those of *Y. glauca* and its fleshy, berry-like fruits are edible. DATILS may be seen in Mesa Verde National Park. The buds on its big, thick flower spike are often tinged with red.

SANDLILY, *Leucocrinum montanum* (36), is a plant of the high plains and foothills from western South Dakota to northern New Mexico and westwards to Oregon, and in the Rockies at elevations of from 3,500 to 8,000 feet. It is often found blooming on vacant lots in Colorado towns and is frequent along the eastern edge of Rocky Mountain National Park. The 6

petals are pure white and the star-like flowers, an inch or more across, are close to the ground, surrounded by a tuft of long, narrow bluish-green leaves. It is one of the earliest spring flowers and may be found at the lower elevations in April. [Color Pl. 2b]

WILD ONION, *Allium.* There are several species of onions growing naturally on the high plains, foot-hills, and mountains of the West. All of them have the characteristic onion odor in their leaves and bulbs and probably all were used as food

37. WILD ONION, ½ ✕

38. NODDING ONION, ½ ✕

36. SANDLILY, ½ ✕

by the Indians and sometimes by the trappers and early settlers.

The small flowers are in umbels carried by slender, leafless stalks. A white-flowered species, *A. textile* (37), is abundant on the plains and dry foothills where it forms clumps, as garden chives do. The Latin word *"textile"* was used in the name of this plant to describe the net-like coat of fibres resembling coarse, woven cloth which covers the bulb. It is frequently found on vacant lots in Colorado Springs and other towns where it blooms in spring.

The species most frequently found at high altitudes is GEYERS ONION, *A geyeri*. It also has a netted bulb coat but its blossoms are usually deep pink. The NODDING ONION, *A. cernuum* (38), with pale pink flowers can be recognized because its umbel is bent down. It blooms in fields and meadows of the montane zone in early summer. Only one species has hollow leaves and that is called WILD CHIVES, *A. schoenoprasum*.

CAMAS, *Camassia quamash (C. esculenta)* (39). The old Latin name *"esculenta"* means edible and the bulbs of this plant were an important food supply for the Indians of Utah, Idaho and Montana where they grow abundantly on the plains and hillsides up to 8,000 feet. The flower stalk, 1 to 2 feet tall, rises from a cluster of strap-shaped, bright green leaves and holds an open raceme of blue flowers. WILD HYACINTH or GOPHERNUT, *Broadiaea douglasii*, has a cluster of funnel-shaped blue flowers at the top of a tall, leafless stalk which grows from an underground corm. It occurs on plains and foothills in western Montana

and southward into Utah and Idaho.

WAND-LILY AND DEATH CAMAS, *Zigadenus*. The common name of some members of this genus indicate its poisonous character and the fact that it must be distinguished from the true CAMAS described above. No parts of any plants of *Zigadenus* should be even tasted. The flowers of all species are greenish or creamy white so the plant when in bloom is easily distinguished from the edible, blue-flowered CAMAS. The leaves and habit of growth are somewhat similar. In one of the most poisonous

39. CAMAS, ½ ×

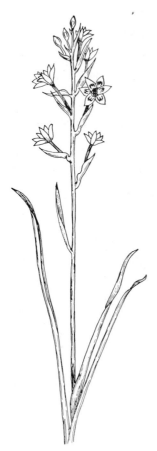

40. WAND-LILY, ½ ×

41. SNOW-LILY, 2/5 ×

species, *Z. venenosus,* the cream-colored flowers are small and arranged in a compact raceme. This plant is sometimes a serious danger to cattle and sheep because the clusters of bright green leaves appear in early spring before there is much other growth to feed on.

The WAND-LILY, *Z. elegans* (40), which is less poisonous, grows in the mountain meadows and into the alpine zone. It has tufts of narrow leaves from which there are some-times several flowering stalks 8 to 18 inches tall. The individual blos-soms are about ½- to ¾-inch across in a star-pointed saucer shape and each petal and sepal has a greenish spot at its base.

Tofieldia glutinosa ssp. *montana,* is a plant with grass-like leaves and a weak stem 1 to 2 feet tall which bears a cluster of small white or greenish flowers. It grows in wet places of the montane regions in northern Wyoming, Montana and northern Idaho. It is found in the Teton, Yellowstone and Glacier National Parks.

SNOW-LILY, *Erythronium grandiflorum* (41). This has one to three bright yellow flowers with turned-back petals, hanging from a slender stalk 6 to 15 inches high. At its base are two bright green, very smooth leaves. It grows in areas of heavy snows and blooms as the drifts melt.

In Colorado the places where it is found are mostly on the western slope with the exception of Wild Basin in the Rocky Mountain National Park. It is particularly conspicuous and abundant in the Rabbit Ears Pass, Steamboat Springs, and Aspen areas of Colo-rado, the Medicine Bow Mountains of Wyoming and on Logan Pass in Glacier National Park. It follows the melting snow up the mountain sides and you can find it in bloom at some altitude from early spring until midsummer.

In Glacier and Mount Rainier National Parks it is called GLACIER-LILY. The beautiful white AVALANCHE-LILY of Mount Rainier is another species of the genus. Its eastern relatives which have mottled leaves are known as TROUTLILIES or FAWNLILIES. Other names are ADDERSTONGUE and DOGTOOTH-VIOLET.

BEADLILY, *Clintonia uniflora,* is a plant of the northern woods which occurs in our range only in Glacier National Park and the mountains of Idaho. Its 6-petaled, white flower is about 1½-inches across, set off by broad, bright green leaves and followed by a bright, metallic-blue berry.

MARIPOSA-LILY, *Calochortus.* Mariposa, the Spanish name for these lovely flowers, means "butterfly." Several species grow in the Rocky Mountains. Their goblet-shaped blossoms have 3 narrow, greenish sepals and 3 broad petals, each with a darker spot at its base. Usually these spots are fringed with yellow hairs. There are one or two slender, grayish leaves at the base and one or two on the stem. They grow on open grassy or sagebrush-covered slopes and in aspen groves of the pine belt.

GUNNISON MARIPOSA, *C. gunnisonii* (42), 10 to 18 inches tall with white, pinkish or lavender flowers is the common one on the eastern side of the Continental Divide and occurs from South Dakota to New Mexico. [Color Pl. 2c]

SEGO-LILY or NUTTALL MARIPOSA, *C. nuttallii,* is the state flower of Utah. Its bulbs were an important article of food for Indians and pioneers. It is frequently found on the western slope in Colorado where its flower is usually an ivory white with a conspicuous dark splotch at the base of each petal. It is also abundant in Utah and is found on both rims of the Grand Canyon. In Dinosaur National Monument there is a brilliant pink form and yellow and orange ones are found in New Mexico and Arizona.

PUSSY-EARS, *C. elegans,* has smaller, creamy-white flowers with hairy petals which are borne singly or 2 or 3 together. It has 1 long leaf ⅛- to ¼-inch wide at its widest point which overtops the flower. It is found in grassy, partially shaded meadows and on slopes of the pine and aspen belts of Montana and westward into Idaho and Oregon. It is frequently seen in Glacier Nation-

42. MARIPOSA-LILY, 2/5 ×

al Park and sometimes in Yellowstone.

The tall *C. macrocarpus* with large purple blossoms in which each petal has a green stripe, grows around Flathead Lake in Montana. Farther west beyond our range there are several other handsome species of *Calochortus*.

ALPLILY, *Lloydia serotina* (43). This slender plant, only about 2 to 6 inches tall with almost thread-like

43. ALPLILY, ½ ×
(See *Color Pl. 2d*)

leaves, grows from little bulbs along a creeping, underground stem and its flowering stalks often stand in a line along the base of rocks. Each holds a single, drooping flower of similar, creamy white sepals and petals which are veined with purple. In the Rockies it is found in the alpine zone, often on the summits of exposed ridges and high peaks, up to 13,000 feet and sometimes at lower altitudes in very cold and exposed situations. It occurs in most of the arctic and many of the alpine regions of the northern hemisphere.

WESTERN TRILLIUM or WAKE-ROBIN, *Trillium ovatum*. Its 3 ovate leaflets and erect flower with 3 white petals make this plant easy

to recognize. It is a rare plant in our area but occurs in deep, moist montane woods in the mountains of northern Colorado and Wyoming and on the western slope in Glacier National Park. Its petals turn from white to pink and finally to purplish. [Color Pl. 2e]

IRIS FAMILY, *Iridaceae*

The plants of this family grow from tough, underground stems. Their stalks are erect, their leaves long and slender and their flower parts in threes. They differ from the lilies in having these parts attached to the top of the ovary instead of at its base.

ROCKY MOUNTAIN IRIS, *Iris missouriensis*, (44). This is a stately plant with large light or purplish blue flowers held on leafless stalks 8 to 12 inches tall. The 3 petals and 3 petal-like style branches are erect; the 3 petal-like sepals curve downward. The long, sword-like leaves form dense clumps. It grows

44. ROCKY   MOUNTAIN   IRIS,
    2/5 ×

throughout the Rocky Mountain states especially in wet meadows but may be found on hillsides or other apparently dry places if there is plenty of spring moisture. Sometimes it is so abundant in mountain meadows that masses of it blooming in June suggest a pale blue lake.

BLUE-EYED GRASS, *Sisyrinchium*. Plants with small blue flowers, usually less than ½-inch broad. The 3 petals and 3 sepals are alike. They grow in meadows where they are rather inconspicuous because of their tufted, grass-like leaves and the fact that their flowers open only in bright sunshine. They are found in nearly all areas of the United States, except deserts. In the Rockies they occur from 4,000 to 10,000 feet. *S. montanum* (45) is the common species in Colorado and Wyoming, and *S. demissum* in New Mexico and Arizona. *S. sarmentosum* is found in Yellowstone National Park.

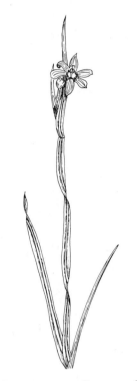

45. BLUE-EYED GRASS, 2/5 ×

ORCHID FAMILY, *Orchidaceae*

This is the largest of all plant families but most of its members live in tropical and subtropical regions. There are about 25 species found in the Rocky Mountains. More than half of these have small, inconspicuous flowers, but, small as they are, each has the distinctive characters of the orchid blossom. These characters are an irregular, that is, a bilaterally symmetrical corolla with the lower petal larger, sometimes spurred and often developed into a sac or pouch; and the stamens and pistil grown together. The flower structure is highly specialized for insect pollination. Some of our species are wholly or partially saprophytic; most of them grow in moist leaf-mold or rotted wood soil under forest trees.

a. Green coloring absent; leaves and stems brown, yellowish or
    reddish   CORAL-ROOT, p. 90.
aa. Green coloring present, at least in leaves.
  b. Flowers one or few; lower petal an inflated sac.
    c. Flower yellow; stem with several leaves
                  LADYSLIPPER, p. 90.
    cc. Flowers not yellow (except sometimes yellowish in
        Brownie Ladyslipper)
      d. Flowers brownish or purplish; stems with one pair of leaves
                  BROWNIE LADYSLIPPER, p. 90.
    dd. Flowers pink; 1 leaf at base of stem
                  FAIRY SLIPPER, p. 91.

bb. Flowers usually several in an erect raceme or spike.
  c. Flowers greenish or purplish, lip over 1/2-inch long
                       HELLEBORINE, p. 91.
  cc. Flowers white, greenish, or yellowish; smaller.
    d. Stalk straight   BOG ORCHIDS and other
                      small species, p. 91.
    dd. Stalk twisted

            LADIES TRESSES, p. 93.

46. YELLOW LADYSLIPPER, ½ ×

47. SPOTTED CORAL-ROOT, ½ ×

times catch the eye of a hiker. Their stems are a translucent reddish-brown and the little laughing flowers show white tongues spotted with purple. These plants are without chlorophyl and are able to absorb their nourishment from rotted wood in the forest soil.

They stand 6 to 18 inches tall with flowers about ½-inch long. This species is frequently found in spruce and pine forests over the United States. Other species found in the Rocky Mountains are the YELLOW STEM CORAL-ROOT, *C. trifida,* with very slender stems and whitish flowers without spots, and the STRIPED CORAL-ROOT, *C. striata,* a stouter plant growing up to 2 feet tall with many purplish flowers. YELLOW LADYSLIPPER, *Cypripedium calceolus* var. *pubescens* (46). This plant is easily recognized by the large, yellow, inflated lip, but it is one of the rarest of Rocky Mountain wildflowers. Its leafy stem grows from 8 inches to 2 feet tall. Here and there in isolated areas a few plants still persist. It should be carefully protected and never picked as it is in danger of extinction. [Color Pl. 2f]

SPOTTED CORAL-ROOT, *Corallorhiza maculata* (47). A few stalks of coral-root, standing in a spot of sunlight on the brown pine needle floor of a mountain forest some-

It grows in moist forest openings and at the edges of meadows from New Mexico and Arizona north into Canada, and throughout most of the United States east of the Rockies. The Rocky Mountain variety of this species has greenish-yellow lateral petals. BROWNIE LADYSLIPPER, *C. fasiculatum,* usually has several stems each with two or three yellowish, brown or purplish flowers 1 to 1½-inches long.

FAIRY SLIPPER, *Calypso bulbosa* (48). A pinkish-brown stalk 4 to 8 inches tall supports a single, fragrant flower with a bright rose, moccasin-shaped lip and slender pink petals. The toe of the moccasin is decorated with spots of yellow and purple. [Color Pl. 3a]

This dainty plant dwells in the cool, moist, coniferous forests of North America and extends south along our high mountains where such forests are present, as far as Arizona. In favorable locations, often north-facing slopes where snow collects in winter, it sometimes occurs in great numbers.

Perhaps because it blooms in late May, before many people visit our mountain forests, it has not suffered the fate of its larger cousin, the LADYSLIPPER. Nevertheless, it should be protected because it is a very fragile plant and picking or transplanting usually destroys the root.

HELLEBORINE, *Epipactis gigantea.* This plant is 8 to 40 inches tall with a leafy stem and a raceme of a few pink, purplish or greenish flowers each placed above a pointed, leaf-like bract. The stalks rise from spreading underground stems which sometimes form large clumps. It grows in wet meadows and especially by seeping springs at the base of cliffs. It is nowhere common but is found at isolated locations in the Arbuckle Mountains of Oklahoma, in Texas, the Grand Canyon of Arizona, in Wyoming, in California and in a few places of central and western Colorado, very often in association with MAIDEN-HAIR FERN, *Adiantum.*

48. FAIRY SLIPPER, ½ ×

BOG-ORCHIDS and others. This group of small-flowered orchids includes the BOG-ORCHIDS, TWAYBLADES, RATTLESNAKE PLANTAIN and ADDERSMOUTH. These all occur in the forested areas of upper montane and subalpine zones. These plants are alike in that their flowers are small and occur in spikes, or racemes, on erect stalks, and are either white or green, some occasionally tinged purplish or yellowish.

Those most frequently seen are the bog-orchids of the genus *Habenaria.* They are distinguished by having a small spur at the base of the lip. They vary in height from a few inches to 2 feet. The WHITE BOG-ORCHID, *H. dilatata,* one of the tallest, has a slender spike of pure white, fragrant flowers. Often several are seen close together in wet grassy spots on stream banks, beside trails, or in boggy ground around ponds and lakes. They are especially abundant and beautiful on roadsides along Lake MacDonald in Glacier National Park.

The GREEN BOG-ORCHIDS, *H. hyperborea* (49), and *H. saccata* are similar except for the green color of the flowers, sometimes tinged with purple, and lack of fragrance. They occur in similar boggy situations. The flowers of *H. hyperborea* are more closely arranged than are those of *H. saccata*. The WOOD-ORCHID, *H. unalaschensis* with small green flowers may be distinguished from the bog-orchids by the fact that its leaves, which are mostly near the base of the stem, wither at about blossoming time. It is found in damp woods.

The TWO-LEAVED WOOD-ORCHID, *H. orbiculata,* which grows in Glacier National Park and thereabouts has greenish-white flowers an inch or more long, and only two, rounded leaves, 6 to 8 inches long, spreading flat on the ground.

The BRACTED BOG-ORCHID, *H. viridis* var. *bracteata* and the ONE-LEAF ORCHID, *H. obtusata* (50), are small plants with greenish flowers sometimes found in permanently wet, shaded situations where the soil contains much humus—such as along small trickling streams in the spruce forests.

In similar places may be found the following species which have no spur: TWAYBLADE, *Listera cordata*

49. GREEN BOG-ORCHID, ½ ×

50. ONE-LEAF ORCHID, ½ ×

52. RATTLESNAKE ORCHID, ½ ×

51. TWAYBLADE, ½ ×, p. 92.

(51), and *L. convallarioides,* delicate plants 3 to 8 inches tall, each having a single pair of leaves at about the middle of the flower stalk. The inflorescence is a few-flowered spike. In the drier parts of spruce and fir forests one may find the RATTLESNAKE ORCHIDS: *Goodyera repens* (52), with flowers in a 1-sided raceme, is rare and *G. oblongifolia,* with its flowers in a loose spiral, is more common. Their dark green, pointed leaves are mottled with white and are in rosettes at the base of the 6 to 8 inch stems which bear small, whitish flowers.

ADDERSMOUTH, *Malaxis soulei,* which has a single leaf clasping the stem and a long, dense spike of tiny, greenish-yellow flowers, is a rare plant sometimes seen in the pine forests on the higher mountains of Arizona and New Mexico.

LADIES TRESSES, *Spiranthes romanzoffiana,* with stems usually 6 to 8 inches tall, is often found in grassy meadows and on stream banks. Its fragrant white flowers are closely set in about 3 ranks, and the stalk is spirally twisted. It blooms in meadows of the montane zone in middle and late summer.

Dicotyledonous Plants (Dicots)

The plants whose seedlings have two seed leaves, *cotyledons,* belong in this group. A familiar example is the cultivated bean. Botanists refer to them as the Dicotyledons or Dicots.

Other characters which distinguish Dicots from Monocots, are the number of flower parts and the type of leaf venation. Dicots usually have flowers built on a basic number pattern of 4 or 5 and their leaves have branched veins which form a network *(Plate B 8).* Frequently the leaves are compound, that is, made up of several leaflets and the edges of the leaves or leaflets may be serrated, or notched, or more or less deeply dissected. These characters contrast with the smooth-edged, undivided monocot leaves.

Observation of them will help in identification. Even if a plant has narrow leaves and apparently parallel veins but its flower parts are in 4's or 5's look for it here, but if its flower parts are in 3's and 6's, look for it under monocots, *(p.68).*

Most dicots have conspicuous petals, and the character of the petals as well as their number helps in identifying a plant. Plants whose flowers have an indefinite number of separate parts are believed to be lower in the evolutionary scale than those whose flowers have few and somewhat united parts.

For the purpose of ease in classification this large group is divided into two sections. The first section includes those plants which have free petals or no petals *(p 94)* and the second section includes those with united petals *(p. 212).*

For those who wish to learn how to identify plants by the use of keys there is a series of diagrams on p. 40. By comparing the structure, leaf shape and individual flower parts with these drawings the reader may easily learn the fundamental principles necessary in simple plant identification.

KEY TO FREE-PETAL DICOT FAMILIES
AND THOSE WITH NO PETALS

a. Plants woody.
  b. Shrubs or vines with conspicuous flowers.
    c. Leaves opposite.
      d. Stems climbing or clambering; flowers blue or white
                CLEMATIS in
                BUTTERCUP FAMILY, p. 123.
      dd. Stems erect, not climbing, petals white.
        e. Stems red, smooth
                RED-OSIER DOGWOOD in
                DOGWOOD FAMILY, p. 212.
        ee. Stems gray or brown, not red.
          f. Petals 4.
            g. Stamens 8
                FENDLERBUSH in
                SAXIFRAGE FAMILY, p. 149.
            gg. Stamens 20 or more
                LITTLELEAF MOCKORANGE in
                SAXIFRAGE FAMILY, p. 150.
          ff. Petals 5
                JAMESIA in
                SAXIFRAGE FAMILY, p. 150.
    cc. Leaves alternate.
      d. Leaves evergreen, compound, leaflets holly-like
                HOLLY-GRAPE in
                BARBERRY FAMILY, p. 137.
      dd. Leaves neither evergreen nor holly-like.
        e. Flowers regular.
          f. Stamens many (except in **HAWTHORN** may be few)
                ROSE FAMILY, p. 158
          ff. Stamens 5 (or 4), as many as the petals or calyx lobes.
            g. Petals with long or short claws, or lacking
                BUCKHORN FAMILY, p. 191.
            gg. Petals without claws, shorter than calyx lobes
                GOOSEBERRY FAMILY, p. 156.
      ee. Flowers irregular, papilionaceus
                NEW MEXICAN LOCUST in
                PEA FAMILY, p 179
  bb. Trees, shrubs or vines with inconpicuous flowers; petals absent or very small.
    c. Flowers, at least the staminate ones, in catkins.
      d. Seeds bearing tufts of hair; buds enclosed in a single bud scale
                WILLOW, in
                WILLOW FAMILY, p. 97
      dd. Seeds without tufts of hair; buds enclosed in overlapping scales.
        e. Seeds are small, winged; both staminate and pistillate flowers in catkins
                BIRCH FAMILY
                Betulaceae, p. 102.
        ee. Seeds are nuts with ''cups'', staminate flowers only in catkins

OAK FAMILY
Fagaceae, p. 103.

cc. Flowers not in catkins.
   d. Plants are vines with tendrils
      GRAPE FAMILY
      Vitaceae, p. 192.

  dd. Plants are erect shrubs.
    e. Leaves are opposite.
      f. Leaves are evergreen
        MOUNTAIN LOVER in
        STAFF-TREE FAMILY, p. 190.

    ff. Leaves are not evergreen.
      g. Leaves lobed and smooth
        MAPLE FAMILY
        Aceraceae, p. 190.

      gg. Leaves entire and scurfy
        Shepherdia in
        OLEASTER FAMILY, p. 201.

   ee. Leaves are alternate.
    f. Leaves compound
      SUMAC FAMILY
      Anacardiaceae, p. 189.

    ff. Leaves simple.
      g. Leaves and berries silvery scurfy
        Eleagnus in
        OLEASTER FAMILY, p. 201

      gg. Leaves green, berries black
        Rhamnus in
        BUCKTHORN FAMILY, p. 192.

aa. Plants herbaceous or only slightly woody at base.
  b. Flowers inconspicuous; petals small or absent.
    c. Plant a twining vine or parasite on conifers.
      d. Plant a twining vine
        Humulus in
        MULBERRY FAMILY, p. 104.

      dd. Plant leafless, parasitic on conifers
        MISTLETOE FAMILY
        Loranthaceae, p. 104.

    cc. Plants neither vines nor parasites.
      d. Leaves opposite; foilage with stinging hairs
        Urtica in
        NETTLE FAMILY, p. 104.

      dd. Leaves alternate; flowers and seeds in lumpy clusters, some-
        times red
        GOOSEFOOT FAMILY
        Chenopodiaceae, p.111.

  bb. Flowers, or at least the inflorescence, conspicuous.
    c. Inflorescence in umbels.
      d. Stems hollow; petioles enlarged and sheathing the stem
        CARROT FAMILY
        Umbelliferae, p. 207.

      dd. Stems not hollow; petioles not enlarged and not sheathing
        the stem.
        e. Leaves compound, of 3 to 5 leaflets, long-petioled

WILD SARSAPARILLA in
GINSENG FAMILY, p. 207

  ee. Leaves always simple

Eriogonum in
BUCKWHEAT FAMILY, p. 108.

cc. Inflorescence not in umbels.
  d. Stamens many, at least more than 10.
    e. Sepals separate.
      f. Sepals 2 or 3

POPPY FAMILY
Papaveraceae, p. 137.

    ff. Sepals more than 3.
      g. Leaves entire, always smooth.
        h. Plants aquatic; flowers yellow, more than 2 inches
        broad

YELLOW PONDLILY in
WATERLILY FAMILY, p. 121.

      hh. Plants not aquatic; flowers pink
BITTERROOT in
PURSLANE FAMILY, p. 115.

    gg. Leaves not usually entire; if entire, flowers not both
    yellow and over 2 inches broad.
      h. Leaves evergreen, compound with 5 to 9 holly-like
      leaflets

HOLLY-GRAPE in
BARBERRY FAMILY, p. 137

      hh. leaves neither evergreen nor holly-like
BUTTERCUP FAMILY
Ranunculaceae, p. 122.

ee. Sepals, calyx, united at least at base.
  f. Ovary superior.
    g. Filaments united into a column
MALLOW FAMILY
Malvaceae, p. 192.

    gg. Filaments separate
ROSE FAMILY
Rosaceae, p. 158.

  ff. Ovary inferior.
    g. Plants usually leafless; stems thick, covered with clus-
    ters of spines
CACTUS FAMILY
Cactaceae, p. 199.

    gg. Plants with leaves, very rough
LOASA FAMILY
Loasaceae, p. 197.

dd. Stamens not more than 10.
  e. Petioles with papery stipules sheathing the stem; or the tiny
  flowers enclosed in corolla-like involucres
BUCKWHEAT FAMILY
Polygonaceae, p. 105.

ee. No such stipules or corolla-like involucre present.
  f. Leaves opposite, stem joints enlarged
PINK FAMILY
Carophyllaceae, p. 117

ff. Leaves alternate, stem joints not conspicuously enlarged.
   g. Flowers irregular.
      h. Sepals 2, separate, dropping early
            FUMITORY FAMILY
            Fumariaceae, p. 138.
      hh. Sepals more than 2, united or at least persistent.
        i. Lower petal spurred
            VIOLET FAMILY
            Violaceae, p. 194
        ii. Lower 2 petals joined into a keel
            PEA FAMILY
            Leguminosae, p. 172.
  gg. Flowers regular.
      h. Stamens as many or twice as many as the petals.
        i. Styles 5, united into a column, petals 5
            GERANIUM FAMILY
            Geraniaceae, p. 185.
        ii. Styles 1 to 5.
          j. Style 1 (may have 4 stigmas), petals 4
            EVENING-PRIMROSE FAMILY
            Onagraceae, p. 201.
        jj. Styles 2 to 5.
          k. Sepals 2 (or several in *Lewisia*)
            PURSLANE FAMILY.
            Portulacaceae, p. 114.
        kk. Sepals 4 or 5.
          l. Plants definately succulent
            STONECROP FAMILY
            Crassulaceae, p. 148.
        ll. Plants not definately succulent
            SAXIFRAGE FAMILY
            Saxifragaceae, p. 149
      hh. Stamens 6, petals 4.
        i. Leaves compound, stamens exserted
            CAPER FAMILY
            Capparidaceae, p. 139.
        ii. Leaves simple (they may be deeply lobed or cut)
          stamens not exserted except in Princes Plume
            MUSTARD FAMILY
            Cruciferae, p. 139.

WILLOW FAMILY, *Salicaceae*

This is a family of trees and shrubs which belongs to a group of wind-pollinated plants. Its petal-less flowers are in catkins, which some botanists call *aments*, with pistillate and staminate catkins usually on different plants. The seeds bear tufts of soft hair. The family contains only two genera and in both of them it is common for leaves on young sprouts to be much larger than those on older branches. Sizes given in the descriptions are for average, normal leaves on second year growth.

POPLAR, *Populus*. This genus includes most of the deciduous trees of our area. Because poplars, often called cottonwoods, were the only broad-leaved trees found growing here by the pioneers they were the first ones planted in the towns. Along the streams, and where planted and watered,they grow to very large size. They gave welcome shade to the early settlers but the female trees are now considered undesirable because of the abundance of "cotton" which fills the air as their seeds are dispersed. However, a cottonwood grove is still a welcome sight on a hot day on the plains or in the foothills.

ASPEN, *P. tremuloides* (53). This is a small or medium-sized tree which forms groves and thickets along streams and on moist soil. It is the only deciduous tree commonly seen in the montane and subalpine zones.

Its white or light greenish bark and small roundish leaves make it easy to recognize. Because the petiole is flattened oppositely to the leaf blade the slightest breeze causes the leaves to quiver. On this account it is called "Quaking Aspen."

Its smooth bark is a favorite food of the beaver. Along streams and ponds one often sees beaver-cut aspen stumps. Beavers also use the small logs and branches in building their dams. Elk browse on the young shoots in winter and also damage the bark by biting and rubbing it with their antlers.

It is found from 6-7,000 feet to timberline and along the higher mountains from Mexico to Alaska. It spreads by root suckers and often covers burned areas where there is sufficient moisture. Its golden autumn coloring is one of the glories of the Rocky Mountains. [Color on Cover]

NARROWLEAF or MOUNTAIN COTTONWOOD, *P. angustifolia* (54). This is a tree of the canyons and streamsides extending from the plains up to 10,000 feet throughout the region. The leaves are lance-shaped, tapering to the tips, 2 to 4 inches long. The brown terminal bud usually has 5 scales, is very resinous and somewhat fragrant. Its bark is smooth and cream colored except near the base where it becomes broken by dark furrows into broad ridges. Its beautiful autumn color is a deeper orange-yellow than that of the Aspen.

In Colorado and northward it is usually a small tree, rarely over 50 feet tall, but along streams in New Mexico it becomes larger.

LANCELEAF COTTONWOOD, *P.*

53. ASPEN, ½ ✕

54. NARROWLEAF COTTONWOOD,

½ ✕

acuminata, is a small tree of the foothill canyons. It often grows with the NARROWLEAF COTTONWOOD and is sometimes difficult to distinguish from it. Leaves of this are rhombic-lance shaped to ovate, 2 to 4 inches long, with an abruptly acuminate tip. The terminal bud in winter has 6 to 7 scales, is somewhat sticky, but not fragrant.

BALSAM POPLAR, *P. balsamifera.* This is a rare tree in the central Rockies but becomes more abundant northwards extending into Alaska and across Canada and the northeastern United States to the Atlantic. In Colorado and southern Wyoming it occurs occasionally in small groves on valley bottoms of the montane zone. Its leaves are usually ovate with sharp pointed tips, 3 to 6 inches long, dark green above and much lighter colored on the under surface. The young leaves and winter buds are fragrant. It can be recognized when not in leaf by the inch-long, pointed, sticky, terminal bud.

PLAINS COTTONWOOD, *P. sargentii,* and VALLEY or RIO GRANDE COTTONWOOD, *P. fremontii* var. *wizlizeni,* are both large trees, sometimes as much as 100 feet tall and 4 feet or more in diameter. They grow along river bottoms and sometimes approach the mountains where the canyons open onto the plains. They have thick, dark, furrowed bark except on the young growth which is light yellowish or pale brown. Their leaves are leathery, somewhat triangular in shape, with toothed or wavy margins.

The first extends along the east side of the mountains from Canada south to central New Mexico. Its leaves usually have more than 10 teeth on each side. The second occurs from central Colorado southwards through New Mexico. Its leaves usually have fewer than 10 teeth on each side.

The firm leaves produce a noticeable rustling sound when set in motion by even a slight breeze.

WILLOW, *Salix.* This is the largest and most widely distributed genus of woody plants in our region. Thirty-one species are known from the state of Wyoming and 30 from Colorado. They range in size from trees 50 feet tall down to tiny creeping shrubs only 2 or 3 inches high. Most of them are medium-sized shrubs.

Some species are "Pussy Willows," that is, their silvery catkins appear before the leaves unfold. Others put out their catkins either with the young leaves or after the leaves have developed. The male and female catkins are on different plants. Branching is alternate and the leaves are always simple.

Members of this genus may be easily recognized by one character. All willows have only one bud scale. The bud covering is in the form of a little cap which is pushed off in one piece when the bud starts to enlarge. Buds of other shrubs have two or more scales which separate when growth starts.

Learning to recognize the different kinds of willows is much more difficult. Many of them are quite similar in general appearance, and identification depends on technical characters. Nearly all of them grow only on moist ground. They border streams from the plains to high mountains and make thickets in wet meadows at all altitudes but especially above timberline. Deer, elk, mountain sheep and domestic animals browse on their twigs and buds and find shelter in their thickets.

Mountain willows contribute much beauty to the landscape. In autumn their green or grayish summer color turns to shades of old gold, bronze and copper. After the leaves drop in late autumn they are still colorful throughout winter and spring because of yellow, orange-brown or maroon bark. Only the most interesting and widely distributed species will be included here. Most of those described occur throughout the Rocky Mountain region.

PEACHLEAF WILLOW, *S. amygdaloides*. This is the only species native in our region which regularly becomes a tree. Its thin leaves are lanceolate to ovate-lanceolate with long pointed tips, 2 to 5 inches long, and pale bluish on their under sides. The twigs are shining dark orange or red-brown, becoming light orange-brown. Bark on trunk and large branches is brown, often tinged with red. It grows on moist soil along stream banks of the upper foothills and lower Ponderosa Pine zones throughout the Rocky Mountains. *S. wrightii* is a similar and closely related species of New Mexico.

BEBB WILLOW, *S. bebbiana*. This is a shrub or small tree 6 to 15 feet tall. It is inclined to have a single trunk and bushy top even when quite small. Occasionally when growing among other trees it may grow to 25 feet in height. Its leaves are elliptical to oblanceolate, 1 to 3 inches long and hairy when young but smooth and strongly veined when old. The catkins appear with the leaves. It is often found along streams but it is one of the few species which is also sometimes found on drier slopes. It occurs throughout our range at altitudes of from 5,000 to 10,000 feet and in Arizona up to 11,000 feet.

SCOULER WILLOW, *S. scouleriana*. A common shrub or small tree usually about 8 to 12 feet tall. Its blooming precedes the leaves and the staminate shrubs are often quite showy when covered with the fluffy, pale-yellow catkins. When the yellow-anthered stamens are extended, the catkins appear oval, about 1½-inches long and 1 inch wide. They offer a feast to hungry, early-season bees. The leaves are oblanceolate with a blunt apex, green above but pale beneath. It grows throughout our range from 8,000 to 10,000 feet mainly along streams but this one is also sometimes found on slopes which dry out in late summer.

BLUESTEM WILLOW, *S. irrorata*. A shrub between 4 and 12 feet tall with dark, straight stems covered with a bluish coating and thickly set with black buds which push out in early spring into silvery catkins. The leaves are dark green, smooth above, usually paler beneath, about 1 to 3 inches long and tapering at both ends. On sprouts in late summer they may be much larger.

It grows along foothill and montane streams; common in Colorado especially on the eastern slope, between elevations of 6,000 and 8,000 feet. It also occurs in Arizona. This is our best native "Pussy Willow."

Another species with bloom on the twigs is GEYER WILLOW, *S. geyeriana* which has smaller leaves and catkins and bears its catkins on short leafy stems. In Colorado it occurs at altitudes from 8000 to 10,000 feet and its range extends northwards through Montana.

YELLOW-TWIGGED WILLOW, *S. monticola,* is the common yellow-colored, very intricately branched shrub of stream-sides in meadows and canyons of the montane zone. It grows from 6 to 15 feet tall and in early spring has many small, silvery-white pussies along its crooked yellow twigs. Its leaves are from 1 to 2 inches long, oblong-lanceolate or oblong-oblanceolate with pointed tips and finely toothed margins. In summer the twigs are yellowish green.

PLANELEAF WILLOW, *S. planifolia*. This has a very wide range in altitude and size. In the upper foothill canyons and up to timberline it may be seen as a shrub from 5 to 10 feet tall. Above timberline it forms large, low patches 1 or 2 feet high or even lower. Its young branches are glossy, dark, reddish brown; its elliptical or obovate leaves are about 1 or 2 inches long and ½-inch wide, green and smooth above, whitish beneath. At high altitudes the catkins precede the leaves; at lower altitudes they come out with them.

The form of this with broadly elliptical leaves and catkins which usually appear with the leaves is *S. planifolia* var. *monica*. It is widely distributed throughout the Rockies from the montane to the alpine zones.

NELSON WILLOW is *S. planifolia* var. *nelsonii* (57). It has oblong, elliptical or oblanceolate leaves, narrower than the last, and its catkins usually appear before the leaves. This is frequently found along the Front Range in Wyoming and Colorado and especially in Rocky Mountain National Park.

BARRENGROUND WILLOW, *S. brachycarpa* (56). This willow grows with the PLANELEAF and NELSON WILLOWS and has much the same habit and range throughout our area, but whereas the PLANELEAF WILLOW has leaves which are smooth and green on their upper surfaces, the BARRENGROUND WILLOW has leaves which are gray-hairy above. Its thickets

can be recognized by their over-all gray-green appearance. This species is widely distributed in the United States. Very similar to this and difficult to distinguish from it is *S. glauca*. The two often occur together.

Curiosities in this genus are the tiny alpine willows found on the

57. NELSON   WILLOW,   ½ ×

56. BARRENGROUND   WILLOW, ½ ×

55. ROCK WILLOW, 2/5 ×; *upper,*
pistillate catkin; *lower,* staminate
catkin.

a small shrub 6 to 8 inches tall with
relatively heavy underground stems,
but higher in the tundra it becomes
a completely prostrate miniature.

S. cascadensis is a very tiny species of the Uintah Mountains and
has been found on Trail Ridge in
Rocky Mountain National Park.

SANDBAR WILLOWS. On the plains
and in the foothills the ditch banks
and streams are often bordered by a
growth of reddish, slender-stemmed
willow shrubs usually about 3 or 4
feet tall, occasionally as much as 10
or 12 feet, with very narrow leaves
about 3 to 5 inches long. There are
two species similar in habit and
general appearance. *S. exigua* has
grayish pubescent, usually entire
leaves and occurs in wet sandy or
gravelly, often alkaline, locations
throughout our range. It is very
common in New Mexico and Arizona where its slender stems are
used in basketry.

S. interior is very similar but its
leaves usually have a few teeth on
their margins and at maturity become smooth at least on the upper
surface. This looks greener than the
first one. It is widely distributed in
the northern United States as far
west as the Rockies in Colorado and
north through Montana.

high tundra. They are closely related to arctic species. Their small
stems are woody but instead of
growing upright they creep, forming
intricately branched mats. Their
twigs are usually only 1 or 2 inches
tall but bear leaves and catkins.
ROCKY MOUNTAIN SNOW WILLOW,
S. reticulata var. *nivalis,* has very
short catkins, ½-inch or less with
few flowers. Its leaves are oval or
roundish, dark green above, whitish
beneath and very strongly netted-
veined. This occurs on the highest
peaks of northern New Mexico and
northwards in alpine situations to
the arctic.

ROCK WILLOW, *S. arctica (S. an-
glorum)* (55), has many-flowered
catkins, an inch or two long, and
strongly veined, but not netted,
leaves which are paler beneath, usually somewhat hairy along the
margins and have yellowish petioles
and mid-veins. At timberline this is

BIRCH FAMILY, *Betulaceae*

This is a family of trees and shrubs. Its flowers are of two kinds but
both kinds are on the same plant. Except for the pistillate flowers of the
hazelnut they are in catkins which are formed in late summer. The staminate catkins of all species release great quantities of pale yellow pollen in
early spring after which they drop off. Most of its members grow only on
moist soil, especially along streams.

WESTERN RED BIRCH or RIVER
BIRCH, *Betula occidentalis, (B. fon-
tinalis).* This shrub, or small tree,

is common along most mountain
streams from the lower foothills
through the montane zone. It grows

in graceful clumps and its several stems are clothed in glossy reddish-brown bark marked by horizontal lenticels. The smallest twigs are roughly glandular; leaves are thin, ovate, and toothed or lobed, tapering to a slender tip, usually turning a clear, light yellow in autumn. The cylindrical staminate catkins are 2 to 2½-inches long at flowering time. The pistillate ones are oval and ripen into light brown papery cones about 1 inch long which hang on the twigs after the flat, winged seeds are dispersed. [Color Pl. 3b]

BOG BIRCH, *B. glandulosa (59)*. This is one of the shrubs found in all the arctic and high mountain areas of North America. It ranges in size from a low spreading shrub only a few inches tall in very exposed locations to a height of about 6 feet along streams or in subalpine bogs. Its leaves are thick, roundish and finely toothed. Its bark is dark and rough, not glossy. It has brilliant autumn coloring in shades from orange to maroon.

THINLEAF ALDER, *Alnus tenuifolia* (58). This species is found in moist situations from Alaska and the Yukon south into New Mexico and Utah. In our range it is restricted to stream-sides from the upper foothill to the lower subalpine zones and is often associated with the red birch. It is a small tree or large shrub, seldom over 30 feet tall, usually having more than one trunk. It is stouter than the birch and has gray, smooth bark. Its staminate catkins are similar but larger and the pistillate ones, when mature, are oval, about ¾-inch long, dark brown, woody and persistent. Its leaves are ovate or oblong-ovate, sharply and doubly toothed, and sometimes abruptly sharp pointed. The commonest alder in Arizona is

A. oblongifolia, which grows to 60 feet in height.

BEAKED HAZELNUT, *Corylus cornuta.* A shrub with smooth, light brownish bark and ovate or obovate, pointed leaves 2 to 5 inches long, found across our northern states to the foothills of the Rockies. It is common in the Black Hills and occurs along streams in some of the deep canyons of the east slope of

59. BOG BIRCH, ½ ×

58. THINLEAF   ALDER,   2/5×

the Continental Divide in Colorado. The husk of the nut has a long "snout." Probably squirrels harvest the nuts because they always seem to disappear before they ripen.

OAK FAMILY, *Fagaceae*

In the foothills from central Col-

62. WILD HOP-VINE, ½ ×

MULBERRY FAMILY, *Moraceae*
WILD HOP-VINE, *Humulus* var. *neomexicanus* (62), is the only species of this family found growing wild in our range. It has opposite, palmately lobed leaves and papery clusters of fruits and is sometimes found clambering over bushes in the canyons.

NETTLE FAMILY, *Urticaceae*
The COMMON NETTLE, *Urtica dioica* ssp. *gracilis,* is sometimes found along streams or on waste ground in the foothill and montane zones. It is a stinging, bristly plant, usually in clumps, with sharply angled stems, opposite, toothed leaves and small clusters of inconspicuous flowers at the nodes.

orado and southwestern Wyoming southward large areas are covered by oak brush. There is considerable variation in the shape of the leaves and the height of the trunks. Some individuals grow into small trees. The commonest species found throughout this region is GAMBEL OAK, *Quercus gambelii* (60).

MISTLETOE FAMILY, *Loranthaceae*
Several species of LESSER MISTLETOE, *Arceuthobium,* are common on trees of the pine family. They can be seen as clusters of smooth, yellowish-brown or greenish stems which erupt from branches

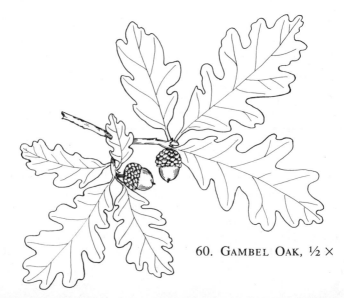

60. GAMBEL OAK, ½ ×

of the host trees. Each species of tree usually has its own species of mistletoe. These plants are parasites and sap the strength of the host tree eventually causing its death. The one most often seen is *A. vaginatum* (61) on PONDEROSA PINES. *A. americanum* grows on LODGEPOLE PINE and *A. douglasii on* DOUGLAS-FIR.

61. PINE MISTLETOE, ½ X

SANDALWOOD FAMILY, *Santalaceae*

The only member of this family commonly found in our range is PALE COMANDRA, *Comandra pallida,* often called "Bastard Toadflax." Its leaves are usually oblong and glaucous; there is a cluster of small, whitish, star-shaped flowers at the top of the 6 to 12 inch stem. This plant is parasitic on others which grow on mesas and foothills. Its root is blue when cut.

BUCKWHEAT FAMILY, *Polygonaceae*

This family is one of the few among the dicots which may have some of its flower parts in 3's or 6's. It may have a 2-to 6-parted perianth, 2 to 9 stamens and 2 or 3 stigmas. Its fruit is an achene, usually 3-sided but sometimes flattened. The individual flowers are always small. It includes many weedy species. In all of ours, except *Eriogonum*, there is a papery sheath around the stem at the nodes.

a. Papery sheaths present on stems; flowers not in involucres nor umbels.
  b. Plant alpine, reddish, less than 1 inch tall, very rare
      KONIGIA, p. 106
  bb. Plants various but more than 1 inch tall.
    c. Flowers green or reddish, in terminal panicles.
      d. Leaves kidney-shaped
          ALPINE SORREL, p. 106.
    dd. Leaves longer than wide; plants stout.
      e. Plants erect, tall and coarse
          WESTERN DOCK, p. 106.
      ee. Plants spreading in patches; panicle bright rose
          BEGONIA DOCK, p. 106.
    cc. Flowers white or pinkish, in axils or in terminal spikes or heads
          POLYGONUM, p. 106.
aa. No papery sheaths present; flowers in corolla-like involucres, and often in umbels
      ERIOGONUM, p. 108.

KONIGIA, *Konigia islandica,* is a very interesting arctic species which occurs in a few arctic-alpine situations in Colorado and Wyoming. It is a very tiny, rarely seen plant—one of the two or three annual species found in the alpine zone. It grows at the edges of small pools or in gravel along streams, forming rosettes of reddish leaves with few, minute, white flowers.

ALPINE SORREL, *Oxyria digyna* (64). A smooth plant, 4 to 12 inches tall with roundish or kidney-shaped leaves which are clustered at the base of an erect stem that holds the elongated panicle of red or greenish-red flowers or fruits. The achenes have membranous wings. This is a plant of cold, wet situations growing in gravel or around rocks near timberline. It is found throughout the arctic and alpine regions of the northern hemisphere. The leaves have a pleasant acid flavor.

DOCK, *Rumex.* This genus includes several large, coarse species, most conspicuous when in fruit. Their fruiting panicles are usually reddish at maturity and then turn rust or dark brown in autumn. Usually the individual achenes are triangular and each has 2 or 3 membranous wings.

BEGONIA-DOCK or SAND-DOCK, *Rumex venosus* (63). This is a plant of sandy ground on the mesas and foothills. It is very showy in fruit because of its bright rose-colored clusters of papery-winged achenes. Each fruiting calyx may be 1 to 2 inches broad. It often forms patches on roadsides. The individual stems are 6 to 15 inches tall.

WESTERN DOCK, *Rumex occidentalis,* is a stout plant which grows from a strong tap-root with a stem 2 to 6 feet tall. Its lower leaves are oblong or lance shaped, sometimes more than a foot long. The long narrow panicle is reddish or rust colored. This plant is frequently seen in wet meadows and on stream banks of the upper montane and subalpine regions.

POLYGONUM, *Polygonum.* This is a large and varied genus with many species in the western United States. It may usually be recognized by the enlarged nodes with papery sheaths surrounding the stem. Because of these large nodes some of the species are called "knotweeds." The achenes are lenticular or tri-

63. BEGONIA-DOCK, ½ ×

winged fruit

64. ALPINE SORREL, ½ ×

angular, often black and shining. This group includes the "smart-weeds," the "sidewalk weeds," and many other small or inconspicuous weedy species.

AMERICAN BISTORT, *P. bistortoides* (65). This plant is one of the most common in subalpine and alpine meadows. Its compact, 2-inch-long head of small white or pink flowers is held on an almost leafless stem a foot or more tall.
On tundra these conspicuous white heads occupy a layer above most of the other alpine flowers and are usually being swayed by the wind. In subalpine meadows they inter-mingle with other lush vegetation. The plant occurs throughout high areas of the mountains.

ALPINE BISTORT, *P. viviparum* (66). A smaller less conspicuous plant than the last, of circumpolar distribution. It has erect stems 4 to 10 inches tall with very narrow, spike-like racemes from 1 to 4 inches long. On the upper part of the raceme there are small white or pinkish flowers which on the lower part are replaced by bulblets. This occurs in our alpine zone and oc-casionally at lower elevations in very cold situations.

WATER BUCKWHEAT or WATER SMARTWEED, *P. amphibium* (67). This plant has oval, floating leaves, which resemble those of some spe-

65. AMERICAN BISTORT, ½ ×

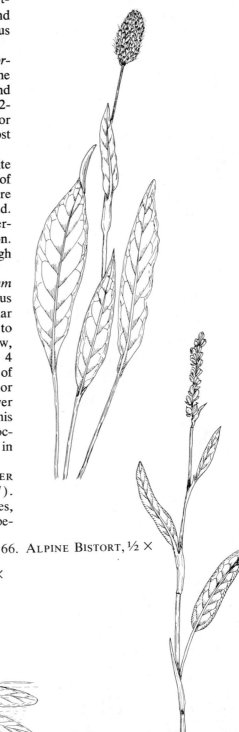

66. ALPINE BISTORT, ½ ×

67. WATER BUCKWHEAT, 2/5 ×

cies of pondweeds, and erect spikes of bright pink flowers ½- to 1-inch long. It grows in ponds and sometimes on their muddy banks, from the plains to the montane zone in the Rockies, and is widely distributed in other parts of the United States.

ERIOGONUM, *Eriogonum*. This is a large genus belonging to western North America. For convenience our species may be divided into three groups. Only a few of the most widespread species can be described here.

At blooming time individual flowers are from 1/16- to ¼-inch long and are held in small clusters, each cluster surrounded by a little, corolla-like involucre. The involucres are variously arranged in the inflorescences and there are usually leaf-like bracts wherever the inflorescence branches; leaves are mostly basal and usually more or less cottony; leaf margins are entire or sometimes wavy. The most conspicuous species in our area have umbellate (umbrella-like) inflorescences.

```
a. Inflorescence umbellate (Group 1).
  b. Flowers bright yellow, fading to rust.
    c. Flower stalks more than 4 inches tall
                  SULPHUR FLOWER, p. 109.
    cc. Flower stalks less than 4 inches tall
                  MAT ERIOGONUM, p. 109.
  bb. Flowers cream, pink, or greenish, turning pink.
    c. Stems unbranched below the umbel
                  SUBALPINE BUCKWHEAT, p. 109.
    cc. Stems forked below the umbels
                  JAMES BUCKWHEAT, p. 109.
aa. Inflorescence not distinctly umbellate.
  b. Plants erect, stems 1 to 3 feet tall. (Group 2).
    c. Stalks green ; flowers in an open panicle
                  WINGED ERIOGONUM, p. 110.
    cc. Stalks whitish with a cottony tomentum.
      d. Inflorescence an irregular corymb
                  ANNUAL ERIOGONUM, p. 110
      dd. Inflorescence a group of 2 or more racemes
                  REDROOT ERIOGONUM, p. 111.
  bb. Plants bushy, usually less than 1 foot tall (Group 3).
    c. Plants shrubby; flowers erect
                  BUSHY ERIOGONUM, p. 111.
    cc. Plants annual; flowers hanging down
                  NODDING ERIOGONUM, p. 111.
```

1. *The largest group consists of the umbrella-form eriogonums which all have their flowers in definite umbels, see Plate F 52.*

Most of these form loose or compact mats of woody stems and the undersides, and sometimes the upper sides, of the leaves are cotton-felted.

Their flower colors are yellow, cream, white or pinkish to begin with, but the yellow forms turn orange to reddish or rust as they age and the cream and white ones turn pink to rusty red. The perianths and the involucres are similar in texture and color and as the seeds ripen they lengthen somewhat and become dry, resembling tissue paper.

The commonly yellow-flowered species sometimes have cream-colored forms and vice-versa. Their perianths may be either smooth or hairy and this character, which can be seen with a hand lens, is helpful in identification.

SULPHUR FLOWER, *E. umbellatum* (68), has several stalks, 4 to 12 inches tall, erect, leafless; umbels usually simple; involucres hairy but perianths smooth; flowers bright yellow; leaves usually with white tomentum on their undersides. *E. flavum* is similar but usually has shorter stalks and leaves tomentose on both sides. Its perianths are hairy. Both are found throughout our range with *E. flavum* the common one above timberline. *E. piperi,* common in Yellowstone and Glacier National Parks, is very similar.

The low-growing MAT ERIOGONUMS, *E. acaule* and *E. caespitosum,* have very compact, woody crowns with white-felted leaves less than ½-inch long and stalks so short that sometimes the flowers are bedded in the leaves. They occur on dry hillsides from Montana to northern Colorado and in Idaho.

SUBALPINE BUCKWHEAT, *E. subalpinum,* has erect stalks, usually simple umbels with cream-colored flowers which turn rose, smooth perianths, and leaves green on upper surfaces. It is abundant, forming large patches in the subalpine zone from southern Colorado northwards.

CUSHION ERIOGONUM, *E. ovalifolium,* is a very compact plant with stalks from only a few inches to nearly a foot tall, yellow, cream or pink flowers, smooth perianths, petioled leaves usually less than an inch long with roundish or elliptic blades; common on dry, rocky ground throughout our range. A close relative similar in appearance

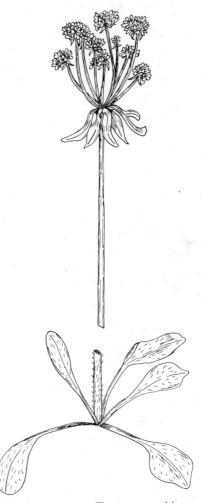

68. SULPHUR   FLOWER,   ½ ×

is *E. depressum* called "silver plant" by prospectors and miners who believed that it indicated the presence of silver ore.

JAMES BUCKWHEAT, *E. jamesii,* has cream, pale greenish or yellow flowers with hairy perianths, stalks 2- or 3-times branched and conspicuous leaf-like bracts below each branch. Common in the foothills and montane zones of Colorado and occurring from Wyoming southward through New Mexico and Arizona.

2. *This group has erect, usually solitary, stalks 1 to 3 feet tall.*

WINGED ERIOGONUM, *E. alatum* (69), is a green plant with elongated basal leaves and tiny yellowish flowers arranged in a large open panicle. When ripe the 3-winged achenes hang from rust-brown involucres. These tall, sparse plants stand erect, scattered singly over the foothill and montane regions of Colorado and southwards.

ANNUAL ERIOGONUM, *E. annuum* (70). These plants are whitish with ragged patches of tomentum on the erect stem and narrow, often twisted leaves. The inflorescence is an uneven corymb of slightly arching branches with numerous white or pinkish flowers usually along their upper sides. It grows abundantly on sandy areas of the plains and up into the foothills from eastern Montana to Mexico.

70. ANNUAL ERIGONUM, ½ ×

69. WINGED ERIOGONUM, ½ ×

REDROOT ERIOGONUM, *E. racemosum*. This plant has stalks up to 2½ feet tall, whitish at least on the lower portions which rise from short woody stems. Its leaves, white at least beneath, are mostly basal on petioles as long or longer than the oval, ovate or oblong blades. The pinkish flowers are in narrow, elongated racemes. It is found from southwestern Colorado through New Mexico, Arizona and Utah, especially in PONDEROSA PINE areas.

3. *The plants of this group are bushy, with wiry stems, seldom more than one foot tall.*

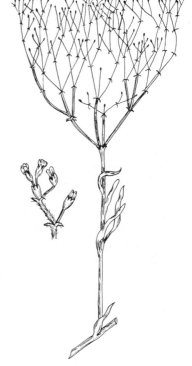

BUSHY ERIOGONUM, *E. effusum* (71), is a shrubby, widely branched plant with small white or pink flower clusters in the axils of the forking branches. The leaves and young branches are tomentose but the branches become smooth and mahogany-colored and foothill slopes covered by this plant are noticeable in fall and winter because of this reddish-brown color. Another woody species of similar aspect but having yellow flowers is *E. microthecum*.

NODDING ERIOGONUM, *E. cernuum*. This is an annual plant with inch-long, roundish leaves all at or near the base of the repeatedly forked stem. It forms a diffusely branched, rounded head with numerous pink or white flower clusters hanging from short stalks. Widely distributed throughout our range on dry hillsides up to 9,500 feet.

71. BUSHY ERIOGONUM, ½ ×

GOOSEFOOT FAMILY, *Chenopodiaceae*

This is a large family of plants which lack showy petals and have unisexual flowers. In some cases the fruits become conspicuous. Many of them are classed as weeds. Some have been introduced from abroad and become widely distributed. Many grow on waste ground and some only on wet, alkali soil. The pollen of several species is believed to cause hay fever. Strictly speaking, only a few properly belong to the mountain flora but some occur in the mountain valleys where there is alkaline soil.

FOURWING SALTBUSH or CHAMISO, *Atriplex canescens* (72), a shrub of sandy and saline soil, widely distributed at altitudes up to 8,000 feet from South Dakota and Oregon to northern Mexico. (New Mexico's "Chamisa" is a different plant—*Chrysothamnus* sp.) Its fo-

72. Fourwing Saltbush, ½ ×

liage is covered with minute silvery scales giving the bushes a gray appearance. The 4-winged fruits occur in conspicuous, often rose-tinged clusters and are very nutritious. It is a valuable food plant for browsing animals, especially sheep. In Arizona's caliche deserts it is an indicator of tillable soil.

Spiny Saltbush or Shadscale, *A. confertifolia,* is similar in appearance and distribution but its twigs become spines and its fruits are flat and wingless. Garden Orache, *A. hortensis,* an annual with round, flat fruits about ½-inch in diameter is a garden escape in some areas. Summer Cypress, *Kochia scoparia,* is an introduced annual weed found along most roadsides. It is finely branched with narrow leaves and forms an erect, bushy plant which often turns red in late summer. The "Burning Bush" of gardens is a form of this.

Russian-thistle, *Salsola kali (S. pestifer),* is one of the commonest "tumbleweeds." This is not a true thistle. It is an annual plant, as all tumbleweeds are, much branched into a rounded form and covered with very slender, stiff, spine-tipped leaves. The stem and main branches are often reddish. It is common in Eurasia from where it has been introduced into our area and is now very common along roadsides and on waste ground.

Greasewood, *Sarcobatus vermiculatus.* A spiny shrub 2 to 8 feet tall, with very slender, fleshy leaves which are well described by the specific name, *vermiculatus* meaning "worm-like." Its staminate flowers are in small greenish or reddish catkin-like spikes at the ends of the branches. The winged fruits, in the axils of the leaves, are sometimes tinged with red. This is a bright green, white-barked shrub growing in large colonies in very drab situations. In general it belongs at altitudes below our range but occurs occasionally in Colorado and Wyoming up to 8,500 feet, always on flat, alkali land.

In the West many different plants are called Greasewood; another example, the Creosote Bush of low Southwestern deserts.

Glasswort or Samphire, *Salicornia rubra,* is a spreading, apparently leafless plant with a fleshy, jointed, oppositely branched stem less than a foot tall. Its leaves are reduced to triangular scales at the joints. The flowers are partially embedded in the fleshy stems and the fruiting spikes, 1 to 2 inches long, turn ruby red at maturity and are so numerous that the plants growing on the borders of alkali ponds sometimes color the whole shoreline, or make patches of brilliant red where a pond has dried up.

Seepweed, *Suaeda depressa.* A fleshy plant, with cylindrical leaves, usually branching from the base but upright in var. *erecta,* growing around alkali lakes where its rusty fall color shows up conspicuously against the white soil.

POVERTY-WEED, *Monolepis nuttalliana,* is a low annual occurring in rosettes on mud or sand along streams and as a weed in gardens. Its leaves are spear-shaped and its small, green flowers are in axillary clusters.

GOOSEFOOT, *Chenopodium.* This genus contains many weeds, some edible wild plants such as "Lambs Quarter," and several vegetables including spinach and beets. The family characteristic of tolerance to alkalinity is a favorable factor for the cultivation of sugar beets in the west where thousands of tons are grown annually on irrigated land.

FREMONT GOOSEFOOT, *C. fremontii,* is an erect plant with thin, triangular leaves somewhat lobed at base and small clusters of green flowers in flexible, sometimes branched spikes. These plants grow in colonies, often under pine trees, and in mid- or late summer turn pinkish or orange. Throughout our range up to 9,000 feet. It furnishes feed for cattle in autumn. There are several other chenopods in the

73. STRAWBERRY BLITE, ½ ×

Rocky Mountains, both native and introduced.

SQUAWPAINT or STRAWBERRY BLITE, *C. capitatum* (73), is interesting with bright green, smooth, triangular and hastately lobed leaves and deep red, fleshy, berry-like clusters of fruits. It grows in rich, moist soil often around old barnyards but also among rocks in the high mountains up to 11,000 feet.

AMARANTH FAMILY, *Amaranthaceae*

This family includes several weedy species besides the horticultural forms of amaranth and cockscomb, *Celosia.* Its flowers are minute but closely compacted together in variously formed clusters which in cultivated species are conspicuous. The commonest native species, often called "Ragweeds," are garden and roadside weeds, the pollen of which bothers many allergic people.

REDROOT PIGWEED, *Amaranthus retroflexus,* is an erect, stout plant from 1 to 5 feet tall with dense, irregular bristly spikes of green flowers. Its stem and the midribs of the pointed, ovate leaves are often reddish and rough with bristly hairs.

FLAT PIGWEED, *A. graecizans,* is a much smoother plant with many prostrate, sometimes reddish branches. Its leaves are oval or spatula-shaped and often white-margined, larger toward the ends of the branches. It produces many, shiny, black seeds.

FOUR-O'CLOCK FAMILY, *Nyctaginaceae*

Our plants of this family have

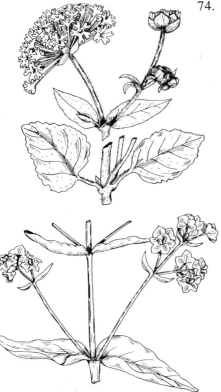

74. SAND VERBENA, 2/5 ×

75. LANCE-LEAVED WILD FOUR-O'CLOCK, 2/5 ×

west and may be found in Colorado up to 8,000 feet.

SAND-VERBENA, *Abronia fragrans* (74), a sprawling plant with whitish, sticky stems and heads of white or pinkish, fragrant flowers. The slender tubular perianths are 1 to 1½-inches long and shorter, papery bracts form a collar beneath the head. The fragrance is especially noticeable at night. A common plant of the western plains extending into the foothills on sandy soil. On shores of Yellowstone Lake the YELLOWSTONE SAND-VERBENA, *A. ammophila,* with pale yellow or greenish flowers, is found.

SHOWY FOUR-O'CLOCK, *Mirabilis multiflora,* is a rounded, compact, very leafy plant with large magenta-colored, funnel-shaped flowers resembling morning-glory blossoms. There are 6 to 8 in each involucre. It is common in the piñon-juniper zone of Colorado and Utah and southward, especially in Grand Canyon and Zion National Parks.

FRINGE-CUP FOUR-O'CLOCK, *Oxybaphus linearis,* is a sprawling, usually sticky, plant with whitish stems, linear leaves and a branched inflorescence of scattered pink to purple flowers which open in late afternoon, found on dry ground throughout our range below 9,000 feet. LANCE-LEAVED WILD FOUR-O'CLOCK, *A. hirsutus* (75), similar but with broader leaves, is sometimes seen.

opposite, simple, entire leaves; stems with enlarged joints; and small, tubular flowers subtended by involucres of separate or united, sometimes petal-like, bracts.

SANDPUFFS or WINGFRUITED SAND VERBENA, *Tripterocalyx micranthus,* has clusters of greenish-white, inch-long flowers which ripen into balls of 3-winged seeds. It is common on sandy plains of the

PURSLANE FAMILY, *Portulacaceae*

Our plants of this family are somewhat succulent with very delicate white, pink or rose-red petals. The flowers open only in sunshine or bright light.

a. Leaves narrow, mostly in basal rosettes.
   b. Flowers not crowded into dense heads.
     c. Flowers 2-3 inches broad; sepals 6-8
                      BITTERROOT, p. 115
   cc. Flowers an inch or less broad; sepals 2.

BITTER-ROOT, *Lewisia rediviva* (76), an amazing plant brought back from Montana by the Lewis and Clark expedition in 1806, "came to life" after many months in a dried condition and, when planted, bloomed. So it was given the name *rediviva,* meaning "to live again." The new genus was named in honor of Meriwether Lewis, leader of the expedition. [Color Pl. 3c]

76. BITTERROOT, ½ ×

The little green tufts of slender leaves come up in winter, on bare ground or under snow, but by late June at blooming time they have withered almost completely away. The showy, many-petaled pink blossoms dot gravelly terraces and stony places which receive abundant moisture in early spring. The thick roots were a staple food for the Indians of the northwest who boiled them until the bitterness disappeared.

The plant is known to grow in only a few places in Colorado and in southern Wyoming, but farther north and west and in the Grand

Canyon area it is abundant. It is the state flower of Montana.

TINY LEWISIA, *L. pygmaea,* is a small rosette plant with narrow leaves about 1 to 2 inches long. The white, pink or rose-red flowers are less than ½-inch broad and have 2 sepals with their upper edges fringed with tiny, glandular teeth. It is found on moist slopes of the subalpine zone and sometimes in cold, wet situations of the upper montane zone such as the Kaibab Plateau.

NEVADA LEWISIA, *L. pygmaea*

var. *nevadensis,* a variety with larger, white flowers and lacking the distinct teeth on the sepals, occurs in the western part of our range. THREE-LEAF LEWISIA, *L. triphylla,* with similar flowers and 2 to 4 leaves in a whorl on the stalk occurs in the subalpine zone from northern Colorado northwestwards.

BIG-ROOTED SPRINGBEAUTY, *Claytonia megarhiza.* This fleshy plant of stony ground and rock crevices of the alpine zone has several flowers to each stem, arranged in a one-sided raceme. Each flower is from ½- to 1-inch across and has 2 greenish sepals, 5 fragile white petals veined with red, 5 stamens each attached to a petal, and 3 thread-like styles. The succulent leaves are in a basal tuft and they vary from spatula-shaped to almost round. A very long, thick purple or reddish-colored root is tucked away between rocks. Blooms soon after the snow is gone, usually late June and July.

LANCE-LEAVED SPRINGBEAUTY,

77. LANCE-LEAVED SPRING-

C. lanceolata (77), has a pair of lanceolate leaves below the terminal raceme of delicate white or pink flowers. The petals are veined with darker pink. It is an early spring flower found throughout our range in moist ravines of the foothills, on open montane fields and in subalpine meadows. *C. rosea* is similar but its stem leaves are narrower and there often are one or more basal leaves. A yellow or orange-flowered species, *C. chrysantha,* grows in Idaho.

WATER SPRINGBEAUTY, or INDIAN LETTUCE, *Montia chamissoi,* is a plant seen along slow moving streams and in wet meadows of the foothills and montane zones. It spreads by long stems which root at the nodes and has paired, oblanceolate leaves and pink-veined, white or pink flowers. (78)

MINERS LETTUCE, *M. perfoliata* is a clump plant with long petioled, roundish basal leaves and a pair of united leaves forming a collar below the small, white flower. This has been used by Indians, pioneers and others as a pot herb and salad plant. It is commonly found in Arizona along brooks and around springs up to 6,000 feet, and less commonly in other parts of the Rockies.

FAME FLOWER, *Talinum parviflorum,* has an erect stalk holding an open cluster of pink flowers which are delicate and short-lived. It grows on dry soil in PONDEROSA PINE forests.

PUSSY-PAWS, *Calyptridium umbellatum (Spraguea multiceps),* the stalks of this plant lie flat, radiating from a rosette of dark leathery leaves. Each tiny, pink flower has 2 papery white or pinkish, persistent

78. WATER SPRINGBEAUTY, 2/5×

sepals and many are gathered together into tightly coiled, ball-like spikes. Several of these balls are clustered on each stalk giving the effect of a cat's foot. It grows on geyser formations and volcanic gravel from northwestern Wyoming into the high mountains of Idaho and westward. In the montane zone its stems may be 5 or 6 inches long, on very dry or alpine situations they may be only 1 inch long.

PINK FAMILY, *Caryophyllaceae*

Plants of this family have opposite, simple, entire leaves; their stems are enlarged at the nodes; they have 5 separate or united sepals. In some species the petals are minute or even absent, but, in general, there are 5 separate petals. In some the petals are composed of a broad blade and a narrow claw *(Plate D 39)* with a small crest at the base of the blade. The ovary is superior and 1-celled. The pinks and carnations of gardens belong to this family.

    a. Plants cushion- or moss-like, without erect stems, alpine.
      b. Flowers white
                              ARCTIC SANDWORT, p. 120.
      bb. Flowers pink or rose, rarely white
                              MOSS CAMPION, p. 117.
    aa. Plants taller with evident stems.
      b. Sepals united; petals clawed.
        c. Styles usually 3
                              CATCHFLY, p. 117.
        cc. Styles usually 5
                              COCKLE, p. 118.
      bb. Sepals separate; petals without claws.
        c. Petals present, white.
          d. Petals deeply notched.
            e. Leaves and stems softly hairy; styles 5
                              MOUSE-EAR CHICKWEED, p. 119.
            ee. Leaves smooth, hairy, or sticky; styles 3
                              STARWORT CHICKWEED p. 119.
          dd. Petals not notched or only slightly so.
            e. Styles 5; capsule with 5 teeth
                              ARCTIC PEARLWORT, p. 120.
            ee. Styles 3; capsule with 3 or 6 teeth.
              f. Petals white ; no stipules present
                              SANDWORT, p. 120.
              ff. Petals pink; thin papery stipules present
                              RED SAND SPURRY, p. 121.
        cc. Petals lacking or very inconspicuous
                              NAILWORT, p. 121.

CATCHFLY or CAMPION, *Silene.* Some plants of this genus are night-blooming and are visited by night-flying insects; their leaves and stems are often more or less sticky; the calyx is united, sometimes inflated and often 10-nerved; the petals are clawed.

MOSS CAMPION or MOSS PINK, *S. acaulis* (79). This cushion plant, starred with pink or rose, almost stemless flowers, is found on

79. MOSS CAMPION, ½ ×

exposed, rocky or gravelly fields above timberline. The blades of its petals are oblong, slightly notched and usually show a little space between them. (Compare ALPINE SANDWORT which has white, rounded petals and shows no space between them.) Its narrow, pointed leaves are from ⅓- to ¾-inch long.

This is a circumpolar species found at sea level in the arctic and at progressively higher elevations along the mountains southward into New Mexico.

It is one of the first colonizers of barren gravel areas in the alpine zone. Each mat of stems and leaves accumulating over many, many years eventually becomes a nursery for other alpine plants. In the slow progress of this vegetation pattern towards a climax community, MOSS CAMPION, which helped to make its beginning possible, is eliminated and is not found in the final stage of the closed sedgegrass community (see p. 35). [Color Pl. 3d]

SLEEPY CATCHFLY, S. antirrhina, is a slender annual plant 1 to 2 feet tall, green and smooth except for dark bands of sticky substance between the upper nodes which prevent insects, such as ants, from climbing up the stem to steal nectar from the flowers. Insects obtaining the nectar in this way do not pay for their food by effecting pollination as flying insects do. The petals are white or pink tipped, usually short,

sometimes lacking. SCOULERS or HALLS CATCHFLY, S. scourleri ssp. hallii, is a tall, branching, sticky, hairy plant with nodding, pinkish flowers which open in late afternoon. Its calyxes are cylindrical in bud but become inflated at flowering time. After flowering they become erect. It grows in aspen groves and on fields of the montane and subalpine zones. MENZIES CATCHFLY, S. menziesii, with repeatedly 2-forked sticky-hairy stems and calyxes less than ¼-inch long, occurs throughout our range, often growing among bushes.

INDIAN PINK, S. laciniata, of the pine forests of New Mexico and Arizona, is the showiest species of the genus within our range. It has brilliant scarlet flowers more than an inch across and each petal is slashed into about 4 divisions. MANY-STEMMED CATCHFLY, S. multicaulis, with several, slender, sticky stems up to 2 feet tall and white or pale red flowers in clusters of threes, grows in the northwestern part of our range, especially Yellowstone and Glacier National Parks.

COCKLE, Lychnis. Plants of this genus are similar in general appearance to those of Silene and sometimes hard to distinguish. Usually they have 5 styles and a 10-ribbed calyx.

ALPINE LANTERNS, L. apetala (L. montana) (80), is a small, compact alpine plant with nodding flowers on stalks usually not over 5 inches tall. The petals are very short but the enlarged, 10-striped

80. ALPINE   LANTERNS,   ½ ×

calyxes suggest Chinese lanterns. *L. kingii* is a similar species with erect, larger flowers but its calyx does not become inflated. Both are rare plants of the alpine zone.

DRUMMONDS COCKLE, *L. drummondii.* Stems more or less sticky, 1 to 2 feet tall; basal leaves oblanceolate, stem leaves linear; calyx cylindric, about ½-inch long, petals included or slightly protruding. This may be distinguished from similar species of *Silene* by examination of the young ovary. In this species it is enlarged near the tip. A plant of dry hillsides and meadows, foothills to alpine.

MOUSE-EAR CHICKWEED, *Cerastium arvense* (81). This plant takes its common name from its small, velvety leaves. It has stems less than a foot tall which tend to spread or lean, and white flowers about ½-inch broad. The petals are deeply cleft. Abundant and widely distributed throughout our range. It begins blooming on the mesas at the base of the foothills in April and proceeds up the slopes to the alpine zone as the season progresses. Often it is the most abundant white flower on open fields and dry meadows in spring and early summer.

The ALPINE MOUSE-EAR, *C. beeringianum,* with shorter stems, broader leaves and shorter petals, is restricted to high altitudes. *C. thermale,* with petals scarcely longer than the sepals and leaves with very thick mid-ribs grows on the geyser basins of the Yellowstone area.

STARWORT CHICKWEED, *Stellaria.* This genus includes several small plants of confusing similarity. Their white petals are deeply 2-cleft. The LONG-LEAVED STARWORT, *S. longifolia,* has linear or lance-linear leaves an inch or more in length

81. MOUSE-EAR CHICKWEED, ½ ×

and many flowers in a spreading cluster; the LONG-STALKED STARWORT, *S. longipes* (82), has shorter, shining leaves and few flowers on erect stalks. Both are found throughout our range but only the

82. LONG-STALKED   STARWORT, ½ ×

latter extends into the alpine zone. JAMES STARWORT, *S. jamesiana,* a glandular pubescent plant with notched petals is found in ravines of the foothill and montane zones.

ARCTIC PEARLWORT, *Sagina saginoides,* is a tiny, bright green plant of wet, cool situations growing among rocks or in mud on the borders of ponds. Its minute, white flowers are on hooked, thread-like stalks.

SANDWORT, *Arenaria (Minuartia).* These plants usually have firm, sometimes stiff, stems and pointed leaves. The leaves are always sessile with their bases clasping the stem.

ARCTIC SANDWORT, *Arenaria obtusiloba (M. obtusiloba)* (83), is a cushion or mat-forming plant. It sometimes makes carpets 2 or 3 feet in diameter of crowded, light green, very tiny leaves, starred with numerous white flowers. The petals of these flowers are oblanceolate and do not have distinct claws but the rounded blade tapers to its base. This is an arctic species which extends south along the high mountains. [Color Pl. 3e]

A. biflora (A. sajanensis), a similar but slightly less compact species having larger leaves, is occasionally found on the tundra. BLUNT-LEAVED SANDWORT, *Arenaria lateriflora,* is a plant with thin, oblong leaves and white petals about twice as long as its sepals, which looks more like a starwort. It occurs in moist, shaded situations of the foothill and montane zones.

83. ALPINE SANDWORT, ½ ×

FENDLER SANDWORT, *A. fendleri* (84), was named for August Fendler, see p. 150. It is a plant of dry, open hillsides from the foothills to the alpine zone. It has tufts of slender, sharp leaves and erect stems from only a few inches tall in the alpine zone to nearly a foot at lower altitudes. The inflorescence is open and bears scattered flowers less than ½-inch broad of 5 white petals against which the 10 red anthers show as dark spots. A closely related species having shorter petals

84. FENDLER SANDWORT, ½ ×

found in western Wyoming, Idaho and Utah is *A. kingii.*

BALLHEAD SANDWORT, *A. congesta.* This species has a tuft of sharp-pointed, grass-like leaves at the base and erect stems with only 2 to 4 pairs of shorter leaves. The white flowers are in dense heads. It grows from Montana to western Colorado and westward, and from foothill to alpine zone. HOOKER SANDWORT, *A. hookeri,* has similar dense flower heads and very sharp leaves which are densely tufted on woody stems often forming large mats. Its flower stalks are 2 to 6 inches tall. It is a dry land plant and its range extends from Montana through Wyoming into the foothills of eastern Colorado.

NAILWORT or WHITLOW-WORT, *Paronychia.* This genus and the next are distinguished from other members of the Pink Family by the presence of thin, silvery stipules. Nailworts have very woody stems and form mats or cushions. They have inconspicuous flowers and a single seed. Most of them are plants of dry regions and in these areas they sometimes extend to high altitudes.

ALPINE NAILWORT, *P. sessiliflora* ssp. *pulvinata,* is a very low, densely caespitose plant of dry tundra with elliptic or oblong leaves less than ¼-inch long. Growing at lower altitudes is a form of this only slightly larger. It has spine-tipped leaves.

JAMES NAILWORT, *P. jamesii,* has stems up to a foot tall. The flowers are in forking clusters, each cluster having a central, stalkless flower. It occurs from Nebraska and Colorado to Arizona on dry plains and hills of the foothill and lower montane zones.

RED SANDSPURRY, *Spergularia rubra,* is a small, low plant with silvery stipules, narrow, clustered leaves and small, pink flowers. It is widely distributed in North America, apparently introduced from Europe. It occurs in a few places in the mountains especially along trails and around camp grounds.

The following members of the Pink Family may be occasionally found as introduced weeds or garden escapes along roadsides, in farmyards, or on waste ground: BOUNCING BET, *Saponaria officinalis,* forms patches, has pale pink flowers in crowded clusters; NIGHT-BLOOMING CATCHFLY, *Silene noctiflora,* and WHITE CAMPION, *Lychnis alba,* both with conspicuous white flowers in the evening, the campion having inflated calyces; COMMON CHICKWEED, *Stellaria media,* a common lawn weed.

WATERLILY FAMILY,
Nymphaceae

YELLOW PONDLILY, *Nuphar luteum* ssp. *polysepalum* (85). This grows in the cold ponds and small lakes of the montane and sub-alpine zones. Its large shining leaves are pushed up from the root, which is embedded in mud, to the surface of the water where they uncurl and

85. YELLOW PONDLILY, 2/5 ×

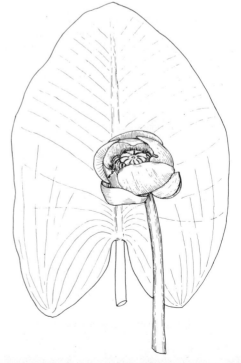

lie flat on the surface. The yellow, cup-like flowers on strong stalks lie at the surface or sometimes just below it. The leaves on seedling pondlilies are very thin and appear like bunches of lettuce growing at the bottom under several feet of water. [Color Pl. 3f]

Pondlilies are found in a few lakes of Rocky Mountain, Yellow- stone and Glacier National Parks and in other areas of the Rocky Mountains. Other subspecies of *Nuphar* are widely distributed across the United States. Their seeds were called "wokas" and were an important food item for the Indians of our Northwest and it is said that moose feed on the large leaves.

BUTTERCUP FAMILY, *Ranunculaceae*

This is a large family including many different-appearing plants. The two characteristics common to all of them are: all flower parts are distinct and separate from each other and the stamens are of an indefinite number. The pistils are from 3 to many, and the fruits may be achenes, follicles, or berries. The leaves are sometimes simple and entire, more often lobed or divided and sometimes compound. Petals are often lacking but in several genera the sepals are petal-like. In general, plants of this family grow in cool, moist situations.

a. Plants aquatic, found floating in water.
  b. Flowers white; leaves brownish
               WATER CROWFOOT, p. 130.
  bb. Flowers yellow; leaves green
               FLOATING BUTTERCUP, p. 130.
aa. Plants terrestial, found growing on the ground.
  b. Plants climbing or trailing; stems more or less woody
               CLEMATIS, p. 123
  bb. Plants not climbing; stems herbaceous.
    c. Leaves made up of many, roundish leaflets.
      d. Flowers conspicuous; petals spurred
               COLUMBINE, p. 124.
      dd. Flowers inconspicuous; stamens like tassels
               MEADOWRUE, p. 126.
    cc. Leaves simple, compound, or variously divided, but not com- posed of many roundish leaflets.
      d. Flowers regular, i.e., radially symmetrical, mostly white or yellow
        e. Flowers bright yellow; leaves various
               BUTTERCUP, p. 127.
        ee. Flowers white, cream, reddish, or lavender.
          f. Leaves undivided, all basal; flowers white.
            g. Leaves 1 to 3 inches long, very narrow
               MOUSETAIL, p. 130.
            gg. Leaves larger, roundish, or oval
               MARSH-MARIGOLD, p. 130.
          ff. Leaves compound, or more or less divided.
            g. Flowers small, many; stamens white.
              h. Leaves ternately compound
               BANEBERRY, p. 131.
             hh. Leaves palmately cleft

FALSE BUGBANE, p. 132.
gg. Flowers larger, 1 or few to each stalk.
  h. Plants usually pubescent; fruit of achenes.
    i. Flowers always subtended by a leafy collar (involucre)
      ANEMONE, p. 132.
    ii. Flowers without involucres; plants bushy
      LEATHER FLOWER, p. 124.
  hh. Plants glabrous; fruit of follicles
    GLOBEFLOWER, p. 134.
dd. Flowers irregular, i.e., bilaterally symmetrical.
  e. Upper sepal spurred
    LARKSPUR, p. 135.
  ee. Upper sepal helmet-shaped
    MONKSHOOD, p. 136.

CLEMATIS, *Clematis.* This is one of the genera which has no petals but its sepals are petal-like. In our species they are usually bluish, purplish or white. There are usually 4 of these sepals and an indefinite number of pistils which develop into plume-tailed achenes. The leaves are compound.

a. Plants with woody stems, climbing or trailing.
  b. Flowers numerous, white, in clusters
    WESTERN VIRGINS BOWER, p. 123.
  bb. Flowers scattered, blue, or lavender.
    c. Leaves with 3 leaflets
      COLUMBIA CLEMATIS, p. 123.
    cc. Leaves twice 3 times compound
      SUBALPINE CLEMATIS, p. 124.
aa. Plants appearing bushy but stems herbaceous
    LEATHER FLOWER, p. 124.

WESTERN VIRGINS BOWER, *C. ligusticifolia,* is often seen along roadsides and in woods on hillsides of the foothill and lower montane zones. It is equally conspicuous in early summer covered with masses of creamy white blossoms and later with its feathery fruiting heads catching the light. Another species, probably introduced, the ORIENTAL CLEMATIS, *C. orientalis,* with larger yellow flowers singly or in small clusters, is sometimes seen.

COLUMBIA CLEMATIS, *C. columbiana* (86), has solitary flowers on stalks several inches long which are bent where the flower is attached.

86. COLUMBIA CLEMATIS, 2/5 ×

The bluish or lavender, long-pointed sepals spread so the flower appears open. Its relative, the Sub-alpine Clematis, *C. pseudoalpina,* is a more dainty plant with twice 3-parted leaves which have deeply toothed or cleft leaflets. Its sepals are not so long-pointed and its flowers are often closed, hanging over the trailing stems like little lavender lanterns. It is found in shaded foothill canyons and occasionally in moist woods nearly up to timberline throughout our region. [Color Pl. 4a]

LEATHER FLOWER, *C. hirsutissima (C. douglasii).* A bushy plant 1 to 2 feet tall with variable but usually finely divided, gray-hairy foliage and nodding, urn-shaped flowers. The thick, leathery sepals with turned back tips are dark purple inside and lighter, because of their pubescence, outside. It grows on dry, open mesas and slopes of the foothill and montane zones from Montana to New Mexico. "Sugar Bowls" is another name for it because of the shape of the flowers. SCOTT CLEMATIS, *C. hirsutissima* var. *scottii* (87), has entire leaflets

and is the one shown in our drawing.

87. SCOTT   CLEMATIS,   2/5 ×

COLUMBINE, *Aquilegia.* This genus is easy to recognize when in flower because the 5 petals are elongated backwards into knob-tipped spurs. There is nectar in these spurs which is sought by long-tongued insects and hummingbirds. Sometimes other insects steal it by biting a hole in the knob. The petals alternate with 5 petal-like sepals. There are many stamens and 5 or more pistils which ripen into many-seeded pods called follicles.

a. Flowers all or partially blue, lavender, or white.
  b. Plants more than 10 inches tall; spurs 1 1/2- to 1 3/4-inches long.
                  COLORADO COLUMBINE, p. 125.
  bb. Plants less than 8 inches tall; leaves tufted.
    c. Spurs 1 to 1 1/2-inches long
                  ROCK COLUMBINE, p. 125.
    cc. Spurs less than an inch long.
      d. Spurs less than 1/3-inch long; leaves green
                  ALPINE COLUMBINE, p. 125-6
      dd. Spurs 1/3- to 1/2-inch long; leaves bluish
                  JONES COLUMBINE, p. 126.
aa. Flowers yellow or partially red.
  b. Flowers golden yellow; spurs more than 2 inches long
                  GOLDEN COLUMBINE, p. 126
  bb. Spurs less than 2 inches long
    c. Flowers pale yellow or pinkish
                  NORTHERN YELLOW COLUMBINE,
          p. 126.

cc. Flowers red and yellow

WESTERN RED COLUMBINE, p. 126.

COLORADO COLUMBINE, *A. caerulea* (88). This handsome plant with its showy blue or lavender and white blossoms 2 to 4 inches broad with long slender spurs, is the state flower of Colorado. It grows tall, with large blue blossoms in the shade of moist aspen groves, and shorter, more bushy, with paler flowers, among rocks of the subalpine and timberline regions. In some areas, especially in Cedar Breaks National Monument, it has pure white flowers. It is found in some form from moist, foothill canyons up to over 12,000 feet throughout the Rocky Mountains.

The Rocky Mountain botanist, Aven Nelson, called it the "Queen of Columbines." [Color Pl. 4b]

In the high mountains of southwestern Wyoming, Utah and Nevada, there is a species called the ROCK COLUMBINE, *A. scopulorum,* which has similar but somewhat smaller flowers with pale blue sepals and yellow or white petals. It is very densely tufted with short-stalked leaves.

ALPINE COLUMBINE, *A. saxi-*

90. WESTERN RED COLUMBINE, 2/5 ×

88. COLORADO COLUMBINE, ½ ×

89. ALPINE COLUMBINE, ½ ×

montana (89), is a charming miniature species found among rocks at high altitudes on the peaks of central and north central Colorado. Its small, drooping flowers have very short spurs. The dainty blossoms suggest a creamy white cup on a blue saucer.

JONES COLUMBINE, *A. jonesii,* is another rare, small, alpine species which occurs in northern Wyoming and Montana. Its tiny bluish-gray leaves are densely tufted and the erect, large, blue flowers are held above them on leafless stalks 1 to 3 inches tall.

GOLDEN COLUMBINE, *A. chrysantha.* This is a handsome, much-branched plant 3 to 5 feet tall, with large, long-spurred, clear yellow flowers which is found in moist ravines of the foothill and montane zones and sometimes up to 11,000 feet, from southern Colorado through New Mexico and Arizona. The NORTHERN YELLOW COLUMBINE, *A. flavescens,* is a species which grows in montane and subalpine woods and is sometimes found above timberline, from Wyoming northward and westward. It is the common kind in Yellowstone and Glacier National Parks. The flowers are pale yellow or sometimes salmon pink.

WESTERN RED COLUMBINE, *A. elegantula* (90), a medium-sized plant rarely more than 1 foot tall with nodding red and yellow flowers is one of the two species that go by this common name. It occurs in southwestern Colorado, northern New Mexico, and Utah. Its flowers are about an inch long, with straight spurs which are abruptly narrowed near the tip. [Color Pl. 4c] A larger species, which also has red and yellow nodding flowers, is *A. formosa.* It barely comes into our range from the northwest.

MEADOWRUE, *Thalictrum.* Most of these plants have ternately compound leaves with small leaflets very much like those of columbine but their petal-less, small, green or purplish flowers which grow in clusters are very different. Some species have perfect flowers but in others they are unisexual (imperfect). The staminate flowers are composed of tassels of yellowish-green stamens. The fruit is a cluster of achenes.

Several species are found in the Rocky Mountains. The ALPINE MEADOWRUE, *T. alpinum* (92), is a tiny plant when growing in the alpine tundra but in subalpine bogs it may be 6 to 12 inches tall. Its leaves are mostly basal and divided into firm, roundish, 3 to 7 lobed leaflets. The few perfect flowers are arranged singly along an upright stalk. This is found from arctic regions through the Rockies as far south as New Mexico.

FENDLER MEADOWRUE, *T. fendleri* (91), is a species having unisexual flowers with the staminate and pistillate usually on separate plants, found in the montane and subalpine zones often in aspen groves and meadows. Its foliage appears a bluish green and its achenes are compressed and strongly nerved. This species is common from northern Wyoming through the southern part of our range.

The FEW-FLOWERED MEADOW-

92. ALPINE MEADOWRUE, ½ ×; left, *flowers;* right, *fruits.*

91. FENDLER MEADOWRUE, ½ ×

Another species of the northern and western part of our region is WESTERN MEADOWRUE, *T. occidentale*, which has slender achenes ¼- to ¾-inch long and grows up to 3½-feet tall. *T. venulosum* is a widespread species with strongly-veined, bluish-green leaflets and oblong, turgid achenes, not over ¼-inch long. Along ditch banks and in wet meadows of the lower montane valleys the tall PURPLE MEADOWRUE, *T. dasycarpum*, with large, purple, pyramid-shaped flower clusters is sometimes seen.

BUTTERCUP, *Ranunculus*. This genus has many species but only a few can be described here. Buttercups have 5 separate sepals and usually 5 petals which are always separate. The sepals are easily detached and frequently drop off before the petals fall.

RUE, *T. sparsiflorum*, has perfect flowers. Its foliage tends to be a more yellowish green than FENDLER MEADOWRUE and its achenes are not strongly nerved. In Colorado the two are often found in the same locations but the range of the FEW-FLOWERED RUE extends farther north and west. It occurs in Yellowstone Park.

Most kinds have bright yellow flowers. One of the best characters by which to distinguish buttercups from other yellow-petaled flowers is the shiny, varnished look on the inner side of the petals. They have many stamens and pistils and each pistil develops into an achene. Most species grow in moist locations.

a. Stems creeping, rooting at the nodes, on wet ground.
  b. Leaves roundish with finely scalloped margins
                    SHORE BUTTERCUP, p. 128.
  bb. Leaves very narrow, entire
                    SPEARWORT, p. 128.
aa. Stems erect or ascending, not rooting at nodes.
  b. Leaves not deeply lobed or divided.
    c. Leaves entire; sepals smooth; petals more than 5
                CALTHA-FLOWERED BUTTER-CUP, p. 128
    cc. Leaves toothed; sepals dark, hairy; petals 5
                MACAULEY BUTTERCUP, p. 129
  bb. At least some of the leaves deeply lobed or divided.
    c. Leaves of 2 forms, some basal ones not deeply divided.
      d. Plants glabrous
                SAGEBRUSH BUTTERCUP, p. 128

dd. Plants pubescent.
  e. Petals 1/2- to 3/4-inch long
                 HEART-LEAF BUTTERCUP, p. 128
  ee. Petals about 1/4-inch long
                 HOMELY BUTTERCUP, p. 128-9
cc. Stem and basal leaves similar, all more or less lobed or divided.
  d. Ultimate leaf divisions linear or oblong.
    e. Leaves finely dissected into thread-like divisions
                 ALPINE BUTTERCUPS, p. 129
    ee. Leaves divided into linear or oblong segments.
      f. Flowers large, 3/4- to 1 inch broad
                 WYOMING BUTTERCUP, p. 129.
      ff. Flowers about 1/2-inch broad or less.
        g. Plants glabrous, montane
                 NUTTALL BUTTERCUP, p. 129-30
        gg. Plants pubescent, subalpine to alpine
                 BIRDFOOT BUTTERCUP, p. 129
  dd. Ultimate leaf divisions rounded; plants glabrous
                 SUBALPINE BUTTERCUP, p. 129.

SHORE BUTTERCUP, *R. cymbalaria,* has small flowers, usually less than ½-inch across and its roundish leaves have heart-shaped bases. It is most common around ponds or on wet ground at middle or lower altitudes. SPEARWORT, *R. flammula,* is found on muddy shores and stream banks in the montane and subalpine regions. Its flowers are slightly less than ½-inch broad.

CALTHA-FLOWERED BUTTERCUP, *R. alismaefolius* (94). This is easily distinguished from all other species by the combination of undivided leaves and 10-petaled flowers. It sometimes covers large areas in wet meadows, blooming in early summer. Found in the subalpine zone from southern Wyoming through Colorado.

SAGEBRUSH BUTTERCUP, *R. glaberrimus (R. ellipticus)* (93), is a very early-blooming species of the foothill and montane zones found throughout our range. Its basal leaves are elliptic or roundish but some of the stem leaves are 3-lobed with the middle lobe the largest. Its sepals are lavender tinged.

HEART-LEAF BUTTERCUP, *R. cardiophyllus,* is a hairy plant of montane and subalpine meadows with at least some of its basal leaves heart-shaped. The flowers are comparatively large, an inch or more across, the sepals are pubescent with long hairs and sometimes there are hairs on the rounded petals. HOMELY BUTTERCUP, *R. inamoenus,* is

93. SAGEBRUSH BUTTERCUP, 2/5 ×

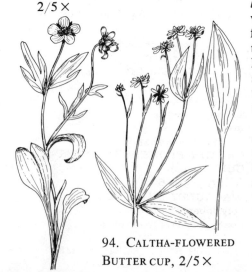

94. CALTHA-FLOWERED BUTTERCUP, 2/5 ×

somewhat similar but has smaller flowers with narrower petals. The WYOMING BUTTERCUP, *R. acriformis* var. *montanensis,* is a plant 12 to 20 inches tall with appressed-pubescent leaves twice 2 or 3 times divided into lanceolate-linear or linear lobes. Its flowers are nearly an inch across and its achenes are smooth and flattened with short, hooked beaks. This grows in wet montane meadows in Montana, Wyoming and adjacent Idaho.

SUBALPINE BUTTERCUP, *R. eschscholtzii.* The leaves of this are deeply 3-lobed, the middle lobe may be 3-lobed or undivided and the lateral lobes are 3 to 7-parted. The plant is very smooth. Its flowers vary in size from ½-inch to fully an inch in diameter. The large-flowered form has been called *R. eximius,* and the small one *R. alpeophilus.* This species occurs throughout our range at altitudes from 9,000 to 12,000 feet. [Color Pl. 4d]

ALPINE BUTTERCUPS. There are several species which qualify for this name. The commonest and most conspicuous in the central part of our region, and the one which is most strictly alpine, is *R. adoneus* (95), SNOW BUTTERCUP. It is characteristic of areas in the Front Range where snow remains late into the summer and in many such places is the first plant out of the ground as the snow melts. Its poppy-like, bright yellow blooms open before the finely cut leaves have a chance to unfold. Some of the places it may be seen are Pikes Peak, Mount Evans and Trail Ridge.

MACAULEY BUTTERCUP, *R. macauleyi,* another large-flowered, showy species with 3-toothed leaves and black, hairy sepals, is found on the high mountains of southern Colorado and New Mexico. In northern Wyoming and Montana (especially in Yellowstone and Glacier National Parks and the Beartooth Range) handsome large-flowered forms of *R. eschscholtzii (R. eximius),* described above, are found in the alpine zone.

The BIRD-FOOT BUTTERCUP, *R. pedatifidus,* is a pubescent plant with erect stems and small flowers which grows in meadows of the montane and subalpine zones and occasionally in the tundra above timberline. May be distinguished from *R. eschscholtzii* by pubescent achenes.

NUTTALL BUTTERCUP, *R. ranunculinus* (96). The basal leaves of this erect, completely smooth plant are 3-times-divided and each division is again divided. It has several to many flowers in a branching inflorescence. Both the petals and sepals are yellow and shiny on the inner surfaces. The petals are sometimes as many as 9, longer but narrower than the sepals. Both petals and sepals fall, or wither, early, leaving heads of plump, green achenes, each with its style forming a little hook at the tip.

Frequent among rocks in the foothills and PONDEROSA PINE zone east of Rocky Mountain National Park and occurring occasionally

95.   SNOW   BUTTERCUP,   ½ ✕

from Wyoming through mountainous regions into northern New Mexico.

WATER CROWFOOT, *Ranunculus aquatilis,* often forms submersed, brownish masses of branched stems and finely-divided leaves which send up numerous dainty, white flowers. It is found in ponds and slow streams throughout the Rockies extending to an altitude of 10,000 feet in Colorado. FLOATING BUTTERCUP, *R. natans,* with shiny yellow petals and floating 3-lobed leaves is found in standing or slow-moving water from the plains to the subalpine zone and from the Yukon through the Rockies into Idaho and southern Colorado. The

lobes of the leaves are more or less notched.

MOUSETAIL, *Myosurus minimus.* A tiny plant with a tuft of linear leaves and white-petaled flowers. It has numerous pistils on a much elongated receptacle which is so long and narrow that it suggests the tail of a mouse. It is occasionally found on muddy banks and shores of ponds in the foothill and montane zones of our region.

WHITE MARSH-MARIGOLD or ELK-SLIP, *Caltha leptosepala* (97). These white and gold flowers without petals are made up of 5 to 15 oblong or oval sepals, arranged around numerous yellow-anthered stamens and several separate pistils which develop into clusters of green seedpods. The sepals are sometimes dark blue on their outer surfaces so that the buds often appear bluish. The leaves are all basal, 3 to 8 inches long, roughly oval or roundish with heart-shaped bases. This is one of the commonest plants of the

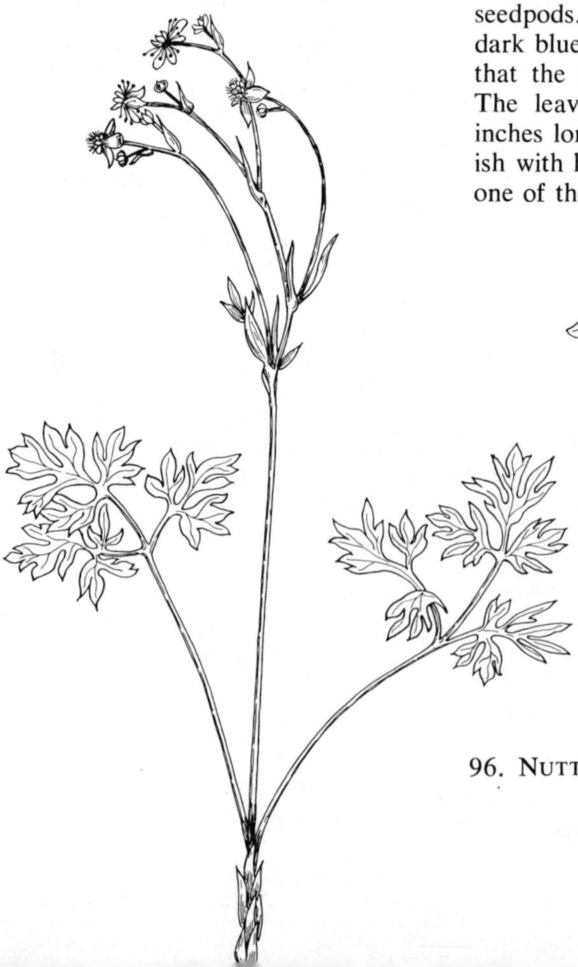

petal

96. NUTTALL BUTTERCUP, ½ ×

97. White Marsh-
Marigold,

subalpine and lower alpine regions, where it often grows in large beds in very wet situations. Often found around melting snowbanks. [Color Pl. 4e]

BANEBERRY, *Actaea rubra* (98). This is a tall plant with thrice compound leaves, the primary divisions long-stalked with pinnately

98. Baneberry, ½ ×

fruits red or
white

arranged, toothed, or lobed leaflets. The small white flowers are on an erect raceme and they mature into shiny, short-stalked, poisonous berries which may be either red or white. It grows in moist woods of the montane and subalpine zones.

FALSE BUGBANE, *Trautvettaria carolinensis*. This is a stout plant 1 to 3 feet tall which has showy panicles of small white flowers. The conspicuous part of each flower is a pompom of white stamens. The seeds are achenes less than ¼-inch long. It grows on wet ground in partial shade in the subalpine zone of southern Colorado, northern New Mexico, Utah and Idaho.

ANEMONE or WIND FLOWER, *Anemone*. Plants of this genus have no petals but their sepals are petal-like in appearance. There are many stamens and pistils. Each pistil ripens into a separate achene. Sometimes the styles develop into long, plumose tails; sometimes the achenes are smooth, sometimes pubescent or woolly. Always in this genus there are leafy collars, called involucres, which are folded around the flower bud and which later encircle the stalk below the flower. Most of the species have their leaves dissected into narrow segments.

```
a. Flowers usually more than 1 inch long, opening before the leaves
     unfold; styles plumose.
   b. Sepals lavender or bluish; involucral leaves sessile
                         PASQUE FLOWER, p. 132
  bb. Sepals cream-colored; involucral leaves short-stalked
                         CHALICE FLOWER, p. 132-3
aa. Flowers usually less than 1 inch long; leaves well developed at
     flowering time.
   b. Plants usually more than 10 inches tall, or, if shorter, sepals red.
     c. Involucral leaves sessile.
       d. Plants alpine; achenes smooth, black
                         ALPINE ANEMONE, p. 133.
      dd. Plants montane; achenes pubescent
                         MEADOW ANEMONE  p. 133
     cc. Involucral leaves short-stalked.
       d. Head of achenes globose or oval; sepals yellowish to red
                         PACIFIC ANEMONE, p. 133
      dd. Head of achenes cylindric; sepals greenish-white
                         CANDLE ANEMONE, p. 133-4
  bb. Plants are less than 10 inches tall.
                         NORTHERN ANEMONE, p. 133
```

PASQUE FLOWER, *Anemone patens (Pulsatilla hirsutissima, P. ludoviciana)* (99). One of the earliest flowers of spring which pushes its furry, lavender-blue, golden-centered cups up into the sun even before the snow is entirely gone. Its stems and finely dissected foliage are covered with silky hairs. When first appearing above ground the buds are protected by the involucral leaves but as the flower develops its stalk lengthens until, by the time the silvery head of long-tailed achenes is mature, it is several inches above the involucre.

This is the state flower of South Dakota and is found most abundantly on open slopes of foothills and montane zones sometimes up to timberline and only on the eastern side of the Continental Divide.

The CHALICE FLOWER, or WESTERN PASQUE FLOWER, *A. occidentale,* is similar in habit but its sepals are cream colored or sometimes white with bluish tinges. Its stems become as much as 18 inches tall in late summer. The achenes turn down as they ripen and the fluffy clusters are quite handsome at first, but after a few rains they appear like bedraggled dish mops. It grows in the northwestern part of our range, particularly in Glacier National Park, and is also found in the Canadian Rockies. Some botanists separate these last two species from *Anemone* on the basis of their long, plumose styles and put them in a genus called *Pulsatilla*.

NORTHERN ANEMONE, *A. parviflora,* is a small dainty plant with 3-parted leaves and a single white or purple-tinged flower which grows in the arctic and is found in cold, moist woods, and sometimes above timberline, in the high mountains.

ALPINE ANEMONE, *A. narcissiflora (A. zephyra)* (100). This plant usually has 3 or more white flowers on stalks 2 to 4 inches long which all rise from the involucre. All the leaves are finely dissected and more or less hairy. The ripened achenes are flattened and black. This species is usually found above timberline in the tundra but may occasionally be seen in subalpine meadows. It grows in the Alps in Europe and from Alaska south through the Rockies to central Colorado.

MEADOW ANEMONE, or NORTHERN ANEMONE, *A. canadensis* (101), is a plant of ditch banks in the foothills and of montane meadows throughout the eastern part of our range. Its white flowers are held on long stalks above the leaves, which are parted into sharply pointed and toothed divisions. The leaves of the involucre are sessile.

PACIFIC ANEMONE, *A. multifida* ssp. *globosa,* is a species which usually has pink or red sepals though

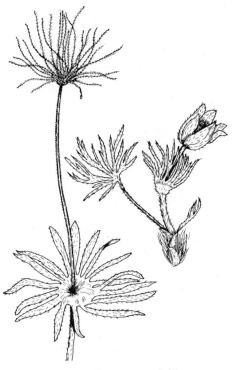

99. PASQUE FLOWER, 2/5×

sometimes they are yellowish. The ripening seed head is roundish and the achenes are densely hairy. This grows from the montane to the alpine zone.

CANDLE ANEMONE, *A. cylin-*

100. ALPINE ANEMONE, ½ ×

drica (102), has whitish sepals and an elongated receptacle covered by the densely woolly achenes. Its involucral leaves are petioled. It grows in the foothill and montane zones. Both species are found throughout our range.

GLOBEFLOWER, *Trollius laxus* var. *albiflorus* (103). This plant usually forms clumps of smooth, long-petioled leaves with several 1-flowered stalks. The sepals are a pale yellow or cream when the flowers open but may become dingy white in fading. There are some very small nectar-bearing petals between the ring of many golden stamens and the sepals. Its leaf blades are roundish in outline but are palmately divided into several lobes which are themselves cut or deeply toothed.

101. MEADOW ANEMONE, 2/5×

102. CANDLE ANEMONE, in fruit, 2/5×

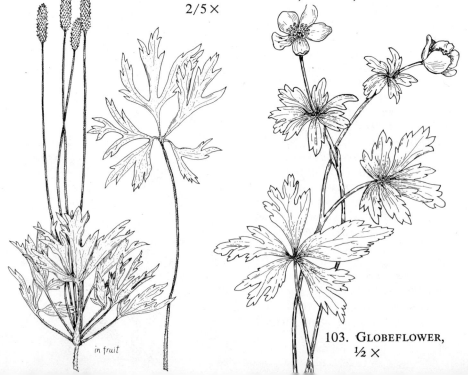

in fruit

103. GLOBEFLOWER, ½ ×

LARKSPUR, *Delphinium*. Wild larkspurs are easily recognized by anyone familiar with the garden varieties, for the structure of the flower is similar and it is distinctive. The irregular flowers have 5 showy sepals and 4 smaller petals. The upper sepal is spurred. The 2 upper petals extend back into the spur. The 4 petals are usually paler than the sepals and together make a sort of knot in the center of the flower which, in the cultivated forms, is called the "bee." The leaves are palmately divided or lobed. Some of the species are poisonous to stock.

a. Flowers whitish or pale
                    PLAINS LARKSPUR, p. 136.
aa. Flowers bright or dark blue or purplish.
  b. Plants from 4 inches to 1 foot tall, smooth; stems usually single; leaves few
                    NELSON LARKSPUR, p. 135.
  bb. Plants 1 to 5 feet tall, leafy either at base or along the stem.
    c. Plants 1 to 2 feet tall; stem and basal leaves densely pubescent
                    GEYER LARKSPUR, p. 135.
    cc. Plants 2 to 4 feet tall; stems leafy, somewhat hairy or glandular.
      d. Flowers in a crowded, unbranched raceme
                    SUBALPINE LARKSPUR, p. 136.
      dd. Flowers usually not crowded; inflorescence often branched
                    TALL MOUNTAIN LARKSPUR, p. 136.

NELSON LARKSPUR, *D. nelsonii* (104). This is one of the spring and early summer flowers of foothill and montane zones throughout our range. Its few leaves are usually dark colored and palmately deeply parted into narrow segments. The stem is between 6 and 12 inches tall, sometimes taller, and bears a raceme of 4 to 10 bright purplish-blue flowers. It is found abundantly on open, sunny hillsides, in meadows and under PONDEROSA PINES. This species was named in honor of Aven Nelson who was Professor of Botany at the University of Wyoming for over 50 years. Two closely related and similar species are *D. bicolor* and *D. scaposum*. [Color Pl. 4f]

GEYER LARKSPUR, *D. geyeri*. The leaves of this plant which are finely divided into narrow segments appear in tufts in early spring. At this

104. NELSON LARKSPUR, 2/5 ×

105. MONKSHOOD, ½ ×

time, on poor pasture where there is little other forage, they are a serious stock poison. The flowers, which come in early summer, are a brilliant and beautiful blue. It grows on the high plains, mesas, and foothill slopes of northern Colorado and Wyoming.

The PLAINS LARKSPUR, *D. virescens (D. penardi),* is a plant with tall, unbranched stems and long racemes of very pale blue or whitish flowers which is found on the plains and lower foothills along the east base of the southern Rocky Mountains.

SUBALPINE LARKSPUR, *D. barbeyi,* is a stout plant with stems from 3 to 6 feet tall which are topped by short, dense racemes of very dark purple flowers. It grows in large clumps or beds in wet meadows and bogs of the subalpine zone in Colorado, Wyoming and Utah.

TALL MOUNTAIN LARKSPUR, *D. occidentale,* is found throughout our area. There are several tall species, similar in appearance and difficult to distinguish, which grow in aspen groves and meadows of the montane zone. They are all between 3 and 6 feet tall. The racemes are usually long, not crowded and sometimes branched. In western Colorado and northwestward *D. ramosum is* common. *D. scopulorum* which has showy indigo-blue flowers and leaves which are dissected into very narrow sharp-pointed segments, is a common one in central Colorado and southwards. It is also reported for Yellowstone National Park. *D. geranifolium* with dense flower spikes occurs in northern Arizona.

MONKSHOOD, *Aconitum columbianum* (105). This is a plant which is found in wet meadows and in thickets of the montane and subalpine zones throughout the Rocky Mountains. Its stems are from 1 to 4 feet tall with hooded flowers widely spaced along them. Usually these are dark blue, but occasionally white-flowered plants are seen.

BARBERRY FAMILY, *Berberidaceae*

Our plants of this family are shrubs with racemes of yellow flowers. There are 6 separate sepals, 6 separate petals, 10 stamens and 1 pistil which ripens into a few-seeded berry. Either the stems or the leaves are spiny. The roots produce a fine yellow dye. Some species are alternate hosts for the stem rust of wheat.

FENDLER BARBERRY, *Berberis fendleri,* with spiny stems and simple, deciduous leaves is found in the upper foothill and lower montane areas of southern Colorado and northern New Mexico.

CREEPING MAHONIA or HOLLY-GRAPE, *Mahonia repens (Berberis repens)* (106). This is a subshrub which spreads by underground stems. It is rarely over a foot tall and has evergreen, compound leaves of 5 or 7 holly-like leaflets; its juicy berries, which make good jelly, are dark blue.

On dry, open hillsides exposed to winter sun its leaves turn red or maroon, but in shaded, moist locations, where it grows more luxuriantly, they remain green. It is a very useful low-growing evergreen for home planting.

FREMONT MAHONIA, *M. fremontii,* is a wide-spreading, erect shrub often 6 or 8 feet tall with compound, leathery evergreen leaves. The 3 to 7 leaflets, which are a beautiful light blue-green, have 3 to 9 spine-tipped teeth on each side. Its abundant yellow flowers are visited by many bees and humming birds. Navajo Indians called this "yellow wood" and used the bark and roots to dye their wool. It grows in the foothill zone, often among piñon pines and junipers, in southwestern Colorado and adjacent Utah and Arizona.

POPPY FAMILY, *Papaveraceae*

The flowers of this family have 2 or 3 sepals which usually fall off when the bud opens, 4 to 6 separate petals which are packed so tightly in the bud that they are always crinkled when they open, many stamens and 1 large pistil with a disk-like, sessile stigma.

They have a yellowish or milky juice which dries into a gummy

106. CREEPING HOLLYGRAPE, ½ ×;

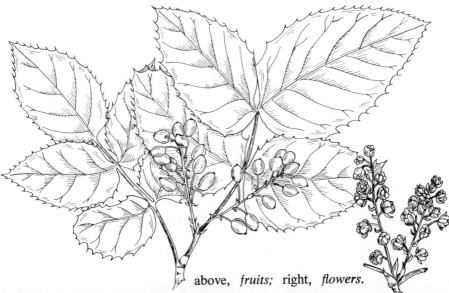

above, *fruits;* right, *flowers.*

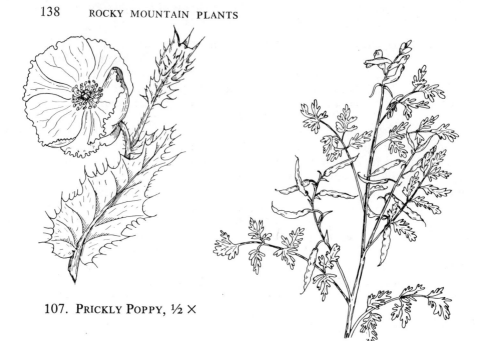

107. PRICKLY POPPY, ½ ×

108. GOLDEN SMOKE, ½ ×

substance. In some cases this forms a seal when the flowers are picked, making it impossible for the stems to absorb water, which explains why poppies often wilt after picking even when placed in water. If the cut end of the stem is put in boiling water or held over a flame for an instant, the substance will be dissolved and then the flowers when put in water will remain fresh.

PRICKLY POPPY, *Argemone polyanthemos, (A. intermedia)* (107), is a gray-leaved, prickly plant with large white, golden-centered blossoms frequently seen along roadsides and on stony slopes of the high plains and foothills from New Mexico to Wyoming. In the middle of the central tuft of bright yellow stamens is the large, black, 4-lobed stigma. The buds become about an inch long before the 3 separate, horned sepals drop off and the wrinkled white petals unfold. *A. hispida (A. platycerus),* is a similar plant which has lots of bristles in addition to the spines on its sepals, stems and leaves.

ALPINE POPPY, *Papaver nudicaule,* is a small plant, very rare in our range, with pubescent, deeply cut foliage and yellow flowers 1 to 2 inches across. Its sepals are thickly set with black hairs, a character easily seen on the buds. It grows in alpine regions on the highest peaks from Glacier Park southward into northern New Mexico.

FUMITORY FAMILY, *Fumariaceae*

The plants of this family have

smooth, finely dissected, often glaucous foliage and irregular flowers with 2 scale-like sepals and 4 petals. The outer petals spread and one or both are spurred; the inner petals are united at their tips and enclose the 6 stamens. The garden BLEEDING HEART and the eastern woodland wild flowers, DUTCHMANS BREECHES and SQUIRREL CORN, are members of this family.

GOLDEN SMOKE, *Corydalis aurea* (108), is a plant with bluish, fern-like foliage and racemes of yellow flowers. The outer petals are unlike —one has a spur at base. Its stems are spreading so the plants are in low clumps. Frequently seen on the disturbed soil of banks and in moist ravines of the montane zone throughout our range.

C. caseana is a tall, stout plant, with flowers similar in form but pink in color, which grows in wet situations of the subalpine zone in Utah and southwestern Colorado.

CAPER FAMILY, *Capparidaceae*

ROCKY MOUNTAIN BEE PLANT, *Cleome serrulata* (109). This plant varies in height from 1 to 3 feet, depending on the amount of moisture available to it. Its leaves are compound, of 3 lanceolate or oblong leaflets. The lower leaves are on long petioles, the upper nearly or quite sessile. The numerous rose or purple, or sometimes white, 4-petaled flowers are in racemes which elongate as the flowers open and usually have buds, flowers and long-stalked pods at the same time.

The flowers secrete much nectar and for that reason fields of these plants provide very good "bee pasture." They grow along roadsides and on overgrazed land of the foothill and lower montane zones throughout the Rocky Mountains. A

109. ROCKY MOUNTAIN BEE PLANT, ½ ×

yellow-flowered species of lower altitudes which has 3 to 7 leaflets is *C. lutea*. This is sometimes seen in western Colorado up to 7,000 feet.

MUSTARD FAMILY, *Cruciferae*

Members of this family are easily recognized by their flowers which have 4 petals arranged in the form of a cross. They usually have 6 stamens, 2 being shorter than the other 4. The leaves are always alternate and in several species their enlarged bases clasp the stem *(see Plate C25)*. The foliage is often covered with hairs or tiny scales which make it rough to the touch or silvery in appearance.

Most of our species have white or yellow flowers—a few are purple or pinkish. Sometimes species which commonly are yellow or white flowered will have pink or purple forms. This is especially true of the wallflowers, *Erysimum*.

The inflorescence is a raceme which is crowded at first but as the outer—or lower—buds open, it elongates. The petal consists of a broad blade attached to a narrow claw *(see Plate D39)*. The distinctive seedpod is 2-celled, short or long, often flattened and sometimes constricted between the ripening seeds which gives it a knobby appearance. These pods are necessary for accurate identification and should always be looked for when plants are collected for study. Usually if the plant has been in bloom for a few days the raceme will have flowers at the top and pods in various stages of development below so that the characteristic shape of the pod may be seen. (Figures given in key are for mature pods.)

This is a very large family including many genera. Some of them contain many species. It includes numerous beautiful wild flowers, several well-known garden plants, several vegetables and numerous weeds with inconspicuous flowers. For accurate identification of the many small-flowered species it will be necessary to consult technical plant manuals. Only those which are important or conspicuous are described here.

a. Flowers yellow.
  b. Pod on a stalk more than 1/2-inch long
                GOLDEN PRINCES PLUME, p. 141
  bb. Pods sessile or on stalks not over 1/8-inch long.
    c. Pods not more than 4 times as long as broad.
      d. Pods inflated.
        e. Pods double
                TWINPOD, p. 142.
      ee. Pods single
                MOUNTAIN BLADDERPOD, p. 142
    dd. Pods not inflated.
      e. Pods flattened, elliptic, or oblong
                DRABA, p. 142
      ee. Pods rounded, pear-shaped
                FALSE-FLAX, p. 147.
  cc. Pods more than 4 times as long as broad.
    d. Leaves entire or wavy-margined, never deeply dissected.
      e. Leaves clasping with heart-shaped bases
                HARES-EAR MUSTARD, p. 147
      ee. Leaves not clasping, narrow
                WILD WALLFLOWER, p. 143
    dd. Some or all of the leaves deeply, pinnately lobed or dissected.
      e. Pods with a stout beak
                BLACK MUSTARD, p. 147
      ee. Pods without a beak.
        f. Pods knobby; plants rough-hairy
                TANSY-MUSTARD, p. 147
        ff. Pods not knobby; plants usually smooth
                TUMBLE-MUSTARD, p. 147
aa. Flower not yellow.
  b. Flowers white, rarely pinkish or lavender.
    c. Pods short, length not over 3 times breadth.

d. Pods ovate or oblong, not over 1/4-inch long
WHITEWEED, p. 147.

dd. Pods over 1/4-inch long, notched at top.
MOUNTAIN CANDYTUFT, p. 144.

cc. Pods long; length more than 3 times breadth.

d. Leaves pinnately dissected.

e. Leaf segments roundish; plants aquatic
WATERCRESS, p. 147.

ee. Leaf segments narrow; plants alpine
FERNLEAF-CANDYTUFT, p. 145.

dd. Leaves not pinnately dissected.

e. Leaves petioled, toothed; base heart-shaped
BROOKCRESS, p. 144.

ee. Leaves clasping the stem.

f. Pods flattened, not knobby
ROCKCRESS, p. 144.

ff. Pods rounded, knobby with a stripe along each side
THELYPODY, p. 146.

bb. Flowers usually purplish, brownish or pinkish.

c. Pods long and slender, knobby.

d. Plants alpine; flowers 1 inch or more broad
PARRYA, p. 146.

dd. Plants not alpine; flowers smaller
BLUE MUSTARD, p. 147

cc. Pods long and slender but not knobby.

d. Calyx closed, flask-like.

e. Stems stout, hollow
WILD CABBAGE, p. 146.

ee. Stems not stout and hollow; outer sepals bulged at base
TWISTFLOWER, p. 146.

dd. Calyx open; outer sepals bulged at base
HESPERIDANTHUS

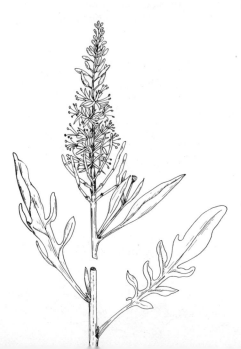

GOLDEN PRINCES PLUME, *Stanleya pinnata* (110). A handsome gray-leaved plant with long sprays of yellow flowers. The narrow petals, stalked pistils and long anthers give a fringed appearance to the racemes. It is common in desert areas and occurs in the mountains only on dry foothill slopes below 8,000 feet. This plant usually indicates the presence in the soil of the poisonous mineral, selenium, which is absorbed into the plant tissues making it poisonous to stock. However, it is said, the Indians of the Southwest use the young leaves as a

110. GOLDEN PRINCES PLUME, 2/5 ×

pot herb after boiling and discarding the first water.

TWINPOD, *Physaria*. These are rosette-type plants with spreading stems, silvery foliage and comparatively large yellow flowers. They begin blooming when very small and compact but the stems elongate later and may become 6 to 10 inches long. They are widely distributed throughout our range on gravelly or sandy foothill slopes or shale banks.

The ALPINE TWINPOD, *P. acutifolia,* grows only in Colorado and is found from 5,000 to 11,000 feet. *P. newberryi* is found in New Mexico, Arizona, and southern Utah. *P. hallii (P. australis)* (111), which has bright yellow flowers and broad leaves which often have two pairs of teeth grows only on shale soils and *P. vitulifera,* with fiddle-shaped or runcinate leaves and crinkled pods occurs on the foothill slopes of Colorado.

BLADDERPOD, *Lesquerella*. This genus is like *Physaria* in general appearance. The plants are usually less compact and the pod is single, but the leaves and stems are cov-

ered with similar silvery scurf which is made up of small star-shaped scales. In these plants the inflorescence elongates in fruit.

MOUNTAIN BLADDERPOD, *L. montana* (112). The stems of this plant are 4 to 8 inches long and usually radiate from the crown of the root, turning up at their tips. Its leaves are petioled, oblanceolate, or obovate with entire or irregularly toothed margins. The flowers are a light yellow on S-shaped pedicels. Found on dry hillsides of the foothill and montane zones from southern Wyoming to northern New Mexico.

DRABA or WHITLOWGRASS, *Draba*. There are many kinds of draba. In general they are smaller plants than most of the members of this family. Their stems are rarely over 6 or 8 inches tall and some species especially the alpine ones, are only an inch or two in height. Their stems rise from rosettes of small leaves with racemes of yellow, or sometimes white, flowers. Their ovate or lanceolate pods are sometimes twisted and one often sees old, dry racemes which show the

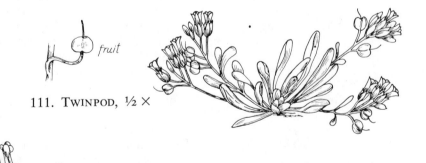

fruit

111. TWINPOD, ½ ×

112. BLADDERPOD, ½ ×

outlines of last year's pods.

GOLDEN DRABA, *D. aurea* (113). This plant usually grows in small clumps of several stems each 2 to 6 inches tall, or rarely taller, each rising from a rosette of small, dark green, spatulate leaves. The stems and leaves are sparsely or densely covered with long hairs. Each raceme has many small, 4-petaled, bright yellow flowers (they become paler as they begin to wither.) It is found from the montane to the alpine zone, commonly under PON-DEROSA PINES in spring, and above timberline in early summer throughout our range. [Color Pl. 5a]

TWISTED-POD DRABA, *D. streptocarpa* is similar but its pods are noticeably twisted. SHINY DRABA, *D. stenoloba,* with smooth shining leaves and a long fruiting raceme occurs in the montane zone.

There are several tiny species found between rocks and on moist ground near and above timberline. Some of them are: THICK-LEAVED DRABA, *D. crassifolia,* which has no leaves on the flower stalks; *D. oligosperma* which has tiny, narrow leaves on which the hairs grow parallel to the mid-rib, and short pods on which there may be short stiff hairs; the WHITE ARCTIC DRABA, *D. fladnizensis,* rare on high tundra.

WILD WALLFLOWER, *Erysimum.* This genus includes the most showy members of the yellow-flowered group of mustard relatives. Their flowers are fragrant and their pods 4-angled.

WESTERN WALLFLOWER, *E. asperum* (114), is a plant 1 to 2 feet tall with bright, orange-yellow, sometimes brownish, 4-petaled flowers in round-topped racemes. Its ripe pods may be ascending or at right angles to the main stalk. Its

113. GOLDEN DRABA, ½ ×

narrow, grayish leaves may be wavy-margined or have scattered, short teeth. Its specific name, *asperum,* refers to the harsh pubescence on stem and leaves which makes it rough to the touch.

It begins to blossom in mid-spring on the mesas and lower grasslands. By mid-June it is in full bloom in the mountain parks and open PON-DEROSA PINE forests. By the 4th of

114. WESTERN   WALLFLOWER, ½ ×

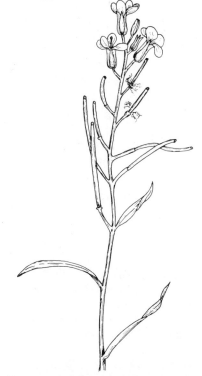

115. MOUNTAIN CANDYTUFT, ½ ×

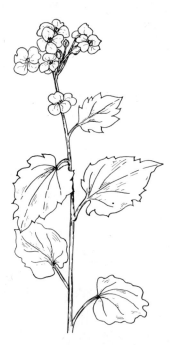

116. BROOKCRESS, ½ ×

July it will be in flower on sunny, subalpine slopes. The plants with deep orange or maroon flowers have been called WHEELER WALLFLOWER, *E. wheeleri.*

WESTERN WALLFLOWER is found throughout the Rockies except in northern Montana where a similar, but smaller-flowered species, *E. inconspicuum,* occurs on the eastern slope in Glacier National Park, and also at low altitudes throughout our whole range.

ALPINE WALLFLOWER, *E. nivale.* This plant is a perennial and, usually has several stems up to 8 inches tall, a stout woody crown and lemon yellow or rarely pink or purple, fragrant flowers. It begins to bloom when the stems are still very short. It is abundant in high tundra in Colorado and in the high mountains of eastern Utah.

MOUNTAIN CANDYTUFT, *Thlaspi alpestre* (115). This plant has short stems from rosettes of grayish or dark green, oval or spatulate leaves. They often grow in little clumps. It begins to bloom when its stalks are only an inch or two tall. They increase in height, as the season advances, to 6 or 8 inches. Each holds a raceme of white flowers. The pods are obcordate. It grows from the foothills, where it is one of the earliest spring flowers in ravines and other moist locations, to the alpine tundra and is found throughout the Rocky Mountains. An introduced weed with smaller flowers and larger flat, round pods called PENNYCRESS, *T. arvense,* is a member of the same genus and is sometimes seen around settlements.

BROOKCRESS, *Cardamine cordifolia* (116), with bright white 4-petaled flowers in round-topped racemes is found along cold mountain streams and around springs of the montane and subalpine zones from Montana and Idaho to New Mexico and Arizona.

ROCKCRESS, *Arabis.* There are several species of this genus in our area. They have tall, unbranched stems, clasping leaves which often have little "ears" called *auricles,* at their bases, small pink or purplish flowers from about ¼ to ⅓ inch broad, and long, usually flat, pods. The pods are necessary for accurate identification.

a. Pods erect or ascending
  b. Plants smooth, glaucous
        DRUMMOND ROCKCRESS, p. 145.
  bb. Plants hairy
        HAIRY ROCKCRESS, p. 145.
aa. Pods not erect, hanging.
  b. Pods uniformly bent down at a sharp angle
        HOLBOELL ROCKCRESS, p. 145.
  bb. Pods spreading or hanging.
    c. Pedicels and fruit arched downward
        FENDLER ROCKCRESS, p. 145.
    cc. Pedicels spreading, slightly up or down but not arched
        SPREADING ROCKCRESS, p. 145.

DRUMMOND ROCKCRESS, *A. drummondii* (117) has the widest pods in our group of species. They are usually over ⅛-inch wide, from 1½- to 4 inches long and stand erect, parallel to the stem and to each other. The small, 4-petaled flowers are white or pinkish. Usually the foliage is smooth and glau-

117. DRUMMOND ROCKCRESS, 2/5
    ×

cous. This is found on rocky slopes of the montane and subalpine zones throughout our range.

HAIRY ROCKCRESS, *A. hirsuta,* is a plant with pubescent stem and thin, oblong, toothed basal leaves; very slender erect pods and white or pink petals. HOLBOELL ROCKCRESS, *A. holboellii,* has several forms and its stems may be anywhere from 4 inches to 3 feet tall, and sometimes one plant has several stems; its basal and lower stem leaves are usually densely pubescent; flowers are white to purple and the pods are more or less reflexed, often sharply so.

FENDLER ROCKCRESS, *A. fendleri.* The basal leaves of this plant are softly hairy, thin, ovate or obovate with tapering bases and more or less toothed margins; the flowers are pink and the pods hang on slender, arching pedicels. SPREADING ROCKCRESS, *A. divaricarpa,* is similar but the pedicels are loosely spreading or ascending.

FERN-LEAF CANDYTUFT, *Smelowskia calycina* (118). This is a small densely caespitose plant which always has old leaf bases clustered on the caudex. Its flowering stalks 2 to 8 inches tall bear

118. FERNLEAF CANDYTUFT, ½ ×

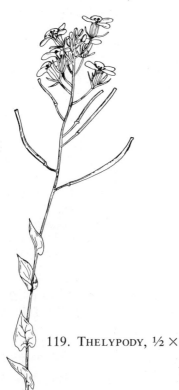

119. THELYPODY, ½ ×

racemes of white, or sometimes rose, flowers with pods ¼- to ½-inch long, tapering to both ends; its hairy leaves are pinnately dissected into narrow segments. Found only above timberline on our highest mountains. A rare and beautiful plant growing on some of the high peaks of Wyoming and Utah is PARRYA, *Parrya nudicaulis,* which has pink or purple flowers nearly an inch across and wavy-margined basal leaves which are 2 to 3 inches long.

THELYPODY, *Thelypodium sagittatum* (119), is a smooth bluish-green herb with white or purplish flowers about ½ inch broad and leaves with little "ears" which clasp the stem. The erect pods are about 1 to 2 inches long and somewhat knobby. Dry ground of the montane zone in Wyoming, Idaho and western Colorado.

WILD CABBAGE, *Caulanthus crassicaulis,* is a smooth, glaucous plant with a leafy, stout, somewhat inflated stem. Its 4-petaled flowers are brownish purple with the sepals curved inwards and the petals curved outwards above them. The pods are 4 or 5 inches long when mature, cylindrical or slightly flattened. This grows on dry soil below 8,000 feet from Wyoming through western Colorado south to Mexico.

TWIST-FLOWER, *Streptanthus cordatus,* grows in the same areas and is another smooth, tall plant with clasping leaves and yellowish-green to purplish flowers with outer sepals bulged at base, but otherwise similar to those of WILD CABBAGE. Its pods are distinctly flattened. Its stems are sometimes branched from the base.

Sisymbrium linearifolium appears somewhat similar to the last two. Its outer sepals are bulged at the base but not constricted above and its petals are pinkish or purple. It is found between 5,000 and 8,000 feet from southern Colorado southward.

MUSTARD, *Brassica*, the genus to which the garden cabbage, cauliflower, and turnips belong, has pale yellow flowers and somewhat knobby pods tipped by strong beaks.

BLACK MUSTARD, *B. nigra*, CHARLOCK, *B. kaber*, and possibly some other species sometimes escape from cultivation and may be found, especially in farming areas.

WATERCRESS, *Rorippa nasturtium-aquaticum*. This plant came from Europe but has become naturalized in cool, running streams throughout the United States. Its stems root at the nodes in shallow water and its leafy shoots make tangled masses of bright green along stream banks. The 4-petaled white flowers are in racemes which elongate as the season advances. The peppery young shoots are used in salads, but one should be careful to pick it only in water known to be uncontaminated.

Several species of this family are more or less conspicuous weeds which have been introduced from Europe or Asia and are now widely distributed in our region. They are usually seen along highways, roads, or trails on soil which has been disturbed and abandoned, or cultivated land. All have 4 petals and 6 stamens.

WHITEWEED or WHITETOP, *Cardaria draba*, is often seen as white patches along roadsides. Its spreading roots make it difficult to eradicate. Its stems are usually between 8 and 26 inches tall with numerous small flowers and tiny, triangular pods. BLUE MUSTARD, *Chorispora tenella*, also occurs in patches, often in grain fields. Its flowers are a bluish-purple or sometimes pinkish. HARES-EAR MUSTARD, *Conringia orientalis*, has pale yellow or whitish petals, long 4-sided pods and clasping leaves which have deeply heart-shaped bases. FALSE-FLAX, *Camelina microcarpa*, has pale yellow petals and long racemes of roundish or pear-shaped pods not over ⅓-inch long. SHEPHERDS PURSE, *Capsella bursa pastoris*, a common weed of gardens, has small white-petaled flowers, triangular pods notched at top, and pinnately lobed or dissected basal leaves. Another weed, found in waste places, is the rough-hairy TANSY-MUSTARD, *Descurania sophia*. Its leaves are twice pinnately dissected into narrow divisions and its pods are somewhat knobby from being slightly constricted between the seeds.

TUMBLE MUSTARD or JIM HILL MUSTARD, *Sisymbrium altissimum*, is a widely-branched annual plant growing up to 3 feet tall with pinnately dissected leaves and numerous pale yellow flowers followed by very slender pods 2½- to 4 inches long.

It has been called "Jim Hill weed" because when the Great Northern Railroad was being built across the western states by the tycoon, James C. Hill, the first season after ground was torn up for track laying this plant appeared and it travelled right along behind the advancing railroad. These dry tumbling weeds scattered their seeds far and wide as winds rolled and bounced them over the high plains and the freshly disturbed soil of the roadbed provided ideal growing conditions for the young seedlings.

SUNDEW FAMILY, *Droseraceae*

The members of this family are of particular interest because they have an ability to trap and digest insects. They are small, inconspicuous plants of bogs or other wet situations with basal rosettes of gland-bearing leaves and slender, leafless stalks holding elongated clusters of tiny white or pinkish flowers. They are widely distributed across the northern part of the United States.

ROUNDLEAF SUNDEW, *Drosera rotundifolia,* has roundish or spatulate, sensitive leaves which are clothed with glistening, reddish, gland-tipped hairs. These secrete a sticky liquid which traps insects that touch it. When an intruder becomes attached to a gland, the other gland-tipped hairs nearby are stimulated to bend toward it until the insect is smothered. Then these glands secrete an enzyme-like substance which digests the soft parts of the insect.

This plant occurs in Yellowstone National Park and both it and the LONGLEAF SUNDEW, *D. anglica, (D. longifolia),* which has more slender leaves, occur in Glacier and other areas of Montana.

STONECROP FAMILY, *Crassulaceae*

The plants of this family are succulents, having fleshy leaves. Many species grow in arid regions as they are well able to withstand drouth. Many are used as ornamentals in rock gardening, such as "HEN-AND-CHICKENS."

STONECROP, *Sedum.* In this genus the sepals, petals and pistils are always of the same number which may be either 4 or 5, and the stamens are twice that number.

YELLOW STONECROP, *S. lanceolatum (S. stenopetalum)* (120), is a very abundant plant throughout our range, occurring at all altitudes.

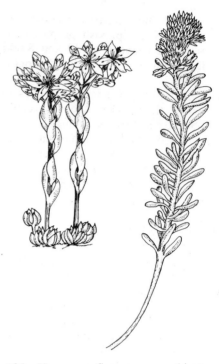

120. YELLOW STONECROP, ½ ×

121. ROSECROWN, ½ ×

Its cylindrical leaves are about ½- to ¾-inch long and form rosettes. In the winter and spring they are brownish green which makes the plants inconspicuous. In early summer each rosette sends up a stalk 2 to 5 inches tall with many bright yellow star-like flowers.

ROSECROWN, QUEENSCROWN, *S. rhodanthum* (121), has leafy stems up to a foot tall with a cluster of rose-colored flowers. Its leaves are thick but flattened. It usually grows in clumps of several stems together in marshy places or on stream banks of the subalpine zone from New Mexico to Montana. [Color Pl. 5b]

KINGSCROWN, *S. rosea* ssp. *integrifolium,* is similar but has dark red or maroon flowers sometimes tinged yellowish or orange; the staminate and pistillate on separate plants.

This is less restricted to wet situations. It occurs in gravelly or rocky places of the subalpine and alpine areas.

SAXIFRAGE FAMILY, *Saxifragaceae*

This is a large. and variable family including both shrubs and herbs. Its flowers have separate or united sepals which are of the same number as the petals which are always separate. Petals may be 4 or 5. The ovary is usually partially inferior. The shrubs have simple leaves and opposite branching. Many of the herbs have only basal leaves. The name means "breaker of rocks" and many of these plants grow in rock crevices.

a. Shrubs with opposite branching.
  b. Petals 4; stamens 8 or many, never 10.
    c. Stamens 8; buds tinged rose
               FENDLERBUSH, p. 149.
    cc. Stamens many; buds green and white
               LITTLELEAF MOCKORANGE, p. 150.
  bb. Petals 5; stamens 10
               JAMESIA, p. 150.
aa. Herbs; leaves mostly basal.
  b. Stamens 4 or 5; flowers white or greenish.
    c. Flowers solitary; clusters of filaments alternating with fertile stamens
               FRINGED PARNASSIA, p. 151.
    cc. Flowers in elongated clusters; no clusters of sterile filaments present.
      d. Petals lobed or dissected; flowers few
               BISHOPS CAP, p. 151.
      dd. Petals entire; flowers many
               ALUMROOT, p. 152.
  bb. Stamens 10; flowers white, yellow, or rose.
    c. Leaves and petals dissected
               WOODLAND-STAR, p. 151.
    cc. Leaves entire, lobed or toothed, never dissected
               SAXIFRAGE, p. 153.

122. FENDLERBUSH, ½ ✕

fruit

FENDLERBUSH, *Fendlera rupicola* (122). This is a shrub with opposite, rigid branches and pale bark. Its leaves are narrow and grayish. Except when in bloom it attracts little attention but when covered with paper-white, 4-petaled blossoms and rose-tinged, squarish buds it is a handsome sight. It grows from southwestern Colorado to Texas and Arizona on rocky slopes of canyons and on mesas. It is particularly abundant and beautiful along the cliffs and canyon rims in

Mesa Verde National Park, usually blooming in late May. [Color Pl. 5c]

This genus was named in honor of Augustus Fendler, a German botanist who came to Houston, Texas, in 1839 and worked there for a time as a market gardener. He later became a very important plant collector in the Southwest, sending his collections to Asa Gray, the famous botanist at Harvard. Some of the plant specimens he collected in the middle 1800's may still be seen in the Gray Herbarium at Cambridge. In describing the new plants which Fendler sent him, Dr. Gray named several of them for the collector.

LITTLE-LEAF MOCKORANGE, *Philadelphus microphyllus* (123), is easily recognized by its white, 4-petaled flowers with many stamens and its opposite branching. It is a fine-textured shrub with slender

124. JAMESIA, ½ ×

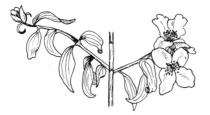

123. LITTLELEAF   MOCKORANGE, ½ ×

twigs and brown and white bark. Its small pale leaves have a slightly silvered aspect. It grows on rocky slopes between 5000 and 8000 feet from Arizona to Texas and northward through southern and western Colorado and Utah into Wyoming.

LEWIS MOCKORANGE, *P. lewisii,* with fragrant flowers and larger leaves occurs in western Montana and in Idaho where it is the state flower. (For Lewis see p. 259)

JAMESIA, CLIFFBUSH or WAX-

FLOWER, *Jamesia americana* (124). This shrub has clusters of 5-petaled creamy-white flowers. Its buds are sometimes faintly tinged with pink. The velvety and beautifully-veined leaves turn to shades of rose and dark red at the end of the growing season. This species is usually found growing from rock crevices or at the base of cliffs.

In autumn a patch of red foliage high up the side of a rock face is almost surely this shrub. It occurs throughout our range and is very abundant in the montane zone along the east side of the Front Range in Colorado. [Color Pl. 5d]

This genus was named for Dr. Edwin James who was the physician-botanist accompanying Major Long on his exploring expedition to the Rocky Mountains in 1820. The expedition discovered the great peak in northern Colorado later named for Major Long, and while they were camped just south of Pikes Peak, Dr. James and two others made the first ascent by white men of that mountain.

This was probably the first time that white Americans had seen the alpine plants of the Rocky Mountains. Dr. James wrote in glowing terms of their beauty and collected several new species which he later described and named.

FRINGED PARNASSIA, *Parnassia fimbriata* (125), is a plant of marshes and wet, mossy places. It usually grows as a clump of bright green, long-petioled, heart-shaped leaves with several slender stalks, each bearing a white flower. These flowers are about one inch across. The rounded petals are clawed and fringed at the sides, and between each anther-bearing stamen is a little bundle of gland-tipped filaments. Each flower stalk has a small, clasping leaf near or above the middle.

SMALL-FLOWERED PARNASSIA, GRASS-OF-PARNASSUS, *P. parviflora*, is similar but lacks the fringe on the petals and the leaf on the stalk is usually below the middle. The latter occurs throughout our range and both species grow in the Colorado mountains and northward into Canada in wet situations of the montane and subalpine regions.

WOODLAND-STAR, FRINGECUP, *Lithophragma glabra* (126), is a very dainty, slender plant with white or pinkish flowers. There are 5 petals and each is cut into 3 or more divisions. The stem is reddish and there are tiny red bulblets in the axils. Clusters of these sometimes replace the flowers. It grows in shaded places of the montane zone and is found from South Dakota and British Columbia west and south through Colorado.

L. parviflora, similar but without the bulblets and the reddish stem color, is found in moist woods from southern Wyoming through western Colorado into New Mexico.

FOAMFLOWER or LACEFLOWER, *Tiarella unifoliata*, is a plant of cool,

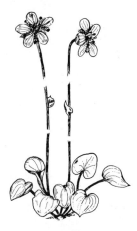

125. FRINGED PARNASSIA, ½ ×

shady situations which is found in the forests of Glacier National Park and northern Idaho. It grows from 8 to 18 inches tall, has heart-shaped and lobed and toothed basal leaves and some smaller but similar stem leaves, and flowers which look like small white pompoms. The white petals are very narrow and there are 10 very long stamens.

BISHOPS CAP or MITREWORT ,

126. WOODLAND STAR, ½ ×

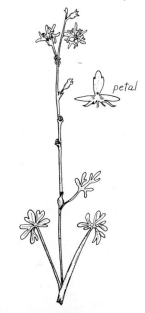

petal

Mitella pentandra (127). This is a plant of moist, shaded forest banks. It is usually found around springs or seepage areas and often grows in moss along with the tiny TWAY-BLADES and ONE-LEAVED BOG-ORCHID. It has a basal rosette of scalloped leaves and an erect stalk holding a raceme of rather widely spaced, small green flowers. The little calyx cup is shallow with 5 pinnatifid petals inserted on its rim. The species grows in subalpine forests from Colorado northward to Alaska.

127. BISHOPS CAP, ½ ×

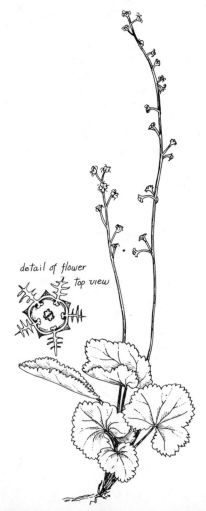

detail of flower
top view

ALUMROOT, *Heuchera.* This genus includes many crevice plants. Its petioled leaves are mostly basal, usually more or less lobed, and are palmately veined. The calyx tube is joined to the lower part of the ovary which develops into a 2-horned capsule. The garden plant CORAL-BELLS belongs here.

BRACTED ALUMROOT, *H. bracteata,* is a plant which forms tufts in rock crevices. Its leaves are bright green, 5 to 7 lobed and sharply toothed. Looking closely one can usually see the rust-colored dried leaves of the previous season around the edges. Its flowers are small, greenish and in compact, one-sided clusters on somewhat scaly but leafless stalks only 4 to 8 inches tall. This is common in the foothill and montane zones of Colorado and Wyoming.

HALLS ALUMROOT, *H. hallii* (128), also grows as tufts and elongated clumps in crevices but its

128. HALLS ALUMROOT, ½ ×

bell-shaped flowers, only about ¼-inch long, are not crowded but hang along slender stalks 4 to 10 inches tall. It is found only in the mountains of central Colorado at altitudes of between 7,500 and 10,000 feet.

COMMON ALUMROOT, *H. parvifolia,* usually grows on the ground under trees with a loose rosette of dark green, long-petioled, roundish leaves which are cordate at base and have 5 to 9 lobes. The margins are toothed. Flowers are tiny in interrupted clusters on stalks 10 inches to 2 feet tall. It grows throughout our range. A similar but smaller and more compact plant is the ALPINE

ALUMROOT, *H. parvifolia* var. *nivalis,* which may be found in rock crevices of the subalpine and alpine zones in Colorado.

SAXIFRAGE, *Saxifraga.* This genus has many species in the mountains and in the northern parts of the northern hemisphere. Its flowers are regular with 5 calyx lobes and 5 petals. The calyx cup is usually joined, at least at base to the ovary and the petals are inserted on its rim. Often the petals are clawed. There are 10 stamens and a 2-celled ovary which develops into a 2-beaked capsule.

a. All leaves basal; petals white.
  b. Leaves ovate; inflorescence compact
                    SNOWBALL SAXIFRAGE, p. 153.
  bb. Leaves round or kidney-shaped; inflorescence open
                    BROOK SAXIFRAGE, p. 153.
aa. At least some small leaves on stem, but larger, basal leaves also present.
  b. Petals white or rose.
    c. Petals white with red and orange dots, not clawed
                    DOTTED SAXIFRAGE, p. 154.
    cc. Petals rose, clawed
                    JAMES SAXIFRAGE, p. 155.
  bb. Petals yellow.
    c. Petals dotted; stems less than 3 inches tall
                    GOLDBLOOM SAXIFRAGE, p. 155.
    cc. Petals not dotted; stems 3 to 8 inches tall.
      d. Runners present; leaf margins fringed with hairs
                    WHIPLASH SAXIFRAGE, p. 155.
      dd. Runners not present; foliage lacking conspicuous hairs
                    ARCTIC SAXIFRAGE, p. 155.

SNOWBALL or DIAMONDLEAF SAXIFRAGE, *S. rhomboidea* (129). This plant sends up a stout, leafless stalk from a flat rosette of very short petioled leaves. At first the inflorescence is a tight ball-like cluster but as it develops it becomes an interrupted panicle having 2 or 3 rather compact clusters of small white flowers, and as it goes to seed it becomes still more open.

It is one of the very early spring flowers of the foothill and montane zones particularly in north central Colorado, and is widely distributed as an early blooming plant of the subalpine and alpine zones throughout our entire range.

BROOK SAXIFRAGE, *S. odontoloma (S. arguta)* (130), is a plant which grows only in very wet places. Its rosette of shiny, green, rounded, strongly-toothed leaves is usually found among stones at the edges of

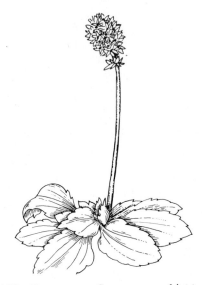

129. Snowball Saxifrage, ½ ✕

subalpine and upper montane zones from Montana south into New Mexico.

Dotted Saxifrage, *S. bronchialis* (131), is a plant frequently found in dry coniferous forests but it also occurs on rocks in the subalpine and alpine regions. Its small, spine-tipped leaves are in tight rosettes. These rosettes often form a mat or carpet covering several square feet of surface. The slender flowering stalks are from 2 to 6 inches tall and bear several white flowers. The 5 oblong petals are distinctly spotted with small orange and red dots. This species is found throughout the Rocky Mountains.

Alpine Saxifrage, *S. caespitosa*, is a tiny, white-flowered plant with crowded, 3-lobed leaves and stems 2 or 3 inches tall, sometimes found in high alpine situations. It is circum-

cold mountain streams. The slender flowering stalk is 10 to 18 inches tall bearing an open panicle of small white-petaled flowers. Their pedicels are often reddish. It grows in the

130. Brook Saxifrage, ½ ✕

131. Dotted Saxifrage, ½ ✕

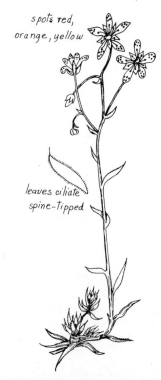

spots red, orange, yellow

leaves ciliate
spine-tipped

boreal and comes as far south as Arizona on the highest mountains.

JAMES SAXIFRAGE, *Telesonix jamesii (Saxifrage jamesii)* (132). A narrow panicle of bright rose-colored flowers from a tuft of green leaves in a rock crevice is apt to be this species. Its petals are distinctly clawed so there are conspicuous spaces between their bases. The petioled, rounded leaves are distinctly toothed.

These plants are found only in granitic rock crevices or, rarely, on very rocky ground in the mountains of central and northcentral Colorado from 9,000 to 10,000 feet. In some older books this species was placed in the genus *Boykinia*.

GOLDBLOOM SAXIFRAGE, *S. serpyllifolia, (S. chrysantha)* (133). This is a tiny alpine plant which has rosettes of smooth leaves ¼- to ½-inch long, and stems usually only 2 or 3 inches tall with comparatively large flowers. The little round buds are on reflexed pedicels but are lifted some when in bloom. Its bright yellow petals are dotted with orange and as the flower ages the ripening pistil becomes bright red. This plant grows in gravelly places on the high mountains of New Mexico and Colorado above 11,000 feet.

WHIPLASH SAXIFRAGE, *S. flagellaris,* is a slightly larger, yellow-flowered alpine with sticky hairs on its leaves and stems. It sends out 1 or 2 runners from the basal rosette which root at their tips and so form new rosettes, as a strawberry plant does. Its capsule is often bright red as it ripens.

132. JAMES SAXIFRAGE, ½ ×

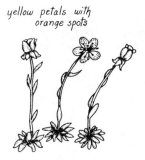

yellow petals with orange spots

133. GOLDBLOOM SAXIFRAGE, ½ ×

A third yellow-flowered species is the ARCTIC SAXIFRAGE, *S. hirculus,* a plant up to 8 inches tall which is sometimes found in subalpine and alpine bogs. This is a circumboreal species which extends south as far as central Colorado.

GOOSEBERRY FAMILY, *Grossulariaceae*

This family is closely related to the Saxifrage Family and in some books is included in that family. It contains only the genus *Ribes,* the gooseberries and currants. These plants are all shrubs, some of them prickly, and their flowers have 5-lobed tubular or saucer-shaped calyxes which may be colored. The small petals are inserted on the calyx. The fruits are juicy berries which are sometimes covered with sticky bristles. The leaves are more or less lobed. These shrubs are browsed by game animals and the berries furnish food for small mammals and birds.

a. Stems without spines or prickles.
  b. Stems erect.
    c. Flowers yellow, fragrant, 1/2-inch or more long; foliage
      smooth
                     GOLDEN CURRANT, p. 156.
    cc. Flowers pink, white, or greenish; foliage sticky.
      d. Leaves usually less than 1 1/2-inches wide; berries red,
        more or less sticky
                     SQUAW CURRANT, p. 156.
     dd. Leaves usually more than 1 1/4-inch wide; berries black, 3/8-
       inch in diameter
                     STICKY CURRANT, p. 157.
  bb. Stems reclining or prostrate
                     COLORADO CURRANT, p. 157.
aa. Stems with spines or prickles.
  b. Flowers bowl- or saucer-shaped; berries bristly, or, at least,
    sticky.
    c. Flowers reddish; berries red, in racemes
                   RED PRICKLY CURRANT, p. 157.
    cc. Flowers greenish, berries black
                   BLACK PRICKLY CURRANT, p. 157.
  bb. Flowers tubular, stems with spines at nodes
                   MOUNTAIN GOOSEBERRY, p. 157.

GOLDEN CURRANT, *Ribes aureum* (134), has smooth foliage which turns rose or red in autumn and the dark red or black berries are edible. It grows in foothill canyons through- out our range. SQUAW CURRANT or WAX CURRANT, *R. cereum* (135), is a very common shrub of sunny, dry foothill and montane slopes.

135. SQUAW CURRANT, ½ ✕

134. GOLDEN CURRANT, ½ ✕

The bright red berries are insipid. It occurs throughout our range. The STICKY CURRANT, *R. viscossismum,* which has sticky stems, leaves and berries is found in mountain woods from Montana south to Colorado. Its black berries are almost dry. COLORADO CURRANT, *R. coloradense,* is most frequently seen in the subalpine forests. Its black berries are slightly sticky. It is found in western Colorado, Utah and New Mexico. A more erect shrub which is otherwise similar to the last is WOLFS CURRANT, *R. wolfii.*

RED PRICKLY CURRANT, *R. montigenum* (136), occurs on rocky montane and subalpine slopes throughout our range and the BLACK PRICKLY CURRANT or SWAMP CURRANT, *R. lacustre,* which occurs in moist, often shaded, locations over much of North America is also found in the montane zone of the Rockies. MOUNTAIN GOOSEBERRY or WHITE-STEMMED GOOSEBERRY, *R. inerme* (137). This is a prickly shrub of moist, shaded ground found throughout our range. It has smooth flowers and its dark purplish, very tart berries make excellent jelly. The specific name, *inerme,* which means "unarmed" is inappropriate because the stems have both prickles and spines. THIN-FLOWERED GOOSEBERRY, *R. leptanthum,* is an excessively prickly shrub found on dry mountain slopes of the southern Rockies which may be distinguished from the last by its pubescent flowers.

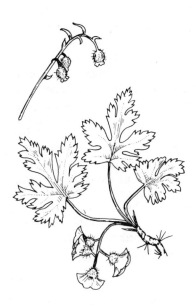

136. RED PRICKLY CURRANT, ½ ×

137. MOUNTAIN   GOOSEBERRY, ½ ×

ROSE FAMILY, *Rosaceae*

This is a very large family and includes plants which differ widely. Some botanists have divided it into several separate families but even then there is great variation within some of the segregated groups. It is treated here in its broadest sense. It includes trees, shrubs and herbs; its members may have simple or compound leaves; there may be one to many pistils. In general: the branching is alternate; the leaves have stipules; the flowers are showy and they are regular with a more or less united calyx and 5 separate petals; the stamens are usually many. By careful observation one may soon learn to recognize combinations of these characters as indicating a member of this family.

Its fruits are variable and apples, plums, raspberries and strawberries are some examples; other rose family fruits are long-tailed achenes or dry seed-pods. Many species of this family—especially the shrubs—are very important food plants for wildlife. Not only the fruits are eaten but game animals browse the foliage and twigs.

a. Plants with woody stems, i. e. , trees, shrubs or undershrubs.
  b. Undershrubs, very low, creeping and matted.
    c. Flowers tiny, in dense, oblong clusters
                ROCKMAT, p. 163.
    cc. Flowers solitary, usually 8-petaled; fruit a cluster of long-tailed achenes; plant alpine
                MOUNTAIN DRYAD, p. 166.
  bb. Medium or tall shrubs or small trees.
    c. Leaves pinnately compound or dissected into narrow lobes.
      d. Leaves compound.
        e. Flowers yellow
                SHRUBBY POTENTILLA, p. 168.
        ee. Flowers pink or white.
          f. Leaflets 3 or 5, coarsely toothed; stems bristly
                WILD RASPBERRY, p. 165.
          ff. Leaflets 5 to 15, finely and evenly toothed.
            g. Stems prickly; flowers large, pink
                WILD ROSE, p. 159.
            gg. Stems smooth; flowers white in clusters; berries orange or red
                MOUNTAIN-ASH, p. 160.
      dd. Leaves small, 3-cleft, or pinnately dissected into narrow lobes but not compound.
        e. Leaves pinnately lobed; pistils several to many, becoming plume-tailed achenes.
          f. Flowers white; pistils many
                APACHE PLUME, p. 161.
          ff. Flowers pale yellow when fresh; pistils 4 to 10
                CLIFFROSE, p. 162.
        ee. Leaves 3-cleft; pistil 1
                ANTELOPE-BRUSH, p. 162.
    cc. Leaves simple, not dissected but may have broad lobes.

d. Leaves palmately veined and lobed; flowers white.
　e. Flowers small, in clusters
　　　　　　　NINEBARK, p. 163.
　ee. Flowers larger, solitary, or 2 to 5 together
　　　　　　　BOULDER RASPBERRY, p. 164.
dd. Leaves pinnately (feather) veined; margins entire, toothed
　or wavy.
　e. Fruits fleshy.
　　f. Fruits like small apples with sepal tips evident.
　　　g. Leaf sharply and coarsely toothed; stout thorns on stems
　　　　　　　HAWTHORN, p. 160.
　　　gg. Leaves entire or with small teeth; no thorns.
　　　　h. Leaves roundish, toothed around upper portion of mar-
　　　　　gin; flowers white
　　　　　　　SERVICEBERRY, p. 161.
　　　　hh. Leaves spatulate or obovate; flowers, or at least buds,
　　　　　pink.
　　　　　　　SQUAW-APPLE, p. 161.
　　ff. Fruits enclosing hard stones, entirely smooth
　　　　　　　PLUMS and CHERRIES, p. 165.
　ee. Fruits dry, of achenes or small pods.
　　f. Flowers inconspicuous; achenes feather-tailed
　　　　　　　MOUNTAIN MAHOGANY, p. 164.
　　ff. Flowers many, in conspicuous clusters.
　　　g. Flower clusters plume-like
　　　　　　　MOUNTAIN SPRAY, p. 162.
　　　gg. Flower clusters flat-topped, rounded or pyramidal
　　　　　　　SPIRAEA, p. 163.
aa. Plants herbaceous, that is, stems not woody; leaves compound.
　b. Flowers yellow; petals always 5.
　　c. Leaflets 3; plants alpine.
　　　d. Petals minute, shorter than sepals
　　　　　　　SIBBALDIA, p. 172.
　　　dd. Petals conspicuous, twice as long as sepals
　　　　　　　ALPINE POTENTILLA, p. 168.
　　cc. Leaflets 5 to 15.
　　　d. Stamens 5; flowers crowded into a head-like cluster
　　　　　　　IVESIA, p. 172.
　　　dd. Stamens many; flowers not tightly crowded.
　　　　e. Style persisting on achene; leaves pinnately compound
　　　　　　　ALPINE AVENS, p. 170.
　　　　ee. Styles withering and falling; leaves either pinnately or palmate-
　　　　　ly compound   POTENTILLA, p. 166.
　bb. Flowers white; leaflets 3; runners present
　　　　　　　WILD STRAWBERRY, p. 171.

WILD ROSE, *Rosa*. The members of this genus are easily recognized as roses but difficult to differentiate. The following three species are the commonest in our range.

ARKANSAS ROSE, *Rosa arkansana,* is usually less than 2 feet tall and its stems often die back to the ground during winter. It has 5 to 7 leaflets and the flowers are usually clustered. It is widely distributed in the western United States. In our area it is most frequently found on railroad embankments, ditch banks and rocky hillsides of the foothill zone.

WOODS ROSE, *R. woodsii (R. fendleri),* is the tallest of the three as it may grow to an extreme of 8 feet, but it averages 4 or 5. Its very fragrant flowers are usually in clusters of 2 to 4 and its fruits are round and hard.

PRICKLY ROSE, *R. acicularis (R. sayi),* may grow up to 6 feet but is usually between 1 and 3 feet tall. Its blossoms are usually solitary but may be 2 together. Its fruits are often elongated and soft when ripe, and its leaves turn beautiful shades of orange, rose and maroon in the fall. It spreads by underground stems and so forms patches. Both the last two are found from the foothills to timberline throughout our area.

MOUNTAIN-ASH, *Sorbus scopulina* (138). This is easily recognized at any time by its symmetrically patterned leaves made up of 11 to 15 evenly and sharply toothed leaflets. In early summer it bears large, flat-topped clusters of white flowers which are followed by orange or red berries. The berries are like tiny apples, each one showing the tips of the 5 calyx lobes. It is found on moist hillsides of the montane and subalpine zones from New Mexico northward. It usually grows as a large shrub and often its main stems are decumbent where they have been bent down by the heavy snow of the subalpine region.

HAWTHORN, *Crataegus.* These thorny shrubs or small trees are difficult to distinguish and identify specifically. They have clusters of white flowers in which the conspicuous anthers may be white, pink, rose or purple. The fruits, called "haws," are berry-like and may be orange, bright or dark red, or black.

COLORADO HAWTHORN, *C. succulenta* var. *coloradensis* (139), has bright red haws. Its leaves are coarsely toothed or shallowly lobed with finely toothed margins. Its young leaves and twigs are more or less hairy and dull. It grows in foothill canyons of central and north-central Colorado.

RED-STEMMED HAWTHORN, *C. erythropoda,* has smooth and shiny leaves and branches and dark red to black haws. It occurrs from New Mexico and Arizona northward into Wyoming on stream banks and in

138. MOUNTAIN ASH, ½ ×

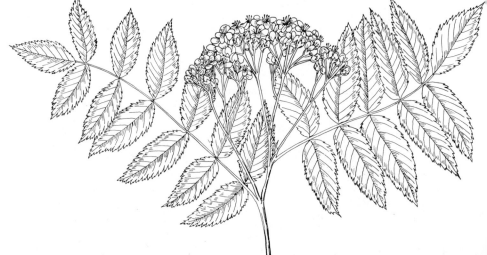

valleys of the foothill and montane zones.

RIVER HAWTHORN, *C. rivularis,* has dark haws and is found in the western part of our range.

DOUGLAS HAWTHORN, *C. douglasii,* is a common species in western Montana and Idaho having black fruits.

SERVICEBERRY, SHADBUSH or JUNEBERRY, *Amelanchier.* Our species are large or small shrubs. They have racemes of white, fragrant flowers and little apple-like fruits. Their bark is gray or reddish-brown. The fruits are eaten by wild animals and were an important food for the Indians. The foliage and twigs are browsed by deer, elk and moose. Their leaves are toothed only from the middle, or a little below it, around the apex.

SASKATOON SERVICEBERRY, *A. alnifolia* (140), with sweet, juicy fruit is the commonest and most widely distributed species in our range. Its foliage is hairy when young but becomes smooth and dull green. UTAH SERVICEBERRY, *A. utahensis,* has grayish hairy leaves and rather dry fruits and is most conspicuous in the higher sections of the Southwest, but its range extends from Montana to New Mexico. It is prominent between Moab, Utah, and the Arches National Monument as large, rounded, grayish shrubs growing singly from crevices in the pavement-like sandstone. The SMOOTH SERVICEBERRY, *A. pumila,* with entirely smooth foliage, is less common but widely distributed throughout our region in the foothill and montane zone.

SQUAW-APPLE, *Peraphyllum ramosissimum.* The Latin adjective used for the specific name of this apple relative means "the most branched" and well describes this

139. COLORADO HAWTHORN, ½ ×
140. SASKATOON   SERVICEBERRY,
     ½ ×

rigid, thicket-forming shrub. It grows up to 6 feet tall, has spatulate leaves which are usually crowded together at the ends of the branchlets, and pink and white flowers resembling apple blossoms. The round fruits are yellowish or reddish brown. It occurs on open fields and slopes at altitudes between 5,500 and 8,000 feet in southwestern Colorado and westward to Oregon and California.

APACHE PLUME, *Fallugia paradoxa* (141). This is a finely branched, white-barked shrub with dainty, dissected leaves and 5-petaled white flowers 1 to 1½-

141. APACHE PLUME, ½ ×

142. ANTELOPEBRUSH,   ½ ×

inches broad. There are several separate pistils each with a long, hairy style. In fruit these styles persist and elongate so there is a cluster of achenes, each with a plumose tail 1 to 2 inches long.

The shrub blooms profusely in May or early June and continues to display a few flowers throughout the summer. The feathery styles are often rose-tinged or rust-colored and a shrub covered with these tufts is a lovely sight, especially if the sun is shining through it. Commonly found along roadsides in the Santa Fe area and around the Grand Canyon, also on the hillsides of northern New Mexico, southern Colorado and adjacent Arizona and Utah. [Color Pl. 5e]

CLIFFROSE, *Cowania mexicana* var. *stansburiana*, is a scraggly shrub or small tree of the high, arid Southwest, which is rather similar to the last in leaves and fruits. Its flowers are rose-like, pale yellow with many yellow-anthered stamens and few pistils, not over 10, which

become feathery-tailed achenes. Both of these are much browsed by livestock and game animals and this, together with the severity of their habitat, results in their rough and gnarled appearance. [Color Pl. 5f]

ANTELOPE-BRUSH or BITTER-BRUSH, *Purshia tridentata* (142). This shrub has 3-toothed leaves and in late May and early June becomes covered with small, half-inch-broad, pale yellow flowers. It looks much like a small copy of the Cliffrose except that each flower has only one pistil that ripens into a large, yellowish brown, pointed achene. All the livestock and game animals browse this extensively so it is usually seen as a low shrub spreading on banks or among rocks. It is found throughout the Rocky Mountains in the foothill and lower montane zones.

MOUNTAIN SPRAY or ROCK-SPIRAEA, *Holodiscus dumosus* (143), is a medium-sized shrub which bears plume-like panicles of very small, creamy white flowers in June. As they fade they turn pinkish and finally become rust colored, persist-

143. MOUNTAIN SPRAY, 2/5 ×

ing on the branches throughout the summer. It grows on shaded, rocky slopes of foothill and montane canyons of Wyoming, Colorado, Utah and southward. Its close relative *H. discolor,* is found in Montana and Idaho.

ROCKY MOUNTAIN NINEBARK, *Physocarpus monogynus* (144). The leaves of this shrub are roundish in outline, 3- to 5-lobed and doubly toothed. The flowers are white, each one about ¼- to 1/3-inch broad and arranged in corymbs along the arching branches. The leaves turn orange and red and are responsible for much of the autumn color on the slopes and in the valleys of the upper foothill and montane regions. They are frequently seen in ravines, under open aspen groves and at the edge of forests. This species occurs from southern Wyoming south through Colorado to New Mexico and Arizona. The TALL NINEBARK, *P. opulifolius,* is larger in every way with leaves usually only 3-lobed and is found in some of the deep foothill canyons in Colorado and in Montana, Wyoming and Utah. *P. malvaceus* is a similar shrub which occurs from Wyoming northwestward.

MEADOWSWEET, *Spiraea lucida* (145), is a plant with stems 8 inches to 2 feet tall, rising singly from a long, woody, underground stem. The upright stems scarcely seem woody. Each bears a flat-topped corymb of many small white, fragrant flowers. The PINK MEADOWSWEET, *S. densiflora,* is a shrub 1 to 5 feet tall with brown, shreddy bark. It has a rounded panicle of pink flowers. ROCKMAT or ROCK SPIRAEA, *S. caespitosum (Petrophyton caespitosum),* is a low plant with creeping, woody stems. Its

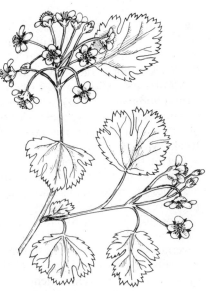

144. ROCKY MOUNTAIN NINEBARK, ½ ×

spatulate, silky-hairy leaves ¼- to ½-inch long, are 1-ribbed and are arranged in crowded rosettes, the whole plant very compact and dense with flowering stalks 1 to 8 inches tall holding short, dense spikes of

145. MEADOWSWEET, ½ ×

small white flowers. It grows on rocks in the upper foothill and lower montane zones throughout the Rockies but is rare in Colorado.

MOUNTAIN MAHOGANY, *Cercocarpus montanus* (146), is a very common shrub on dry, rocky slopes of the foothills throughout the Rocky Mountains. It grows to 8 or 9 feet in favorable locations but is commonly 4 to 6 feet tall. Its branches are rigid and its bark gray. Its leaves are 1 to 2 inches long, oval or obovate with rounded apex. They are whitish beneath with a covering of fine hairs. The flowers are without petals and the 1 pistil ripens into a pubescent achene with conspicuously twisted and plumose tail 3 to 4 inches long. This has been called "mahogany" because the wood is very hard and heavy and in areas where it is available it is considered an excellent fuel.

CURL-LEAF MOUNTAIN MAHOGANY, *C. ledifolius,* is a shrub or small round-topped tree which often has a twisted trunk. Its small leaves are dark green above, light beneath with inrolled margins. They are leathery and evergreen. Its flowers and long-tailed fruits are similar to the last.

BOULDER RASPBERRY or ROCKY MOUNTAIN THIMBLEBERRY, *Rubus deliciosus* (147). This is a handsome shrub with rounded and more or less lobed, bright green leaves and white, rose-like flowers 2 to 3 inches across. It grows from 2 to 5 feet tall with arching branches clothed with light brown, shreddy bark. The young tips and sprouts are bright rose color during the growing season. Its raspberry-like, insipid fruit is eaten by birds and animals.

This grows on rocky slopes and banks of the foothill and montane

146. MOUNTAIN MAHOGANY, ½ ×

zones in Colorado and southern Wyoming, mostly on the eastern slope. It is one of the best of our native shrubs for garden use.

R. neomexicanus, of New Mexico and Arizona, has slightly smaller flowers and more sharply lobed leaves but is otherwise similar. THIMBLEBERRY, *Rubus parviflorus* (148), is a related shrub with smaller, more cup-shaped flowers and large, angular, 3- to 5-lobed leaves. It occurs over a wide area from Alaska to Mexico and is found in a few moist, shaded canyons on the eastern slope in Colorado and

147. BOULDER RASPBERRY, ½ ×

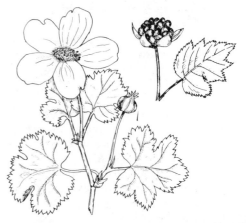

148. THIMBLEBERRY,   2/5 ×

149. WILD PLUM, 2/5 ×

much more abundantly in the north central mountains.

WILD RED RASPBERRY, *Rubus idaeus (R. strigosus)*. This is a bristly shrub with compound leaves of 3 or 5 leaflets which are usually white on their under surfaces and sharply toothed. The white flowers which are in terminal and axillary clusters are followed by typical raspberry fruits of excellent flavor. It grows along trails, roadsides and rocky slopes from the foothills to the alpine zone throughout mountainous areas of the United States. Recently burned areas are often invaded by it.

PLUMS and CHERRIES, *Prunus*. The flowers in this genus have 5 separate petals, many stamens which are inserted on the edge of the calyx tube and 1 superior pistil which develops into a fleshy fruit containing a hard stone and is called a drupe. In general the stones of plums are flattened and of cherries are round.

WILD PLUM, *P. americana* (149), is a rigid, much branched, thicket-forming, somewhat spiny shrub or small tree with grayish bark and few-flowered umbels of white, fragrant flowers which open before the leaves. The petals are

rounded and from ¼- to ½-inch long. Its leaves are 2 to 4 inches long and taper-pointed at apex. The plums are about an inch long, orange to red or purplish when ripe and much sought after by both birds and humans. They have a fine flavor for eating raw or making into jelly. This species is widely distributed from the Atlantic coast to the Rocky Mountains and is found in our area in foothill canyons and along streams on the eastern side of the Continental Divide.

PIN or BIRD CHERRY, *P. pennsylvanica* (150), is less rigid than the plum and its bark, except on old trunks, is glossy brown with horizontal markings. Its flowers are similar but the fruits are small, bright red cherries. They also are very desirable for jelly. This blooms as the leaves are unfolding. This species is widely distributed east of the Rockies. It is a small tree in

150. PIN CHERRY, 2/5 ×

151. CHOKECHERRY, ½ ×

canyons at elevations between 6,000 and 7,000 feet, but becomes a shrub at higher altitudes. In Colorado it is found as a low shrub even as high as the subalpine zone.

CHOKECHERRY, *P. virginiana* (151). This is the common choke-cherry of the United States. It may grow from 2 to 30 feet tall but rarely exceeds 8 to 12 feet in the Rocky Mountain region where it is called var. *melanocarpa*. The

152. MOUNTAIN DRYAD, ½ ×,

bark is reddish brown, the leaves taper to both ends and the creamy white flowers hang in racemes.

Its abundant dark red or black fruit is an important food for bears, small animals and birds. The cherries are somewhat puckery in flavor but make delicious syrup and can be used for jelly by combining them with apple juice or other pectin. These shrubs form thickets in valleys and on hillsides of the foothill and montane zones throughout our range. Their rosy red color adds a brilliant touch to the autumn scenery.

MOUNTAIN DRYAD, *Dryas octopetala* (152). This plant is easy to recognize because its flowers have 8 creamy white petals and no other flower of our region regularly has 8 petals. Even if the petals have fallen you can still recognize it by the 8 sepals, plus the clusters of long, plumy styles. It is an arctic plant which extends south along our mountain tops. Its leaves are ½- to 1 inch long, finely scalloped, white beneath, and with their veins conspicuously impressed. These leaves furnish an important source of food for the ptarmigan, large grouse-like birds with protective coloration which live on the tundra.

POTENTILLA or CINQUEFOIL, *Potentilla*. This genus has many representatives in western America. Their flowers are so similar that when one learns one species the others are easy to recognize as belonging to the same clan. These flowers have 5 separate heart-shaped petals which are usually yellow and have an orange spot at base. The 5 sepals are united into a calyx resembling a 5-pointed, saucer-shaped star to which 5 extra, narrower points have been attached which alternate with the main calyx

Pl. 1a-ALPINE LADY FERN, *Athyrium alpestre* var. *americanum* (7), p. 57.

Pl. 1b-WHITE FIR, *Abies concolor*, p. 65.

Pl. 1c-ENGELMANN SPRUCE, *Picea engelmanni* (16), p. 66, and BIG SAGE, *Artemisia tridentata*, p. 306.

Pl. 1d-CREEPING JUNIPER, *Juniper horizontalis*, p. 67.

Pl. 1e-WESTERN SPIDERWORT, *Tradescantia occidentalis* (25), p. 78.

Pl. 1f-WOODLILY, *Lilium philadelphicum* (33), p. 82.

Color Plate 2

Pl. 2a-YELLOWBELLS, *Fritillaria pudica* (35), p. 82.

Pl. 2b-SANDLILY, *Leucocrinum montanum* (36), p. 84.

Pl. 2c-MARIPOSA LILY, *Calochortus gunnisonii* (42), p. 87.

Pl. 2d-ALPLILY,*Lloydia serotina* (43), p. 88.

Pl. 2e-WESTERN TRILLIUM, *Trillium ovatum*, p. 88.

Pl. 2f-YELLOW LADY SLIPPER, *Cypripedium calceolus* (46) p. 90.

Pl. 3a-FAIRY SLIPPER, *Calypso bulbosa* (48), p. 91.

Pl. 3b-Leaves of W. RED BIRCH, *Betula occidentalis,* in autumn, p. 102.

Pl. 3c-BITTER ROOT, *Lewisia rediviva* (76), p. 115.

Pl. 3d-MOSS CAMPION, *Silene acaulis,* (79), p. 117.

Pl. 3e-ARCTIC SANDWORT, *Arenaria obtusiloba* (83), p. 120.

Pl. 3f-YELLOW PONDLILY, *Nuphar luteum* var. *polysepalum* (85), p. 121.

Color Plate 4

Pl. 4a-Subalpine Clematis, *Clematis pseudoalpina*, p. 124.

Pl. 4b-Colorado Columbine, *Aquilegia caerulea* (88), p. 125.

Pl. 4c-W. Red Columbine, *Aquilegia elegantula* (90), p. 126.

Pl. 4d-Subalpine Buttercup, *Ranunculus eschscholtzia*, p. 129.

Pl. 4e-White Marsh-marigold, *Caltha leptosepala* (97), p. 130.

Pl. 4f-Nelson Larkspur, *Delphinium nelsonii* (104), p. 135.

Pl. 5a-GOLDEN DRABA, *Draba aurea* (113), p. 143.

Pl. 5b-ROSECROWN, *Sedum rhodanthum* (121), p. 148.

Pl. 5c-FENDLERBUSH, *Fendler rupicola* (122), p. 149.

Pl. 5d-JAMESIA, *Jamesia americana,* in autumn (124), p. 150.

Pl. 5e-APACHE PLUME, *Fallugia para-doxa* (141), p. 161.

Pl. 5f-CLIFF ROSE, *Cowania mexicana,* p. 162.

Color Plate 6

Pl. 6a-DWARF or DEER CLOVER, *Trifolium nanum* (164), p. 177.

Pl. 6b-NEW MEXICAN LOCUST, *Robinia neomexicana* (169), p. 179.

Pl. 6c-LAMBERT LOCO-WEED, *Oxytropis lambertii* (176), p. 184.

Pl. 6d-SHELTON VIOLET, *Viola sheltonii,* p. 195.

Pl. 6e-HUNGER CACTUS, *Optunia polyacaniha* (206), p. 200.

Pl. 6f-GREEN-FLOWERED HEDGEHOG CACTUS, *Echinocereus viridiflorus* (207), p. 200.

Pl. 7a-MOUNTAIN BALL CACTUS, *Pedio-cactus simpsonii* (208), p. 200.

Pl. 7b-ALPINE FIREWEED, *Epilobium latifolium* (211), p. 203.

Pl. 7c-CUT-LEAF EVENING PRIMROSE, *Oenothera coronopifolia* (217), p. 206.

Pl. 7d-GRAYS ANGELICA, *Angelica grayi,* p. 210.

Pl. 7e-PINEDROPS, *Pterospora andromeda,* (229), p. 215.

Pl. 7f-KINNIKINNIK in blossom, *Arctos-taphylos uva-ursi* (234), p. 217.

Color Plate 8

Pl. 8a-Kinnikinnik berries, *Arctostaphylos uva-ursi* (234), p. 217.

Pl. 8b-W. Shooting-star, *Dodecathon pulchellum* (237). Photo by Matthews. p. 219.

Pl. 8c-Fairy Primrose, *Primula angustifolia* (238), p. 220.

Pl. 8d-Parry Primrose, *primula parryi* (239), p. 220.

Pl. 8e-Rocky Mtn. Fringed Gentian, *Gentiana thermalis* (245), p. 223.

Pl. 8f-Arctic Gentian, *Gentiana algida* (249), p. 225.

Pl. 9a-SPREADING PHLOX, *Phlox diffusa,* ssp. *subcarinata* p. 229.

Pl. 9b-SCARLET GILIA, *Gilia aggregata* (258), p. 231.

Pl. 9c-ALPINE FORGET-ME-NOT, *Eritrichium elongatum* (267), p. 237.

Pl. 9d-NARROW-LEAF PUCCOON, *Lithospermum incisum,* p. 237.

Pl. 9e-EATON PENSTEMON, *Penstemon eatonii,* p. 248.

Pl. 9f-PIKES PEAK PENSTEMON, *P. alpinus* (282), p. 250.

Pl. 10a-SAND PENSTEMON, *Penstemon ambiguus*, p. 251.

Pl. 10b-WHIPPLES PENSTEMON, *Penstemon whippleanus*, p. 251.

Pl. 10c-WESTERN PAINTBRUSH, *Castilleja occidentalis* (287), p. 255.

Pl. 10d,e-ROSY or SUBALPINE PAINT-BRUSH, *C. rhexifolia*, p. 255.

Pl. 10d,e-ROSY or SUBALPINE PAINT-BRUSH, *C. rhexifolia*, p. 255.

Pl. 10f-FOOTHILL PAINTBRUSH, *Castilleja integra*, p. 254.

Pl. 11a-ELEPHANTELLA, *Pedicularis groenlandia* (289), p. 257.

Pl. 11b-LEWIS MIMULUS, *Mimulus lewisii*, p. 259.

Pl. 11c-TWINFLOWER, *Linnaea borealis* (296), p. 261.

Pl. 11d-HAREBELL, *C. rotundifolia* (306), p. 266. Photo by Matthews.

Pl. 11e-PARRY HAREBELL, *Campanula parryi* (308), p. 267.

Pl. 11f-COLORADO ASTER, *Aster coloradoensis*, p. 277.

Pl. 12a-SUBALPINE ERIGERON, *E. pere-grinus* (317), p. 280. Photo by Bettie E. Willard.

Pl. 12b-SUBALPINE ERIGERON and AR-ROWLEAF SENECIO. Photo by Bettie E. Willard.

Pl. 12c-FIVE-NERVED HELIANTHELLA, *H. quinquenervis* (325), p. 284.

Pl. 12d-RYDBERGIA, *Hymenoxys grandi-flora* 329), p. 286.

Pl. 12e-RYDBERGIA (329) as seen from Trail Ridge Road, R.M. Nat'l Park.

Pl. 12f-BLACK-TIPPED SENECIO, *Senecio atratus,* p. 299.

lobes and give the calyx a 10-lobed appearance. These extra segments are called bractlets.

This type of calyx which is illustrated on *Plate E41,* is found only in the Rose Family and mainly in this genus and a few other closely related ones. It is a positive character by which to distinguish these plants from yellow-flowered plants of other families such as the buttercups. The leaves of potentillas are always compound, either palmate or pinnate, and always have stipules attached at the base of the petioles.

The old common name of this plant, Cinquefoil, which is a French word meaning "5 leaf," was originally applied to a European species which had 5 leaflets. Among the large number of American species most have more than 5 leaflets, so that name is not appropriate for the whole genus.

a. Plants woody, small shrubs with narrow leaflets
           SHRUBBY POTENTILLA, p. 168.
aa. Plants herbaceous, not woody except at the crown.
  b. Leaves palmate with not over 7 leaflets.
    c. Basal leaves with 3 leaflets
           ALPINE POTENTILLA, p. 168.
   ·cc. Basal leaves with 5 or more leaflets.
      d. Leaflets green at least above.
        e. Leaflets dark green above, white-felted beneath
           BEAUTY POTENTILLA, p. 168.
       ee. Leaflets green above and below, somewhat silky
           GOLDCUP POTENTILLA, p. 168.
      dd. Leaflets gray or bluish both sides
           BLUELEAF POTENTILLA, p. 168.
  bb. Leaves pinnately compound with 7 or more leaflets.
    c. Petals bright yellow, longer than the sepals.
      d. Plants prostrate and trailing by means of runners which root
           SILVERWEED, p. 168.
      dd. Plants with erect stems.
        e. Leaflets deeply dissected into narrow lobes
           PRAIRIE POTENTILLA, p. 168.
       ee. Leaflets more or less toothed, not deeply dissected.
          f. Inflorescence open, widely branching; petioles more than
             half as long as the rachis.
            g. Leaves bicolored, green above, white beneath
           BEAUTY POTENTILLA, p. 168.
           gg. Leaves gray hairy on both sides
           SILVERY POTENTILLA, p. 169.
          ff. Inflorescence narrow; petioles less than half as long
             as leaf rachis
           LEAFY POTENTILLA, p. 169.
   cc. Petals not bright yellow.
      d. Petals white or cream color
           STICKY POTENTILLA, p. 170.
      dd. Petals and stamens red; petals shorter than sepals
           MARSH POTENTILLA, p. 170.

153. SHRUBBY POTENTILLA, ½ ×

SHRUBBY POTENTILLA, *P. fruticosa (Dasiphora fruticosa)* (153). This shrub grows from 1 to 3 feet tall and is found on moist hillsides and in meadows. It is noticeable during winter as compact, rounded dark brown or grayish bushes scattered over grassland. In summer these little shrubs are covered with bright yellow, rose-like blossoms 1- to 1½-inches broad. The plant is widely distributed in arctic and northern regions of the world and extends southward along mountain ranges. It occurs in our area from the foothills to the alpine zone and the higher you find it the brighter and bigger the flowers seem to be.

ALPINE POTENTILLA, *P. nivea,* is a small, tomentose plant with trifoliate leaves and bright yellow, comparatively large, ½-inch-broad flowers. The leaflets are white-felted at least on their lower surfaces. This is an arctic-alpine plant which extends southward to the high mountains of Colorado. The very small, 1-flowered forms of this have been called *P. uniflora.*

GOLDCUP POTENTILLA, *P. gracilis.* This plant is usually from 1 to 2 feet tall with many flowers in an open, flat-topped cluster. Each petal has an orange spot at base. It grows in meadows and on open slopes of the montane and subalpine zones from Alaska south through Colorado.

BLUELEAF POTENTILLA, *P. diversifolia,* has spreading stems not over a foot long. Its basal leaves usually have 5 leaflets. It occurs in moist meadows of the subalpine and alpine regions from the Canadian Rockies south to New Mexico.

SILVERWEED, *P. anserina,* is a plant of wet soil with long, pinnate leaves which may have as many as 31 leaflets. These are sometimes silvery on both sides but may be green above and white beneath. It spreads by means of runners which root at their tips. It is found along ditch banks and in meadows from the plains to the subalpine zone throughout our range. The specific name *anserina* means "of geese" in reference to the plant being eaten by geese. Its root was used by Indians as both food and medicine.

PRAIRIE POTENTILLA, *P. pennsylvanica (P. strigosa),* has 5 to 9 leaflets which are cut about halfway to the midrib and pinnately arranged. They are sometime so crowded as to appear almost palmate. The leaflets are more or less hairy on their upper surfaces and usually tomentose beneath. Flowers are about ½-inch broad. Found throughout our range on dry hillsides and fields in the foothill and montane zones.

NELSON POTENTILLA, *P. plattensis (P. nelsoniana),* is similar to the last but its leaves are mostly basal and may have as many as 17 leaflets. It is pubescent but never tomentose.

BEAUTY POTENTILLA, *P. pulcherrima* (154). The stems of this are 1 to 2 feet tall. Most of its

155. Leafy Potentilla, ½ ×

154. Beauty Potentilla, ½ ×

leaves are basal on long petioles
and they may be either palmate or
pinnate. There are usually 7 leaflets but there may be from 5 to 11.
They are dark green above and
white beneath, obovate or oblanceolate with sharp teeth cut less than
halfway to the midrib. The flowers
are ½- to ¾-inch broad. Found in
meadows and on mountain slopes
throughout the Rockies up to timberline.

P. concinna, is a low, silvery
plant which has 5 leaflets and grows
on dry meadows and rocky hillsides, usually in the subalpine zone.

Silvery Potentilla, *P. hippi-
ana,* is a leafy stemmed plant, the
leaves having 7 to 13 toothed leaflets which are gray with hairs on
both surfaces. It is common on
fields and hillsides of the foothill
and montane zones throughout our
range.

Leafy Potentilla, *P. fissa*
(155). This is a very abundant
plant 8 to 12 inches tall and easy
to recognize. Its stems are erect and
the flowers in a narrow cluster are
comparatively large, up to an inch
broad, and usually of a paler shade
of yellow than the other species. Its

short-petioled leaves have 9 to 13 broad leaflets which decrease in size from the terminal one to the basal pair. The plant is rather shaggy with brown, sticky hairs. It grows on rocky slopes and along roads and trails from the foothills to the subalpine zone in South Dakota, Wyoming, Colorado and New Mexico.

P. glandulosa is a related species which seems to replace the LEAFY POTENTILLA in Montana and Idaho. It is taller, sometimes has reddish stamens and its petioles are long and slender.

STICKY POTENTILLA, *P. arguta,* is a tall, rather weedy plant with sticky, hairy foliage and crowded, cream colored or white flowers. At first the petals are slightly longer than the calyx lobes but in fruit the calyx lobes enlarge and bend together over the cluster of achenes. It grows in meadows throughout our range except in the alpine zone.

MARSH POTENTILLA, *P. palustris (Comarum palustris),* may be recognized by its red petals which are shorter than the reddish sepals. Its leaves are pinnately compound with sharply toothed leaflets which are

156. ALPINE AVENS, ½ ×

pale beneath. It grows in swamps and bogs from Alaska to southern Wyoming.

ALPINE AVENS, *Geum rossii (G. turbinatum, Sieversia turbinata)* (156). A 5-petaled yellow-flowered plant with finely dissected leaves somewhat similar to potentilla but with its calyx tube top-shaped so that the flower is somewhat depressed at its center instead of being flat.

In many alpine locations in the Rockies this appears to be the most abundant and conspicuous plant throughout the season. It blooms profusely in late June and early July and scatteringly during the rest of the summer. Its leaves indicate the coming of autumn by beginning to turn bronze or maroon in late August. It is found in the subalpine and alpine zones of the high mountains from Montana to New Mexico and Arizona.

Another plant of the same genus is BUR AVENS, *G. macrophyllum.* It grows to 3 feet in height, has yellow flowers and compound leaves with the rounded, terminal leaflet much bigger than the others. The styles which persist on the many achenes are jointed and bent so that the fruit becomes a bur. This grows in meadows throughout the northern part of North America and in the mountains is found in the foothill and montane zones.

PINK PLUMES or PRAIRIE SMOKE, *Geum triflorum (Sieversia ciliata)* (157), has finely dissected leaves and nodding flowers, usually 3 on a stalk. The whole inflorescence is rose-colored. The calyx lobes overlap to form a sort of urn from which whitish or pale yellow petals protrude slightly. In fruit the plumose styles elongate to 1 or 2

158. Wild Strawberry, ½ ×

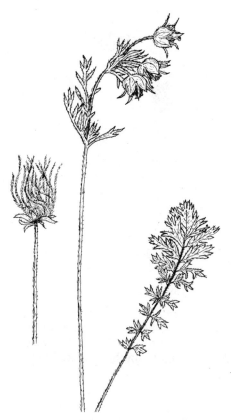

157. Pink Plumes, ½ ×

inches, forming a tuft of rose-colored fluff.

AGRIMONY, *Agrimonia striata,* is an erect plant which grows up to 3 feet tall with pinnately compound leaves and a spike-like raceme of small yellow flowers which develop into burs with hooked prickles. There are 7 to 13 leaflets, alternating large and small. It occurs in meadows and open wooded areas of the foothill and montane zones.

NUTTALL CHAMAERHODOS, *Chamaerhodos nuttallii,* has many small, white flowers on a much-branched stem up to 1 foot tall rising from a rosette of finely divided leaves. It occurs in central Colorado and Utah and extends north to Alaska.

WILD STRAWBERRY, *Fragaria ovalis (F. glauca)* (158). Strawberry flowers are much like potentilla flowers except that the 5 petals are white instead of yellow. These plants may be recognized by their compound leaves made up of 3 toothed, slightly bluish leaflets. The flowers have many separate pistils and as they go to seed the receptacle to which these pistils are attached enlarges and becomes a strawberry. Each pistil develops into an achene seated on the juicy red receptacle. Strawberry seeds are on the outside of the fruit. In this species they are in little pits. It grows throughout the western part of the United States and Canada in meadows and on open slopes.

WOODLAND STRAWBERRY, *F. americana,* has greener leaflets and the seeds are in very shallow depressions on the surface of the receptacle. It is less common than the first and often is found at the edge of woods, sometimes in the shade of open coniferous forests.

SIBBALDIA, *Sibbaldia procumbens,* is a dwarf, tufted, cushion plant with bluish, trifoliate, compound leaves. The leaflets are less than an inch long and 3- to 5-toothed at apex. The calyx of the small flowers is 5-lobed with 5 alternating bractlets and there are 5 minute yellow petals, shorter than the sepals. This plant is circumpolar and alpine in the northern hemisphere. In the Rockies it occurs on gravelly tundra from timberline to above 13,000 feet.

IVESIA, *Ivesia gordonii (Horkelia gordonii)* (159). This plant is closely related to the potentillas. Its small flowers are clustered in a compact, head-like inflorescence and the leaflets of the pinnately compound leaves are dissected into many narrow lobes. The flower

159. IVESIA, ½ ×

clusters are yellow at first and then turn reddish brown. It occurs from the montane to the alpine zone and from Montana south through Colorado.

PEA FAMILY, *Leguminosae*

It is easy to recognize the members of this family because of their distinctive, irregular corollas. All species commonly found within the range of this book have *papilionaceous* corollas, see *Plate E49*. These flowers are composed of a united calyx, 5 petals including a *banner,* 2 *wings* and 2 lower petals joined to form the *keel,* 10 stamens and 1 pistil which develops into a one-celled, usually several-seeded, pod called a *legume.* The stamens and pistil are usually enclosed by the keel. Sweet Pea and clover blossoms are typical papilionaceous flowers and bean and pea pods are typical legumes. Many plants of this family have 9 of the stamens joined together by their filaments and 1 separate. Most of the plants of the family have compound leaves and they usually have stipules.

a. Leaflets 3 or more, palmately arranged.
  b. Leaflets 5 or more.
                 LUPINE, p. 173.
  bb. Leaflets 3 (except DEERVETCH which may have 3 to 6).
    c. Flowers bright yellow or orange.
      d. Stipules large, leaf-like; stamens all separate
                GOLDEN BANNER, p. 175.
     dd. Stipules less conspicuous; some of stamens joined.
      e. Inflorescence from leaf axils.
        f. Flowers 1 to 3
            DEERVETCH, p. 176.

ff. Flowers many, in racemes
SWEET-CLOVER, p. 178.
ee. Inflorescence terminal, in head-like clusters
JAMES DALEA, p. 176.
cc. Flowers not bright yellow.
d. Leaves minutely dotted; plants of sandy ground
SCURFPEA, p. 176.
dd. Leaves not dotted; plants of meadows or rocky ground
CLOVER, p. 176.
aa. Leaflets pinnately arranged, usually more than 5.
b. Leaves usually tipped with a tendril or bristle.
c. Style with a tuft of hairs near tip; stems trailing or climbing
CLIMBING VETCH, p. 178.
cc. Style hairy along one side
PEAVINE, p. 178.
bb. Leaves odd-pinnate, without tendrils (see Plate 9B).
c. Shrubs with pink or lavender flowers
NEW MEXICAN LOCUST, p. 179.
cc. Herbs.
d. Pod a prickly bur; stems coarse and stout
WILD LICORICE, p. 179.
dd. Pod never prickly.
e. Pod various but never jointed in segments.
f. Keel of corolla pointed
LOCO, p. 183.
ff. Keel of corolla blunt
MILKVETCH, p. 180.
ee. Pod composed of jointed segments
SWEETVETCH, p. 179.

PURPLE PRAIRIE CLOVER, *Dalea purpurea (Petalostemum purpureum)* (160). This plant usually has several erect or ascending leafy stems 8 to 20 inches tall. The leaves are short petioled of 3 to 5 leaflets; leaflets are usually folded and there are small dots on their lower surfaces. Small purple flowers are in dense terminal spikes, 1 to 2 inches long. It grows on the plains and foothills from the mountains eastward.

LUPINE, *Lupinus.* All plants in this genus may be recognized by their distinctive leaves which are composed of from 5 to 9 long, narrow leaflets, all evenly attached at the tip of the petiole. Sometimes they are silky, sometimes almost bristly, but always more or less hairy. The pea-form flowers are

160. PURPLE PRAIRIE CLOVER, ½ ×

usually blue, sometimes two-toned. One of our species often has dingy white blossoms.

a. Plants rarely over 8 inches tall; flower clusters scarcely exceeding leaves.
  b. Plants with short, leafy stems.
    c. Stem silky-pubescent; hairs sometimes tawny
                KINGS LUPINE, p. 174.
    cc. Stem with long, stiff hairs; plant grayish
                LOW LUPINE, p. 174.
  bb. Leaves all basal; flowers never exceeding leaves
                CUSHION LUPINE, p. 174.
aa. Plants usually more than 10 inches tall; flowers in racemes above the leaves.
  b. Flowers blue or bi-colored.
    c. Flowers blue with purple spot, more than 1/2-inch long
                NEBRASKA LUPINE, p. 174.
    cc. Flowers blue, about 1/2-inch long
                SILVERY LUPINE, p. 174.
  bb. Flowers whitish or tinged with blue, about 1/3-inch long
                LODGEPOLE LUPINE, p. 174.

KINGS LUPINE, *L. kingii,* is a low annual or biennial plant, usually having dark blue flowers, found on dry ground of the foothills in Utah, New Mexico, Arizona and west of the Continental Divide in Colorado LOW LUPINE, *L. pusillus,* is a somewhat similar annual plant with pale or almost white flowers found on sandy soil of the foothills and plains along the eastern side of the Rockies from Canada south into New Mexico. CUSHION LUPINE, *L. lepidus* var. *utahensis (L. caespitosus),* is a mat-forming perennial species with leaflets not over an inch long and very short clusters of pale blue or lavender flowers which are partly buried in the leaves. It grows on dry hills in the montane zone from Montana to central Colorado and is often seen in Yellowstone National Park. A form of this with very small leaves and comparatively large flowers found in Glacier National Park was called *L. minimus.*

NEBRASKA LUPINE, *L. plattensis,* is a showy plant between 1 and 2 feet tall, found on the high plains and in the foothills of Nebraska, Wyoming, western Kansas, and eastern Colorado. It often grows among sagebrush and is easily recognized by the large, bicolored corolla.

SILVERY LUPINE, *L. argenteus (L. alpestris)* (161), is a common blue-flowered, or sometimes bicolored, lupine of the mountains. It is found from the foothills through the subalpine zone, and from Montana to New Mexico and Arizona, and occurs in all the National parks of the Rocky Mountain region. It is frequently found at the edges of woods or other partly shaded places but grows in the open at the higher altitudes.

SILKY LUPINE, *L. sericeus (L. flexuosus),* is a large, branched plant usually having several stems 12 to 24 inches tall. It is a very silky and conspicuous species found on fields and open slopes often with sagebrush throughout the western parts of the Rocky Mountains and particularly in Glacier and Yellowstone National Parks.

LODGEPOLE LUPINE, *L. parviflorus,* is a species with long racemes of dingy white or bluish flowers

162. GOLDEN BANNER, 2/5 ×

161. SILVERY LUPINE, ½ ×

which turn brown as they fade; the commonest small-flowered lupine found in the montane zone throughout our range.

GOLDEN BANNER, GOLDENPEA, *Thermopsis*. These plants have compound leaves of 3 leaflets with large, leaflike stipules, showy yellow pea blossoms and bean-like pods. Because of their vigorous-spreading, underground stems they tend to occur in patches and often take over banks and roadsides. In our area there are three species similar in appearance. For accurate identification pods are necessary. The earliest to bloom is *T. rhombifolia*. It is rarely over a foot tall and grows on sandy soil on the plains from North Dakota to Nebraska and westwards to the foothills of the

Rockies in Montana, Wyoming and Colorado. Its pod is curved, sometimes forming a half circle, and is finally bent down.

The other two species are from 1 to 2 feet tall, bloom in late spring and early summer, occur from the foothills up to timberline and can be distinguished only by the position of the pod and the locality where found growing.

T. divaricarpa (162), has slightly hairy pods that spread away from the stalk almost at right angles. It is abundant from central Colorado northward through Wyoming on the eastern side of the Continental Divide. Occasionally it may also be found in New Mexico and Utah and scatteringly throughout the mountainous parts of Colorado. *T. montana* has pods which are very hairy and are held erect close to the stalk. It occurs abundantly in the mountains of southern Colorado and through Utah and Nevada to Montana and Oregon.

WRIGHT DEERVETCH, *Lotus wrightii,* is a plant with spreading, branching stems covered with grayish hairs, and yellow or orange flowers which turn reddish as they fade. It has 3 to 6 crowded leaflets. This grows on rocky slopes, often in shade, from southwestern Colorado into Utah, Arizona and New Mexico. Its seeds and foliage are a valuable source of food for wildlife.

JAMES DALEA, *Dalea jamesii,* has numerous silky, somewhat decumbent stems from 2 to 10 inches long which are tufted at the top of a thick, woody root. Its leaves are of 3 silky leaflets, less than an inch long, and the yellow flowers are in dense, woolly clusters. They turn rose or purple as they dry. It grows on dry plains and hillsides of the foothills and lower montane zones

from Kansas and Colorado south into Mexico.

SCURF PEA, *Psoralea lanceolata,* is a plant which usually grows in sandy soil and has very long, creeping underground stems. The tiny white or purple-tipped flowers are in dense clusters not over an inch long. There are 3 leaflets which are conspicuously dotted with glandular spots. This is found on plains and foothills along the eastern slope of the Rocky Mountains.

CLOVER, *Trifolium.* The wild clovers of the mountains have 3-foliate leaves and compact heads of papilionaceous flowers much like those of the cultivated species. Some species have papery bracts below the heads which form involucres. The presence or absence of an involucre is a character which is helpful in identification. The seeds and leaves of most clovers are eaten by large and small mammals and by some birds.

a. Plants acaulescent, i.e., leaves all basal; native, high altitude species.
  b. Flowers 1/3- to 2/3-inch long; keel cream-colored or pinkish; banner and wings darker
                      WHIPROOT CLOVER, p. 177.
  bb. Flowers 2/3- to 1 inch long.
    c. Flowers 6 to 15 in a loose head; lower ones reflexed
                      BRANDEGEE CLOVER, p. 177.
    cc. Flowers 2 to 3, 1/2- to 3/4-inch long, pink, turning brown
                  DWARF or DEER CLOVER, p. 177.
aa. Plants caulescent; i.e., stems leafy.
  b. Heads on leafy stalks; no green leaves just below head.
    c. Flowers 1/3- to 3/4-inch long, native species.
      d. Flowers 1/3- to 1/2-inch long; greenish involucre present
                  FENDLER CLOVER, p. 178.
      dd. Flowers 1/2- to 3/4-inch long.
        e. Flowers rose; papery, blue-veined involucre present
                  PARRY CLOVER, p. 177.
        ee. Flowers white to rose; involucre absent
                  RYDBERG CLOVER, p. 177.
    cc. Individual flowers not over 1/4-inch long; species escaped from cultivation.
      d. Stems creeping and rooting
                  WHITE CLOVER, p. 178.

dd. Stems erect; flower reflexed in fruit
ALSIKE CLOVER, p. 178.
bb. Heads just above an involucre of green leaves
RED CLOVER, p. 178.

There are three cushion-type species. The commonest and most widely distributed is WHIPROOT CLOVER, *T. dasyphyllum* (163). It has 2-toned flowers and hairy leaflets which are usually about an inch long and is found at high altitudes throughout the southern Rocky Mountains, i.e. from southern Wyoming southward. It grows in exposed rocky situations of the subalpine zone and on gravelly areas above timberline. The DWARF or DEER CLOVER, *T. nanum* (164), is a compact, mat-forming, alpine plant with leaflets usually not over ½-inch long. Each head is composed of only 2 or 3 comparatively large, rose-colored flowers which turn brown as they age. [Color Pl. 6a]

Another alpine species of the high mountains of Colorado and New Mexico is BRANDEGEE CLOVER, *T. brandegei*, which has several purple flowers in a loose head. The lower ones soon become conspicuously reflexed. J. S. Brandegee, a railroad engineer with the Santa Fe and topographer with the Havden Survey in 1875, made botanical collections in Colorado.

Among the taller, native species PARRY CLOVER, *T. parryi* (165), is the showiest. The compact heads of bright rose-pink flowers are raised on long peduncles above the green, glabrous leaves and surrounded by papery involucres. It occurs from Wyoming and Utah southward through the mountains of Colorado, especially in the timberline region of the subalpine zone but also in moist alpine meadows.

RYDBERG CLOVER, *T. longipes*, a plant of the montane and sub-

163. WHIPROOT CLOVER, ½ ×

164. DWARF CLOVER, 1 ×

164. DWARF CLOVER, 1 ×

165. PARRY CLOVER, ½ ×

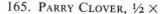

165. PARRY CLOVER, ½ ×

alpine regions has leafy stems up to 18 inches long, sharply toothed and strongly veined leaflets, the veins ending in little, sharp teeth. The white or rose-colored flowers become reflexed as they age. Often there are silky hairs on one half of the lower surface of a leaflet.

FENDLER CLOVER, *T. fendleri,* has leafy stems up to 18 inches tall, rounded, long-stalked heads of white or rose flowers surrounded by green involucres. It occurs in montane meadows from central Colorado into New Mexico, Arizona and Utah.

The common cultivated species RED CLOVER, *T. pratense,* WHITE or DUTCH CLOVER, *T. repens,* and ALSIKE, *T. hybridum,* have become established in meadows and along roads and trails throughout our area and may be identified by the characters given in the key.

YELLOW SWEETCLOVER, *Melilotus officinalis* (166), is another escape from cultivation which has become very widely distributed especially along roadsides and in fields below 8,000 feet. It is usually a tall, branched, bright green plant with many short racemes of heavily

166. YELLOW SWEETCLOVER, ½ ×

sweet-scented yellow flowers but sometimes after the original upright stems have been cut off by road machinery the plant sends out lateral branches near the ground and goes right on blooming, appearing like a low, yellow-flowered, ground cover. WHITE SWEETCLOVER, *M. alba,* grows in similar locations. Both furnish good forage for livestock when young, and the sweet-scented flowers provide excellent "bee pasture."

CLIMBING VETCH, *Vicia.* This genus is easily recognized by the fine tendrils which tip its pinnately compound leaves and by which it attaches itself to other plants. AMERICAN VETCH, *V. americana* (167), is our most common species. It has few-flowered racemes of showy, purple pea-blossoms which are followed by inch-long pods. This is widely distributed over the United States and is found trailing on the ground or clambering over bushes in the foothills and montane zones of the Rockies.

PEAVINE or WILD SWEETPEA, *Lathyrus.* Plants of this genus have their leaves tipped either with tendrils or with bristles but our common native species are usually more bushy and less inclined to trail or climb than those of CLIMBING

167. AMERICAN VETCH, ½ ×

VETCH, and their flowers are usually larger. Some species are very fragrant. The cultivated SWEETPEA belongs to this genus.

WHITE-FLOWERED PEAVINE, *L. leucanthus* (168), has cream-colored flowers which turn light brown as they fade. Sometimes its leaves end in short tendrils, sometimes only in bristles. It occurs in large patches on banks of gulches and on hillsides from the foothills to timberline, from Wyoming and Utah through Colorado into New Mexico and Arizona. PURPLE PEAVINE, *L. eucosmus,* which has climbing tendrils, at least on the upper leaves, and rose or purple flowers, grows in the foothills from Colorado and Utah to Mexico.

LOCUST, *Robinia,* is a woody genus with odd pinnate leaves and racemes of pink or white, papilionaceous flowers. Our only native species is the NEW MEXICAN LOCUST, *R. neomexicana* (169), having pale pink to rose or lavender flowers, which grows as a large shrub on foothill slopes and along roads from southern Colorado into Texas, New Mexico, Mexico, Arizona, and Nevada. [Color Pl. 6b]

WILD LICORICE, *Glycyrrhiza lepidota* is a stout, weedy, widely distributed plant of ditch banks and moist, sandy soil sometimes found

168. WHITE-FLOWERED PEAVINE, ½ ×

in the foothills. It has dotted leaves and greenish white flowers in compact, axillary clusters. The fruits are brown, prickly burs. The common licorice used to flavor candy is a different species but the root of our species is equally sweet and is used as food by the Indians.

SWEETVETCH, *Hedysarum*. Plants of this genus look very much like

169. NEW MEXICO LOCUST, ½ ×

170. Northern   Sweetvetch,
½ ×

the milkvetches but may be distinguished by their pods which are pendant and made up of separable segments. Northern Sweetvetch, *H. boreale* (170), is a beautiful plant with racemes of rose or purple flowers with the pod divided into 2 to 4 round segments. It grows in rocky places throughout North America and in the higher mountains as far south as Utah and New Mexico. The roots of this plant are eaten by Indians and Eskimos. Western Sweetvetch, *H. occidentale,* is similar but the segments of the fruit are elliptic and sometimes narrowly winged. It occurs in Wyoming, Idaho and southwestern Colorado.

Milkvetch, *Astragalus*. This is a very large genus including many species which differ widely in general appearance and many others which are so similar that identification depends on small technical features. Even botanists consider it difficult. Accurate determination is usually impossible without well developed pods. The flowers vary in size but are quite constant in

form and structure. At flowering time the calyx is a sleeve-like tube with 5-pointed teeth. It enlarges or is split open as the legume develops. The papilionaceous flower is whitish, bluish, rose or purple and has the tip of the keel rounded. (This character distinguishes it from the oxytropes or "locoweeds" of the genus *Oxytropis* which have a sharply pointed keel.)

A few species are cushion or mat plants with their leaves reduced to one or few leaflets, a few others are of low habit and more or less caespitose, but most have erect or ascending, branched stems and odd-pinnate leaves with numerous leaflets.

Many species grow on alkali or "badland" type soils where *selenium* is present and absorb this poisonous mineral into their foliage. In such cases they become dangerously poisonous to livestock eating them and are sometimes called "locoweeds" by ranchers and stockmen but that name is used more properly for plants of the genus *Oxytropis,* mentioned above. Most of the seleniferous species are found at altitudes below our range. A few of the species most commonly seen in the mountains are described here, but anyone needing accurate identification will do well to send specimens including flowers and well-developed legumes to one of the experiment stations or herbaria. (See p. 51)

Matvetch, *Astragalus kentrophyta* var. *implexus (A. tegetarius).* This is a very low cushion or mat-forming plant with tiny stiff, spine-tipped leaflets and small purple flowers which are partly hidden among the leaves. It is occasionally found on moist, granitic soils in openly wooded areas from Montana and Idaho south to Colorado. The TUFTED MILKVETCH, *A. spatulatus (A. caespitosas)*, is a species somewhat similar in habit of growth but with softer, spineless leaves which usually have only one long, slender leaflet and numerous clusters of purple or sometimes cream-colored flowers held above the foliage on slender stalks. This grows on dry, sandy, exposed areas at altitudes of from 5,000 to 9,000 feet, from Canada along the mountains into northern Colorado.

171. EARLY PURPLE MILKVETCH, ½ ×

EARLY PURPLE MILKVETCH, *A. shortianus* (171), is a plant of the mesas and lower foothills, especially along the eastern slope, which has stems about 4 inches tall, each bearing a crowded cluster of rose-purple, inch-long flowers. The rounded leaflets are covered with silky hairs and the pods are 1 to 2 inches long and curved. It occurs from southern Wyoming to northern New Mexico.

172. PARRY MILKVETCH, 2/5 ×

PARRY MILKVETCH, *A. parryi* (172), is a tufted, gray-hairy plant with creamy white blossoms which have a purple-tipped keel and are sometimes tinged with pink. Its pods are about 1 inch long. It is found along the eastern slope on dry fields and open areas of the foothill and montane zones from southern Wyoming to central Colorado. PURSHES MILKVETCH, *A. purshii*, is similar but has very woolly pods and is frequently found in the western part of our range.

173. GROUNDPLUM, ½ ×

GROUNDPLUM, *A. crassicarpus (A. succulentus)* (173), is another low-growing species with stems 6 to 12 inches long. Its flowers are white with blue or purple tips and the fruits are round, smooth and fleshy. When ripe they are hard and do not split open. Found on high plains and fields of the foothill zone from Canada to Colorado.

INDIAN MILKVETCH, *A. aboriginum,* has 4 to 12 inch stems in tufts which grow from large, woody taproots. The flowers are whitish with purple tips and the linear or oblong leaflets are usually covered with curly hairs. The smooth thin pods are from ¾- to 1¼-inches long and hang from the calyx on slender stalks. Its roots were used for food by Indians. This plant occurs from the Yukon south into Nevada and Colorado in open woods and on hillsides, often on limestone, from 7,000 to 10,000 feet and is found in Yellowstone and Glacier National Parks.

ARCTIC MILKVETCH, *A. eucosmus,* is a tufted plant with several erect or ascending stems which grow from a woody taproot. The leaves are green with oblong leaflets which have appressed hairs on their under sides. The dark purple or blue flowers are 5/16-inch long, in a loose, often one-sided, raceme, and the pendant pods which are also appressed-hairy are comparatively short and thick, not over ¾-inch long. It grows in partly shaded situations on moist stream banks and borders of lakes in the montane and subalpine zones from arctic America through Montana and Wyoming into the Colorado mountains.

Several of the larger species of the genus *Astragalus* become conspicuous in early summer in fields and pastures and along roadsides on the mesas, high plains and mountain valleys. These plants may be from 1 to 2 feet tall with several leafy stems forming clumps. One of the most frequently seen is the TWO-GROOVED MILKVETCH, *A. bisulcatus.* It has erect stems and numerous rose-purple flowers which are usually bent downwards and arranged in compact racemes. The

pods are ½- to ¾-inch long with 2 grooves along the upper surface. This is one of the worst of the stock-poisoning plants. It grows on alkali and seleniferous soils, usually below 7,000 feet from Canada southwards into New Mexico.

Another species which has rose or purple flowers is HALL MILKVETCH, *A. hallii,* which is found in the montane zone in Colorado, especially in the intermountain valleys. It differs from the last one by having its stems somewhat decumbent at base and its inflated pods without grooves.

DRUMMOND MILKVETCH, *A. drummondii,* (174), is a plant with erect, bunched stems, conspicuously gray-hairy foliage, whitish or cream-colored flowers and pods 1 to 2 inches long which are stipitate and protrude from the more or less black-hairy calyx. It grows on dry fields of the foothill and lower montane zone from Canada to northern New Mexico, mostly east of the Continental Divide.

174. DRUMMOND   MILKVETCH,

½ ×

A. tenellus is another species having cream-colored flowers. Its leaflets are green, narrow and usually smooth and its 10 to 18 inch long stems are often reddish at least towards the base, and more or less decumbent. Its thin-walled pods are ⅓- to ½-inch long. It occurs from Canada southward to Colorado and Nevada.

ALPINE MILKVETCH, *A. alpinus* (175), is a dainty plant with conspicuously two-toned flowers. The banner and wings are pale bluish, violet or sometimes white and the keel is purple; the stems are from 4 to 12 inches in height; the leaflets are oval and notched at apex; the calyx is covered with black hairs and the stipitate, slightly inflated pods are pendant. It grows in shaded locations from the upper montane through the subalpine zone. This species is circumboreal in distribution, occurring throughout the northern and mountainous regions of America, Europe, and Asia.

LIMBER VETCH or WIRE MILKVETCH, *A. flexuousus,* is a sprawling plant with stems from 6 to 20 inches long, racemes of small pink or yellowish blossoms, and narrow leaflets. The calyxes are covered

175. ALPINE MILKVETCH, ½ ×

with short, appressed hairs, some of which are black and the slender, cylindric pods are usually less than an inch long. It grows on fields and hillsides of the foothill and montane zones from Montana into Utah and New Mexico.

Still another vetch is *A. diversifolius* which has its upper leaves so reduced that the plant appears rush-like. Its whitish flowers are about ⅜-inch long with an erect banner. It has creeping rootstocks with stems 6 to 18 inches long. It grows on dry slopes, often among sagebrush, in the foothill and lower montane zones from Montana to Colorado and northeastern Arizona.

LOCO, OXYTROPE, or CRAZYWEED, *Oxytropis.* The plants of this genus are often confused with the milkvetches. Some species of each are poisonous to stock and are indiscriminately called "locoweeds." Both have pinnately compound leaves, usually of numerous leaflets and papilionaceous flowers.

In general the milkvetches are leafy-stemmed plants and the oxytropes are acaulescent, i.e. all the leaves are basal. But there are exceptions in both groups. The best character by which to distinguish the two is the shape of the keel. The milkvetches have the tip of the keel blunt but in the oxytropes it is pointed, *Plate E 49.* The poisonous element in these plants is said to be derived from soils which contain the mineral *barium* and it acts as a narcotic on animals which eat considerable amounts of it. They become addicted to it and at times it causes them to "go crazy."

a. Plants usually with leafy stems; pods pendant
DROP-POD LOCO, p. 184.

aa. Plants with all leaves basal; pods erect or spreading.
  b. Flower brilliant rose purple.
    c. Plants caespitose; pods inflated
TUFTED LOCO, p. 185.
    cc. Plants with flower stalks 6 to 12 inches tall.
      d. Leaflets in opposite pairs
LAMBERT LOCO, p. 184.

      dd. Leaflets in whorls
SHOWY LOCO, p. 184.
  bb. Flowers blue, white, pink, or yellowish.
    c. Plants glandular and sticky; flowers blue
YELLOWHAIR LOCO, p. 185

    cc. Plants neither glandular nor sticky.
      d. Flowers yellowish, 1 to 1 1/3-inches long
FIELD LOCO, p. 185.

      dd. Flowers white, pink, or lavender
ROCKY MOUNTAIN LOCO, p. 185.

176. LAMBERT
LOCO, ½ ×
[Color Pl. 6c]

177. SHOWY
LOCO, ½ ×
(leaf only)

LAMBERT LOCO, *O. lambertii* (176). This is one of the most conspicuous and beautiful wildflowers of the Rocky Mountains. Its foliage is silvery with appressed silky hairs and the bright rose-purple flowers are held erect in racemes on leafless stalks. *O. parryi* is a somewhat similar but smaller, alpine species found at high altitudes throughout the Rocky Mountains.

SHOWY LOCO, *O. Splendens* (177), is a handsome plant with silvery, silky, foliage, rose-colored flowers, and numerous leaflets arranged in whorls. It grows in the montane zone.

DROP-POD LOCO, *O. deflexa*. This plant has many-flowered, crowded racemes of whitish, sometimes purple-tipped, flowers which elongate in fruit. There are some black hairs mixed with light ones on the calyx. As the pods ripen they hang down. The leaflets are so spaced that the leaves have a ladder-like appearance. It grows on hillsides and especially in LODGEPOLE PINE forests from Canada to New Mexico, and is circumboreal in distribution.

TUFTED LOCO, *O. multiceps* (178), often grows in a low circle. Its leaves are gray with silky hairs. Each short stem bears only a few rose-colored flowers and as the petals fade the calyx turns red and becomes inflated so that the plant appears as a mat of gray, rose and red. It is found on granitic gravel from northwestern Nebraska and Wyoming to central Colorado in the foothill and montane zones.

YELLOWHAIR LOCO, or STICKY CRAZYWEED, *O. viscida (O. viscidula)*, is an erect plant with sticky green foliage and blue flowers. It is a rare alpine in Colorado but occurs more abundantly farther north, especially in Yellowstone National Park. FIELD LOCO, *O. campestris*, is a taller plant than most of the other species, with flower stalks 12 to 20 inches high and crowded racemes of yellowish flowers which grows on rocky or gravelly slopes of the montane and subalpine zones from Canada southward to Colorado.

ROCKY MOUNTAIN LOCO, *O. sericea (O. saximontana)*, is a handsome plant which usually grows in clumps with numerous flower stalks 10 to 18 inches tall. Its leaves are silvery-pubescent. It occurs in Wyoming, Colorado, New Mexico and

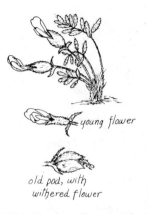

young flower

old pod, with
withered flower

178. TUFTED LOCO. ½ ×

Utah on gravelly slopes and open fields of the montane and subalpine zones.

In the true species the flowers are white with a purple-tipped keel, but LAMBERT LOCO and this hybridize. Their seedlings retain the vigor and clump habit of ROCKY MOUNTAIN LOCO but take on various amounts of color from the other parent so that where these two species grow together one often finds beautiful fields of plants with flowers ranging in color from white through lavender and pink to deep rose. One place where this occurs is along U. S. Highway 24, near Divide, Colorado, west of Colorado Springs, and another place is the Centennial Valley west of Laramie, Wyoming.

GERANIUM FAMILY, *Geraniaceae*

This family is characterized by having regular flowers with 5 sepals and petals and 10 stamens. The sepals are united at base and usually awn-tipped; the petals are separate; the pistil is compound of 5 1-seeded carpels which separate at maturity. The 5 styles which are united into an elongated beak separate as the seed ripens.

STORKSBILL, FILAREE, *Erodium cicutarium* (179), is one of the earliest flowers to bloom on the mesas and in the lower foothills, especially on over-grazed fields. It

has pinnately compound, much dissected leaves and small, bright pink flowers and is easily recognized by this combination of characters plus the corkscrew-like "tails" of the

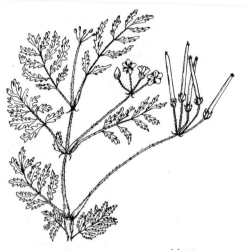

179. STORKSBILL, ½ ×

fruits. When dry these are coiled but when moist they uncoil and this action drives the pointed tip containing the seed into the soil. This plant, the *Alfilaria* of the Spaniards, introduced from Europe, is widely distributed as a weed in the United States. It is also a valuable forage plant throughout the Southwest.

180. FREMONT GERANIUM, 2/5 ×

GERANIUM or CRANESBILL, *Geranium*. The plants of this genus all have palmately lobed leaves and, in our species, the flowers are pink, purplish, or white. The styles separate at the base and recoil at maturity but are not twisted. The ones included here are all perennials. The house plants commonly called "geraniums" belong to a related genus, *Pelargonium*. Our pink- and purple-flowered species are usually caespitose with several stems from a tuft of long petioled leaves and they look much alike.

FREMONT GERANIUM, *G. fremontii* (180), is common in the foothill and montane zones of the central Rockies. The petioles of its basal and lower leaves are hairy but not sticky. Its flowers are pink. PARRY GERANIUM, *G. parryi,* is a plant with sticky leaves and stems. Its flowers are usually a deep rose-purple. It occurs from southern Wyoming southwestward through Colorado into Utah and Arizona. JAMES GERANIUM, *G. caespitosum (G. atropurpureum)* is pubescent but not at all sticky. It may be erect and up to 3 feet tall but sometimes its stems are decumbent and rooting at the nodes. Its flowers are usually deep rose-purple and it also grows abundantly in southwestern Colorado, and adjoining states, in the PONDEROSA PINE forests. STICKY GERANIUM, *G. viscosissimum,* is a stout, many-flowered plant, somewhat flat-topped, of the northern part of our range. Its flowers are bright rose-purple and it is very sticky. This is conspicuous in the montane zone in both Yellowstone and Glacier National Parks.

RICHARDSON GERANIUM, *G. richardsonii,* has white or very pale lavender flowers; its stems are usually single and it grows in moist, usually shaded locations throughout our range, from the foothills to timberline.

WOODSORREL FAMILY, *Oxalidaceae*

This family has only one common species in our area, the YELLOW WOODSORREL, *Oxalis stricta,* which is a small plant with 3-foliate, compound leaves which are acid-flavored. The erect or decumbent stems bear 2 or 3 yellow flowers. It occurs as a weed in gardens throughout most of North America and is occasionally found in woods or along roads of the foothill and lower montane zones.

FLAX FAMILY, *Linaceae*

This family has regular, 5-merous flowers. Its petals are very fragile; its leaves are narrow and small and its stems very tough.

WILD BLUE FLAX or LEWIS FLAX, *Linum lewisii* (181). This is a perennial and is similar in general appearance to the annual species cultivated for oil and fiber. Nothing else in our region has such a symmetrical, clear sky-blue blossom. Early morning of a sunny day is the time to see it, because the petals wither and fall under a hot sun. It usually has several ascending stems clothed up to the inflorescence with numerous, narrow leaves. Usually only one flower is in bloom at a time on each stem, but a fresh one opens each morning during the blooming season. As this progresses, a row of round seed pods, each on a curved pedicel, lines the stalk. This plant was named in honor of Meriwether Lewis, see p. 259, and the naming was appropriate because it occurs over the entire western territory first explored for the United States by the Lewis and Clark Expedition.

YELLOW FLAX, *L. rigidum,* has pale yellow petals which turn to apricot as they fade. A plant of the plains and foothills, it occurs from Canada south to Colorado and Texas. Another yellow-flowered flax is *L. kingii* which has a narrow, crowded inflorescence and very leafy, tufted stems with many, narrow leaves. It grows from a few inches to a foot tall from a woody base. This occurs in the montane zone of the high mountains of Wyoming, southeastern Idaho and south to Colorado and Utah.

RUE FAMILY, *Rutaceae*

WAFER-ASH or HOPTREE, *Ptelea trifoliata* (182), is our only representative of this family. It is a shrub or small tree with 3-foliate leaves and small greenish flowers which produce clusters of roundish, veiny-winged fruits, each about an inch broad. The foliage is bright green, glossy, and strong-scented. It grows in canyons of southern Colorado and southward.

181. WILD BLUE FLAX, ½ ×

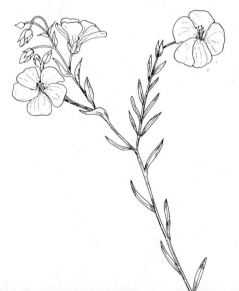

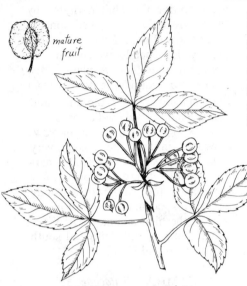

mature fruit

182. WAFER-ASH, ½ ×

SPURGE FAMILY,
Euphorbiaceae
This interesting family includes

184. ROCKY MOUNTAIN SPURGE,
2/5 ×

some very curious plants, many inconspicuous ones, as well as the showy POINSETTIA and CROWN-OF-THORNS and some strange, cactus-like succulents of Africa. The small flowers are unisexual and in our species both kinds are gathered in few-flowered clusters.

Our most conspicuous species is

SNOW-ON-THE-MOUNTAIN, *Euphorbia marginata* (183), which scarcely qualifies as a mountain plant. It grows from 1 to 2 feet tall with an umbel-like inflorescence in which the showy parts are the numerous white-margined floral leaves. This is abundant on the plains and is sometimes found along the eastern foothills up to 7,000 feet. It is occasionally grown in gardens.

ROCKY MOUNTAIN SPURGE, *E. robusta* (184), is an entirely green plant. Its small flowers are surrounded by involucres and each involucre contains 4 crescent-shaped glands. Its stems are 6 inches to a foot tall, usually clustered, sometimes reddish at base, and each bears a 3- to 5-rayed umbel. This plant occurs in the Ponderosa Pine areas throughout our area.

SIDEWALK-WEED or THYME-LEAVED SPURGE, *E. serpyllifolia,* is a small, annual plant which lies flat on the ground. It has zigzag stems and smooth green leaves which are less than ½-inch long, oval or oblong, often finely toothed around the apex and unequal at the base. The flowers have appendages which appear as small white petals. This is a widely distributed weed of gardens and is often seen growing in the cracks of sidewalks.

183. SNOW-ON-THE-MOUNTAIN,
2/5 ×

WATER STARWORT FAMILY, *Callitrichaceae*

WATER STARWORT, *Callitriche palustris*. This is a water plant with narrow, one-nerved submersed leaves about an inch long and shorter, broader floating leaves arranged in little rosettes. There are tiny 4-seeded fruits in the leaf axils. It has been found in shallow ponds and in rock pools in Colorado up to 11,500 feet and is widely distributed throughout the northern hemisphere. AUTUMN WATER STARWORT, *C. hermaphroditica,* is a completely submersed plant having only narrow, one-nerved leaves. It has the same distribution.

185. SMOOTH SUMAC, 2/5 ×

SUMAC FAMILY, *Anacardiaceae*

This is a family of shrubs, trees or woody climbers, with compound leaves and small flowers in axillary or terminal panicles. Our only genus is SUMAC, *Rhus*.

SMOOTH SUMAC, *Rhus glabra* (185), is a shrub 2 to 6 feet tall with stout stems having few branches and pinnately compound leaves of 11 to 21 lanceolate, toothed leaflets which are green above but whitish beneath. The small, cream-colored flowers in dense, pointed clusters become dark red, velvety, berry-like fruits. The leaves turn brilliant red in autumn. This shrub grows on banks, dry hillsides and along roads in the foothill zone throughout our range and in much of North America.

THREE-LEAF SUMAC or SQUAW-BUSH, *R. trilobata* (186), is a much branched, rounded shrub with bright green, 3-foliate leaves and light brown bark. Its flowers appear before the leaves in crowded, catkin-like clusters and are followed by flattened, velvety red or orange berries. These have an acid flavor

and have been used to make a pretty good substitute for lemonade. On this account the plant is sometimes called "LEMONADEBUSH."

Because of the strong odor of its foliage it is also called "SKUNK-BUSH," and it gets its name of "SQUAWBUSH" because the long, slender young branches were split by Indian women and used in basketry. It occurs on dry, sunny foothill and montane slopes throughout the Rockies.

A relative of the sumac is POISON IVY or POISON OAK, *R. radicans* (187), which occurs throughout the

186. THREE-LEAF SUMAC, ½ ×

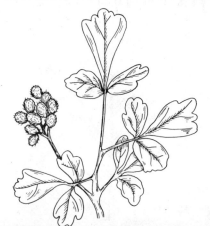

187. POISON IVY, ½ ×

United States and is occasionally found on hillsides and foothill canyons of the Rocky Mountain region. It is either a low, single-stemmed shrub or a woody climber clinging to tree trunks. It may be recognized by its bright green, compound leaves of 3 shiny, ovate leaflets and clusters of small yellowish-white flowers or white, smooth berries ¼-inch in diameter. The leaves turn brilliant shades of orange or red in autumn. The foliage of this plant is poisonous to some people but a thorough washing with strong soap after exposure will usually prevent bad results. Immediate application of household ammonia stops the itching.

188. MOUNTAIN-LOVER, 2/5 ×

STAFF-TREE FAMILY, *Celastraceae*

This is the family to which the BITTERSWEET, WAHOO or "BURN-ING BUSH" and the many deciduous and evergreen species of Euonymous belong. Our only native representative is MOUNTAIN-LOVER or MYRTLE PACHYSTIMA, *Pachystima myrsinites* (188). It is a low shrub with neat, opposite, evergreen leaves and small, 4-pointed, greenish-brown, or dark reddish flowers. The leaves are thick, usually about ½-inch long, oval or oblong, and finely toothed around the upper half. It grows in moist forests of the montane and subalpine zones from Canada to New Mexico and California.

MAPLE FAMILY, *Aceraceae*

This is a family of trees and shrubs native in the cool regions of the northern hemisphere. All North American species belong to the genus *Acer*. It is characterized by opposite, and usually palmately lobed, leaves and winged and paired fruits. Three species occur in our area.

ROCKY MOUNTAIN MAPLE, *A. glabrum* (189), is a large shrub or small tree with gray bark. Its young twigs are smooth and dark red and its winter buds are bright red. The leaves are palmately 3- to 5-lobed and sometimes 3-foliate, always

189. ROCKY MOUNTAIN MAPLE, 2/5 ×

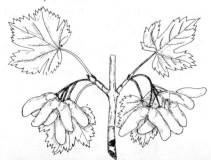

sharply toothed. Its small chartreuse-colored flowers are fragrant
and in the center of the female ones
you can see the young ovary already
in the shape of the double "key"
which is the maple fruit. As these
ripen they are often tinged with red.
There is an insect which frequently
attacks this maple, its egg clusters
appearing as crimson blotches on
the leaves. It always grows with
several trunks in a clump. These
may be from ½-inch to 5 inches in
diameter and from 6 to 30 feet tall.
It is found from Wyoming and
Idaho south to Nebraska, New
Mexico and Utah and is common in
the canyons and on hillsides of the
foothill and montane zones throughout Colorado.

WASATCH or BIGTOOTH MAPLE,
A. grandidentatum (190), is a small
tree which grows in groves or
thickets on moist canyon sides and
along streams. Its leaves are 3-lobed
with rounded sinuses and bluntly
pointed tips. They turn rose or red
in autumn and some seasons make
a very spectacular color display.
This species is found from western
Wyoming through the mountainous
parts of Utah to Arizona, New
Mexico and west Texas.

BOXELDER, *A. negundo,* is a tree
found along streams of the high
plains and foothill canyons. It differs
from our other maples in having a
pinnately compound leaf and flowers and fruits in pendant clusters.

BUCKTHORN FAMILY,
Rhamnaceae

A family of woody plants—most
of ours are low shrubs. Their small,
white petals are clawed and inserted
on the calyx tube.

MOUNTAIN-BALM or SNOWBRUSH,
Ceanothus velutinus (191), has
oval, leathery leaves which appear

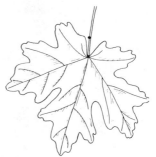

190. WASATCH MAPLE, 2/5 ×

as though varnished. Its twigs are
olive green and its evergreen leaves
dark green above, lighter beneath,
strongly 3-veined and fragrant. Its
small flowers are creamy white in
dense clusters and the small, dry,
3-lobed capsules often persist for
2 or 3 seasons. The shrubs are 2 to
6 feet tall and frequently form large
patches on montane hillsides. It is
found from South Dakota to British
Columbia and south through Wyoming and Colorado to California.

REDROOT CEANOTHUS or NEW
JERSEY TEA, *C. ovatus* (192), is a
shrub 1 to 2 feet tall with oblong
to ovate-lanceolate leaves 1 to 2
inches long and crowded, corym-
bose clusters of small white flowers
which is found on sandy soil from
New England to the foothills of
Colorado and New Mexico.

191. MOUNTAIN-BALM, 2/5 ×

192. REDROOT CEANOTHUS, 2/5 ×

193. FOX GRAPE, 2/5 ×

FENDLER CEANOTHUS or BUCK-BRUSH, *C. fendleri,* is a low, thorny shrub with white flowers in umbel-like clusters which are arranged in terminal racemes. Its small leaves are pale beneath. It is much browsed by deer. This is a plant of the foothill and montane zones, often forming patches under pines, in Colorado, Utah and south to Texas, Mexico and Arizona.

SMITH BUCKTHORN, *Rhamnus smithii,* is a shrub with alternate or nearly opposite, elliptical to oblong-lanceolate leaves about 1 to 1½-inches long, which are yellow-ish beneath. The small, unisexual flowers are 2 or 3 together in the leaf axils. The fruits are smooth, black berries about ⅓-inch long. This grows on hillsides and in valleys of the upper foothill and lower montane zones in western Colorado and New Mexico. DWARF BUCKTHORN, *R. alnifolia,* grows in northwestern Wyoming, Montana and Idaho.

GRAPE FAMILY, *Vitaceae*
  Members of this family have palmately lobed, or palmately com-pound leaves and most of them have tendrils. This is the family to which all the varieties of cultivated grapes and the many wild species belong but in our range there is only one native species of grape,

the FOX GRAPE, *Vitis riparia (V. vulpina)* (193), which grows on banks and slopes of the foothills.

Its relative, VIRGINIA CREEPER or WOODBINE, *Parthenocissus inserta* (194), is more inclined to climb and is found on trees, fences or old buildings. It has a palmately compound leaf of 5 to 7, long, pointed leaflets and its berries resemble small grapes. This fur-nishes some of our red autumn color.

MALLOW FAMILY, *Malvaceae*
  The mallow family is represented in our gardens by the familiar holly-hocks and hibiscus. Cotton and

194. VIRGINIA CREEPER, 2/5 ×

okra also belong here. The wild species resemble these in their flower structure. There are 5 sepals, united at base and sometimes a calyx-like involucre outside of them; 5 petals united to each other and to the united stamens which form a column. The superior ovary which is inside the stamen column is made up of several carpels with the lower part of their styles united. The fruit is dry and the carpels usually separate from each other at maturity.

MODEST MALLOW or WHITE CHECKERMALLOW, *Sidalcea candida* (195), is a plant growing unbranched 1 to 3 feet tall which spreads by a system of underground stems so forming patches. Its smooth, basal leaves are round, palmately 7-lobed and coarsely toothed. Its upper leaves are deeply dissected into several narrow segments. The dainty white flowers are in terminal racemes. This grows in moist meadows and on stream banks from the foothills to timberline and from Wyoming to Nevada, Colorado, New Mexico and Utah.

NEW MEXICO MALLOW or PURPLE CHECKERMALLOW, *S. neomexicana,* grows from a woody root with one or more erect stems which are often branched. It does not spread freely, as the former does, by underground stems. Its foliage is hairy. The lower leaves are round and scalloped or shallowly lobed, the upper ones deeply dissected. The corollas are rose or purplish. Its range is similar to the last except that it does not extend much above the montane zone.

COPPER MALLOW or SCARLET GLOBEMALLOW, *Sphaeralcea coccinea* (196), is a low, gray foliaged plant of the roadsides and fields with brick-red blossoms. Its deeply dissected leaves are covered with

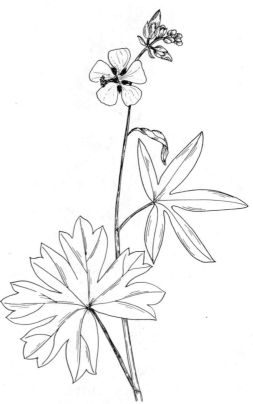

195. MODEST MALLOW, ½ ×

196. COPPER MALLOW, ½ ×

197. Mountain Hollyhock, 2/5×

small, star-shaped scales or hairs which give them their gray color. These can be seen with the aid of

198. Western St. Johnswort, ½ ×

a 10-power hand lens. A taller, greener species with leaves less dissected which grows in Montana, Wyoming and Utah is called Munroe Globemallow, *S. munroana.* There are several other very handsome species with tall stems bearing pink or salmon-red blossoms found in the arid regions of the Southwest.

Mountain Hollyhock, *Illiamna rivularis* (197), is a large plant with clumps of stems 2 to 6 feet tall. Its leaves are heart-shaped or roundish and deeply 5- to 7-lobed. The flowers are 1 to 2 inches across, white or pink. This handsome species grows on banks and in meadows on the western slope in Colorado and from New Mexico, Arizona, and Nevada to Canada. Montane and subalpine. It is often seen along roadsides in Grand Teton, Yellowstone, and Glacier National Parks.

ST. JOHNSWORT FAMILY, *Hypericaceae*

The family is characterized by opposite leaves having black or translucent dots. Our only species is Western St. Johnswort, *Hypericum formosum* (198). This is a smooth plant with 5-petaled, bright yellow flowers about 1 inch broad with many stamens. The buds are often tinged with red. Stems are 8 inches to 2 feet tall. It grows in meadows and on moist banks throughout our range. A form with shorter stems and larger flowers is found in alpine meadows of Glacier National Park where it sometimes forms mats or clumps covered with golden flowers.

VIOLET FAMILY, *Violaceae*

This family is distinguished by having simple leaves with petioles and stipules, and irregular flowers with 5 separate petals. Garden pansies and violas belong here. *Viola* is our only conspicuous genus. Its flowers have the lower petal spurred. These plants may be either leafy stemmed (caulescent) or acaulescent, that is, with all leaves and flower stalks rising from a thick, short stem at ground level. Most of these are spring-blooming plants but those found at the higher altitudes may be seen in bloom during the summer months.

a. Flowers yellow; petals may be purple-tinged on back.
  b. At least some of the leaves deeply or shallowly lobed or toothed.
    c. Some leaves shallowly lobed or toothed
                        GOOSEFOOT VIOLET, p. 195.
    cc. All leaves deeply, palmately lobed
                        SHELTON VIOLET, p. 195.
  bb. None of the leaves lobed or deeply toothed.
    c. Leaves longer than wide
                        NUTTALL VIOLET, p. 195.
    cc. Leaves rounded, heart-shaped at base
                        NORTHERN YELLOW VIOLET, p. 196.
aa. Flowers white, blue, or purple.
  b. Plants leafy stemmed.
    c. Flowers blue
                        SUBALPINE BLUE VIOLET, p. 197.
    cc. Flowers white, or mostly white.
      d. Flowers entirely white; leaves with rounded tips
                        WHITE MARSH VIOLET, p. 196.
      dd. Flowers with purplish tinge on back of petals
                        CANADA VIOLET, p. 196.
  bb. Plants acaulescent, i.e., with basal leaves only.
    c. Leaves not dissected
                        NORTHERN BOG VIOLET, p. 197.
    cc. Leaves deeply, palmately dissected into narrow divisions
                        PRAIRIE VIOLET, p. 197.

GOOSEFOOT VIOLET or PINE VIOLET, *V. purpurea* ssp. *atriplicifolia.* A small plant with its stems partly under ground, sometimes only 1 to 3 inches tall, but may be up to 8 inches, above ground level. The leaves are variable from entire to rather deeply lobed; on their lower surfaces the veins are purplish. Petals yellow, the backs of the upper ones tinged purplish and the lower ones veined with purple. This is found on open slopes in pine forests and sometimes above timberline from Montana south to New Mexico and Arizona.

SHELTON VIOLET, *V. sheltonii.* The palmately, deeply-lobed leaves of this plant are mostly in a basal tuft and on petioles from 1 to 5 inches long. Its bright yellow flowers are held slightly above the leaves. Found on meadows and hillsides in rich soil, sometimes in partial shade, from Montana to southwestern Colorado and westward, montane zone. [Color Pl. 6d]

NUTTALL VIOLET or WESTERN YELLOW VIOLET, *V. nuttallii* (199). This plant appears acaulescent in spring when first coming into bloom but later develops several leafy stems 5 to 20 inches tall. Its leaves are from 2 to 4 inches long and vary from linear-lanceolate to ovate in shape. The yellow petals may be veined with purple or the upper ones tinged with reddish on the

199. NUTTALL VIOLET, ½ ×

back. The subalpine YELLOW VI-
OLET, *V. praemorsa,* is similar.

NUTTALL VIOLET grows on
banks and open hillsides of the
foothill, montane and subalpine
zones throughout our range, especially in rich, moist soil. Thomas
Nuttall, a naturalist of the early
19th century, was interested in both
birds and plants. He was professor
of Botany at Harvard and collected
in Wyoming and other parts of the
west.

NORTHERN YELLOW VIOLET or
TWINFLOWER VIOLET, *V. biflora*
(200), is a delicate, leafy-stemmed
plant with ascending stems and
rounded or kidney-shaped leaves.
The peduncles rise from the axils
and hold yellow flowers (usually

200. NORTHERN YELLOW VIOLET,
½ ×

2) above the leaves. This is a plant
of arctic regions and occurs occasionally in cold, wet situations of
the high Colorado mountains. The
SMOOTH YELLOW VIOLET, *V. glabella,* which is similar but larger
occurs in moist mountain woods
from Alaska to Montana, northern
Idaho and California. It is found in
Glacier National Park where it
blooms during the summer and
often forms large beds near snow
banks at timberline.

CANADA VIOLET, *V. canadensis*
(201), is a leafy-stemmed species,
6 inches to a foot tall, with broadly
heart-shaped leaves which have a
slender tip. The flower stalks rise
from leaf axils. The petals are white
on their faces but more or less
purplish-red on the reverse side. A
plant of moist, shaded ravines and
slopes of the foothill and montane
zones. *V. rugulosa* is closely related
and very similar but has larger
flowers with more purple on the
backs of the petals.

WHITE MARSH VIOLET, *V. pal-
lens,* is a smooth plant spreading by
slender stems which creep over wet,
mossy banks. The leaves are rather
light green, 1 to 2 inches long
and usually broader, heart-shaped,
round or kidney-shaped. The petals
are white, sometimes finely veined
with purple or lightly purple-tinged.

201. CANADA VIOLET, 2/5 ×

Found in wet meadows or forest bogs across the northern part of North America, and in the sub-alpine zone of the mountains.

NORTHERN BOG VIOLET, *V. ne-phrophylla* (202), is a smooth, acaulescent plant with flower stalks 3 to 10 inches tall. Its leaves are heart-shaped or kidney-shaped, often purplish beneath, with finely toothed margins and sometimes short-pointed tips. The flowers are nearly an inch broad with thick spurs and violet petals which are paler and purple veined at base. This is a common spring flower of meadows and mountain valleys throughout our range. The PRAIRIE VIOLET, *V. pedatifida,* is a dark purple-flowered, acaulescent species with much dissected leaves which occurs on the high plains and reaches the lower slopes of the foot-hills in Colorado and New Mexico.

SUBALPINE BLUE VIOLET, *V. adunca* var. *bellidifolia* (203). The subalpine and alpine forms of this plant are quite compact with short stems, small roundish-ovate leaves and comparatively large bluish-violet flowers. This is frequently found along streams, at edges of subalpine meadows and on moist slopes above timberline where it is seen in bloom during the summer.

202. NORTHERN BOG VIOLET, ½ ×

203. SUBALPINE BLUE VIOLET, ½ ×

The species, *V. adunca,* grows taller with a definitely leafy stem and occurs throughout the Rockies from moist foothill ravines to timberline.

LOASA FAMILY, *Loasaceae*

The members of this family have their leaves covered with stiff, barbed hairs which cause them to stick tightly to clothing. The leaves are usually pinnately lobed or dissected and the stems are often white and shining. The flowers are regular with 5 calyx lobes, 5 or 10 petals, a completely inferior ovary and from 10 to many stamens. In some species some of the filaments become petal-like. These plants frequently grow in sandy soil. Petals and filaments are yellow or whitish and in some species the flowers open only late in the afternoon. All ours belong to the genus *Mentzelia.* The following key may help to distinguish them.

a. Flowers bright yellow.
  b. Petals small, less than 1/2-inch long
    SMALL-FLOWERED STICKLEAF, p. 198.

bb. Petals more than 1/2-inch long.
  c. Plants more than 1 foot tall

                  MANY-FLOWERED EVENING-
                  STAR, p. 198.
  cc. Plants less than 1 foot tall

                  YELLOW EVENING-STAR, p. 198.
aa. Flowers pale yellow or creamy white.
  b. Petals 1 to 2 inches long

                  WHITE EVENING-STAR, p. 198.
  bb. Petals 2 to 4 inches long

                  GIANT EVENING-STAR, p. 198-9.

204. MANY-FLOWERED
     EVENING-STAR, ½ ×
205. WHITE EVENING-STAR, ½ ×

SMALL-FLOWERED STICKLEAF, *Mentzelia albicaulis,* has small yellow flowers which bloom in the daytime and white stems. Most of its leaves are pinnately lobed. It grows on dry banks of the foothills from Wyoming south to New Mexico. *M. dispersa* is similar and has about the same range. Most of its leaves are entire or slightly toothed. The seeds of both were used for food by the Indians. MANY-FLOWERED EVENINGSTAR, *M. speciosa (M. multiflora)* (204), is a branching plant, 1 to 2 feet tall with bright yellow flowers 1½ to 2 inches across which usually open in the afternoon and close before the sun is high the next forenoon. It grows on dry banks and roadsides of the foothill and montane zones from Wyoming south through our range. Yellow Evening-star, *M. pumila,* is very similar but not so tall.

WHITE EVENING-STAR, *M. nuda* (205), is a rough looking, much-branched plant 12 to 20 inches tall which in late afternoon covers itself with cream-colored blossoms 2 to 4 inches broad. It grows on dry, sandy banks of the foothills and mesas, often along highways. If one passes during the middle of the day and sees only sparse, weedy vegetation he may be amazed on returning at dusk to find great beds of these luminous blossoms. The GIANT EVENING-STAR, *M. decape-*

tala, is similar but with much larger blossoms. It is much less commonly seen than the last because it grows only on a certain type of shale soil. One place to see it is along the Woodman Valley Road north of the Garden of the Gods, near Colorado Springs.

CACTUS FAMILY, *Cactaceae*

The plants of this family are succulents. They store water in their thick stems. But not all succulents are cacti. To be a true cactus a plant must have spines on its stems arranged in little groups called *areoles.* The areoles are arranged in definite patterns. Cactus flowers have many sepals, petals and stamens and a large pistil. Their petals usually have a satiny sheen. Some species never have any leaves, others have small leaves which appear when moisture is plentiful but soon shrivel and drop off. The usual functions of leaves are carried on by the green-colored bark of the stems. Only a few species of cacti occur naturally in our mountains.

a. Stems made up of joints.
  b. Joints flattened
                PRICKLY PEAR, p. 199.
  bb. Joints nearly cylindrical
                BRITTLE CACTUS, p. 199
aa. Stems cylindrical or ball-shaped, not jointed.
  b. Stems in large clumps, cylindrical
                KINGS CROWN CACTUS, p. 199.
  bb. Stems not in large clumps, either solitary or with one or a few offsets.
    c. Stems with parallel ridges: flowers greenish
              GREEN-FLOWERED HEDGEHOG CACTUS, p. 199.
    cc. Stems with nipple-like tubercles.
      d. Flowers on spine-bearing tubercles
              MOUNTAIN BALL CACTUS, p. 200.
      dd. Flowers from between the tubercles
              BALL NIPPLE CACTUS, p. 200

PRICKLY PEAR, *Opuntia.* Two species of this large genus extend into the mountains. The HUNGER CACTUS, *O. polyacantha* (206), has flat joints 3 to 6 inches long and yellow flowers which appear on the edges of the joints or pads. They turn orange as they fade. The fruits are spiny. The BRITTLE CACTUS, *O. fragilis,* has shorter, nearly cylindrical joints and yellow or pinkish flowers. Both grow on sunny, rocky slopes of the foothills. [Color Pl. 6e]

KINGS CROWN CACTUS, *Echinocereus triglochidiatus* var. *melanacanthus,* belongs to the group referred to as "hedgehog cacti." It forms mounds, sometimes 2 or 3 feet in diameter, and is very handsome in bloom. The flowers are a rich, brilliant red with a knot of green stigmas at the center. Its spines are angled. This grows on warm, rocky hillsides of foothill canyons from southern Colorado to Texas and New Mexico.

GREEN-FLOWERED HEDGEHOG CACTUS, *Echinocereus viridiflorus* (207), grows singly or in small clusters. The stems are about 3 inches tall, longitudinally ribbed with the areoles along the ridges; these sometimes more or less spiral. The chartreuse-colored flow-

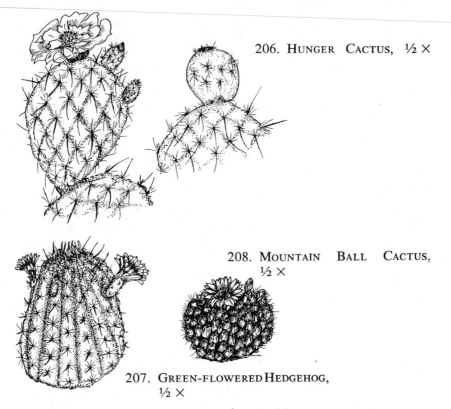

206. Hunger Cactus, ½ ×

208. Mountain Ball Cactus, ½ ×

207. Green-flowered Hedgehog, ½ ×

ers come out from the ribs often near the base of the plant. It grows on grassy mesas and hillsides of the foothill zone from Wyoming south to New Mexico mainly on the eastern side of the Continental Divide. [Color Pl. 6f]

Mountain Ball Cactus or Pincushion Cactus, *Pediocactus simpsonii (Echinocactus simpsonii)* (208). The fragrant, pink satin flowers of this prickly ball grow from its top like a crown. Instead of ribs its surface is covered with tubercles arranged in rows which are somewhat spiral. Its stem is a slightly flattened ball 2 to 6 inches in diameter. This species reaches the highest altitude of any of our cacti and is frequently seen on sunny, rocky situations in the montane zone, even as high as 10,000

feet. It blooms from mid April to late May. [Color Pl. 7a]

A close relative of this having longer spines and flowers which vary in color from white through green to purplish grows on south-facing slopes at Monarch Pass, Colorado. The Ball Nipple Cactus, *Coryphantha vivipara (Mamillaria vivipara),* is somewhat similar but the globular plant body is not depressed and its tubercles are more conspicuous. It has pink or rose-purple flowers. This grows 1½- to 2½-inches tall and is found on mesas and dry slopes of the foothill and lower montane zones. Its relative, the Mesa Nipple Cactus, *C. missouriensis (Mammillaria missouriensis),* has inconspicuous, yellow or greenish flowers and occurs on mesas and foothill slopes from Montana south to Texas.

OLEASTER FAMILY,
Eleagnaceae

All our members of this family are shrubs with simple, entire leaves. The young twigs and leaves are scurfy with silvery or rusty scales. Usually the male and female flowers are on different plants. The fruit is a dry or juicy berry.

BITTER BUFFALOBERRY, *Shepherdia canadensis* (209), is the most commonly seen. It is a low shrub of shaded, rocky hillsides in the montane zone having opposite, ovate, dark green leaves and, in the autumn, orange-red, juicy, but very bitter, berries. The buds and under leaf surfaces are distinctly rusty as are the small axillary, clustered, round flower buds which are formed in late summer.

SILVER BUFFALOBERRY, *S. argentea,* is a taller, erect shrub of bottom lands and streamsides of the foothills often found on alkaline soil and especially on the western slope. Its leaves are silvery and its branches thorny. The female shrubs bear quantities of oval,

209. BITTER BUFFALOBERRY, 2/5 ×

quarter-inch-long, red or orange berries which are sour and edible.

SILVERBERRY, *Eleagnus commutata,* is a stout shrub with mahogany-colored stems and oval or ovate silvery leaves. Its fruit is an olive-shaped, dry, silvery berry which furnishes food for many birds. It is closely related to the small tree called "RUSSIAN OLIVE," *Elaeagnus angustifolia,* which is much planted throughout our area and sometimes escapes.

EVENING PRIMROSE FAMILY, *Onagraceae*

The plants of this family are easy to recognize because in our species the flowers have 4 petals and an inferior ovary. (Flowers in the Mustard Family, also 4-petaled, have a superior ovary). The ovary is usually long and slender and often 4-sided. There are usually 8 stamens and the stigma is often 4-lobed. It is a large family with many native representatives in this region and includes several cultivated species—FUSCHIA is one—and a good many weeds.

a. Flowers scarlet or partially scarlet; leaves opposite or mostly so.
  b. Seeds with tufts of hair
           FIRECHALLIS, p. 202.
  bb. Seeds lacking tufts of hair; fruits nut-like
           GAURA, p. 202.
aa. Flowers white, yellow, rose or rose-purple.
  b. Seeds bearing a tuft of hairs at one end
           EPILOBIUM or WILLOWHERB, p. 202.
  bb. Seeds without such hairs.
    c. Flowers not over 1/4-inch across
           GROUNDSMOKE, p. 203.

cc. Flowers usually 1 inch or more across
EVENING PRIMROSE, p. 203.

FIRECHALLIS or HUMMINGBIRD-TRUMPET, *Zauschneria garrettii*. A plant with spikes of very showy scarlet flowers having a long tube which is inflated just above the ovary. This grows in the mountains of Utah, southern Wyoming and Idaho.

GAURA, *Gaura coccinea* (210), is a perennial plant, usually branched from the base and having several stems with terminal spikes of spidery flowers. The petals are pinkish turning red; found in dry situations of the foothills, often along roadsides.

EPILOBIUM or WILLOWHERB, *Epilobium*. The botanical name of this genus is Greek and means "on a pod," describing the elongated ovary bearing the other flower parts on its tip. Its English name refers to the tuft of hairs at the end of each seed similar to that on willow seeds. Usually a plant in flower will have at least a few pods beginning to burst so that this character may be seen.

COMMON FIREWEED or GIANT WILLOWHERB, *E. angustifolium* (211), is one of our most common and widespread plants due, largely, to the ease with which its seeds are distributed by the wind. It often grows in masses on burned over areas, hence its name of FIREWEED, or along roadsides. It has tall stems bearing spire-like racemes of bright rose-purple flowers and occurs in mountainous areas throughout the western United States and into

211. FIREWEED, ½ ×

seeds with coma (x10)

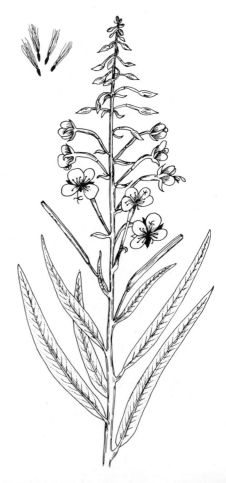

210. GAURA, ½ ×

Canada and Alaska. In autumn the leaves turn a brilliant red.

ALPINE or BROAD-LEAVED FIRE-WEED, *E. latifolium,* has similar but larger flowers in which the crimson sepals contrast with the rose petals. It has shorter stems and grayish leaves and is found on moist gravelly slopes and along stream beds in the subalpine and alpine regions of the Rockies, becoming more abundant northward. [Color Pl. 7b]

There are several smaller species of willowherb. Some are found in moist places, others on dry, waste ground. ALPINE WILLOWHERB, *E. alpinum* (212), with pink flowers about ⅓-inch across and S-shaped stems occurs in subalpine and lower alpine meadows; *E. hornemanni,* about the same size is more common in spruce forests; and *E. lactiflorum,* with white flowers is found along subalpine streams. PANICLED WILLOWHERB, *E. paniculatum,* with shreddy bark on the stems and small pink or lilac blooms, grows on dry ground in the foothill zone. CLARKIA or PINK FAIRIES, *Clarkia pulchella,* which slightly resembles Fireweed but has 3-lobed petals, is a plant sometimes found in the northern and western part of our range. GROUNDSMOKE or BABYS-BREATH, *Gayophytum racemosum* (213), is a delicate, much-branched plant with tiny pinkish flowers found on dry fields and slopes of the foothill and montane zones.

EVENING-PRIMROSE, *Oenothera.* This large genus has many species in the Rockies. The 4-petaled flowers are white or yellow, the white ones fade to pink and the yellow to orange or reddish. Many of them are fragrant and open in the late afternoon or evening and these usually wither when the sun becomes bright the following day.

212. ALPINE WILLOWHERB, ½ ×

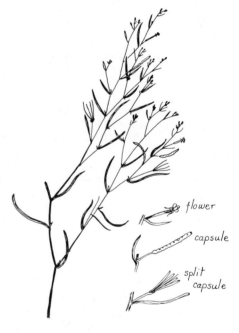

flower

capsule

split capsule

213. GROUNDSMOKE,   ½ ×

An individual flower does not reopen but there are usually buds ready to open the next evening. They all have a tube called a *hypanthium* which is really part of the calyx though it might be mistaken for a stem. Through it the style, which in some species may be from 4 to 6 inches long, connects the stigma and the ovary.

a. Flowers yellow.
 b. Flowers opening in evening and withering in bright sun.
  c. Plants rosette-like; petals about 2 inches long
                    YELLOW STEMLESS EVENING-
                    PRIMROSE, p. 204
  cc. Plants with tall stems.
   d. Petals not over 1 inch long
                    COMMON EVENING-PRIMROSE,
                    p. 204.
   dd. Petals 1 to 2 inches long
                    HOOKER EVENING-PRIMROSE,
                    p. 204.
 bb. Flowers remaining open during day.
  c. Hypanthium tube less than 1 inch long
                    SUNDROPS, p. 205.
  cc. Hypanthium tube 1 to 2 inches long
                    GALPINSIA, p. 205.
aa. Flowers white or pinkish, opening in afternoon.
 b. Plant in rosette form, stemless
                    WHITE STEMLESS EVENING-
                    PRIMROSE, p. 205.
 bb. Plant with branching stems, 6 to 30 inches tall.
  c. Leaves entire
   d. Plants perennial; stems white and shining
                    NUTTALL EVENING-PRIMROSE,
                    p. 206.
   dd. Plants annual from winter rosettes; stems pubescent
                    PRAIRIE EVENING-PRIMROSE, p. 206.
  cc. Leaves pinnatifid; stems somewhat pubescent
                    CUTLEAF EVENING-PRIMROSE,
                    p. 206.

YELLOW STEMLESS EVENING-PRIMROSE, *O. brachycarpa* (compare with No. 215). This large, bright yellow flower appearing in a rosette of long, green leaves, has a very long hypanthium. The plant grows on shale banks in the foothills and on the mesas throughout the Rockies. HOOKER EVENING-PRIMROSE, *O. hookeri.* Stem 1 to 4 feet tall; flowers in a terminal, elongated raceme interspersed with leafy bracts. The hypanthium and sepals are reddish and the yellow petals turn red or purplish as they age. Grows in New Mexico, Arizona, southern Colorado, and Utah to Idaho, in foothills and montane zones. The COMMON EVENING-PRIMROSE, *O. strigosa* (214), is similar but has smaller flowers and is common throughout the western United States, often occurring as a weed.

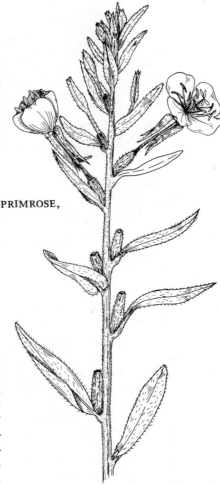

214. COMMON EVENING-PRIMROSE, ½ ×

SUNDROPS or MERILYX, *O. serrulata,* is a small bushy plant of the high plains and foothills found on dry ground and mostly east of the Continental Divide. GALPINSIA, or PUCKERED SUNDROPS, *O. lavendulaefolia,* is a plant of similar habitats with larger, paler yellow flowers which have a squarish outline. The petals are usually crinkled. WHITE STEMLESS EVENING-PRIMROSE or FRAGRANT MORNING PRIMROSE, *O. caespitosa* (215), is a lovely fragrant flower with several common names. One is "GUMBOLILY" but its 4 petals and 4-parted stigma tell the observer right away that it is not a true lily. It grows on clay banks, often on red shale, also in gravel, from the foothills to the subalpine regions, throughout our range. It is similar to its close relative, the YELLOW STEMLESS PRIMROSE, p. 204.

215. WHITE-STEMLESS EVENING PRIMROSE, ¼ X

winter rosette; its stems branch and often form a bushy plant. Found on the high plains and foothills.

CUT-LEAF EVENING-PRIMROSE, *O. coronopifolia* (217), is a white-flowered species of smaller size than the last two. It has leaves which are **sharply toothed or divided and always** seems to show some pink withered flowers. It is found on foothill and montane fields, often along roadsides, throughout our region. [Color Pl. 7c]

216. NUTTALL EVENING-PRIMROSE, ½ ×

NUTTALL EVENING PRIMROSE, *O. nuttallii* (216), is a leafy-stemmed plant which grows from a spreading underground root so it is often found in patches. It has a shiny white stem from which the outer bark peels off in shreds. The tips of its stems with unopened buds are usually somewhat bent down. Occurs in montane zone. Another white-flowered species is the PRAIRIE EVENING-PRIMROSE, *O. albicaulis,* with similar flowers but different in habit as it grows from a

WATER MILFOIL FAMILY, *Haloragaceae*

This is a family of water plants which are not very conspicuous in our area. MARESTAIL, *Hippuris vulgaris,* has narrow, simple leaves about one inch long arranged in whorls. The tiny flowers occur in their axils. Usually the whole plant is submersed but sometimes part of it extends above the water. In the submersed form the leaves are very limp. It is found from Greenland throughout North and South America and in Europe and Asia. In the Rockies it occurs in ponds up to 10,000 feet. PARROT FEATHER or WATER MILFOIL, *Myriophyllum exalbescens,* with leaves dissected into thread-like divisions occurs in quiet water of ponds and slow streams almost throughout the United States and in the Rockies up to about 8,500 feet.

217. CUTLEAF EVENING-PRIMROSE, ½ ×

GINSENG FAMILY, *Araliaceae*

WILD SARSAPARILLA, *Aralia nudicaulis* (218), is about a foot tall with long-petioled leaves rising from an underground rootstock. Each leaf is divided into 3 sections and each section consists of 3 to 5 finely toothed leaflets. In autumn these often turn a bronze or maroon color. The greenish flowers are very small, in ball-like umbels on a leafless stalk, and ripen into dark berries.

CARROT FAMILY, *Umbelliferae*

This is a very large family. It is characterized by having small, usually numerous, flowers in umbels, see p. 45. The umbels are often compound, that is, made up of smaller umbels. Stems hollow; leaves compound with petioles having sheathing bases. The flowers are nearly always white or yellow. Some species are diminutive alpines, others are stout plants up to 6 feet tall. There is much similarity in general appearance due to the umbrella-like inflorescence but identification of species is often difficult. Only a few of the most common and easily recognized are described here.

The family includes several common vegetables and culinary herbs. Carrots, parsnips, parsley, caraway seed and angelica are a few of them. The thick starchy roots of some wild species were used as food by Indians and early settlers. Several species are poisonous, so it is important to know the plants before eating them.

Some of the very earliest spring-blooming wild flowers belong in this family. BISCUITROOT or SALT AND PEPPER, *Lomatium orientale (Cogswelia orientalis)* (219), with whitish flowers and finely divided gray-

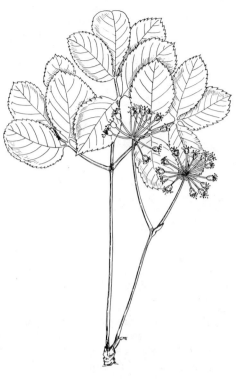

218. WILD SARSAPARILLA, 2/5 ×

ish leaves is one of the first plants to appear on dry plains, mesas and foothills. To begin with, its leaves spread flat against the ground and

219. BISCUITROOT, ½ ×

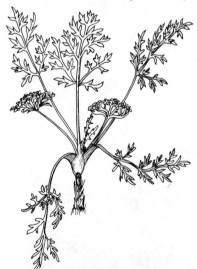

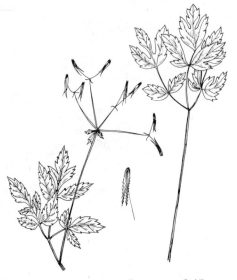

220a. SWEET CICELY, 2/5 ×

its speckled flower clusters seem
almost stemless. Later the stems
may become several inches long.
Found from Minnesota to Montana

220b. SWEET CICELY, in fruit
2/5 ×

and south to Missouri and northeastern Colorado. The thick starchy
roots were used by Indians and
pioneers for food.

Two species of *Cymopteris* are
somewhat similar in habit and
appearance. *C. montanus* has pink
or purplish flowers and gray leaves
and *C. acaulis* has white flowers
and shiny green leaves. INDIAN-
POTATO, *Orogenia linearifolia,* is a
small smooth plant 2 to 6 inches
tall which grows from a tuber. Its
2 or 3 leaves are made up of narrow
divisions. The rays of the umbel are
few and of unequal length, each
bears a small tight cluster of white
or pinkish flowers. It is sometimes
found on mountain slopes blooming
as soon as the snow melts.

SWEET CICELY, *Osmorhiza de-
pauperata* (220 a. and b.), 6 to 25
inches tall, is a plant of moist
shaded woods that hardly looks like
a member of this family. Its umbels
have only 2 to 5 rays which are
long and spreading or reflexed. The
club-shaped fruits are about half an
inch long.

WESTERN SWEETROOT, *O. occidentalis,* is from 1 to 3 feet tall
with 5 to 12 rays to an umbel. The
flowers are yellowish and the linear,
erect fruits are ½- to ¾-inch long.
When nearly ripe each pair becomes
detached and separate at the base,
while still attached at the tip.

YAMPA, *Perideridia gairdneri,* is
a slender plant 1 to 3 feet tall with
compound leaves of narrow, grass-
like leaflets 1 to 6 inches long which
soon wither. The small white flowers
are in compound umbels. This
grows from tubers like small sweet
potatoes. It is one of the best wild
food plants of the Rocky Mountains
and was an important food used by
the Indians and the early explorers.
But if you wish to eat it be sure you

have the correct identification of the plant. Some in this family are poisonous. The grass-like leaflets are the distinguishing character of YAMPA.

MOUNTAIN PARSLEY, *Pseudocymopteris montanus* (221), is a yellow-flowered plant which grows in moist meadows and aspen groves from the foothills to the subalpine zone. Its stems may be from 8 inches to 2 feet tall. It occurs from Wyoming and Utah southward in the mountains. WHISKBROOM PARSLEY, *Harbouria trachypleura* (222), also has yellow flowers but its stems are usually in tufts and it is found on dry hillsides of the montane

zone. The two may be distinguished by reference to figs. 221 and 222, as the shape of the ultimate leaf segments is different. INDIAN BALSAM, *Lomatium dissectum,* is a stout species with stems from 1 to 3 feet tall. Its flowers are usually yellow but may be purplish. It grows in the upper foothill and lower montane zone throughout our range. ALPINE PARSLEY, *Oreoxis alpina* (223), is

223. ALPINE PARSLEY, ½ ×

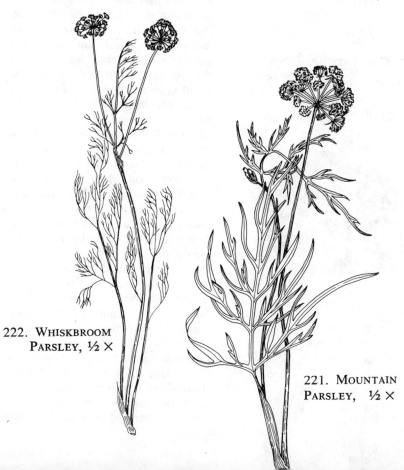

222. WHISKBROOM PARSLEY, ½ ×

221. MOUNTAIN PARSLEY, ½ ×

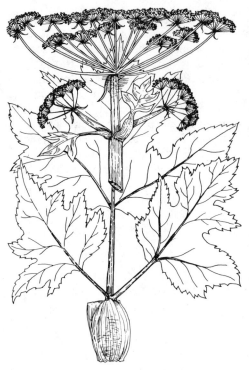

224. Cow Parsnip, 2/5×
225. Giant Angelica, 2/5×

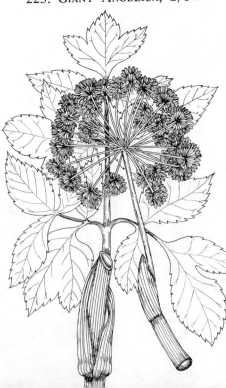

a low, mat-forming plant found on gravel slopes and among rocks of the alpine zone. The yellow-flowered umbels are compact, rarely over ½-inch in diameter on stalks from 1 to 4 inches tall and the leaves are finely dissected. It is found on high mountains from Wyoming and Utah south to New Mexico and Arizona.

Cow Parsnip, *Heracleum lanatum* (224), is a stout plant up to 5 to 8 feet tall with hollow stems. The huge leaves are compound of 3 coarsely toothed leaflets, and the white flowers are in large, flat-topped, compound umbels. The flowers at the edge of the umbels are larger than the inner ones, and the stem leaves have conspicuously enlarged and dilated sheaths.

Giant Angelica, *Angelica ampla* (225), has stout stems often more than 5 feet tall and large pinnately compound leaves. Both the big compound umbels and the small ones are globular. This character plus its size makes the plant easy to recognize. The flowers are white but after the petals drop and the fruits develop the umbels look greenish or brown. This plant grows on moist soil often in shade in montane meadows of Wyoming and Colorado. Grays Angelica, *A. grayi,* is a stout plant not over 2 feet tall but it is large for the conditions under which it grows. Its flowers are greenish and its umbels are globular. This is found in the subalpine and alpine zones on high mountains often among rocks, in Wyoming and Colorado. [Color Pl. 7d]

Rose Angelica, *A. roseana,* a stout plant which has white or pink flowers and less symmetrical umbels than the last is common in the northern part of our range. Pin-

NATE-LEAVED ANGELICA, *A. pinnata,* is a comparatively slender plant with stems up to 3 feet tall and flattened umbels of white or pinkish flowers which grows in the montane and subalpine zones from Montana south to New Mexico.

PORTER LOVAGE, *Ligusticum porteri* (226), has stems from 18 inches to 3 feet tall with white-flowered, flattened, compound umbels. It grows in meadows of the montane and subalpine zones from Wyoming south and west through our region. It somewhat resembles QUEEN ANNES LACE of the eastern states. FENDLER OXYPOLIS, or COWBANE, *Oxypolis fendleri,* is a slender, smooth plant with stems from 1½- to 3 feet tall. The small, dainty umbels are white-flowered and the pinnate leaves are somewhat suggestive of celery. This is a plant of wet, shaded locations such as stream sides and bogs of the subalpine zone. It occurs from Wyoming and Utah south to New Mexico.

POISON HEMLOCK, *Conium maculatum,* has branched, spotted stems from 3 to 9 feet tall. Its numerous, tiny white flowers in open, compound umbels give a lacy effect. It grows on waste, moist soil along roadsides and on ditch banks over much of the world and is found in western Colorado at elevations from 5,000 to 9,000 feet. Beware of any such plant that has a spotted stem.

Another poisonous species is WATER HEMLOCK, *Cicuta douglasii,* with stems 2 to 4 feet tall. It has an open inflorescence of compound umbels. In old plants cross partitions are developed in the roots and the base of the stem. This is a poisonous plant and it may be distinguished from similar-appearing, non-poisonous plants by the char-

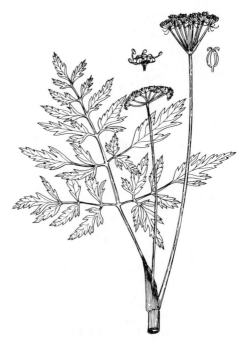

226. PORTERS LOVAGE, 2/5 ×

acter of the leaf veining. In this plant the secondary veins of the leaflets end in the notches between the teeth. It occurs on wet ground from Alaska south in the mountains to Mexico. This plant resembles WATER PARSNIP, *Sium suave (S. cicutaefolium),* which is not poisonous. The veins of WATER PARSNIP leaves run toward the tips of the teeth.

DOGWOOD FAMILY, *Cornaceae*

Most members of this family are trees or shrubs but of the two species commonly found in the Rockies one is a low, herbaceous plant. Ours have opposite or whorled leaves, which turn dark red in autumn, and small flowers in flattened or headlike clusters.

BUNCHBERRY or DWARF CORNEL, *Cornus canadensis,* (227), with stems only 4 to 10 inches tall from a creeping, underground rootstock

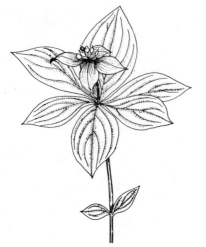

227. BUNCHBERRY, ½ ×

228. RED-OSIER DOGWOOD, 2/5 ×

may form carpets in moist forests. The small, clustered flowers are surrounded by 4 white, petal-like bracts, as is the case with the flowering dogwood trees of our eastern states and of California. The fruit is a cluster of red berries. BUNCHBERRY is rare in Colorado and in most of our range but becomes more abundant in the Northwest and in the Canadian Rockies.

RED-OSIER DOGWOOD, *C. stolo-* *nifera* (228), is an oppositely-branched shrub in our area usually from 2 to 8 feet tall, with smooth, red stems and ovate, pinnately-veined leaves. Its small white flowers occur in flat-topped clusters and are followed by whitish berries which provide good food for birds. It grows along streams of the foothill and montane zones and is easily recognized in winter by its red bark.

KEY TO UNITED-PETAL DICOT FAMILIES

a. Plants with woody stems.
  b. Leaves opposite or whorled; stamens 5
          HONEYSUCKLE FAMILY
          Caprifoliaceae, p. 261.
  bb. Leaves alternate (except in **KALMIA** which has 10 stamens)
          HEALTH FAMILY
          Ericaceae, p. 214.
aa. Plants not woody; stems herbaceous.
  b. Ovaries superior.
    c. Flowers regular.
      d. Plants with milky juice; seed pods often in pairs.
        e. Plants with alternately forking stems
            DOGBANE FAMILY
            Apocynaceae, p. 226.
      ee. Plants with stems mainly unbranched
            MILKWEED FAMILY
            Asclepiadaceae, p. 226.
    dd. Plants without milky juice.

e. Plants saprophytic, lacking green coloring
> PINEDROPS in
> HEALTH FAMILY, p. 215.

ee. Plants with green foilage.

  f. Fruits are capsules with several to many seeds.

    g. Anthers on long slender filaments conspicuously exserted from corolla
> WATERLEAF FAMILY
> *Hydrophyllaceae*, p. 233.

  gg. Anthers on short filaments, exserted only in SHOOTING-STAR.

    h. Leaves all basal and corollas salver-form
> PRIMROSE FAMILY
> *Primulaceae*, p. 219.

    hh. Leaves not all basal; corollas salver-form, funnel-form, or rotate.

      i. Stigmas 3-lobed
> PHLOX FAMILY
> *Polemoniaceae*, p. 228.

      ii. Stigmas 2-lobed or entire.

        j. Leaves opposite or whorled; foilage smooth
> GENTIAN FAMILY
> *Gentianaceae*, p. 221.

        jj. Leaves usually alternate
> POTATO FAMILY
> *Solanaceae*, p. 242.

  ff. Fruits are small nutlets; ovules 4, sometimes only 2 or 3 maturing
> BORAGE FAMILY
> *Boraginaceae*, p. 234.

cc. Flowers irregular, 2-lipped; functional stamens 4 (or 2).

  d. Plant parasitic, without green coloring
> TUFTED BROOMRAPE in
> BROOMRAPE FAMILY, p. 259.

  dd. Plants with green leaves.

    e. Fruits are 4 small nutlets; stems square
> MINT FAMILY
> *Labiatae*, p. 239.

    ee. Fruits are 2-celled capsules with several or many seeds
> FIGWORT FAMILY
> *Scrophulariaceae*, p. 244.

bb. Ovaries inferior.

  c. Inflorescence a compact head of small individual florets surrounded by an involucre (see Plate G).
> COMPOSITE FAMILY
> *Compositae*, p. 268.

  cc. Inflorescence various but not a compact head of florets surrounded by an involucre.

    d. Calyx lobes of plumose bristles which unroll after flowering
> VALERIAN FAMILY
> *Valerianaceae*, p. 264.

  dd. Calyx lobes not as above.

e. Plants trailing or climbing by tendrils
>GOURD FAMILY
>*Cucurbitaceae,* p. 265.

ee. Plants without tendrils.
>f. Leaves opposite; stems square
>>MADDER FAMILY
>>*Rubiaceae,* p. 260.

>ff. Leaves alternate; flowers blue
>>BELLFLOWER FAMILY
>>*Campanulaceae,* p. 266.

HEATH FAMILY, *Ericaceae*

In general the plants of this family have woody stems though some are very low creepers. Of our species several have evergreen leaves but some have deciduous leaves and two are without any green coloring; mostly the corollas are more or less united and have 4 or 5 lobes or petals, the stamens are twice as many as the corolla lobes or, rarely, of the same number. Most of these plants grow on acid soil, either under coniferous trees or in bogs. The family includes the rhododendrons and other handsome, cultivated ornamentals.

a. Plants entirely reddish or brown, hairy; no green leaves
>PINEDROPS, p. 215.

aa. Plants with green leaves.
>b. Petals appearing separate.
>>c. Plants low, not obviously shrubby.
>>>d. Flower 1, white, star-shaped
>>>>WOODNYMPH, p. 215.
>>>dd. Flowers several.
>>>>e. Flower stalks rising from a rosette of basal leaves
>>>>>PYROLA or WINTERGREEN, p. 215.
>>>>ee. Flower stalks rising from a whorl of stem leaves
>>>>>PIPSISSIWA, p. 216.
>>cc. Plants are shrubs; leaves whitish beneath
>>>LEDUM, p. 217.
>bb. Petals plainly united.
>>c. Plants creeping and forming mats.
>>>d. Plants very low; flowers solitary in leaf axils
>>>>CREEPING WINTERGREEN, p. 216.
>>>dd. Plants 4 to 6 inches tall; flowers terminal in clusters
>>>>KINNIKINNIK, p. 217.
>>cc. Plants usually erect (alpine forms may appear creeping).
>>>d. Corollas urn-shaped.
>>>>e. Leaves green and smooth
>>>>>*Vaccinium* (BLUEBERRIES), p. 218.
>>>>ee. Leaves rusty-hairy above, lighter beneath
>>>>>RUSTY-LEAF MENZIESIA, p. 218.
>>>dd. Corollas saucer, cup, or bell-shaped.
>>>>e. Corollas bright pink; leaves narrow with inrolled margins.
>>>>>f. Leaves opposite
>>>>>>BOG KALMIA, p. 217.

ff. **Leaves** alternate but very crowded
PINK MOUNTAINHEATH, p. 218.
ee. **Corollas** white, pinkish, or yellowish.
f. **Plants** are shrubs 1 to 4 feet tall
ROCKY MOUNTAIN AZALEA, p. 217.
ff. **Plants** are less than 1 foot tall
MOUNTAINHEATH, p. 218.

PINEDROPS, *Pterospora androme-da* (229). This interesting plant will be found in dry coniferous woods, often under LODGEPOLE PINES. It is called a *saprophyte* because it derives its food from dead vegetable matter such as rotting wood. In July it sends up stout, brownish-pink, hairy stems which may be from 10 inches to 3 feet tall. From each stalk hangs a series of bell-like flowers with whitish petals. The whole plant becomes rusty brown as it matures and the seed capsules are persistent. These dry, brown stalks are often seen in winter stand-ing up from the pine needle carpet. [Color Pl. 7e]

Another leafless plant sometimes found is PINESAP, *Monotropa hypopitys, which is related to the* INDIANPIPE, but of a yellowish or reddish color and shorter and stouter than PINEDROPS.

PYROLA or WINTERGREEN, *Pyrola.* This genus contains several rather similar species. Their leaves are evergreen, their flowers are spaced along an erect stalk, and are made up of 5 rounded or oval petals, 10 stamens and a superior ovary. In all but one of our species the styles are long and bent down. They grow in damp forests or bogs and are called "wintergreens" because the simple, rounded or ovate leaves are evergreen but these plants do not have the aromatic flavor associated with creeping winter-green.

WOODNYMPH, or SINGLE-DELIGHT, *Pyrola uniflora (Moneses uniflora)* (230), is one of the most charming flowers of the spruce

229. PINEDROPS, ½ × (old plants hairy and reddish brown)

230. WOODNYMPH,   2/5 ×

231. ONE-SIDED PYROLA, ½ ×

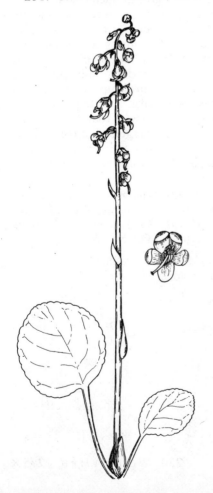

forests. It is a shy thing, growing in shade and hanging its head, about 4 inches tall and may have either 4 or 5 petals. It is well worth getting down on one's knees for a look into its star-like face and a whiff of its lovely perfume. Found in moist woods of the subalpine zone throughout the Rockies and in boreal forests around the world.

ONE-SIDED PYROLA or SIDEBELLS WINTERGREEN, *P. secunda* (231), often occurs in small beds. Its leaves are ovate and its white or greenish flowers are along one side of the 4 to 8 inch stalk which is often slightly curved. It somewhat suggests a lily-of-the-valley to which it is in no way related.

PINKFLOWERED PYROLA or BOG WINTERGREEN, *P. asarifolia (P. uliginosa* (232), has round leaves, a stalk up to 12 inches tall which holds a raceme of several to many pink flowers. It grows around forest springs, along stream banks and in bogs. Two other species having white or greenish flowers may be found. The SPOTTED SHINLEAF, *P. picta,* occurs in Yellowstone and Glacier National Parks and throughout the northern part of our range. LESSER WINTERGREEN, *P. minor,* has short styles and is found in boreal woods around the world. WESTERN CREEPING WINTERGREEN, *Gaultheria humifusa,* is a lowly plant which embeds itself in moss on moist ground and is rarely noticed except when its bright red edible berries ripen in late summer. PIPSISSEWA or PRINCES-PINE, *Chimaphila umbellata* (233). The dark green, stiff and glossy leaves are in whorls on a stem about 4 to 6 inches tall and from this the flower stalk rises another 2 to 6 inches, holding several round, pink

232. PINK-FLOWERED PYROLA, ½ ×

233. PIPSISSEWA, ½ ×

buds or open flowers. This can be one of the delightful finds on a walk through coniferous forests of the Rockies.

LEDUM, *Ledum glandulosum,* a shrub with fragrant, oval leaves which are white beneath, and long-stalked, terminal clusters of white flowers with separate petals which are about ¼-inch long, grows in swamps in Yellowstone and Glacier National Parks and surrounding areas. It is related to the more northern Labrador Tea.

KINNIKINNIK, *Arctostaphylos uva-ursi* (234), is probably the commonest evergreen plant, aside from members of the Pine Family, found in the whole Rocky Mountain region. Its leaves are firm, bright

234. KINNIKINNIK, 2/5 ×

green and shiny. It spreads over rocky or gravelly soil forming big or little carpets 4 to 6 inches thick and is important in the soil building process. Its flowers are dainty pink and white jugs on curved pedicels, which are followed in autumn by scarlet berries. Both leaves and berries provide important food for wildlife and were also used by the Indians. [Color Pls. 7f and 8a]

A related species is GREENLEAF or UTAH MANZANITA, *A. patula,* a shrub with smooth reddish branches growing in western Colorado on the Uncompahgre Plateau and in the mountains of Utah.

ROCKY MOUNTAIN AZALEA, *Rhododendron albiflorus,* is a loosely growing shrub with deciduous, pale green, thin leaves and saucer or bell-shaped white flowers about an inch long. The flower buds are often pink-tinged. It occurs from the Canadian Rockies south into Oregon and is found in one area of moist, rich forest in northern Colorado.

BOG KALMIA or BOG-LAUREL, *Kalmia polifolia* (235), is a diminu-

235. BOG KALMIA, ½ ×

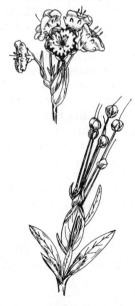

tive relative of the eastern MOUN-
TAIN LAUREL and has rose-colored
flowers which hang from erect pedicels. Its opposite leaves appear
narrow because their margins are
inrolled. It may be from 4 to 18
inches tall and grows in cold, peaty
bogs of the subalpine zone throughout the Rocky Mountains. At timberline it sometimes appears almost
creeping. Closely related are the
Mountainheaths of the genus *Phyl-
lodoce*. PINK MOUNTAINHEATH, *P.
empetriformis,* is a low evergreen
shrub with small, crowded leaves
which when not in bloom might
suggest some kind of a juniper or
spruce relative. But it bears bell-
shaped, pink blossoms. It covers
large areas with mats of densely
branched stems a foot or less in
height. CREAM MOUNTAINHEATH,
P. glanduliflora, is similar, except
that the yellowish corollas are constricted at the throat and covered
with sticky hairs. CASSIOPE or
WHITE MOUNTAINHEATH, *Cassiope
mertensiana,* is another little shrub
with very small, 4-ranked leaves
and pure white, urn-shaped corollas
set off by red sepals and pedicels,
which occurs in the northern Rockies and in southern Montana and
northern Idaho.

BLUEBERRY, HUCKLEBERRY, *Vac-
cinium.* Our species are small shrubs
with urn-shaped greenish, white or
pink flowers and juicy edible berries. DWARF BLUEBERRY or BIL-
BERRY, *V. caespitosum* (236), has
brown, round stems from 2 to 10
inches tall, often tufted and usually
found in timberline regions although
in Glacier Park it is said to be
very common at low altitudes and
reaches a height of 15 inches.
MYRTLE-LEAF BLUEBERRY, *V. myr-
tillus,* is similar but usually slightly
taller and not so densely tufted. It

236. DWARF BLUEBERRY, ½ ×

grows among rocks in the subalpine
zone and in good seasons bears
quantities of delicious bluish-black
berries. GROUSEBERRY or RED
WHORTLEBERRY, *V. scoparium,* has
green, angled stems, thin bright
green leaves and small red berries.
In many areas it is almost the only
plant growing under coniferous
trees, especially in ENGELMANN
SPRUCE forests where it makes a
lacy ground cover. These three species occur throughout our range.
From northern Wyoming northward in moist areas of the foothills
and montane zones the TALL WHOR-
TLEBERRY or THIN-LEAVED HUCKLE-
BERRY occurs. This grows from 2 to
6 feet tall and bears delicious black
fruits nearly ½-inch in diameter.

SMOOTH MENZIESIA, *Menziesia
glabella,* an erect shrub 6 to 10 feet
tall with thin, oblong leaves which
are paler beneath is common in
wooded parts of western Montana
and northern Idaho. Its urn-shaped
yellowish or bronze flowers are
similar to those of the huckleberry
but its fruits are dry capsules so
it is sometimes called "Fool's
huckleberry." The RUSTY-LEAF
MENZIESIA, *M. ferruginia,* which is
similar except that its leaves are

narrower with pointed tips and are clothed with reddish-brown hairs, is common in Yellowstone National Park. This genus was named in honor of Archibald Menzies, the surgeon and naturalist who accompanied Vancouver on his exploration of the Puget Sound area in 1790 to 1795, one of the first botanists to collect plants in that area.

PRIMROSE FAMILY, *Primulaceae*

Our plants of this family have united corollas made up of a *tube* and a *limb* (see *Plate E 46}.* The place where the tube expands into the limb is the *throat.* Five stamens are attached inside the tube opposite the lobes of the corolla and there is 1 pistil. In SHOOTINGSTAR the tube is very short. The 5-merous flowers distinguish this family from the Evening-primrose Family which has 4-merous flowers.

a. Plants stemless; all the leaves basal.
  b. Flowers bright rose, 1/2-inch or more in diameter or length.
    c. Corolla lobes reflexed; anthers forming a dark point
                SHOOTINGSTAR, p. 219.
    cc. Corolla lobes rounded; limb at right angle to tube
                PRIMROSE, p. 219.
  bb. Flowers white, not over 1/3-inch in diameter
                ANDROSACE, p. 220.
aa. Plants with leafy stems.
  b. Stems low and matted; leaves moss-like
                DOUGLASIA, p. 221.
  bb. Stems upright; leaves whorled
                LOOSESTRIFE, p. 220.

WESTERN SHOOTINGSTAR, *Dodecatheon pulchellum (D. pauciflorum)* (237). These clusters of bright pink flowers with their corolla lobes turned back from a point of dark colored anthers are easily recognized. They are held on slender, leafless stalks above basal rosettes of smooth, bright-green leaves. They bloom along mossy stream banks in the foothills in spring and in wet montane and subalpine meadows in early summer. In some areas, such as South Park, Colorado, they are so abundant as to color whole meadows pink. The turned-back petals suggest their relationship to the genus *Cyclamen,* of this same family. [Color Pl. 8b]

PRIMROSE, *Primula.* These plants have erect flower stalks from

237. WESTERN SHOOTINGSTAR,
    ½ ×

238. FAIRY PRIMROSE, ½ ×

239. PARRY PRIMROSE, ½ ×

rosettes of basal leaves. Their corollas are salver-form, marked by a yellow eye. FAIRY PRIMROSE, *P. angustifolia* (238), is a dainty alpine with stems 2 to 3 inches tall and rose-colored flowers with bright yellow eye, ½- to 1-inch across. It grows singly or in clumps in very exposed, alpine locations. Sometimes on mountaintop boulder fields this "fairy" takes advantage of a sheltered nook between rocks. [Color Pl. 8c]

PARRY PRIMROSE, *P. parryi* (239), which has similar, but larger, flowers is a much taller plant, up to 15 inches in height. The rather stout stalks hold umbels of bright rose, yellow-centered, flowers. It is usually found along subalpine and alpine streams, often growing in the edge of the water, though it sometimes occurs in bogs. The flowers and foliage are disagreeably strong-scented. This handsome species was named for the botanist Parry (see p. 74). The plant is found from southern Montana and Idaho southward into the mountains of northern New Mexico and Arizona and is frequently seen at high altitudes in Rocky Mountain National Park. [Color Pl. 8d]

BIRDSEYE PRIMROSE, *P. incana,* a smaller plant of wet meadows of the foothill and montane regions has crowded umbels of lilac flowers and white powdered leaves.

TUFTED LOOSESTRIFE, *Lysimachia thyrsiflora,* is a plant of wet ground with small yellow flowers in crowded tufts.

ROCK-JASMINE, *Androsace*. Diminutive primrose relatives are these inconspicuous, white-flowered plants. ALPINE ROCK-JASMINE, *A. chamaejasme* ssp. *carinata* (240). is a tiny, cushion-type alpine 2 to 3 inches tall with silvery hairs on

240. ALPINE ROCK-JASMINE, 4 ×

stem and leaves and a cluster of
fragrant flowers which might suggest a Forget-me-not. The creamy
white corolla has a tiny yellow eye
which turns pink as the flower ages.
NORTHERN ROCKJASMINE, *A. sep-*
tentrionalis (241), is an annual with
smooth, wiry stems and tiny, white,
5-lobed corollas. At high altitudes
the stems are short and the plant
may be only 1 to 2 inches tall and
quite compact. At lower altitudes
the stems grow to several inches and
become diffusely and always umbel-
lately branched. DOUGLASIA, *Doug-*
lasia montana, another matted,
moss-like plant with small, crowded
leaves starred with short-stemmed,
phlox-like, lilac or rose flowers is
found on dry hills and mountain
tops of Montana and Idaho.

241. NORTHERN ROCK-JASMINE,
2/5 × *(left,* low elevation
form; *right,* alpine form).

OLIVE FAMILY, *Oleaceae*

One species, FORESTIERA or
MOUNTAIN PRIVET, *Forestiera neo-*
mexicana (242), a large shrub with
pale gray or greenish bark and
opposite branching, is found in
valleys and on canyon sides of the
foothills of southwestern Colorado,
New Mexico and Arizona. Its small,
clustered yellow, dioecious flowers

242. FORESTIERA, ½ ×

appear before the leaves and its
fruits are oval or oblong, bluish-
black berries relished by birds.

GENTIAN FAMILY, *Gentianaceae*

The most conspicuous members of this family found in our range
have bright blue or purplish-blue flowers; a few have white or greenish
corollas; the united corollas may be saucer-shape *(rotate),* funnel-form,
or tubular with more or less spreading lobes, and the lobes may be either
4 or 5. In general the leaves are opposite, whorled or all basal; the foliage
and stems are always smooth. The blossoms of several species close when
shaded so they are often overlooked on cloudy days.

a. Leaves simple; plants of meadows or fields.
  b. Corollas rotate (see page 44).
    c. Corollas dark purplish-blue
STAR-GENTIAN, p. 222.
    cc. Corollas white or greenish.
      d. Corolla white; plant not over 18 inches tall
MARSH FELWORT, p. 222.

dd. Corollas greenish; plant 1 to 6 feet tall
MONUMENT PLANT, p. 222.
bb. Corollas tubular, cup-shaped, or funnel-form.
c. Corollas bright blue or purplish-blue.
d. Corolla lobes 4, fringed
R. MTN. FRINGED GENTIAN, p. 223.
dd. Corolla lobes entire, usually 5, with pleats at the sinuses.
e. Plants tiny; stems thread-like.
MOSS GENTIAN, p. 224.
ee. Plants 4 to 20 inches tall .
f. Flowers 1 to 5, 1 to 1 1/2-inches long
PARRY GENTIAN, p. 224.
ff. Flowers several to many, not over 1 inch long
PRAIRIE GENTIAN, p. 225.
cc. Corollas white, greenish, pinkish, or pale blue.
d. Flowers 1 to 2 inches long, greenish with dark streaks
ARCTIC GENTIAN, p. 225.
dd. Flowers less than an inch long.
e. Flowers solitary, white or pale bluish.
f. Stems stiffly erect; capsule conspicuously protruded
FREMONT GENTIAN, p. 224.
ff. Stems weak; flowers on long peduncles, plant alpine
ONE-FLOWERED GENTIAN, p. 224.
ee. Flowers several to many, lilac or whitish
AMARELLA, p. 224.
aa. Leaves trifoliate; plants growing in water or very wet situations
BUCKBEAN, p. 226.

243. STAR GENTIAN, ½ ×

STAR GENTIAN, *Swertia perennis* (243). Stems 6 to 12 inches tall from a basal rosette of smooth, lanceolate or elliptic leaves with a long narrow cluster of dull blue, star-shaped flowers; corolla lobes 5 or 4. Found in wet meadows and on stream banks in the subalpine and alpine zones of the Rocky Mountains and in boreal regions around the world. MARSH FEL-WORT, *Lomatogonium rotatum,* is a white-flowered plant somewhat similar to the STAR GENTIAN occasionally found in mountain bogs and wet meadows of northwestern America.

MONUMENT PLANT or GREEN GENTIAN, *Frasera speciosa* (244). This is a stout, pale green plant which sometimes becomes very conspicuous in middle and late summer on montane hillsides and at the

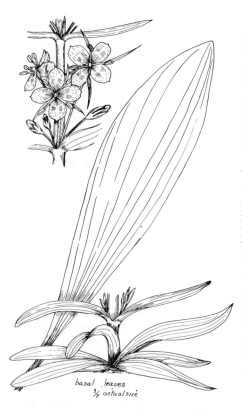

244. MONUMENT PLANT, ½ ×

basal leaves
½ actual size

edges of meadows. Its stems are from 1 to 6 feet tall from a basal rosette of long smooth leaves; stem leaves are in whorls and are progressively smaller upwards. There are numerous flowers on short stalks from each of the middle and upper whorls. These have 4-lobed corollas and are pale green with purplish markings and fringed appendages. This is a biennial plant and its rosettes of large pale (sometimes purple-tinged), oblong or spatulate leaves are conspicuous during its first summer. The following season when the flower stalk begins to develop, the basal leaves gradually wither and after flowering the plant dies. The dry stalks often persist through the winter.

GENTIAN, *Gentiana.* The flowers of this group of gentians may have 4 or 5 corolla lobes with no pleats nor small extra lobes between them. Some have the margins of the corolla lobes fringed, others have small fringes at the throat of the corolla. All are annuals except the perennial fringed gentian.

ROCKY MOUNTAIN FRINGED GENTIAN, *G. thermalis (G. elegans)* (245). The flowers of this slender erect annual plant have 4 lobes with fringed margins. On a dull day the lobes are erect and twisted together but in bright sunlight they spread widely, displaying their brilliant purplish-blue color. The plants are found in moist meadows and on margins of ponds and streams from the montane to the alpine throughout the Rockies. It was chosen the Park flower of Yellowstone because of its abundance in that area. [Color Pl. 8e]

This plant has had a confusing number of Latin names given to it by different botanists. One found it growing around the hot springs of

245. ROCKY MOUNTAIN FRINGED GENTIAN, ½ ×

Yellowstone National Park and called it *thermalis.* Another, not knowing it had already been named gave it the more appropriate name of *elegans,* then a third decided it should be put into a distinct genus and called it *Gentianopsis thermalis.*

PERENNIAL or FRAGRANT FRINGED GENTIAN, *G. barbellata,* is somewhat similar in general appearance. Its delicately fragrant flowers vary from rather light grayish-blue to dark purplish but are never such a bright color as the R. MTN. FRINGED GENTIAN, and its corolla lobes are narrower and usually twisted. This is a rare plant found occasionally at the edges of coniferous forests or on open slopes of the subalpine zone in the central and southern Rockies. It should be protected. It blooms late and may often be found in flower in September.

AMARELLA or ROSE GENTIAN, *G. amarella,* is a variable plant of very wide distribution. Its flowers may have 4 or 5 lobes. The lobes are pointed and there is a fringed crown at the throat of the corolla. There may be from one to many flowers. The plants are usually erect and often have several erect branches. Flowers are dull rose or lilac. (This is a plant of marshy ground and occurs throughout our range from the montane zone to the alpine.)

A similar and closely related plant is *G. strictiflora* with white or bluish blossoms. ONE-FLOWERED GENTIAN, *G. tenella,* is a tiny plant with its ½-inch long pale blue flower on the end of a thread-like stalk. It grows in grassy tundra from the arctic south in the high mountains to Arizona.

PLEATED GENTIANS, *Gentiana.* Plants of this group usually have 5 corolla lobes with folds or pleats between them which end in small teeth. Most of these are perennial plants.

MOSS GENTIAN, *G. prostrata,* is a very small slender plant found in moss or in the grassy alpine tundra. It has a blue star-like flower not over ⅓-inch broad when open. It is so sensitive to light that it will close immediately if a cloud passes over or even if a hand is held over it for an instant. A closely related species is FREMONT GENTIAN, *G. fremontii* (246), which has an erect stem and a whitish flower. It is sometimes abundant in wet subalpine meadows and when it goes to seed the capsule is pushed up above the calyx and splits, showing two spatula-shaped valves. This species was named for General John C. Fremont who explored, mapped, and collected plants in the Colorado Rockies in 1842 and 1843.

PARRY or MOUNTAIN GENTIAN *G. parryi* (247), is the largest-flowered and probably the most frequently seen of any of our gentians. The corollas are goblet-shaped 1-½ to 2 inches deep, bright

246. FREMONT GENTIAN, ½ ×

247. MOUNTAIN GENTIAN, ½ ×

248. PRAIRIE GENTIAN, ½ ×

clear blue with dark greenish stripes on the outside so that when closed they are inconspicuous. The plant usually has several stems from a perennial crown. Each stem may have 1 to several blossoms. This grows on open fields and meadows of the subalpine zone throughout our range.

FORWOOD GENTIAN, *G. forwoodii,* is an erect plant with stems 6 to 15 inches tall. Each one holds several to many bright blue, narrowly funnel-form blossoms. The calyx is short and split at one side and the corolla lobes are short and pointed. This grows in moist meadows and along streams of the montane zone.

A closely related plant is PRAIRIE GENTIAN, *G. affinis (G. bigelovii)* (248), which grows on dry fields of the mesas and foothills. It is a tufted plant with stems which are decumbent at base, and blue flowers which appear closed except in bright sunlight.

ARCTIC GENTIAN, *G. algida (G. romanzoffiana)* (249). This is a tundra plant and occurs in our region on grassy alpine meadows. It usually has several stems each bearing a compact cluster of flowers. The deep cup-shaped corollas are greenish-white with dark blue or purplish streaks on the outside of each lobe. The buds and closed flowers appear dark in color. Inside are 5 salmon-colored anthers. This species occurs from Siberia and Alaska south

249. ARCTIC GENTIAN, ½ ×

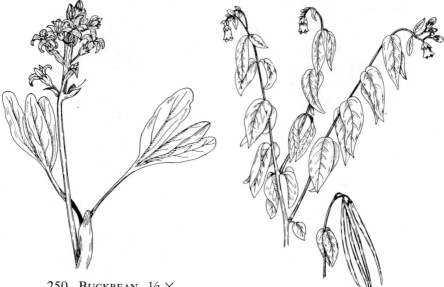

250. BUCKBEAN, ½ ×

251. DOGBANE, 2/5 ×

through the high mountains into Utah and northern New Mexico. It is the latest of the alpine plants to bloom and is rarely seen in flower before August. [Color Pl. 8f] At that time the fern-like leaves of its companion, ALPINE AVENS (156), have already turned maroon color.

BUCKBEAN, *Menyanthes trifoliata* (250), is a plant of cold bogs and ponds of the subalpine zone. Its leaves are made up of three oval, thick leaflets on long petioles. The white, fringed and often pink-tinged flowers are in short spikes. Its leaves and flowers are sometimes seen standing in shallow water. Found in northern North America and occasionally in the Rockies. In some books this plant is placed in a separate family, the *Menyanthaceae*.

DOGBANE FAMILY, *Apocynaceae*

DOGBANE, *Apocynum androsaemifolium* (251). Erect plants having forked branching and smooth, ovate or oblong leaves, clusters of small white or pink flowers, and a milky juice which is said to be poisonous. The pods are in pairs, 3 to 6 inches long and very slender; each seed has a tuft of silky hairs at one end. Dogbane grows from the foothills to the subalpine zone on dry hillsides and along roads throughout our range. The leaves which usually hang down turn yellow in autumn. The stems contain strong fibers and a related species, INDIAN HEMP, *A. cannabinum*, which is taller and grows at lower altitudes, was used by the Indians for making string and rope.

MILKWEED FAMILY, *Asclepiadaceae*

These plants have their flowers in umbels; they have milky juice and pods containing silky tufted seeds, as do the Dogbanes, but milkweed flowers are elaborately constructed. In each individual flower there is a *corona* of hooded appendages between the 5 stamens and the pistil. These flower parts are so arranged as to trap any insect which visits the flower and make it impossible for him to get away without carrying some pollen to the next flower he visits. Milkweed flowers are very attractive to butterflies, especially the handsome Monarch Butterfly whose green and black banded caterpillars feed on the milkweed plants.

SHOWY MILKWEED, *Asclepias speciosa* (252), is our most common species. It has thick, short petioled, oblong to ovate-lanceolate, opposite leaves 4 to 10 inches long which may be smooth or more or less woolly. The flowers are pink or whitish. The asymmetric fat, usually rough, pods may be in pairs or single. There are 2 ovaries but sometimes only one matures. This plant grows from 18 inches to 5 feet tall forming clumps and sometimes extensive beds along roadsides and on ditch banks. It is found throughout our area, usually at the lower altitudes but seems to be extending its range into the montane zone and occasionally higher. BUTTERFLYWEED, *A. tuberosa* ssp. *interior,* with clusters of brilliant orange flowers and narrow, hairy leaves is an exception in this group as it does not have the milky juice of its relatives. It is occasionally seen along roadsides in the foothills.

MORNING-GLORY FAMILY, *Convolvulaceae*

This family includes some garden flowers and several very persistent weeds. The stems climb by twining around any available supports or

252. SHOWY MILKWEED, 2/5 ×

253. BINDWEED, 2/5 ×

trail over the ground. The flowers are broadly funnel form.

BINDWEED, *Convolvulus arvensis* (253), has white or pinkish flowers 1 to 2 inches long, most conspicuous in the mornings. It has a deep, wide-spreading root, very difficult to eradicate, and occurs as a weed in cultivated fields and along roadsides.

PHLOX FAMILY, *Polemoniaceae*

This family is characterized by having regular, united corollas which may be rotate, funnel-form, campanulate or salver-form. In the bud the corolla lobes are always folded in a certain way so that the edge of one overlaps the edge of the next and they appear twisted. When buds are so arranged they are said to be *convolute*. The 5 (rarely 4) stamens are attached inside the corolla tube and there is a 3-celled, superior ovary.

```
a. Corollas salver-form.
   b. Leaves simple and entire.
      c. Flowers in dense,terminal, leafy-bracted heads
                            COLLOMIA, p. 228.
      cc. Flowers not in dense heads; corolla lobes broad
                            PHLOX, p. 228.
   bb. Leaves lobed, dissected, or compound; corolla lobes pointed
                            GILIA, p. 229.
aa. Corolla rotate or funnel-form

                            POLEMONIUM, p. 231.
```

COLLOMIA, *Collomia linearis,* is a weedy plant with narrow, tapering leaves and very small, trumpet-shaped pinkish flowers about ¼-inch across in a dense cluster which is interspersed with leafy bracts. Found on disturbed ground and along roadsides. LARGE-FLOWERED COLLOMIA, *C. grandiflora,* has white to orange flowers which are about ½-inch across and occurs in the western part of our range.

PHLOX, *Phlox.* Our plants of this genus may be loosely spreading or very compact in dense mats, carpets or cushions. Their leaves are opposite and often closely crowded. The corolla is always salverform with slender tube and spreading limb. Usually there are 5 broad lobes. The buds show the characteristic convolute folding. Flowers on different species vary in size but otherwise are so similar that when you learn one kind other members of the genus are easily recognized. There may be considerable color variation in any given species. Some kinds are more or less woody at base.

```
a. Plants 4 to 10 inches tall; leaves over 1/2-inch long.
   b. Leaves 1 1/2- to 3 inches long
                            LONG-LEAF PHLOX, p. 229.
   bb. Leaves 1/2-inch to 1 inch long.
      c. Plants are low, succulent shrubs
                            MARSH PHLOX, p. 229.
      cc. Plants are not succulent shrubs
                            ROCKY MOUNTAIN PHLOX, p. 229.
aa. Plants are less than 4 inches tall; leaves less than 1/2-inch long.
   b. Stems and leaves whitish with dense, cobwebby hairs
                            MOSS PHLOX, p. 229.
   bb. Stems and leaves smooth or with few hairs.
      c. Plants of the high mountains
                            ALPINE PHLOX, p. 229.
   cc. Plants of plains and foothills
                            CARPET PHLOX, p. 229.
```

LONG-LEAF PHLOX, *P. longifolia.* This is a loosely-spreading plant with stems from 4 to 12 inches long which may be erect or decumbent. Its slender pointed leaves are from 1 to 3 inches long and are always in pairs. The corolla tube is from ½- to ⅝-inch long and the flower is about ½-inch across, varying from white to bright pink or lilac. It grows throughout our range and is commonly found in the foothills of the Colorado Rockies but is reported to occur at all altitudes in Idaho.

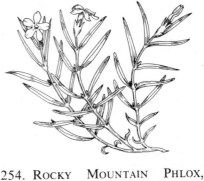

254. ROCKY MOUNTAIN PHLOX, 2/5×

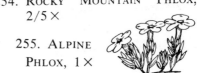

255. ALPINE PHLOX, 1×

ROCKY MOUNTAIN PHLOX or Yellowstone Phlox, *P. multiflora* (254), has shorter stems and leaves than the preceding and forms rather loose mats. It has white, bluish or lavender flowers and is often found among shrubs, especially under sage brush. This is our most widespread and commonly seen species occurring throughout the Rockies.

MARSH PHLOX, *P. kelseyi,* is a low, half-shrubby plant of alkaline or salty marshes with bright blue or lavender, fragrant flowers found at low elevations in Montana, Wyoming and Idaho.

ALPINE PHLOX, *P. pulvinata (P. caespitosa)* (255), is a compact, cushion plant with crowded leaves from ¼- to ½-inch long and short-stemmed white or bluish flowers which grows on rocky alpine fields and occasionally at lower altitudes. MOSS PHLOX or SQUARESTEM PHLOX, *P. bryoides,* is a very low-growing cushion plant with tiny, crowded, gray, 2-ranked leaves which give the shoots a square appearance. Its flowers are usually white and about ⅓-inch across. Found on open, dry, rocky slopes and valleys of the foothills from Montana south to Colorado and Utah. CARPET PHLOX, *P. hoodii, (P. glabrata),* is a variable species as to size of flowers and leaves but well described by its common name as it carpets large areas of gravelly soil on the foothills and high plains. In many of these areas it is the earliest flower to bloom; its small white flowers appear in late April and it is locally known as "MAYFLOWER" by Wyoming children, which illustrates the fact that common plant names are not meaningful outside the locality of their origin.

SPREADING PHLOX, *P. diffusa* ssp. *subcarinata,* with bright pink or white flowers, occurs in northern Arizona, especially in the Kaibab forest and northward to Idaho and Washington. [Color Pl. 9a]

GILIA. The large and variable group of related plants all of which at one time or another have been classified in the genus *Gilia,* have been more recently segregated into several genera on botanical characters not easily evident to amateurs. Because GILIA is still applied to them as a common name, they will be considered here in one group and the writer hopes that the following key will help to distinguish and identify them. All have salverform corollas with slender tubes and most have divided leaves. In some cases the leaves are so deeply divided that the segments appear as very narrow, simple leaves.

a. Plants with leaves palmately divided into needle-like segments.
  b. Plants low shrubs with spine-tipped leaf segments
                   SPINY GILIA, p. 230.
 bb. Plants not shrubby nor spiny; leaf segments soft
                 NUTTALL GILIA, p. 230.
aa. Plants with leaves pinnately more or less divided.
  b. Flowers in compact spikes or globular heads.
    c. Flowers in globular heads
              ALPINE BALL-HEAD GILIA, p. 231.
    cc. Flower clusters in dense spikes
                 SPIKE GILIA, p. 231.
 bb. Flowers in open elongated clusters.
   c. Flowers white, pink, or scarlet, over 1 inch long.
    d. Flowers scarlet
              SCARLET GILIA, p. 231.
    dd. Flowers white, pink, or salmon color
              FAIRY TRUMPET GILIA, p. 231.
   cc. Flowers whitish to blue, not over 1/2-inch long
             PINNATE-LEAF GILIA, p. 231.

256. NUTTALL GILIA, 2/5×

258. SCARLET GILIA, 2/5×

257. ALPINE BALL-HEAD GILIA, 2/5×

SPINY GILIA, *Leptodactylon pungens (Gilia pungens)*. This is a small, dry, spiny looking shrub not over 1 foot tall with its leaves deeply divided into slender, stiff, sharp segments. Its white, yellow or pinkish flowers resemble those of a phlox. It grows in dry rocky or sandy situations of the foothill and montane zones throughout our range. The very appropriate specific name *pungens* means "sharp pointed."

NUTTALL GILIA, *Linanthastrum nuttalli (Gilia nuttallii)* (256), is a tufted plant with opposite leaves that are deeply divided into 3 to 7 narrow linear segments which appear as whorls or tiers on each stem. The flowers, on very short pedicels, are small, phlox-like, white with yellow eye and tube, and are clustered at the tips of the branches.

PINCUSHION PLANT, *Navarretia breweri (G. breweri)* is a low stout usually branched plant with spine-tipped leaves and white or yellow flowers crowded into dense heads surrounded by spine-tipped bracts. Grows in Yellowstone National Park and southwards through Wyoming and western Colorado into Arizona.

ALPINE BALL-HEAD GILIA, *Ipomopsis globularis* (257), with round silky clusters of very fragrant cream-colored flowers and having cobwebby hairs on the stem and leaves, is an alpine plant found on the high mountains of Colorado. The COMMON BALL-HEAD GILIA, *I. congesta (Gilia congesta),* is a similar, though usually taller, plant up to 1 foot in height, with heads of small white flowers having blue anthers. It is occasionally found growing on dry and rocky or sandy hillsides and valleys of the foothills. SPIKE GILIA, *Ipomopsis spicata (G. spicata).* This is a woolly plant with tight balls of whitish or cream-colored flowers arranged in a spike-like inflorescence which is found on the high plains and foothills of Colorado, New Mexico and Utah.

SCARLET GILIA or SKYROCKET GILIA, *Ipomopsis aggregata* (258). Plants 1 to 3 feet tall with many scarlet, trumpet-shaped flowers, each 1 to 2 inches long arranged along the stems in a narrow or open, elongated cluster. The pointed corolla lobes are turned back and often there are yellow markings on the inside of the corolla. Leaves are pinnately divided into narrow lobes. These plants are biennial. The rosettes of leaves become established in the first season and the next summer the flowering stalk is developed. After it goes to seed the plant usually dies but if you look around carefully you will discover some seedling rosettes preparing to furnish flowers for the next season. These plants bloom in July along roadsides and on banks in the foothills and montane zone throughout the Rocky Mountains. [Color Pl. 9b]

FAIRY TRUMPET, *I. aggregata* ssp. *candida,* similar except that the corollas are sometimes longer and vary from a glistening pinkish-white to rose or salmon color, is found in Colorado and New Mexico. PINNATE-LEAF GILIA, *Gilia pinnatifida,* is an inconspicuous plant with an erect branched stem, small bluish flowers and sticky foliage, which grows on open sandy ground from Wyoming to New Mexico and at all altitudes up to timberline.

JACOBS LADDER or SKY PILOT, *Polemonium.* Plants of this genus have rotate or funnel-form corollas and pinnately compound leaves

259. DELICATE JACOBS LADDER, ½ ×

260. SKY PILOT, ½ ×

261. LEAFY POLEMONIUM, ½ ×

which are very strong and disagreeably scented. This accounts for the name of "skunk leaf" or "skunk plant" given to some species.

DELICATE JACOBS LADDER, *P. delicatum, (P. pulcherrimum)* (259). The ovate-lanceolate or elliptical leaflets are 2-ranked so that they suggest a ladder. This plant is well named. Its clustered stems are slender and decumbent, its leaflets are thin and pale green, its dainty wide open flowers are sky blue. It is usually found under "wind timber," the dwarf bent and twisted trees at timberline, or in lightly shaded areas of the upper spruce forests. It grows in Wyoming, Colorado, New Mexico, Arizona, Utah and Idaho.

SKY PILOT, *P. viscosum (P. confertum)* (260), has its flowers crowded into compact clusters; the funnel-form corollas are violet blue or purplish. Against this color the orange anthers of the 5 stamens show up beautifully. Leaves are mostly basal of numerous tiny oval leaflets crowded along the rachis. Grows on the tundra and most frequently in places where the soil has been recently disturbed by road work or by pocket gopher diggings. White- flowered plants are seen and there is a cream-colored form.

LEAFY POLEMONIUM, *P. foliosissimum* (261), is a stout, branched, sticky plant 1 to 3 feet tall with a skunk-like odor. It has many short, open funnel-form, blue flowers. Its leaves have 12 to 25 2-ranked, lanceolate to oblong, leaflets, the upper ones often confluent. Found along ditches and roadsides at middle elevations throughout our area. WESTERN JACOBS LADDER, *P. caer-*

uleum (P. occidentale), is a more slender unbranched plant with similar flowers which grows in moist meadows and open woods of the montane and subalpine zones from the Arctic south to Colorado, Utah, and California.

WATERLEAF FAMILY, *Hydrophyllaceae*
The flowers in this family have 5-lobed bell-shaped corollas with 5 stamens which are attached to the tube of the corolla. The filaments and styles are longer than the corollas and this gives most of these flowers a fringed appearance. Their leaves are usually more or less lobed or divided.

FENDLER WATERLEAF, *Hydrophyllum fendleri* (262). A plant 1 to 3 feet tall of moist shaded situations with large leaves pinnately divided into 9 to 13 long-pointed, main divisions, which are toothed or again divided. The pale flowers are in loose clusters on stalks taller than the leaves; found in moist, shaded situations of foothill and montane zones from Wyoming to New Mexico and Utah. BALL-HEAD WATERLEAF, *H. capitatum,* is a smaller plant with round clusters of lavender or light purple flowers on

stalks shorter than the leaf stalks; found in moist locations of the montane zone from the Canadian Rockies south to western Colorado.

PURPLE FRINGE, *Phacelia sericea* (263), has silky silvery foliage and stems from 4 inches to a foot tall which are often clustered. The crowded spike-like inflorescences

263. PURPLE FRINGE, ½ ×

262. FENDLER WATERLEAF, 2/5 ×

are composed of purple flowers from which the stamens and pistils protrude conspicuously. It grows on roadsides, banks and sandy or gravelly hillsides, especially in disturbed soil, from the montane through the alpine zones throughout our range.

SILVER SCORPIONWEED, *P. hastata (P. leucophylla),* is a branching, spreading plant with similar but paler flowers in coiled clusters and silvery, irregularly lobed foliage. *P. heterophylla* is closely related and both are common weeds on disturbed soil throughout our range.

The STICKY SCORPIONWEED, *P. glandulosa,* is an erect glandular-hairy species which always looks dark-colored. Its insignificant flowers are on erect 1-sided racemes of which there are usually several. It is widely distributed as a weed. THREADLEAF PHACELIA, *P. linearis,* is an annual erect, rough-hairy plant with a simple or branched stem 4 to 15 inches tall. Its flowers are saucer-shaped, bright blue or white, about ½-inch broad. This grows in Yellowstone National Park and on plains and hills in Idaho and Utah.

BORAGE FAMILY, *Boraginaceae*

Our plants of this family have united, 5-lobed, symmetrical corollas with 5 stamens attached to the corolla tube and alternating with its lobes. The flowers are usually white, blue or yellow and with the exception of the MERTENSIAS and LITHOSPERMUMS, which have long corolla tubes, they are on the same pattern as forget-me-not flowers, i.e. a short, inconspicuous tube with 5 spreading rounded lobes and little crests at the throat. The ovary is superior and the fruit consists of 4 separate seeds or nutlets though sometimes not all four mature. The branches of the inflorescence are often scorpioid, i.e., coiled to one side. In many species the plants are bristly-hairy.

a. Flowers blue; foliage may be hairy, but not bristly.
  b. Corollas with obvious tubes, longer than calyx lobes
                MERTENSIA, p. 235.
  bb. Corolla tubes short, hidden by calyx lobes .
    c. Plants 1 to 3 feet tall; nutlets prickly-edged
                STICKSEED FORGET-ME-NOT, p. 236.
    cc. Plants not over 1 foot tall; nutlet edges smooth.
      d. Cushion-type plants of alpine regions
                ALPINE FORGET-ME-NOT, p. 237.
      dd. Erect tufted plants; stems not over 1 foot tall
                MOUNTAIN FORGET-ME-NOT, p. 237.
aa. Flowers yellow or white; foliage with bristly hairs.
  b. Flowers yellow or orange.
    c. Corolla lobes toothed or fringed
                PUCCOON, p. 237.
    cc. Corolla lobes entire.
      d. Flowers orange
                FIDDLENECK, p. 238.
      dd. Flowers light yellow
                GOLDEN CRYPTANTHA, p. 239.
  bb. Flowers white or very pale bluish.
    c. Nutlets with prickles
                STICKSEED, p. 237.

cc. Nutlets without prickles but foliage bristly
MINERS CANDLE, p. 238.

MERTENSIA, CHIMINGBELLS or
MOUNTAIN BLUEBELL, *Mertensia.*
This genus has many species in the
mountains of western North America. It may be recognized by the
combination of blue, tubular, often
pendant, 5-lobed corollas and the
4-parted ovary which develops into
4 nutlets. Buds are often lavender
or pinkish and the leaves always
have entire margins.

a. Plants 1 to 3 feet tall; leaves with obvious side veins
TALL CHIMINGBELLS, p. 235.
aa. Plants rarely over 15 inches tall; leaves without side veins.
b. Stamens attached near throat; anthers easily visible.
c. Plants 6 to 15 inches tall; dry foothill and montane slopes
FOOTHILL MERTENSIA, p. 235.
cc. Plants usually less than 1 foot tall; moist locations
UTAH MERTENSIA, p. 235.
bb. Stamens attached in tube; anthers not easily visible.
c. Corollas 1/2- to 1 inch long; funnel-form.
d. Roots tuber-like, shallowly seated
LONG-FLOWER MERTENSIA, p. 235.
dd. Roots fibrous, deep seated
GREENLEAF MERTENSIA, p. 236.
cc. Corollas usually not over 1/2-inch long, bell-shaped
ALPINE MERTENSIA, p. 235.

TALL CHIMINGBELLS or MOUN-
TAIN BLUEBELLS, *M. ciliata* (264),
has smooth, entire, bluish-green
leaves with a few strong lateral
veins; dusty blue flowers which
hang in clusters are ½ to ¾ inch
long; buds pinkish; one of the most
lush plants of the high mountains.
Montana to New Mexico, often forming large clumps or beds along
streams and in wet places of subalpine zone. *M. franciscana* is similar
but has short stiff appressed hairs
on the upper leaf surface. It gradually replaces the former in the
southwest part of our range.

FOOTHILL MERTENSIA, *M. lanceolata.* Plant 10 to 15 inches tall with
stems often slanting upwards;
leaves usually smooth beneath and
more or less pubescent above, dull
green or distinctly bluish. The pink-
tinged buds are in tight clusters

which later become panicles. This
plant blooms in early spring and is
frequently seen on mesas, foothills
and in the montane zone on dry,
sunny fields and slopes, from Saskatchewan to New Mexico. In the
western part of our area from Montana through Wyoming and Utah is
the smaller *M. oblongifolia.*

UTAH MERTENSIA, *M. fusiformis,*
has erect stems from deep spindle-
shaped rootstocks and may be distinguished from other similar-
species by the character of its leaf
hairs which, on the upper leaf surface, always point towards the
margin of the leaf. Moist situations
of the montane and subalpine,
western Colorado and Utah. LONG-
FLOWER MERTENSIA, *M. longi-
flora,* with bright blue long-tubed
flowers, Montana to northeastern
California.

265. ALPINE MERTENSIA,   ½ ×

STICKSEED FORGET-ME-NOT, *Hackelia floribunda (Lappula floribunda)* (266), is usually a coarse tall plant up to 3 feet in height with blue flowers ⅛- to ⅓-inch across. The 4 (or 3) nutlets are armed

264. TALL CHIMINGBELLS, ½ ×

ALPINE MERTENSIA, *M. alpina* (265). The flowers of this have comparatively short tubes and spreading limb with rounded lobes which make them more showy than some other species. It is a rare plant of the upper subalpine and alpine zones from Montana to Idaho and New Mexico. GREENLEAF MERTENSIA, *M. viridis,* which grows in leafy tufts with stems 6 to 12 inches tall is the more common alpine species, especially in Colorado. It has fragrant bright blue flowers with corollas about ½-inch long and occurs on tundra meadows from Montana to Colorado and Utah.

266. STICKSEED   FORGET-ME-NOT,   ½ ×

with hooked prickles which assures their distribution as they catch in animal fur or human clothing. This often grows among bushes. COMMON STICKSEED, *Lappula redowskii,* has similar but much smaller flowers and seeds. Its flowers are usually white, less than ¼-inch in diameter. Both grow around buildings and along trails and roadsides throughout our area. HOUNDSTONGUE, *Cynoglossum officinale,* is another plant having prickly nutlets. It is an introduced weed, is tall, stout and erect, with oblong to lance-shaped white-velvety leaves and scorpioid racemes of small reddish-purple flowers; found along roads and around buildings.

ALPINE FORGET-ME-NOT, *Eritrichium elongatum (E. argenteum)* (267), is a cushion plant of the alpine meadows with fragrant, brilliantly blue, or sometimes white, yellow-eyed flowers. Its stems, from 1 to 3 inches tall, rise from compact rosettes of tiny silver-hairy leaves. [Color Pl. 9c]

This is one of the delightful alpine discoveries and a finder should go down on his knees to properly appreciate it. HOWARD ERITRICHIUM, *E. howardii,* which is similar but may be a little taller with darker blue flowers is found on dry hilltops in Montana. MOUNTAIN FORGET-ME-NOT, *Myosotis alpestris* (268), is closely related to the cultivated varieties and resembles them but usually its flowers are a deeper blue. Its stems are from 4 to 12 inches tall, usually tufted, and the individual flowers are ¼- to ⅓-inch in diameter. It grows in meadows and other moist places in the montane and subalpine zones from northwestern Colorado northward to Alaska.

PUCCOON, *Lithospermum.* Our plants of this genus are yellow-flowered with narrow, pubescent leaves. Their nutlets which are very hard are whitish, shiny and smooth and are well described by the generic name *Lithospermum* which means "stone-seed." NARROW-LEAF PUCCOON, *L. incisum,* has stems 6 to 18 inches tall, usually several in a clump. The yellow corollas are from ½- to 1½-inches long, salver-form with a slender tube and toothed or finely slashed lobes. The descriptive specific name *incisum* means "cut" or "slashed." Found on dry valleys and slopes of the mesas, foothills and lower montane zone throughout the Rockies. [Color Pl. 9d]

MANY-FLOWER PUCCOON, *L. multiflorum* (269), has smaller orange-yellow flowers and corolla lobes with entire margins. It occurs from the foothills to the subalpine zone

267. ALPINE FORGET-ME-NOT, ½ ×

268. MOUNTAIN FORGET-ME-NOT, ½ ×

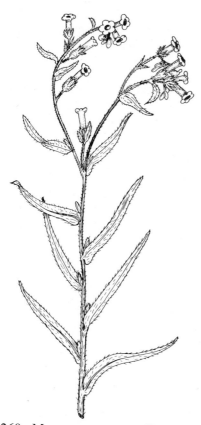

269. MANY-FLOWERED PUCCOON, ½ ×

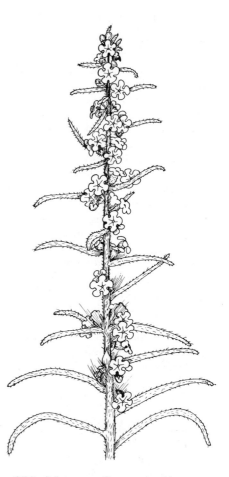

270. MINERS CANDLE, ½ ×

and from Wyoming to Mexico. WAYSIDE GROMWELL, *L. ruderale,* has many unbranched stems and very small pale yellow flowers almost hidden by long upper leaves. Its big woody root was cooked and eaten by Indians. FIDDLENECK, *Amsinkia rugosa (A. retrorsa),* is a very rough plant covered with bristly hairs. It has orange flowers arranged in a one-sided, coiled spike which resembles a fiddle neck. This is found in Idaho, Utah and probably western Colorado on fields and waste ground.

MINERS CANDLE, *Cryptantha virgata* (270). Stems 10 inches to 2 feet tall, unbranched; covered with bristly hairs; flowers white, like forget-me-nots, in short coiled clusters along the erect stem, interspersed with linear, leaf-like bracts longer than the flower clusters. Found on open dry fields and hillsides of Wyoming and Colorado from 5,000 to 9,000 feet.

BUSHY CRYPTANTHA, *C. thyrsiflora,* with 1 to several stout stems and a broad round-topped inflorescence is common on dry foothill slopes along the eastern side of the Continental Divide from Wyoming to New Mexico. These plants usually die after blooming but the dry bristly stalks often stand through the winter.

The common MINERS CANDLE in Montana is *C. bradburiana* which is found on dry plains and hills and is even more prickly than the first one and there are several other bristly species with similar white flowers in the semi-arid regions of our area.

GOLDEN CRYPTANTHA, *C. flava,* is a yellow-flowered species having several stems with narrow crowded inflorescences. It occurs on dry foothill fields and slopes from Wyoming and Utah through western Colorado to New Mexico and Arizona.

POPCORN FLOWER, *Plagiobothrys scopulorum,* is a much branched annual plant of sandy or moist soil found at the lower altitudes in our area. Its lower leaves are opposite.

VERBENA FAMILY,
Verbenaceae

The plants of this family have opposite or whorled leaves which, in our species, are toothed or more or less lobed or divided. The blue, purple or rose-colored flowers have 4 stamens and the united corollas, which may be slightly irregular, have 4 or 5 lobes. Most species of this family grow at altitudes below our range.

WILD VERBENA, *Verbena ambrosifolia,* is occasionally found on the high plains and lower foothills along the eastern and southern fringes of the Rockies. It is a branching plant with decumbent stems, deeply pinnatifid leaves and clusters of showy rose-purple flowers.

VERVAIN, *V. bracteata,* is similar in habit of branching but has small light blue or purplish flowers in conspicuously bracted spikes. It occurs as a weed in gardens, fields and along roadsides over most of North America and is found up to 7,500 feet in Colorado.

MINT FAMILY, *Labiatae*

The plants of this family have opposite leaves, square stems, irregular flowers with 2-lipped corollas and some have aromatic foliage. Leaves are simple but usually their margins are more or less toothed or finely scalloped. The stamens are 4 or 2 and the 4-lobed ovary ripens into 4 small nutlets, each containing one seed.

a. Stamens 2.
  b. Foliage fragrantly aromatic.
    c. Flowers rose purple, in heads
               MONARDA, p. 240.
    cc. Flowers pink, in small axillary clusters
               PENNYROYAL, p. 240.
  bb. Foliage not strongly fragrant; flowers white or bluish
               LANCELEAF SAGE, p. 242.
aa. Stamens 4.
  b. Foliage strongly aromatic.
    c. Flowers in terminal, globose clusters
               CLOVERHEAD HORSEMINT, p. 240.
    cc. Flowers in axillary clusters
               WILD MINT, p. 242.
  bb. Foliage not strongly aromatic.
    c. Flowers in pairs, blue-purple
               SKULLCAP, p. 240.

240   ROCKY MOUNTAIN PLANTS

cc. Flowers in dense spikes or heads.
  d. Leaves and bracts spine-tipped
                    DRAGONHEAD, p. 242.
  dd. Leaves and bracts not spine-tipped.
    e. Foliage usually smooth.
      f. Stems 2 to 6 feet tall
                    GIANT HYSSOP, p. 241.
    ff. Stems less than 1 foot tall
                    PRUNELLA, p. 242.
    ee. Foliage definitely hairy.
      f. Flower spikes compact, under 1 inch diameter
                    GERMANDER, p. 241.
    ff. Flower spikes loose, 1 inch or over in diameter
                    WOUNDWORT, p. 241.

Monarda, Horsemint or Bergamot, *Monarda fistulosa (M. menthaefolia)* (271). A showy perennial plant with rounded rose-colored heads, each individual flower about 1½-inch long. Each corolla is slashed into 2 lips; the 2 stamens protrude from the upper one, the lower is 3-lobed and spreading; the stems are 1 to 2 feet tall with fragrant, opposite, ovate-lanceolate, serrate leaves on short petioles. Grows in meadows and ravines and along roadsides, often in clumps or patches, in the foothill and montane zones throughout our range. The flowers are frequently visited by bees and humming birds.

Whorled Monarda, *M. pectinata,* is an annual plant branched from the base, 6 to 15 inches tall,

271. Monarda, ½ ×

with smaller pinkish flowers arranged in tiers around the stems. It occurs in the foothill zone from Colorado and Utah south to Mexico.

Cloverhead Horsemint, *Monardella odoratissima,* has a base of woody twisted stems with branches not over a foot tall which are softly hairy. The pale purple flowers are in small clusters surrounded by purplish bracts. The Latin adjective *odoratissima* means "most fragrant." This occurs in the montane zone from Montana through western Colorado to Utah and New Mexico.

Pennyroyal, *Hedeoma drummondii,* is a bushy little gray plant, 3 to 10 inches tall, with slender pink blossoms in the leaf axils, which grows on dry ground of the foothill ridges throughout the Rockies.

Skullcap, *Scutellaria brittonii* (272). A plant with erect stems 4 to 10 inches tall which grow from creeping underground rootstocks. The rich purplish-blue flowers are in pairs, standing erect in the leaf axils. This plant takes its common name from the cap-shaped calyx. It is found on slopes of the foothill and montane zones from Wyoming to New Mexico.

A similar but larger plant is the Marsh Skullcap, *S. galericulata,* which occurs on wet ground around

272. SKULLCAP, ½ ×

273. WOUNDWORT, ½ ×

lakes and ponds and on ditch banks of the foothills and lower montane zone and is widely distributed in northern North America, Europe and Asia.

NARROW-LEAF SKULLCAP, *S. angustifolia,* has long petioled lower leaves and much narrower, almost sessile, upper ones. The axillary flowers are from nearly 1 inch to 1½-inches long. This species occurs on moist soil from Montana and Idaho to Utah.

GIANT HYSSOP, *Agastache urticifolia,* has stems from 2 to 6 feet tall and terminal, compact spike-like clusters of white, rose or purplish flowers from 2 to 6 inches long. Its ovate to triangular-ovate leaves are usually smooth at least above and lighter colored beneath. It occurs on moist soil of the mon-

tane and lower subalpine zones throughout our range.

WOUNDWORT, *Stachys palustris* (273), is a somewhat similar but smaller and distinctly hairy plant. It rarely exceeds 2½-feet in height and its inflorescence is less dense. The flowers are usually in threes in the axils of leafy bracts and are pale lavender with darker spots on the lip. This species grows on moist soil and is widely distributed in North America.

GERMANDER, *Teucrium canadense,* a plant 1 to 2 feet tall has unbranched stems, except sometimes branching in the inflorescence. Flowers small, purple, in slender compact spikes 4 to 8 inches long; calyx covered with long soft sticky hairs; stem 4-angled; leaves narrow, pointed, opposite, 2 to 4 inches

274. PRUNELLA, ½ ×

long. Moist soil in foothills of the Rockies and widespread throughout North America.

PRUNELLA or SELFHEAL, *Prunella vulgaris* (274), has short blunt spikes of purple flowers interspersed with broad clasping bracts, and opposite entire leaves. It grows on more or less shaded, moist soil of meadows and roadsides of the upper foothill and montane zones, and is widely distributed in the cooler parts of North America, Europe and Asia.

WILD MINT, *Mentha arvensis (M. canadensis),* is an aromatic plant with pale lavender or pinkish flowers in dense clusters in the leaf axils, which grows from 4 to 15 inches tall. Its leaves are oblong, rounded at base and pointed at tip, the margins with rounded or sharp teeth; a circumpolar species found on moist meadows of the Rockies up to an elevation of 9,500 feet. Its leaves are useful for flavoring beverages.

There are two widely distributed annual weedy species in this family found on waste ground or disturbed soil; LANCELEAF SAGE, *Salvia reflexa (S. lanceolata),* an inconspicuous plant with pale blue or whitish flowers in the leaf axils usually seen as a weed in gardens or on vacant lots and DRAGONHEAD, *Moldavica parviflora (Dracocephalum parviflorum),* which has dense spikes of blue or pinkish flowers interspersed with spine-tipped, pectinate (comblike) bracts and is frequently seen on burned-over areas.

POTATO FAMILY, *Solanaceae*

Plants of this family have flowers with regular, united, usually 5-lobed corollas which may be from tubular to wheel-shaped, and 2-celled ovaries which ripen into several-seeded berries or dry capsules. Often the fruits are enclosed in the enlarged calyx. Some of the species are poisonous and the family also includes several important vegetables such as, potatos, tomatos, egg-plant and green and red peppers, besides tobacco and petunias.

a. Fruits are dry capsules.
  b. Corolla open funnel-form.
    c. Flowers 2 to 5 inches long, white or violet
                JIMSON WEED, p. 243.
    cc. Flowers 1/2- to 1 inch long, greenish or purplish
                HENBANE, p. 243.
  bb. Corolla tubular, funnel-form, or salver-shaped
                WILD TOBACCO, p. 243.

aa. Fruits are berries but sometimes enclosed in a spiny or papery husk.

   b. Plant very bristly; leaves pinnately lobed
BUFFALO-BUR, p. 243.

  bb. Plant not spiny; leaves not lobed.

   c. Berry enclosed in the enlarged, papery calyx
FENDLER GROUNDCHERRY, p. 244.

  cc. Berry not so enclosed
WILD POTATO, p. 243.

JIMSON WEED or THORNAPPLE, *Datura stramonium,* is a stout, coarse plant with large irregularly toothed leaves 4 to 8 inches long. The calyx is 5-angled and the large white or violet, funnel-form corolla is plaited with little pointed tips on each lobe. The thorny ovoid fruit is about 2 inches high. This introduced plant has a worldwide distribution as a weed on waste or cultivated ground and is sometimes seen in our foothill region.

Another widely distributed, introduced weed is HENBANE, *Hyocyanus niger,* which is a coarse, strong-scented, sticky plant which has greenish-yellow flowers with purplish veins occuring in the upper leaf axils and in terminal racemes. The seed capsules are vase-shaped. Seeds and foliage are poisonous. Found around buildings and along roadsides.

WILD TOBACCO, *Nicotiana attenuata,* is an annual, sticky, usually-branched plant 1 to 2 feet tall, with terminal clusters of greenish-white flowers. The corollas are 1 to 2 inches long, tubular with spreading lobes. The lower leaves are ovate, the middle ones lanceolate with the upper becoming linear. Found on sandy ground of the foothills from Montana to Utah and New Mexico.

BUFFALO-BUR, *Solanum rostratum* (275). A branched plant with saucer-shaped yellow flowers an inch or more across, and irregularly pinnately lobed leaves covered with yellowish bristles. The leaf lobes are rounded. The fruit is enclosed in the bristly calyx. This is seen on waste ground, roadsides and overgrazed pastures of the high plains and lower foothills.

WILD POTATO, *S. jamesii.* This is a true potato, closely related to our cultivated variety and bears small round tubers on its underground stems. The leaves are compound, made up of 5 to 9 lance-shaped to ovate-oblong leaflets. The corollas are ½- to 1-inch across, usually white, deeply 5-lobed. It was used by the Indians of the Southwest as food and grown by them in their gardens. It is found in southern Colorado, Utah, Arizona, and New Mexico, growing mostly in the

275. BUFFALO-BUR, 2/5 ×

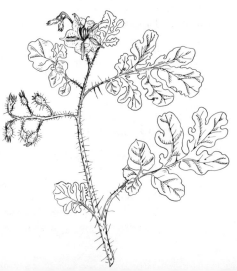

coniferous forests of the montane zone.

FENDLER GROUNDCHERRY, *Physalis fendleri* (276), has ovate or triangular leaves with somewhat wavy margins and dull yellowish flowers with brownish centers. The corolla is open bell-shaped ½- to 1-inch wide. As the fruit ripens, the calyx enlarges and encloses the berry in a papery, lantern-like husk. These berries were gathered for food by Southwestern Indians. The plants grow on rocky ground of dry plains and hills from Colorado and Utah southwards.

276. FENDLER   GROUNDCHERRY,
2/5 ×

FIGWORT FAMILY, *Scrophulariaceae*

Many beautiful wildflowers are found in this family. Their corollas are irregular, mostly 2-lipped and the lips are usually lobed. There is a superior ovary which ripens into a 2-celled seed capsule. The leaves are frequently but not always opposite. Stamens are 2, 4 or 5, but except in the first genus, MULLEIN, never more than 4 are anther bearing. A more or less reduced, sterile stamen, called a *staminode*, is sometimes present. Some plants of this family which have opposite leaves also have 4-angled stems and so might be confused with members of the mint family but plants of the Figwort Family may always be distinguished by the 2-celled ovary which ripens into a dry, many-seeded capsule, whereas members of the mint family have fruits consisting of 4 nutlets. The cultivated snapdragons and several other garden flowers belong here.

```
a. Corollas only slightly irregular, nearly rotate.
  b. Flowers yellow or white
                        MULLEIN, - p. 245.
  bb. Flowers blue
                        VERONICA, p. 246.
aa. Corollas strongly irregular, definitely 2-lipped
  b. Corolla spurred
                        BUTTER-AND-EGGS, p. 245.
  bb. Corolla not spurred.
    c. Stamens only 2
                        KITTENTAILS, p. 246.
  cc. Stamens 4 or 5 but only 4 with anthers.
    d. Stamens 5 but 1 sterile and sometimes inconspicuous.
      e. Flowers many, greenish, or brown
                        LANCELEAF FIGWORT, p. 247.
```

ee. Flowers few to many, bright colored or white
PENSTEMON, p. 247.
dd. Stamens 4 and all with anthers.
  e. Flowers in terminal brush-like clusters .
    f. Upper corolla lip much longer than lower
PAINTBRUSH, p. 254.
    ff. Upper corolla lip not much longer than lower
OWLCLOVER, p. 256.
  ee. Flowers not in brush-like clusters.
    f. Upper lip of corolla arched upward at center; leaves
      opposite.
      g. Stem 4-angled; calyx enlarged in fruit
YELLOW-RATTLE, p. 256.
      gg. Stems round; calyx not conspicuously enlarged
LOUSEWORT, p. 256.
    ff. Upper lip of corolla not conspicuously arched upward at
      center.
      g. Leaves alternate
BIRDSBEAK, p. 256.
      gg. Leaves opposite
MONKEY-FLOWER, p. 258.

COMMON MULLEIN, *Verbascum thapsus,* is a tall weed of roadsides, banks and waste ground. It is biennial and during the first season it develops beautiful pale green rosettes which may become as large as plates. The leaves are covered with tangled, yellowish, wool-like hairs. The second season an erect stem develops which may grow to a height of 6 feet and bears a long spike of yellow saucer-shaped flowers which are only slightly irregular. The corolla is 5-lobed and in the bud is always folded so that one lobe is entirely outside the others. This has 5 fertile stamens, and the three upper ones have their filaments decorated with longish hairs.

MOTH MULLEIN, *V. blatteria,* is smaller with almost smooth leaves and is less frequently seen. Its stamens all have knob-tipped, purple hairs along the filaments. Both species have been introduced from Europe.

Another introduced plant frequently seen around settlements and along roadsides is BUTTER-AND-EGGS, *Linaria vulgaris* (277), with its racemes of pale yellow and

277. BUTTER-AND-EGGS,   ½ ×

bright orange, long-spurred flowers.

TOAD-FLAX, *L. canadensis (L. texana),* is a native species with blue flowers ¾- to 1-inch long. About ⅓ of this length consists of the spur. It grows in the eastern part of our range below 7500 feet.

BLUE-EYED MARY, *Collinsia parviflora,* is a delicate plant with pale blue or white corollas not over ¼-inch long. The pointed, sometimes purplish, leaves are opposite on the lower stem and whorled above. In the whorls there are usually 2 to 5 flowers. It grows on shaded ground where other vegetation is sparse, in the foothill and montane zones throughout the Rockies.

VERONICA or SPEEDWELL, *Veronica.* Our species of this genus are small plants which grow in wet or moist places, with blue or rarely whitish, flowers in terminal or axillary racemes. The corollas are rotate and 4-lobed and there are only 2 stamens.

ALPINE VERONICA or ALPINE SPEEDWELL, *V. wormskjoldii (V. alpina)* (278), is a slender erect plant usually about 4 to 8 inches tall with a terminal raceme of dark blue flowers, and opposite, sessile, ovate to oblong leaves. The flattened capsule is slightly notched at the top. This occurs in moist tundra among grasses and sedges and in wet mountain meadows of northern North America from the Arctic south to New Hampshire, New Mexico and California and is found in the Rockies up to 12,500 feet.

AMERICAN SPEEDWELL, *V. americana,* is a trailing plant of wet locations with opposite, ovate or lanceolate leaves and axillary racemes of small blue flowers. It grows in shallow water or mud around springs and along streams

and is widely distributed in North America.

THYMELEAF SPEEDWELL, *V. serpyllifolia* var. *humifusa,* is a creeping plant with stems to a foot long which root at the lower axils and end in racemes of blue or sometimes white flowers. It is widely distributed in moist soil.

KITTENTAILS, *Besseya plantaginea* (279), has a basal rosette of rounded or oval, petioled leaves and erect spikes from 8 to 15 inches tall. The individual flowers are white to pinkish but very small and densely crowded. This occurs on moist wooded slopes of the foothill and

278. ALPINE VERONICA, 2/5 ×

279. KITTENTAILS, 2/5 ×

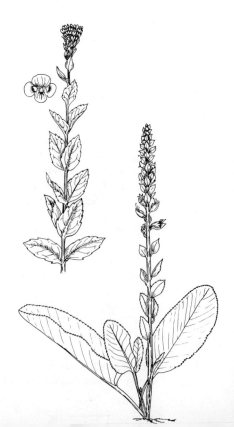

montane zones from Wyoming to New Mexico. In Colorado it is only on the eastern side of the Continental Divide, but there is a similar plant having yellowish flowers called *B. ritteriana* in the mountains of southwestern Colorado.

ALPINE KITTENTAILS, *B. alpina,* with somewhat woolly foliage and fuzzy purplish spikes from 2 to 6 inches tall, occurs among rocks of the alpine zone from Wyoming and Utah to New Mexico. This might be confused with PURPLE FRINGE, fig. 263, but the latter has fern-like leaves. This genus was named in honor of Charles Edwin Bessey, for many years professor of botany at the University of Nebraska.

LANCELEAF FIGWORT, *Scrophularia lanceolata* (280), is another weedy plant found on disturbed soil of roadbanks and around buildings. It grows from 1½ to 4 feet tall, is coarse and has a narrow inflorescence of small green or greenish-brown flowers. The 2 lobes of its upper lip stand erect. This occurs occasionally throughout our region in the foothill and montane zones.

280. LANCE-LEAF FIGWORT, 2/5 ×

PENSTEMON or BEARDTONGUE, *Penstemon.* The name means "5 stamens" and refers to the fact that although most members of this family have only 4 stamens, this genus regularly has 5, but the fifth has no anther and is, therefore, not functional. It is called a staminode and differs somewhat from the 4 fertile stamens in shape. In many species it has a tuft or brush of hairs at its tip or along one side. From this character comes the common name BEARDTONGUE. The united corolla is irregular and 2-lipped, the upper lip has 2 lobes, the lower 3; it may be tubular-funnelform or it may be bulged or inflated above a short, slender tube. The leaves are opposite, the inflorescence often one-sided.

Since there are so many more or less similar species the following key only divides them into groups according to color, size and habit of growth. Most of the normally tall ones may begin blooming when their stems are very short, especially if the season or location is unfavorable. The blue and purple kinds vary a good deal in color, and sometimes have pink or white forms.

Flower size is about the most dependable character. The species descriptions and distributional notes will help to distinguish individual species. One should look around for more plants of the same kind and take the average to get an estimate of size and height.

Several Penstemon species are restricted in their distribution to rather small areas in the Colorado mountains, and in a different locality will be replaced by a similar but different species. Less than half the kinds known to grow in the Rocky Mountains can be described here.

a. Flowers bright, scarlet red
> The SCARLET-FLOWERED PEN-STEMONS, p. 248.

aa. Flowers blue, purple, rose, or white.
  b. Plants with creeping stems, forming mats, usually less than 6 inches high
> The CREEPING PENSTEMONS, p. 249.

  bb. Plants with erect stems from 4 to 40 inches tall.
    c. Flowers averaging from 2/3- to over 1 inch long.
      d. Stems mostly over 15 inches tall
> The LARGE-FLOWERED TALL PENSTEMONS, p. 250.

      dd. Stems mostly less than 20 inches tall
> The LARGE-FLOWERED LOW PENSTEMONS, p. 251.

    cc. Flowers usually averaging less than 3/4-inches long.
      d. Inflorescence interrupted; flowers in clusters
> The CLUSTERED PENSTEMONS, p. 251.

      dd. Inflorescence elongated, usually in narrow clusters.
        e. Stems usually over 12 inches tall
> The SMALL-FLOWERED TALL PENSTEMONS, p. 252.

        ee. Stems usually less than 12 inches tall
> The SMALL-FLOWERED LOW PENSTEMONS, p. 253.

SCARLET-FLOWERED PENTSTEMONS

SCARLET BUGLER, *P. barbatus,* or TORREY PENSTEMON has stems 15 inches to 3 feet tall, solitary or in clumps, with a spire-like panicle of brilliant scarlet tubular flowers. The 3 lobes of the lower corolla lip are reflexed. The leaves and smooth stem are often dark and tinged with reddish. This is found from the Pikes Peak region of Colorado south and west to New Mexico and Arizona in the montane zone. (285)

EATON PENSTEMON, FIRECRACK-ER PENSTEMON, *P. eatonii,* is similar but has somewhat shorter stems and the corollas are scarcely 2-lipped, their short lobes not reflexed. It occurs from Mesa Verde National Park, where it is quite common around the ruins, southwestward. [Color Pl. 9e]

BRIDGES PENSTEMON, *P. bridgesii,* has stems to 2 feet tall, the upper part often branched, from a somewhat woody base. The scarlet corollas are strongly 2-lipped with the upper lip erect and the lower reflexed. It grows in the oak-piñon-juniper areas of the southwest with a range similar to the last.

281. CRANDALL PENSTEMON, ½ ×

crandallii

barbatus

285.   SCARLET BUGLER or TORREY
PENSTEMON 2/5 ×

CREEPING and MAT-FORMING PENSTEMONS

CRANDALL PENSTEMON, *P. crandallii* (281), forms a mat 4 to 6 inches thick of small green leaves, mostly less than an inch long and not over ¼-inch wide, which may become covered, in May or early June, with blue or purple, inch-long flowers. This grows on loamy soils of the montane and lower subalpine zones from central Colorado south and west into Utah. C. S. Crandall was professor of botany at Colorado Agricultural College (now Colorado State University) from 1889 to 1899. During those years he made extensive botanical collections in the state which became the basis for early publications on the flora of Colorado.

GRAYLEAF CREEPING PENSTEMON or GERMANDER PENSTEMON, *P. teucrioides,* has slender stems and small narrow leaves covered with very fine gray hairs; the flowers are pale purple, nearly an inch long. This low, creeping plant is usually found growing among sagebrush on dry slopes of the montane zone in central and southwestern Colorado.

HARBOUR ALPINE PENSTEMON, *P. harbourii,* is a creeping plant, the stems not rising higher than 6 inches, the leaves dull green or grayish, from ½- to 1-inch long and ¼-inch wide. The corollas are almost an inch long, light purple and hairy inside and outside. It is strictly an alpine species, found only on scree or gravel slopes of the high Colorado peaks.

MAT PENSTEMON, *P. caespitosus,* has stems not over 3 inches high but spreads into mats as large as 4 feet in diameter. The leaves which are usually less than 1 inch long and ¼-inch wide, may be grayish or green; flowers are ½- to ¾-inch long, light blue or purplish. It may be distinguished from the last two by its thin, compact, carpet-like mat. It occurs in western Wyoming, northwestern Colorado, and northeastern Utah on clay or rocky soil in sagebrush country between 6000 and 9000 feet.

ROCKVINE PENSTEMON or ALPINE BEARDTONGUE, *P. ellipticus,* forms loose mats. It is somewhat woody at base with smooth leaves ½- to 1¼-inches long and showy, light violet-colored flowers 1½-inches long with the staminode heavily bearded with long yellow hairs. It grows on rock slides and cliff faces above and below timberline from the Canadian Rockies into western Montana and northern Idaho and is especially conspicuous in Glacier National Park.

LARGE-FLOWERED TALL PENSTEMONS

ONESIDE, or TALL PENSTEMON, *P. unilateralis,* is a very showy species with stems up to 2 feet in height which are usually slightly curved upwards from the base. It has blue and purple expanded corollas. The anthers are always smooth and the staminode usually smooth. In northern Colorado it grows as a biennial or short-lived perennial on overgrazed pastures and areas of disturbed soil, often producing fields of bluish-purple color. In some areas it appears to be perennial. From southeastern Wyoming to southern Colorado along the eastern slope of the mountains and up to 10,000 feet, it is the commonest tall penstemon. In New Mexico and Arizona it is replaced by the similar *P. virgatus.*

ROCKY MOUNTAIN PENSTEMON, *P. strictus,* has larger, darker blue flowers, is somewhat 1-sided with stems from 8 inches to 2¼-feet tall, has long hairs on the anthers and the staminode is usually bearded. It is widely distributed from southern Wyoming to Arizona but is most common on the western side of the Continental Divide.

MOUNTAIN BEARDTONGUE or PIKES PEAK PENSTEMON, *P. alpinus,* (282), is another very showy species. Its stems are stouter and usually not so tall as the last two; the stalks often grow in clumps and the 1-sided inflorescence is rather stubby at apex. The flowers are usually a clear, intense blue. It occurs on gravelly soils, being especially luxuriant in places on the red granitic gravel of the Pikes Peak region and is sometimes seen on earth dams. It is one of the species collected by Edwin James on that first ascent, by white men, of this

282. MOUNTAIN   BEARDTONGUE,
     ½ ×

famous mountain in July of 1820 (see p.150). It grows from southeastern Wyoming to northern New Mexico extending up to 11,000 feet, along the eastern slope. [Color Pl. 9f]

WASATCH PENSTEMON, *P. cyan-* *thus,* is a tall, handsome blue-flowered species found from southwestern Montana through western Wyoming and eastern Idaho into the Wasatch Mountains of Utah. Its anthers are covered with short, stiff hairs.

LARGE-FLOWERED LOW PENSTEMONS

CRESTED PENSTEMON, *P. eriantherus,* has stems from 5 to 15 inches tall; stems and leaves are sticky-hairy; flowers are an inch or more long, usually pinkish or pale purple and the staminode, which is bearded with long yellow hairs, protrudes conspicuously. This is a plant of the high plains and foothills North Dakota to northern Colorado and northwestward to Canada.

BUSH PENSTEMON, *P. fruticosus,* forms a wide, dense clump 4 to 20 inches high from a woody base. The leaves are thick and shiny, more or less toothed, ½- to 2½-inches long; the inflorescence is somewhat 1-sided with bright lavender-blue flowers about 1½-inches long and ½-inch wide. It has hairy anthers and a yellowbearded staminode. This is found on rocky slopes in openings of the coniferous forests from the mountains of Montana and Wyoming westward.

A similar but smaller plant is CORDROOT PENSTEMON, *P. montanus,* which has sharply toothed leaves and a smooth staminode. It occurs on stony montane and subalpine slopes in Wyoming, Idaho and Montana.

WHIPPLE PENSTEMON or DARK PENSTEMON, *P. whippleanus,* is easily recognized in its most common from by the very dark wine red or purple, almost black, bell-shaped corollas. These flowers, about 1½-inches long, are in whorls more or less separated, or sometimes in single head-like clusters. The stems vary from 4 to 18 inches in height and the plants are found on rocky or openly wooded slopes or along trails, from the montane to the alpine zones, most abundantly in the subalpine region. Idaho, Wyoming, Colorado, Utah to Arizona and New Mexico. There are forms of this species which have dingy blue or whitish flowers. [Color Pl. 10b]

HALLS ALPINE PENSTEMON, *P. hallii,* usually has several erect stems 4 to 8 inches tall from tufts of smooth, oblanceolate leaves. The flowers are in rather few-flowered clusters on the shorter plants or in an elongated, 1-sided inflorescence on the taller ones. The corollas are about an inch long, bright reddish purple or violet with white markings at the throat and are abruptly inflated. It grows in rocky or gravelly situations on the higher peaks of central and southern Colorado from 10,000 to 13,000 feet.

SAND PENSTEMON, *P. ambiguous,* with phlox-like pink and white flowers occurs on the eastern plains and foothills. [Color Pl. 10a]

CLUSTERED PENSTEMONS

CLUSTERED OR TINY-BLOOM PENSTEMON, *P. procerus (P. micran- thus)* (283). The erect stems are from 4 to 12 inches tall and the

½ ×

283. CLUSTERED PENSTEMON,

small, tubular, dark blue, slightly 2-lipped flowers, which occur in whorls or separated clusters, are usually not more than ½-inch long. The plant grows in moist meadows of the montane and subalpine zones, and is sometimes found as high as 12,000 feet. It occurs from Alaska to southcentral Colorado, especially in the eastern part of our range.

A similar but larger species found farther west is RYDBERG PENSTEMON, *P. rydbergii.*

YELLOW PENSTEMON, *P. confertus.* The slender stems are usually clustered, 7 to 24 inches tall, with interrupted inflorescences made up of clusters of half-inch-long, light yellow or whitish, tubular corollas. Brown hairs inside the lower lip. Range is northern; common in Glacier.

SMALL-FLOWERED TALL PENSTEMONS

WATSON PENSTEMON, *P. watsonii,* usually grows in clumps having several stems 1 to 2 feet tall. There is no basal rosette and the upper leaves are ¾- to 2½-inches long and larger than the lower ones. Its many blue or purplish flowers have the staminode bearded with long yellow hairs. This occurs from southwestern Wyoming through western Colorado and Utah to northwestern Arizona, and in Idaho and Nevada. It grows among sagebrush or other brushy vegetation.

SLENDER PENSTEMON, *P. gracilis,* has stems from 10 to 20 inches tall which usually grow alone or sometimes a few together. The leaves are entire or finely toothed, the basal ones blunt and the upper ones long pointed. The flowers are pale blue or lavender, somewhat sticky outside and with hairs inside. The lower lip projects beyond the upper one. The staminode is densely bearded but does not stick out. This is an eastern species growing from Ontario and Wisconsin to the eastern slope of the Rockies where it occurs along the base of the mountains among scrub oak or pines and in foothill meadows, from Alberta to New Mexico.

SIDEBELLS PENSTEMON or PURPLE BEARDTONGUE, *P. secundiflorus* (284), with stems from 4 to 20 inches tall, is one of our most charming wildflowers. The leaves clasp the stem and are smooth, thick and glaucous (light gray or bluish) and make a beautiful combination with the rose, lilac or purple blossoms. The slender, definitely one-sided inflorescence often has its tip slightly curved down, especially when still partly in bud. The corolla flares into an open throat showing the staminode strongly-bearded with dark yellow hairs. This grows on hillsides of the foothill and montane zones from southern Wyoming through central Colorado into New Mexico.

MATROOT PENSTEMON, *P. radicosus,* forms clumps of slender stems up to 14 inches tall; its leaves are grayish and its flowers, in rather compact clusters, vary from pale to dark blue. This is found in Yellowstone National Park and from Montana southward through western Wyoming and Idaho to north central Colorado. It grows in the montane zone, often in rocky or sagebrush areas.

Secund forms

284. SIDEBELLS PENSTEMON, ½ ×

SMALL-FLOWERED LOW PENSTEMONS

SIDEBELLS PENSTEMON, fig. 284, and MATROOT PENSTEMON, often have stems less than a foot tall, for descriptions see above.

COLORADO PENSTEMON, *P. linarioides* ssp. *coloradoensis,* is a plant with wiry stems from 4 to 10 inches tall from a heavy woody base. Its leaves are narrow, crowded and grayish. The inflorescence is 1-sided of lavender or lilac-colored flowers about ¾-inch long, corollas strongly inflated and lightly bearded inside. This is found on rocky ground and among sagebrush on the upper foothill and montane zones of southwestern Colorado and northwestern New Mexico.

SKYBLUE PENSTEMON, *P. angustifolius,* has rather stout stems from 4 to 10 inches tall with glaucous leaves which have prominent midribs, and cylindrical inflorescences of pale or bright blue flowers less than 1 inch long. The buds and some of the corollas are often tinged with pink. This is a plant of the mesas and lower foothills along the eastern slope and is sometimes found on vacant lots in the towns, where it is one of the spring-blooming flowers. It occurs from North Dakota and eastern Montana to New Mexico.

BLUE-MIST PENSTEMON or GREENLEAF PENSTEMON, *P. virens.* This plant has numerous erect stems which may be from 4 to 14 inches tall but are usually between 6 and 10 inches, from mats of bright green, shiny leaves. It blooms in such masses on some foothill slopes as to give them a misty blue appearance from a distance. It is especially noticeable during late May in the scrub-oak country between Castle Rock and Colorado Springs and from there along Highway 24 up Ute Pass. Its range extends up to 10,500 feet along the eastern slope of the Divide from southern Wyoming through Colorado. At the higher altitudes it blooms in June or early July.

LOW PENSTEMON, *P. humilis,* is a rather similar plant with duller leaves which is found in Yellowstone National Park and through western Wyoming into northwestern Colorado and Idaho.

NELSON LARCHLEAF PENSTEMON, *P. laricifolius* var. *exilifolius,* is a plant with several, slender stems 5 to 9 inches tall from a cushion of very narrow, bright green leaves. The dainty white, greenish or sometimes pinkish, corolla is from ½- to ¾-inch long, the tube abruptly inflated and with spreading lips. This occurs on the dry rocky plains and hills of north central Colorado and southeastern Wyoming between the altitudes of 7000 and 9000 feet.

SNOWLOVER, *Chionophila jamesii,* is a small alpine plant similar to and closely related to the penstemons. Its stems are rarely more than 4 inches tall with short, 1-sided spikes of white or cream-colored flowers. The staminode is shorter than the stamens and smooth. This grows on moist, gravel slopes of high mountains in Wyoming and Colorado.

INDIAN PAINTBRUSH or PAINTED CUP, *Castilleja.* Many plants with gay colors belong to this group but the flowers themselves are inconspicuous. Red, orange, pink or white calyxes and leafy bracts surrounding the flowers in brush-like inflorescences produce the showy effect. Some of the species have a wide range of color variation and several are difficult to identify accurately. The corolla is 2-lipped with the upper lip extended into a long beak-like *galea* which includes the 4-stamens and the much shorter lower lip is tucked up under it.

a. Bracts orange or some shade of rose or red.
  b. Bracts orange-red; spring-blooming plants of the foothills
              FOOTHILLS PAINTBRUSH, p. 254.
  bb. Bracts scarlet, crimson, or rose
    c. Stems branched; green corollas protruding; bracts scarlet
              WYOMING PAINTBRUSH, p. 254.
    cc. Stems usually unbranched.
      d. Bracts entire or shallowly lobed, scarlet
              SCARLET PAINTBRUSH, p. 255.
      dd. Bracts, at least some of them, deeply lobed
              ROSY PAINTBRUSH, p. 255.
aa. Bracts whitish or yellowish.
  b. Stems often branched; bracts whitish or greenish
              NORTHERN PAINTBRUSH, p. 255.
  bb. Stems unbranched, in clumps; bracts yellow
              WESTERN PAINTBRUSH, p. 255.

FOOTHILLS or ORANGE PAINTBRUSH, *C. integra,* is a spring-blooming plant of mesas and lower foothills growing in clumps with stems from 4 to 12 inches tall and with its showy bracts mostly entire; found from Wyoming to Oregon and south to New Mexico. [Pl. 10f.]

NELSON PAINTBRUSH, *C. chromosa,* is rather similar as to color, but the upper leaves and bracts are divided into narrow lobes. It occurs in Wyoming on dry, high plains, mesas and foothills and southward to New Mexico.

WYOMING PAINTBRUSH, *C. linariaefolia* (286), is a branched plant up to 2 feet or more in height with 'brushes" of scarlet bracts and calyxes from which the green, general its bracts are not scarlet. They may be crimson, rose, purple or pink, or even 2-toned. These varying color forms may be of hybrid origin. It is a subalpine species and sometimes provides beautiful displays of color in the high meadows throughout our range. [Color Pl. 10d,e]

NORTHERN PAINTBRUSH, *C. septentrionalis,* has whitish bracts; its stems are solitary or few together and are sometimes branched at least once. It grows in moist aspen groves and shaded meadows of the montane and subalpine zones of the Rockies and also in moist meadows of eastern Canada and New England.

WESTERN YELLOW PAINTBRUSH, *C. occidentalis* (287), grows in clumps with stems 3 to 8 inches

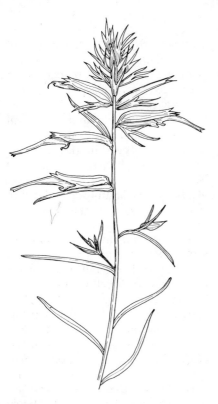

286. WYOMING PAINTBRUSH, ½ ×

red-edged, corollas protrude conspicuously. This plant often grows among shrubs, sometimes coming up through sagebrush or antelope-brush. It is found mostly in the montane zone and occurs from Wyoming to Oregon and south to New Mexico and California. It is the state flower of Wyoming.

SCARLET PAINTBRUSH, *C. miniata,* is another species usually found in the montane zone having erect, unbranched stems 1 to 2 feet tall, sometimes several from the same root. The corollas of this do not project so conspicuously as in the Wyoming Paintbrush. It grows from the Canadian Rockies southward throughout our range.

ROSY or SUBALPINE PAINTBRUSH, *C. rhexifolia,* is sometimes hard to distinguish from the last, but in

287. WESTERN YELLOW PAINTBRUSH, ½ ×

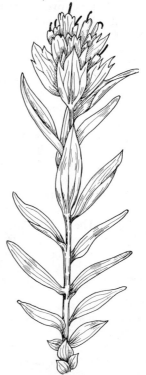

288. YELLOW OWLCLOVER, ½ ✕

tall. The bracts are greenish yellow or sometimes purplish. It is an alpine and subalpine species of Colorado, Utah and New Mexico. [Color Pl. 10c] See cover color photo.

YELLOW OWLCLOVER or GOLD-TONGUE, *Orthocarpus luteus* (288), is an erect annual plant 4 to 12 inches tall with narrow leaves and flowers in a terminal, clubshaped inflorescence, which grows abun-dantly on dry fields and slopes of the foothill and montane zones, blooming in early summer. It is often seen in overgrazed pastures.

PURPLE OWLCLOVER, *O. pur-pureo-albus,* is similar in habit but has white and pink or purplish flowers. It occurs in the montane zone of southwestern Colorado, New Mexico and Arizona. These plants are not in any way related to the true clovers of the Pea Fam-ily

YELLOW-RATTLE or PAPER-BAG-PLANT, *Rhinanthus rigidus,* is from 8 inches to 2 feet tall with narrow leaves and small yellow flowers in a leafy-bracted spike. The 4-toothed, papery calyx which becomes inflat-ed after flowering, makes the plant conspicuous. It grows in meadows of the montane and subalpine zones from Alberta to Arizona.

BRANCHED BIRDBEAK, *Cordylan-thus ramosus,* has grayish, finely divided leaves and head-like clusters of yellowish flowers. Individual flowers are from ⅔- to ¾-inch long with tubular, 2-lipped corollas resembling birds' beaks. It occurs on dry foothills from Montana through Colorado.

LOUSEWORT or WOODBETONY, *Pedicularis.* This genus has curiously shaped flowers. Its corolla is strongly 2-lipped with the upper lip or *galea,* arched and sometimes elongated into a beak. There are 4 stamens in two pairs, one pair longer than the other and all included in the galea. In most species the leaves are pinnately divided, sometimes into comb-like divisions or, in other species, into fern-like patterns. These plants usually grow in moist places. The name "lousewort" is an old English plant name and *Pedicularis* is merely the Latin form of it. It was once believed that cows which ate this plant became infested with lice.

a. Flowers rose or purple, resembling elephant heads
aa. Flowers not resembling elephant heads.
  b. Flowers rose or purple.
    c. Leaves divided into narrow segments, comb-like

cc. Leaves very finely and doubly scalloped
PURPLE LOUSEWORT, p. 257.
bb. Flowers white, yellowish, or greenish.
c. Plants not over 15 inches tall
d. Flowers white; leaves minutely toothed
SICKLETOP LOUSEWORT, p. 257.
dd. Flowers cream or yellowish; leaves pinnately divided.
e. Leaf segments comb-like; plants alpine
PARRY LOUSEWORT, p. 258.
ee. Leaf segments not comb-like; plants montane
CANADA LOUSEWORT, p. 258.
cc. Plants 1 to 4 feet tall; leaves fernlike.
d. Flowers about 1 inch long
FERN-LEAF LOUSEWORT, p. 258.
dd. Flowers 1 to 1 1/2-inches long
GRAYS LOUSEWORT, p. 258.

ELEPHANTELLA, ELEPHANTHEAD or LITTLE-RED-ELEPHANT, *P. groenlandica* (289), can always be recognized by its long twisted beak, resembling an elephant's trunk. It grows from 6 inches to 2 feet tall and its slender spike of purple or rose-colored flowers is frequently seen in wet meadows, on pond margins and along stream banks, most commonly in the subalpine zone but sometimes at either lower or higher altitudes. It ranges across Arctic America and southward in the mountains to New Mexico and California. [Color Pl. 11a]

ALPINE LOUSEWORT, *P. sudetica* var. *scopulorum,* is a rare plant with rose-colored flowers, leaves divided into comb-like teeth and stems 4 to 8 inches tall, found in the alpine tundra from Montana to southern Colorado.

PURPLE LOUSEWORT or PURPLE WOODBETONY, *P. crenulata,* has similar flowers but its long, slender leaves are finely scalloped and there are long hairs on the stem. It grows in wet montane meadows and sometimes becomes a weed in hay fields.

SICKLETOP LOUSEWORT or MOUNTAIN FIGWORT, *P. racemosa* (290). This plant usually has several stems in a clump; stems and leaves

289. ELEPHANTELLA, ½ ×

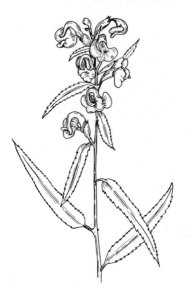

290. SICKLETOP LOUSEWORT, ½ ×

are reddish, flowers white or creamy with a curved and somewhat twisted galea. It grows in dry coniferous forests of the upper montane and subalpine zones from Canada south to New Mexico and California.

291. PARRY LOUSEWORT, ½ ×

PARRY LOUSEWORT, *P. parryi*, (291), is an alpine plant with creamy or yellowish flowers on erect stalks from 4 to 12 inches tall, and leaves divided nearly to the midrib into regular, narrow, toothed segments, found from Montana south to New Mexico and Arizona. CANADA LOUSEWORT or WOODBETONY, *P. canadensis*, has yellow or sometimes reddish flowers and its leaves are divided not more than ⅔ of the way to the midrib. It occurs in meadows and open woods and is widely distributed throughout North America south of the Arctic.

FERN-LEAF LOUSEWORT, *P. bracteosa* var. *paysoniana*, has stems from 1 to 3 feet tall and fern-like leaves to 6 inches long. The yellow-ish, inch-long flowers are in a dense spike; the erect galea is curved at the top. This is a plant of moist woods and shaded meadows of the subalpine zone from Montana south to Colorado and Utah.

GRAYS FERN-LEAF LOUSEWORT or INDIAN WARRIOR, *P. grayi*, is even larger with stems to nearly 4 feet tall and leaves sometimes a foot or more in length. Its flowers are dingy yellow, often streaked with red. It grows in montane woods from Wyoming and Utah to New Mexico and Arizona.

MONKEYFLOWER, *Mimulus*. Flow-ers of these plants have 5-lobed and more or less 2-lipped corollas with 2 ridges extending back from the lower lip into the throat. The leaves are opposite and the stems square. The plants grow in moist places. See LEWIS MIMULUS *M. lewisii*, Color Pl. 11b.

COMMON MONKEYFLOWER, *M. guttatus*, (*M. langsdorfii*) (292), has stems which may be erect or decumbent and from a few inches to 18 inches long, and yellow flow-

292. MONKEY-FLOWER, ½ ×

ers spotted with red; corollas an inch or more in length with closed throats. This is found around springs and on mossy stream banks, sometimes in wet gravel, usually in the subalpine zone, throughout our range.

A smaller, branched plant of the montane zone, with similar but smaller flowers with open throats, is the MANY-FLOWERED MONKEY-FLOWER, *M. floribundus.*

LITTLE RED MIMULUS, *M. rubellus,* is a small, annual plant with flowers from ¼- to ½-inch long on stalks longer than the flowers. The funnel-form corollas are usually red, sometimes white or yellow. This rare plant grows on mossy banks of the montane and subalpine zones.

LEWIS MIMULUS, *M. lewisii,* has unbranched finely hairy and rather sticky stems 1 to 2 feet tall and rose-red corollas 1 to 2 inches long. The anthers are hairy and the 2 ridges on the lower part of the thtoat are bearded with orange hairs. A showy plant, it is abundant along mountain streams, in moist ravines and around seepage areas of the montane and subalpine re-

gions of Grand Teton, Yellowstone, Glacier, and Mt. Rainier National Parks and the surrounding areas. The species was named in honor of Captain Meriwether Lewis of the Lewis and Clark Expedition. (See Color Pl. 11b)

BROOMRAPE FAMILY, *Orobanchaceae*

These are parasitic plants without green coloring but having flowers similar to those of the Figwort Family. The stems are fleshy, finely hairy, and pinkish-brown. The species most frequently seen is TUFTED BROOMRAPE, *Orobanche fasciculata* (293), which has several dull yellow or purplish flowers on thick straight stalks standing erect from the fleshy stem. It occurs throughout our range evidently being parasitic on species of *Eriogonum, Artemisia* (sagebrush), and other plants.

293. TUFTED BROOMRAPE, ½ ×

BLADDERWORT FAMILY, *Lentibulariaceae*

The members of this family grow in water or in very wet situations. Most of them are insectivorous. They have irregular, 2-lipped corollas which are usually spurred.

COMMON BLADDERWORT, *Utricularia vulgaris,* is a floating plant with very finely divided leaves. There are little inflated bladders on the leaf segments which act as floats and also trap insects. The yellow flowers are about ½-inch long. Occasionally seen in ponds of our region.

BUTTERWORT, *Pinguicula vulgaris,* grows on mud or wet rocks and has a basal rosette of yellowish-green leaves which have a grease-like, sticky substance on their surfaces which traps and digests insects. The violet-like flowers are on leafless stalks 2 to 4 inches tall. This is a northern plant, perhaps in our range only in Glacier National Park.

PLANTAIN FAMILY, *Plantaginaceae*

The flowers in this family are very small, without bright color and crowded into compact spikes. Leaves are basal and usually prominently ribbed. It includes some common lawn weeds which have been introduced from Europe and naturalized here but there are also several native species.

REDWOOL PLANTAIN, *Plantago eriopoda* (294), has a basal rosette of oblong or oblanceolate leaves 3 to 8 inches long and 3 to 9 ribbed which have reddish woolly hairs at their bases. The compact, cylindrical flower spikes are from 2 to 5 inches long on stalks 5 to 15 inches tall. This occurs on plains, hills and mountain slopes (up to 10,000 feet in Colorado) throughout the Rockies.

MADDER FAMILY, *Rubiaceae*

Plants of this family have 4-angled stems with opposite or whorled leaves, small flowers with regular, 4-lobed corollas and a 2-celled inferior ovary which becomes a 2-lobed fruit. Only one genus of the family is commonly seen in our area and except for one species the members are inconspicuous.

NORTHERN BEDSTRAW, *Galium boreale* (295), is an erect plant 8 inches to 2 feet tall, with 4 narrow, 3-nerved leaves at each node and masses of tiny white, fragrant flowers. It grows throughout the area from foothills to timberline and there is considerable difference in

294. REDWOOL PLANTAIN, ½ ×

appearance between plants growing in sunny, dry situations and those in moist, shaded places. The shade plants are larger, greener and less compact.

FRAGRANT BEDSTRAW, *G. triflorum,* has longer stems which are inclined to lean on the surrounding vegetation. Its 1-nerved leaves are in whorls of 5 or 6 and its few flowers are greenish or purplish. In this species it is the foliage which is fragrant. It grows in moist, shaded locations of the montane zone throughout the Rockies.

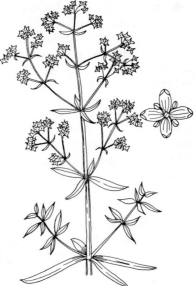

295. NORTHERN BEDSTRAW, ½ ×

HONEYSUCKLE FAMILY, *Caprifoliaceae*

Most of the plants of this family are woody. Our species are shrubs or vines. All have opposite leaves and some have paired flowers. They have united corollas with 5 stamens inserted in the corolla tube and inferior ovaries. In all but one of our genera the fruits are fleshy and berry-like.

a. Plant a low, trailing vine; flowers in pairs
          TWINFLOWER, p. 261.

aa. Plants erect shrubs.
  b. Leaves pinnately compound
        ELDERBERRY, p. 262.

  bb. Leaves not compound but sometimes lobed.
    c. Flowers white, in flat-topped clusters
        HIGH-BUSH CRANBERRY, p. 262.

    cc. Flowers not in flat-topped clusters.
      d. Flowers yellowish, in pairs; berries black or red
        HONEYSUCKLE, p. 262.

      dd. Flowers pinkish; berries white or greenish
        SNOWBERRY, p. 263.

TWINFLOWER, *Linnaea borealis (L. americana)* (296). This is a slender trailing plant with paired evergreen leaves which grows in moist shaded situations, usually under coniferous trees. The flower stalks are very slender, 2 to 4 inches tall, from the leaf axils and each bears a pair of fragrant, pink, funnel-form blooms ⅓- to ⅔-inch long. It occurs in the upper mon-

296. TWINFLOWER, ½ ×

tane and subalpine zones through-out our range and in favorable locations across the northern United States and Europe. It was the favor-ite flower of the great Swedish botanist, Carolus Linnaeus, and was named in his honor. [Color Pl. 11c]

ELDERBERRY, *Sambucus.* In our region these are stout shrubs with large, pinnately compound, opposite leaves and clusters of small white flowers which are followed by many small berries.

BLUE ELDERBERRY, *S. coerulea,* has large flat-topped clusters of small white flowers and bluish berries. At lower altitudes it be-comes a small tree. It grows in the foothill and montane zones.

The BLACK ELDERBERRY, *S. mel-anocarpa,* and the RED ELDERBER-RY, *S. racemosa* ssp. *pubens (S. microbotrys)* (297), are similar in general appearance. Their flower clusters are somewhat pyramid-shaped. The first has slightly larger

flower clusters and black berries. It grows along stream banks and on moist slopes of the montane and lower subalpine areas. The RED ELDERBERRY has orange or red berries and is usually found on sub-alpine slopes. All are widely distrib-uted throughout our region.

HIGH-BUSH CRANBERRY or AR-ROW-WOOD, *Viburnum edule, (V. pauciflorum),* (298), is a shrub 3 to

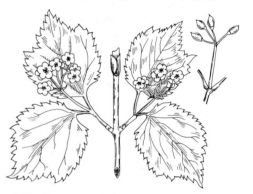

298. HIGHBUSH CRANBERRY, 2/5 ✕

6 feet tall with opposite, toothed leaves, some of which are lobed like maple leaves. It has small clusters of white flowers which are followed by red, juicy, edible berry-like drupes containing flat stones. This shrub is widely distributed in Can-ada and the northern United States where the fruits are often used for jelly. It extends south in the mon-tane and subalpine zones of the Rockies as far as central Colorado.

TWINBERRY HONEYSUCKLE or

297. RED ELDERBERRY, 2/5 ✕

299. TWINBERRY HONEYSUCKLE, 2/5 ✕

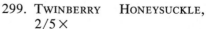

INVOLUCRED HONEYSUCKLE, *Lonicera involucrata* (299), is an erect leafy shrub from 2 to 9 feet tall. Its opposite leaves are 2 to 6 inches long, from obovate to oval or ovate-oblong and pointed at tip. The flowers are in pairs on a common stalk in the upper leaf axils. They are tubular, about ½-inch long, light yellow and enclosed in an involucre of leafy bracts which enlarges and turns red as the twin berries ripen and become glossy black. This is commonly seen along mountain streams and on moist slopes of the subalpine zone throughout our range.

UTAH HONEYSUCKLE, *L. utahensis,* is a smaller shrub growing from 3 to 6 feet in height with pale leaves which are glaucous beneath and 1 to 3 inches long. It lacks the conspicuous involucres of the last but has a handsome bright red 2-lobed berry.

ARIZONA HONEYSUCKLE, *L. arizonica,* is a clambering plant with clustered red or orange flowers, each 1 to 1½- inches in length. The upper pair of leaves is joined around the stem like a collar. This is found in the montane zone of Utah, Arizona and New Mexico.

MOUNTAIN SNOWBERRY, *Symph-oricarpos oreophilus* (300), is a much-branched shrub from 1 to 3 feet tall with shredding bark and roundish to ovate leaves about 1 inch long which are pale beneath. It has small, tubular or funnel-shaped, pink flowers nearly ½-inch long followed by white berries about ⅓-inch in diameter. This grows on slopes and in ravines of the montane zone from the Canadian Rockies south through Colorado.

BUCKBRUSH or SNOWBERRY, *S. albus* (301), is similar but its flowers are bell-shaped and about ¼-inch long. It is found in valleys and on hillsides of the montane and lower subalpine zones from Montana through Colorado.

WOLFBERRY, *S. occidentalis,* is an erect shrub from 1½- to 5 feet tall with oval leaves, sometimes wavy-margined or lobed, 1 to 4 inches long, and short spikes of pinkish flowers in the upper leaf axils followed by clusters of pale greenish berries. This grows in ravines and along sandy stream banks of the foothills and lower montane zone throughout our range.

MOSCHATEL FAMILY,
Adoxaceae

This family contains only one species, MUSK-ROOT, *Adoxa mos-*

300. MOUNTAIN SNOWBERRY, ½ ×

301. BUCKBRUSH or SNOWBERRY, ½ ×

302. Musk-root, ½ ×

chatellina (302), which is a delicate, smooth herb. It has long-
petioled basal leaves 3 times divided
into 3-lobed segments and a pair of
3-parted leaves on the flower stalk.
The inflorescence is a few, small,
greenish-yellow flowers in a tight
cluster. The top flower has a 4 or
5-lobed corolla and the others are
5 or 6 lobed. This plant has a wide,
scattered distribution in arctic
America and in moist soil of the
subalpine zone of the Rocky Mountains, but is seldom seen.

VALERIAN FAMILY,
Valerianaceae

Only one genus of this family is
represented in our region, VALER-
IAN, *Valeriana*. Its flowers are small
with calyx lobes modified into plumose bristles which unroll as the
seeds ripen and act as parachutes to
aid their dispersal.

TALL or EDIBLE VALERIAN, *V.
edulis,* is usually a foot or 2 tall
with a very open, branched inflorescence. The thick smooth, pale
green basal leaves have several
veins parallel to the midrib, and

some of them usually have a few
lobes. This grows from a stout tap-
root which has a distinctive odor.
These roots were cooked and used
for food by the Indians of the
Northwest. They are said to be
poisonous unless cooked. The plant
grows on moist meadows, ravines
and open hillsides of the montane
and subalpine zones throughout the
Rockies.

SUBALPINE VALERIAN, *V. capi-
tata, (V. acutiloba),* is a smooth
plant with stems from 6 to 18 inches
tall and clusters of tiny pink or
whitish flowers, each about 3/16-
inch long. The clusters are at first
compact but become more open as
they develop. There are 2 to 4 pairs
of leaves on the stem which usually
have 2 or more thumb-like lobes.
This is a plant of moist, shaded
ground, often found in aspen groves
and edges of spruce forest and
sometimes even above timberline,
from Wyoming to New Mexico and
Arizona.

WESTERN VALERIAN, *V. occidentalis* (303), is similar but the
flowers are even smaller and the
leaves more lobed. It grows from
Montana to Arizona and is found
in the foothill and montane zones.
It is sometimes seen in early spring
on moist foothill slopes beginning
to bloom with a short-stemmed
cluster of tiny pink buds centered
in the basal rosette of pinnately
lobed leaves.

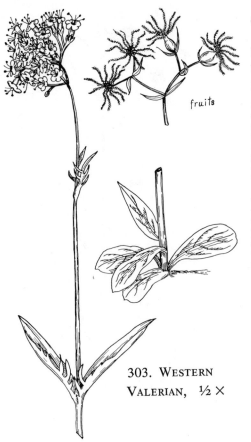

fruits

303. WESTERN
VALERIAN, ½ ×

GOURD FAMILY, *Cucurbitaceae*

All the squashes, melons, pumpkins, gourds and cucumbers, belong to this family. In general they are plants of warm climates.

WILD GOURD, *Cucurbita foetidissima* (304), is a coarse, trailing plant with large triangular, grayish leaves and yellow, bell-shaped flowers from 1 to over 2 inches long. It grows on roadsides, dry banks and, very often, along railroad embankments. The fruits are mottled dark and light green but turn yellowish after the first frost which by killing the leaves often reveals several of the baseball-like gourds lying on the ground attached to a withered stem. This is a plains plant which approaches the eastern mesas and foothills and is found from Colorado south to Mexico.

MOCK CUCUMBER, *Echinocystis lobata,* is an annual plant which climbs by tendrils over shrubs and low trees. Its leaves are thin and palmately lobed into 3 to 7 divisions. The light greenish-yellow,

304. WILD GOURD, ½ ×

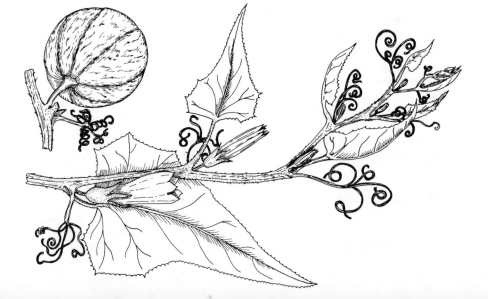

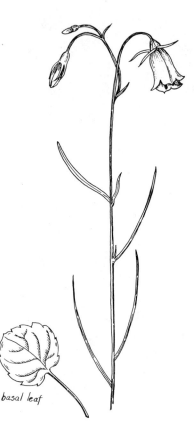

basal leaf

305. Venus Looking-glass, ½ ×

306. Harebell, ½ ×

staminate flowers are small but numerous in clusters from the leaf axils. Pistillate flowers are solitary or few from the same leaf axils. Egg-shaped, pendant fruits are about 2 inches long, covered with soft spines and, when ripe, contain several, large, flat black seeds. This is commonly found in the eastern United States and is sometimes seen along the high plains and foothills from Montana to Texas and Arizona.

BELLFLOWER FAMILY,
Campanulaceae

Members of this family have united 5-lobed corollas and inferior ova-

ries. The native species have blue flowers.

Venus Looking-glass, *Triodanis perfoliata (Specularia perfoliata)* (305), is an annual plant having stems which are usually erect and unbranched with alternate, cordate-clasping leaves and bracts. The leaves merge into the bracts and there are blue or purplish, half-inch broad flowers in their axils. It occurs occasionally on dry slopes of the foothills and lower montane zone throughout our range.

Harebell, *Campanula rotundifolia* (306), with its truly bell-like, lavender-blue flowers hanging from slender stems, is frequently seen

307. ALPINE HAREBELL, ½ ×

308. PARRY HAREBELL, ½ ×

from the foothills to the alpine zone throughout the Rockies. In spite of its specific name which means "round leaf," its leaves are seldom round. The basal ones are usually somewhat cordate and the stem leaves are linear or linear-lanceolate. At lower altitudes the plants may be a foot tall but at timberline and above the stems are shorter, sometimes only 2 or 3 inches high, but the flowers are just as large, from ½- to ¾-inch long. This plant is widely distributed around the world in northern countries and is the famous "bluebell" of Scotland. [Color Pl. 11d]

ALPINE or ONE-FLOWERED HAREBELL, *C. uniflora* (307), is a diminutive relative with slender stems 4 inches tall and a corolla less than ½-inch long having slender, pointed lobes. It grows in the dense grass and sedge sod of the tundra and has a wide distribution in arctic and alpine regions.

PARRY HAREBELL, *C. parryi* (308), has slender, usually one-flowered stems and erect, violet-col-

ored or purple, open funnel-form corollas. It is a plant of moist meadows and edges of aspen groves in the montane and subalpine zone from Wyoming and Utah to New Mexico and Arizona. [Color Pl. 11e]

CARDINAL FLOWER, *Lobelia cardinalis,* included by some botanists in the Bellflower Family and by others in a separate one, the Lobelia Family, *Lobeliaceae,* is found in our range only in New Mexico and Arizona where it is sometimes seen in moist situations up to 7000 feet. It does occur in southeastern Colorado but below 5000 feet. It is easily recognized by its brilliant red, irregular corolla, 1 to 1½-inches long.

COMPOSITE FAMILY, *Compositae*

The Composites make up one of the largest families of seed plants. Its members vary greatly but all have the inflorescnce arranged according to a similar pattern. They have been streamlined by nature for efficiency in the matters of reproduction and distribution. Species of this family are considered difficult to identify but they are not impossible if one is willing to devote some time to learning the fundamental characteristics of the family and its different genera. A good 10x hand lens is necessary because many of the individual flowers are very small. They are called *composites* because their inflorescences have become crowded into compact heads which simulate individual blossoms. Sunflowers, thistles and dandelions are well-known examples.

If you cut open a dandelion or sunflower head you will find that it is made up of numerous separate flowers. In the case of the dandelion all these flowers are alike. Each has a strap-shaped corolla formed into a short tube at the base which surrounds a ring of 5 stamens. The ovary is inferior, one-seeded, and there is a very slender style and two stigmas. Attached to the top of the ovary and surrounding the base of the corolla is a tuft of white hairs. This represents the calyx and is called the *pappus*. In the case of the sunflower you will find that the head is made up of two different kinds of flowers. Around the outside are flowers similar to those of the dandelion. They have long, flat corollas and are called *ray* flowers. In the center of the head are numerous flowers with tubular, 5-toothed corollas. These are called *disk* flowers. In the sunflower the pappus consists of scales or awns.

In both cases the flowers are all attached to the enlarged top of a stalk and this structure is called a *receptacle*. Originating at the edge of the receptacle and surrounding the cluster of flowers is a series of green bracts, the *phyllaries,* and together they make up the *involucre*. This involucre simulates a calyx. In the dandelion head all the flowers are perfect and each produces a seed-like fruit called an *achene*. In the sunflower the ray flowers are pistillate but sterile and the disk flowers are perfect and each produces an achene.

Many variations occur in different members of the family. In some species the ray flowers produce achenes and the disk flowers are sterile. In some only disk flowers are present. The pappus may consist of soft hairs, of stiff bristles or of scales. In many of the species it serves to insure wide distribution of the seeds. Those achenes which have a pappus of soft hairs or bristles are carried long distances by the wind, those with scales are often blown along the ground, those with barbed bristles hook into the hair of animals or man's clothing for transportation.

The receptacle may be flat, convex or concave; sometimes it is elevated into a cone or column; sometimes it is pitted and often it bears scales or bristles between the flowers. Often the anthers cohere in a ring around the styles which are usually 2-branched. At one stage the stigmas are elevated to protrude above the ring of anthers, at another stage the anther ring is pushed up. The phyllaries are usually separate but may be joined together; they may be in one or more rows; often they overlap symmetrically as shingles on a roof and then they are said to be *imbricated;* sometimes they are colored other than green; sometimes they are thin and papery.

Some of these plants bloom in early spring and summer but a majority of composite species are late-blooming. From mid-August until frost the wild flower show is dominated by plants of this family.

The family is represented by more than 500 species in the Rocky Mountain region. Because of the efficiency of its distribution devices it includes a large number of weeds. Many of its species are abundant in our flora but little noticed because their flowers are inconspicuous. It is impossible to include more than a small proportion of the total number present in a book of this sort, and difficult to decide on the few which should be included. The author has endeavored to describe, or at least mention, all of those which are generally looked on by non-botanists as "wildflowers," and has endeavored by means of illustrations and keys to present this great and interesting family in a non-formidable aspect. In many cases the Latin generic names have been applied as common names because common names in this group are in a very indefinite and confused state. Only generic names are used in the key. Many of these plants have no generally accepted common names. Readers will find some common names given second place and listed in the index.

For convenience the family may be divided into 3 groups:
Group I includes the genera having radiate heads, i.e., those in which both ray and disk flowers are present. Occasionally in some of these species forms without rays will be found.
Group II includes those genera which usually have only discoid heads, i.e., where ray flowers are lacking.
Group III includes those with only strap-shaped corollas. This last group is sometimes considered as a separate family called the *Cichoriaceae.*

KEY TO THE GENERA OF THE COMPOSITE FAMILY

Group 1. Heads usually with both disk and ray flowers.
a. Ray flowers white, pinkish, lavender, or purple; never yellow; disk flowers yellow, except white in ACHILLEA.
  b. Leaves pinnately lobed or finely divided.
    c. Leaves unevenly pinnately lobed; disk yellow
                CHRYSANTHEMUM, p. 273.
    cc. Leaves deeply and finely divided.
      d. Heads about 1/3-inch broad; leaves aromatic
                ACHILLEA, p. 273.
      dd. Heads about 1 inch broad
                LEUCAMPYX, p. 273.
  bb. Leaves entire or wavy-margined.
    c. Ray flowers conspicuous, several or numerous.
      d. Plants usually branched with few to many heads.
        e. Phyllaries flat; tips not recurved; plants perennial
                ASTER, p. 275.
        ee. Phyllaries with recurved tips; plants usually annual or biennial
                MACHAERANTHERA, p. 277.

  dd. Plants caespitose or taller with stems little-branched and single or few heads.
   e. Phyllaries many, imbricated
       TOWNSENDIA, p. 274.
   ee. Phyllaries fewer, usually in 1 series
       ERIGERON, p. 278.
  cc. Ray flowers small, inconspicuous; basal leaves large, triangular, white beneath
       PETASITES, p. 282.
aa. Ray flowers yellow or orange.
 b. Leaves, at least the lower ones, opposite.
  c. Plants smooth; leaves divided into thread-like divisions
       THELESPERMA, p. 283.
  cc. Plants hairy; leaves not divided.
   d. Pappus conspicuous, of white or tawny bristles
       ARNICA, p. 292.
   dd. Pappus none or of scales or awns.
    e. Pappus none; foliage with very fine hairs
       VIGUIERA, p. 283.
    ee. Pappus of scales or awns; foliage often rough.
     f. Achenes flattened, with thin edges

       HELIANTHELLA, p. 284.
     ff. Achenes not flattened
       HELIANTHUS, p. 283.
bb. Leaves either all basal or alternate on stem, not opposite.
 c. Plants with leaves all, or mostly, basal.
  d. Leaves 4 to 12 inches long.
   e. Leaves green, ovate, oblong, or lanceolate
       WYETHIA, p. 285.
   ee. Leaves gray, arrowhead-shaped
       BALSAMORHIZA, p. 285.
  dd. Leaves 1 to 4 inches long, silvery or white wooly
       HYMENOXYS, p. 286.
 cc. Plants with some leaves along the stems.
  d. Disk flowers dark colored.
   e. Disk flowers dark red
       GAILLARDIA, p. 287.
   ee. Disk flowers black, brown, or greenish.
    f. Receptacle cone-shaped
       RUDBECKIA, p. 288.
    ff. Receptacle cylindric or columnar
       RATIBIDA, p. 289.
  dd. Disk flowers yellow or orange.
   e. Heads 1/2-inch or more broad.
    f. Involucres saucer-shaped, or of 2 or 3 series of narrow phyllaries
       HELENIUM, p. 289.
    ff. Involucre hemispheric or cylindric.
     g. Phyllaries tightly appressed.
      h. Involucre hemispheric
       BAHIA, p. 289.
      hh. Involucre cylindric.

i. Plants more or less rough hairy
       CHRYSOPSIS, p. 290.
ii. Plants smooth or more or less cottony or wooly
       SENECIO, p. 295.
gg. Phyllaries many, loose, and leafy, or narrow and bristle-
    tipped, or with tips recurved.
h. Phyllaries with strongly recurved tips
       GRINDELIA, p. 290.
hh. Phyllaries loose and leafy or bristle-tipped
       HAPLOPAPPUS, p. 290.
ee. Heads less than 1/3-inch broad, numerous.
f. A bushy plant with very narrow leaves
       GUTIERREZIA, p. 301.
ff. Stems usually unbranched; inflorescence often 1-sided
    and arched
       SOLIDAGO, p. 300.

Group II   Heads made up of disk flowers (i.e., those having tubular
       corollas) only, or, rarely, with a few inconspicuous ray
       flowers present.

a. Phyllaries papery or cartilaginous; the head white, pink, or
  brownish.
b. Heads yellowish or cream-colored; phyllaries satiny
       GNAPHALIUM, p. 301.
bb. Heads white, pink, or brownish; phyllaries papery.
c. Plants 10 to 18 inches tall, mainly subalpine in distribution;
  phyllaries pure white
       ANAPHALIS, p. 301.
cc. Plants 2 to 10 inches tall, or, if taller, of montane woods
       ANTENNARIA, p. 301.
aa. Phyllaries green, gray, yellowish, or purplish, but not papery.
b. Plants with foliage, and often stems, spiny
       CIRSIUM (Carduus), p. 302.
bb. Plants without spines on foliage.
c. Flowers bright yellow.
d. Plants woody at least at base.
e. Phyllaries and flowers only 4 in each head
       TETRADYMIA, p. 304.
ee. Phyllaries and flowers more than 4 in each head
       CHRYSOTHAMNUS, p. 304.
dd. Plants not woody.
e. Leaves opposite.
f. Leaves triangular or heart-shaped with attenuate tips, very
  smooth
       PERICOME, p. 305.
ff. Leaves lanceolate, glandular hairy
       Arnica parryi, p. 293.
ee. Leaves alternate.
f. Phyllaries in one even row with sometimes a few shorter
  ones at base of involucre
       SENECIO, p. 295.
ff. Phyllaries in 2 or more overlapping rows
       ERIGERON, p. 278.

cc. Flowers not bright yellow.
　d. Leaves opposite or in whorls.
　　e. Heads cream-colored, nodding; leaves opposite
　　　　　　　BRICKELIA (KUHNIA), p. 305.
　　ee. Heads whitish or purple, erect; leaves whorled
　　　　　　　EUPATORIUM, p. 306.
　dd. Leaves alternate or all basal.
　　e. Leaves all basal; flowers whitish
　　　　　　　PETASITES, p. 282.
　　ee. Leaves alternate.
　　　f. Plants with numerous, small, grayish or yellowish heads;
　　　　foliage aromatic
　　　　　　　ARTEMISIA, p. 306.
　　　ff. Plants with heads over 1/2-inch high.
　　　　g. Leaves narrow, entire; heads bright rose purple
　　　　　　　LIATRIS, p. 307.
　　　　gg. Leaves pinnately divided; heads whitish or pinkish.
　　　　　h. Phyllaries green; pappus scales 4 to 10
　　　　　　　CHAENACTIS, p. 308.
　　　　　hh. Phyllaries with papery margins; pappus scales 10 to 20
　　　　　　　Hymenopappus arenosus, p. 308.

Group III Heads in general made up of flowers with strap-shaped
　　　corollas (like those of the dandelion); plants with
　　　milky juice.
a. Plants with all leaves strictly basal; stems unbranched and with
　only 1 head to each stem.
　b. Leaves with white tomentose margins
　　　　　　　NOTHOCALAIS, p. 311.
　bb. Leaves without white tomentose margins.
　　c. Phyllaries imbricated in several rows
　　　　　　　AGOSERIS, p. 308.
　　cc. Phyllaries in one main row, usually a few, small, short ones
　　　at base of involucre; stalks hollow
　　　　　　　TARAXACUM, p. 308.
aa. Plants with at least a few leaves or bracts on the stems.
　b. Most of the leaves at or near the base; or upper leaves much
　　smaller; stems branched.
　　c. Flowers pinkish, rose, or blue.
　　　d. Flowers bright blue
　　　　　　　CICHORIUM p. 311.
　　　dd. Flowers pinkish or rose.
　　　　e. Pappus bristles feathery
　　　　　　　STEPHANOMERIA p. 311.
　　　　ee. Pappus bristles simple
　　　　　　　LYGODESMIA, p. 310.
　cc. Flowers yellow.

d. Pappus of small scales, each tipped with a feathery bristle
MICROSERIS, p. 311.
dd. Pappus not of bristle-tipped scales.
e. Pappus double; outer ring of scales and inner ring of longer bristles
KRIGIA, p. 311.
ee. Pappus single of long, soft bristles.
f. Pappus bristles usually white
CREPIS, p. 309.
ff. Pappus bristles usually tan
HIERACIUM, p. 309.
bb. Plants with stems equally leafy to the inflorescence.
c. Leaves long and grass-like; fruiting heads spherical, 2 to 3 inches in diameter
TRAGOPOGON, p. 310.
cc. Leaves not grass-like; fruiting heads smaller.
d. Flowers rose; inflorescence a raceme
PRENANTHES, p. 310.
dd. Flowers blue or dark purplish; infloresence an open panicle
LACTUCA, p. 311.

Group I. Heads usually having both disk and ray flowers.

OXEYE DAISY, *Chrysanthemum leucanthemum.* T h i s golden-centered and white-rayed daisy is becoming established along roadsides of our area. Its ancestors arrived from Europe with early colonists and for many generations their progeny have been establishing themselves in hay meadows and fields of the eastern states where the plant is considered by farmers as a troublesome weed. Gradually it has worked its way westward and today occurs in some mountain areas, especially along highways. Narrow leaves with wavy or toothed margins form low, green rosettes; flower stalks are erect, 10 to 24 inches tall, almost leafless, one-flowered; phyllaries are pointed, light green lined with brown.

YARROW, *Achillea l a n u l o s a* (309). A strongly aromatic plant with grayish leaves finely divided into numerous, extremely narrow segments. Flowering stems are 6 to 24 inches tall with flat-topped clusters of numerous small white heads. Widely distributed throughout our area. Closely related and similar to the weedy COMMON YARROW, *A. millefolium.*

LEUCAMPYX or WILD-COSMOS, *Leucampyx newberryi.* A plant with alternate, mostly basal leaves which are somewhat cottony and twice or

309. YARROW, ½ ×

thrice pinnately parted into linear segments. The stems are 8 to 20 inches tall with conspicuous white flowers 1 to 2 inches broad; rays are 3-toothed and phyllaries broad with papery margins. Found in the upper foothills and montane zones of northern New Mexico and central and southwestern Colorado.

EASTER TOWNSENDIA or EASTER-DAISY, *Townsendia exscapa* (310). This is a low cushion-like plant with

310. EASTER TOWNSENDIA or DAISY, ½ ×

white or pinkish flower heads nestled in a dense tuft of narrow grayish leaves. Heads about an inch broad when fully open; phyllaries in 4 to 6 series, linear, having irregular papery margins. *T. hookeri*

is very similar but may be distinguished by the tufts of tangled hairs at the tips of its phyllaries.

J. D. Hooker, who was director of the Royal Botanic Garden at Kew, visited the Rocky Mountains with Asa Gray, F. V. Hayden, and others in 1877, collecting and studying alpine plants.

EASTER TOWNSENDIA is usually the first plant to bloom and may be found in flower in March, or sometimes even earlier, on the mesas and lower foothills. By April it is blooming on fields of the montane zone. Found throughout our range.

SHOWY TOWNSENDIA, *T. grandiflora*. Stems 2 to 8 inches tall, leafy, branching at base; basal leaves oblanceolate, upper ones lanceolate; rays pink or rose-purple; phyllaries in about 3 series, lanceolate with long sharp points and irregular papery margins. A summer blooming plant found on dry slopes of mesas and foothills of South Dakota, Wyoming, Colorado and New Mexico. Somewhat similar but taller is *T. eximia*, which grows in the montane zone of southern Colorado and New Mexico. Its rays are bluish or purple.

PARRY TOWNSENDIA, *T. parryi*. Stems 1 to few, 2 to 10 inches tall with a single head to each stem; rays pale purplish-blue; basal leaves spatulate, entire or 3-toothed upper leaves much smaller. Occurs in the northern part of our range, especially in Teton, Yellowstone, and Glacier National Parks. Dry hillsides and rocky slopes up to timberline. This may be distinguished from species of aster and erigeron by the large size of the head and by its pappus which consists of bristles plus long flat scales.

ASTER, *Aster*. This is a genus of numerous and rather similar species. The ray flowers in this group are most often in shades of blue or purple but a few species have white rays and several have pale lavender, pinkish or rose-colored ones. The pappus is a tuft of soft, white or tawny bristles. The plants vary in height from a few inches to 3 or 4 feet. In our species the leaves are nearly always longer than wide. Most true asters have entire, or rarely slightly irregular, margins and are perennials. There may be one to many heads in the inflorescence, and seldom more than 25 rays to each head. The involucre is usually composed of more than 2 series of phyllaries in an imbricated arrangement.

For a comparison of aster and erigeron involucres see *Plate G, figs. 62* and *63* and also read the erigeron description on page 278. These plants resemble, and are often confused with, members of the genus *Erigeron*. In general asters have more heads per stalk, fewer and broader ray flowers and more definitely imbricated phyllaries than do erigerons. Asters bloom in late summer and fall. As an aid to identification they are here divided into two groups according to color.

Asters with blue, violet, rose or purple ray flowers.

311. SUN-LOVING ASTER, ½ ×

SUN-LOVING ASTER, *A. foliaceous* var. *apricus* (311). A low-growing, usually tufted plant with violet or bright rose rays and one or few heads on decumbent, leafy stems. The phyllaries are loose and somewhat leafy, often purple-edged. Alpine and subalpine zones on moist gravel. This is a variety of the LEAFY-BRACT ASTER, *A. foliaceus*, which has many forms and may become from one to 3 feet tall. It is widely distributed in our area from the upper foothills to the subalpine zone.

A rather similar species having ray flowers which may vary from violet to bright rose is the FREMONT ASTER, *A. occidentalis*. Comparing the SUN-LOVING and FREMONT ASTERS, the latter usually has fewer, taller, more erect and often reddish, stems which are without leaves on their upper portions. It occurs in the upper montane and subalpine zones from Canada south to Colorado.

PACIFIC ASTER, *A. chilensis (A.* *adscendens)*. A very common, variable, and widely distributed plant. It has a creeping rootstock so it forms clumps or beds. The ray flowers are usually pale, either lavender or pinkish; phyllaries imbricated in 3 to 4 rows, blunt or bristle tipped, white at base; stems usually about a foot tall but may be less or up to 2 feet and the plants may be quite smooth or moderately or

312. SMOOTH ASTER, ½ ×

densely hairy. It grows along road-sides, in marshes and on hillsides of the foothill, montane and lower subalpine zones.

SMOOTH ASTER, *A. laevis* (312). Rays blue and stems 1 to 3 feet tall. One of the few asters having entirely smooth foliage. The lower leaves are short petioled and may be up to 6 inches long, the upper ones are noticeably smaller and clasp the stems; heads ½- to 1-inch broad. This is the common, blue-flowered, late summer and fall aster from the Rockies eastward to the Atlantic coast. Found on moist soil of the foothill and montane zones.

SKYBLUE ASTER, *A. hesperius* (*A. coerulescens*), is a tall plant of swampy places at lower altitudes, with numerous, small heads; rays commonly pale blue but may some-times be whitish or pinkish; stems marked lengthwise with lines of hairs and leaves willow-like.

SHOWY ASTER, *A. conspicuus*, a

stout plant 1 to 3 feet tall with large, stiff, sharply-toothed leaves and many heads in a much branched inflorescence; heads about one inch broad with 15 to 35 violet rays; involucre sticky; phyllaries with re-curved tips, imbricated in about 5 rows. Found in open woods of the montane zone, northern Wyoming, Montana and Idaho, especially in Yellowstone and Glacier National Parks.

HAYDEN ASTER, *A. alpigenus* var. *haydeni (Oreastrum haydeni)*. A small plant with spreading, single-headed stalks 3 to 6 inches long, and slender basal leaves about 2 to 4 inches long. The heads are com-paratively large and showy, with bright purple rays and yellow disks. It occurs in the alpine zone of Wyoming, Idaho, and Montana. This variety was named in honor of Dr. F. V. Hayden, famous geologist and one of the most important American explorers of the region which now contains Yellowstone Park. He became director of the

313. TANSY ASTER, ½ ×

rays purple

U.S. Geological Survey of the Territories and headed expeditions into the Yellowstone country in the early 1870's. He was one of the small group of men directly responsible for the Act of Congress which set this area apart as a National Park.

TANSY - ASTER, *Machaeranthera bigelovii (Aster bigelovii)* (313). A widely branched, annual or biennial, sticky plant with numerous, brilliant reddish-purple flower heads; the leaves are lanceolate or oblanceolate and usually have sharply toothed or wavy margins; the sticky phyllaries taper into slender, recurved tips. This is the best character by which to distinguish this plant from the true asters. (See *Plate G, fig. 64*). *M. tanacetifolia* is similar but its leaves are once- or twice-pinnately-divided into narrow segments. The flower heads are distinctive in color and in late summer a border of bright reddish purple along a highway is an almost sure sign of the presence of tansy-asters.

COLORADO TANSY-ASTER, *M. coloradoensis,* has violet to rose-purple ray flowers, heads about an inch broad, leaves appressed-hairy with spine-tipped teeth and sharp-pointed phyllaries. This little plant, usually not over 5 inches tall, is limited in its distribution to the subalpine zone in central and southwestern Colorado. (Color Pl. 11f)

Asters with pure white, pale pinkish or lavender rays.

PORTER ASTER, *A. porteri* (314). A plant with smooth stems and leaves and bright white rays; stems branched, 8 to 20 inches tall; heads ½- to ¾-inch in diameter. As the flowers age the orange disk turns dark red. It occurs on montane fields and meadows of New Mexico and Colorado.

A rough-hairy plant with white ray flowers and bristle-tipped leaves and phyllaries is the ROUGH WHITE ASTER, *A. falcatus (A. commutatus).* It has a creeping underground rootstock so is usually found in patches or large clumps. Along roadsides, on banks and in meadows of the foothill zone throughout the Rockies.

ENGELMANN ASTER, *A. engelmannii,* is a stout plant 1⅓ to 4 feet tall with numerous white or pinkish, rather ragged, flower heads. The leaves are ovate-oblong to broadly lanceolate, 2 to 4 inches long; phyllaries are tough and papery, often purple tinged, imbricated in several

rays white

314. PORTER ASTER, ½ ×

rows. Found on moist banks and in woods of the montane and lower subalpine zones from Canada south to Colorado and Nevada.

GLAUCOUS ASTER, *A. glaucodes,* 10 to 15 inches tall with gray-green, narrow, blunt leaves and pale lavender flowers is sometimes seen as long clumps along mountain roads or among rocks of the montane and subalpine zones of Wyoming, Colorado, Utah and Arizona.

SAND ASTER, *Aster arenosus,* *(Leucelene ericoides),* is a little tufted plant usually not over 5 inches tall with wiry stems and tiny leaves. Each branch bears a single white-rayed and yellow-centered head. The phyllaries, imbricated in several rows, are pointed and have green midribs and papery margins. Found on sandy soil of the foothills and plains from Wyoming to Texas and westward.

ERIGERON, *Erigeron.* This genus contains many beautiful species which appear similar to each other and are often confused with asters. To aid in their identification readers are advised to study the information on aster, page 275, and *Plate G, figs. 62* and *63.*

Most erigerons are perennial and in general they have very numerous (30 to 150) and very narrow ray flowers. Their rays range in color from violet, pinkish or white to blue and purple. Farther west and in the Canadian Rockies there are some with bright yellow rays. Many kinds have only one head to each stem and most have fewer than five. (Most asters have several to many heads). The phyllaries in erigerons are of nearly equal length, rarely in more than two rows. The pappus is a tuft of rather brittle bristles sometimes with an outer ring of shorter bristles or scales.

Erigerons usually bloom in spring and early summer while asters are late summer and fall bloomers. These plants have been called "Fleabane" and "Mountain Daisies" but so many different plants in this family have been called "daisies" that confusion results from the use of that name and the same is true of "fleabane." The only way to be sure we know what plant we are talking about is to use the generic name, (pronounced e rij' eron) as a common name.

As an aid to identification our species may be divided into three groups on the basis of habit. But it should be remembered that there may be considerable overlapping, and also that only a portion of the many species found growing in the Rocky Mountains can be described here.

Foothill Erigerons with heads 1-inch broad or less.

BRANCHING ERIGERON, *E. divergens.* This is easily distinguished from other erigerons by its widely branching habit and its many flower heads. It may be distinguished from asters by its numerous and very narrow rays which are light purple or pinkish. The plant is softly hairy all over and its basal leaves are oblanceolate to spatulate with entire or somewhat lobed margins. It occurs on sandy ground and rocky slopes of the foothills throughout our range.

WHIPLASH ERIGERON, *E. flagellaris* (315). A plant of foothill and

315. WHIPLASH ERIGERON, ½ ×

montane meadows with stems 4 to 10 inches tall. Its heads are always bent down in bud and appear pink due to coloring on the outside of the rays. These are usually white inside so when erect and fully open the flower head is white. Most of the leaves are basal and oblanceolate. It begins to bloom in spring and continues into summer when it develops long runners which may root at the tips, producing new plants in the manner of strawberry plants. Occurs throughout our range.

EARLY WHITE ERIGERON, *E. pumilus.* A hairy plant with white rays usually found in tufts growing from a woody caudex. Stems several, 3 to 10 inches tall; leaves narrow and up to 3 inches long. On dry mesas and plains from Colorado south to Arizona. It occurs among oaks and service-berry bushes in Mesa Verde National Park and may also be found in Dinosaur National Monument. Similar species found on rocky slopes and in dry open woods of the foothills and lower montane zone are *E. engelmannii* which has almost leafless stalks and occurs

mostly on the western slope, and *E. eatonii* which has 3-nerved basal leaves up to 6 inches long and is often found among sagebrush. They are usually white flowered but their rays may vary to blue or pink.

EARLY BLUE ERIGERON, *E. vetensis,* is a tufted, somewhat sticky plant with several stems, 6 to 10 inches tall, from a heavy, woody caudex; leaves mostly basal, oblanceolate, with a fringe of stiff hairs along their edges. The stalks are leafless but there are many old dry leaf bases on the caudex. Occurs in dry woods of the foothill and montane zones from Wyoming to New Mexico.

CUT-LEAF ERIGERON, *E. compositus* (316). A little tufted plant with stems 2 to 6 inches tall; rays usually white but may be bluish or purple, especially at high altitudes; leaves mostly basal and once or twice 3-parted into narrow, blunt lobes, the very few small stem leaves entire. One form of this quite often seen which has no ray flowers, just the yellow disk, has been called "GOLD BUTTONS." CUT-LEAF ERIGERON begins to bloom in the foothills in early spring and as the sea-

316. CUT-LEAF ERIGERON, ½ ×

son advances it comes into flower at higher altitudes. It is abundant on openings in the ponderosa pine forest in June and is found on the tundra in July and August. Widely distributed throughout the Rockies.

Erigerons of the montane and subalpine zones, mostly tall species with heads from 1- to 2- inches broad and with more or less leafy stems.

(The CUT-LEAF and EARLY BLUE ERIGERONS, described above, may also be found here).

317. SUBALPINE ERIGERON, ½ ✕

phyllaries covered with pink wool

318. PINK-HEAD ERIGERON, ½ ✕

319. ASPEN ERIGERON, ½ ✕

SUBALPINE ERIGERON, *E. peregrinus (E. salsuginosus)* (317). Stems usually about 12 to 15 inches tall, it may occasionally reach 2 feet and in exposed alpine situations it sometimes attains only a few inches. The heads are large and showy with comparatively broad (1/8 to 3/16-inch) rose-purple or violet rays and orange-yellow disks; phyllaries are attenuated into loose tips; usually only 1 head to a stem. The foliage is mostly glabrous; basal leaves oblanceolate and petioled, stem leaves smaller and often clasping. This is one of the conspicuous flowers of subalpine meadows in July and early August. Occurs in subalpine meadows from Alaska to New Mexico and California. [Color Pl. 12a, b].

PINK-HEAD ERIGERON, *E. elatior* (318). One of the tallest of erigerons with erect stems up to 2 feet in height; heads solitary or 2 or 3 on one stem, in bud usually bent down; rays numerous, narrow, pink or rose; involucres very woolly with pinkish hairs. This pink effect is produced by red coloring in the crosswalls of the hairs.

PALE ERIGERON, *E. eximius (E. superbus)*. Stems from one to 2 feet tall, smooth except sometimes a little sticky in the inflorescence, stem leaves more or less 3-nerved, few, far apart; rays light pinkish, lavender or sometimes white; heads noticeably bent down in bud. Stream banks and moist forest glades, montane and subalpine zones, Wyoming and Utah south to Texas and Arizona.

SHOWY ERIGERON, *E. speciosus*. Stems 1 to 2 feet tall, each with from 1 to 10 heads; rays many (75-150) and narrow, blue or violet; involucres usually somewhat glandular (sticky) and with some long non-glandular hairs; leaves usually 3-nerved, mostly smooth, basal ones oblanceolate, petioled, stem leaves lanceolate or ovate, not noticeably smaller. Found along roadsides, on open slopes, and among rocks throughout our range.

The form of this most commonly seen in Colorado is the ASPEN ERIGERON or ASPEN-DAISY, *E. speciosus* var. *macranthus* (319). Its stems tend to lean and usually have from 3 to 5 heads which lack the long hairs on the involucre. This occurs commonly in aspen groves

and on montane and subalpine meadows and margins of forests. A similar but more hairy plant which usually grows in clumps having several stems which are curved at base is *E. formosissimus*. It occurs on open ground throughout our range from the foothills to timberline.

The COULTER ERIGERON, *E. coulteri*, is a hairy plant, 10 to 20 inches tall with 50 to 100 white rays and a slightly woolly involucre. The hairs here are long but not as long and dense as those on the PINK-HEAD and they darken the involucre because near the base of each hair there are dark crosswalls. The lower leaves are broadly oblanceolate, or oval, petioled, the upper ones broadly lanceolate, clasping and occasionally dentate. Grows in meadows and at edges of forest, in montane and subalpine zones from Wyoming to Washington and south to New Mexico and California. In Colorado it is common on the western slope but rare east of the Continental Divide.

This was named for Dr. John M. Coulter, for many years a well-known professor of botany at the University of Chicago, who, as a young man, had accompanied F. V. Hayden on exploring expeditions in the Rocky Mountains and collected plants at high altitudes in Colorado.

Dr. Coulter prepared the first manual of Rocky Mountain botany, which was later revised and greatly expanded by Aven Nelson.

Erigerons of the alpine and subalpine zones, usually less than 8-inches tall. (CUT-LEAF ERIGERON (fig. 316) *occurs here also).*

BLACK-HEADED ERIGERON, *E. melanocephalus.* Stems 2 to 6 inches tall, each with a single head; rays white, involucres dark purplish and woolly with long hairs, the dark effect caused by purple pigment in the crosswalls of these hairs. (The specific name, *melanocephalus,* means "black-head"). A plant of the subalpine and alpine regions especially around melting snow. Wyoming to Utah and New Mexico.

320. ONE-FLOWERED ERIGERON, ½ ×

ONE-FLOWERED ERIGERON, *E. simplex (E. uniflorus)* (320). Stems 2 to 8 inches, leaves mostly basal, oblanceolate, entire; heads solitary; rays blue or purplish; involucre woolly with long white or grayish hairs. Alpine tundra from Montana south to New Mexico and Arizona.

ROCK-SLIDE ERIGERON, *E. leiomeris.* Stems scattered or few together from a long taproot or branching caudex extending among loose rocks; basal leaves clustered, spatulate and petioled, stem leaves few and much smaller; heads solitary, rays blue or violet. Rockslides in the subalpine and alpine zones from Wyoming and Idaho south to New Mexico and Nevada.

PINNATE-LEAF ERIGERON, *E. pinnatisectus* (321), is a tundra plant

321. PINNATE-LEAF ERIGERON, ½ ×

forming tufts of fern-like leaves with stems 4 to 5 inches tall; heads about an inch broad with purple rays and bright yellow or orange disks. Alpine regions from Wyoming to New Mexico.

SWEET COLTSFOOT, *Petasites sagittata.* A rare plant which grows from a thick creeping rootstock and has large, triangular leaves which are white on their undersides. The leaves have heart-shaped or arrow-shaped bases and wavy margins and may be as much as a foot long. The flower stalks are unbranched and without leaves. They hold clusters of small whitish heads which are most conspicuous as they go to seed and display tufts of silvery-white pappus. This is a northern bog plant which extends southward from Labrador and Alaska to Minnesota and Colorado; occasionally found in cold mountain bogs.

GREENTHREAD or FIELD-COREOPSIS, *Thelesperma filifolium* (322). A much-branched plant with bright green, smooth stem and leaves and large, bright yellow flower heads on long stalks. The rays are 3-lobed and the phyllaries are in 2 rows, the inner ones broad and united into a cup-shaped involucre, the outer ones slender and spreading; leaves pinnately divided into very slender thread-like segments. A plant of the high plains, mesas and foothills along the east side of the mountains from Nebraska and Colorado to New Mexico and Texas.

GOLDENEYE or SUNSPOTS, *Viguiera multiflora* (323). A much-branched plant having many yellow flower heads suggesting small sunflowers. The leaves are rough, 1 to 3 inches long, mostly opposite. Common on dry slopes in the foothill and montane zones throughout our range.

BUSH SUNFLOWER, *Helianthus pumilus* (324). Several stiff stems 1 to 2½ feet tall from a woody, perennial crown give this plant a bushy appearance. The opposite leaves are ovate to lanceolate with short petioles, very rough and dull green; heads are 1½- to 3 inches broad with yellow rays and dingy yellow or brownish disks. The name *Helianthus* comes from two Greek words, *helios,* the sun, and *anthos,* a flower. Common on dry slopes of the foothills in Wyoming and Colorado, mostly on the eastern slope.

NUTTALL SUNFLOWER, *H. nuttallii,* has erect, unbranched stems up to 8 feet tall with several entirely bright yellow heads 2 to 4 inches broad on short branches along their

322. GREENTHREAD, 2/5 ×

upper portions. This is closely related to *H. tuberosus,* the "Jerusalem artichoke" and like that plant has tubers on its roots which are dug by bears and other animals for food. It grows in marshy places and along ditch banks of the foothill and montane zones from Alberta south to New Mexico and Arizona.

323. GOLDENEYE, ½ ×

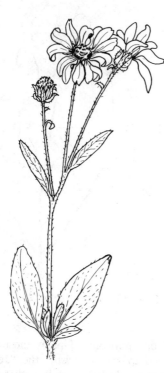

324. BUSH SUNFLOWER, ½ ×

325. FIVE-NERVED HELIANTHELLA, ½ ×

KANSAS SUNFLOWER, *H. annuus,* is the one commonly seen along roadsides, on fields and on dry plains, with heads 2 to 4 inches broad, bright yellow rays and dark brown or black disks; phyllaries have long-pointed tips and are bristly-hairy with bristle-fringed margins.

PRAIRIE SUNFLOWER, *H. petiolaris,* is very similar except that its phyllaries lack the bristly fringe and the long tips. The two are often found growing together and hybridize freely. Their brilliant coloring characterizes the scenery of the western plains and foothills during late summer from Canada to Mexico. Seeds of all the sunflowers furnish important food for birds and small mammals.

FIVE-NERVE HELIANTHELLA or LITTLE-SUNFLOWER, *Helianthella quinquenervis* (325), is closely related and similar to the true sunflowers. Its erect stems are 1 to 4 feet tall, unbranched, usually with large basal leaves which may be a foot or more long; stem leaves usually 4 pairs, shiny, 5-nerved; heads 3 to 4 inches broad, solitary or sometimes a few smaller ones below, rays light yellow, disk darker. The stalk is bent so that the flower head is in a perpendicular position. Found in open, moist woods montane and subalpine, from Montana to Mexico. [Color Pl. 12c]

ONE-FLOWER HELIANTHELLA, *H. uniflora,* is similar but lacks the large basal leaves and has erect heads; both rays and disk are bright yellow; leaves 3-nerved. It is one of the conspicuous plants of Yellowstone National Park and occurs from Montana through Wyoming to northwestern Colorado.

PARRY HELIANTHELLA, *H. parryi,* is a smaller plant, about a foot tall, with many long-petioled basal leaves and only 1 or 2 pairs of much smaller, 3-nerved stem leaves. Its yellow heads are about 2 inches broad. Montane and subalpine zones, especially ponderosa pine forests, from central Colorado south to New Mexico and Arizona.

MULE-EARS, *Wyethia amplexicaulis* (326). A coarse plant with large, leathery, elliptic, basal leaves about a foot long. The leaves have a varnished look and may be somewhat sticky; the smaller upper ones clasp the stems; heads 3 to 5 inches broad, yellow, usually several with the terminal one largest; phyllaries more or less leafy. Moist soil, montane and subalpine zones from northwestern Colorado to Nevada and Montana, blooming from May to July.

326. MULE-EARS, 2/5 ×

ARIZONA MULE-EARS, *W. arizonica,* is a hairy plant but otherwise similar which occurs in southwestern Colorado and southward to New Mexico and Arizona. Where the distribution of the two species overlaps, hybridization takes place and plants intermediate in appearance are found. MULE-EARS sometimes usurps whole meadows, probably as a result of overgrazing.

WHITE MULE-EARS, *W. helianthoides,* with white or cream-colored rays has heads 4 to 6 inches broad. Its leaves and phyllaries are finely fringed with marginal hairs. Found on moist soil in Yellowstone Park and west to Oregon and Washington.

ARROWLEAF BALSAMROOT, *Balsamorhiza sagittata* (327). A coarse plant with many leaves from a stout

327. ARROWLEAF BALSAMROOT, 2/5 ×

tap-root. Basal leaves are 8 to 15 inches long including the long petiole, grayish-velvety and arrow-shaped. Flower stalks are 8 to 24 inches tall, with only a few small leaves; heads yellow, usually solitary, 2 to 4 inches broad; involucre white with matted hairs, phyllaries with long, slender tips. Hillsides and open ground, upper foothill and montane zones throughout the Rockies. These plants begin to bloom in April or May and continue into the summer. Both wild game and domestic animals like to feed on them and they survive well under heavy grazing.

HOARY BALSAMROOT, *B. incana,* has a similar habit of growth but its leaves are silvery white and pinnate-ly parted into narrow segments. *(Incana* means "white"). Its range is from western Wyoming and southwestern Montana westward to Washington and Oregon. Another BALSAMROOT, *B. pinnatifida,* occurs in the western part of our range. It has green, pinnately divided leaves.

ACTINEA, *Hymenoxys acaulis, (Actinea acaulis, Actinella acaulis)* (328). An interesting plant with silvery-silky or woolly leaves and bright yellow heads. Leaves narrow, 1 to 2 inches long, crowded on a caespitose caudex; heads embedded in the leaves or on slender leafless stalks which may be from 2 to 15 inches tall. The ray-flowers are usually 3-toothed and have orange veins. Grows in rocky places of the foothill and alpine zones. Blooms in early spring in the foothills with very short stalks, later in the season it has taller ones. In late June or July you may find it on the tundra with its yellow heads nestled among the silvery leaves. This alpine form is called var. *caespitosa.*

RYDBERGIA or ALPINE-SUNFLOWER, *H. grandiflora, (Rydbergia grandiflora)* (329). With its large golden

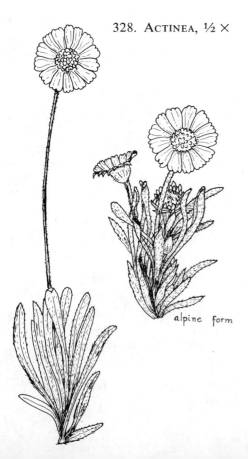

328. ACTINEA, ½ ✕

alpine form

329. RYDBERGIA, 2/5 ✕

heads and comparatively short stems this plant is the most showy and easiest to recognize of all our alpine wild flowers. Heads 2 to 4 inches broad, rays crowded, 3-lobed; foliage and involucre woolly or cottony, leaves divided into slender segments. Abundant on exposed alpine ridges, from southwestern Montana and east central Idaho to New Mexico and Utah. Its heads always face toward the rising sun and remain facing eastward. Abundant on Trail Ridge in Rocky Mountain National Park, and on the Beartooth Plateau northeast of Yellowstone. Named in honor of Per Axel Rydberg, a Swedish-born American botanist, who spent many years in botanical field work and study on the Rocky Mountain flora. [Color Pl. 12d, e] *H. brandegei,* of the southern Rockies is similar.

COLORADO RUBBER PLANT, *H. richardsonii,* is a relative of AC-TINEA and RYDBERGIA but quite different in general appearance. It is a much-branched plant with several stems from a branched woody caudex between 4 and 18 inches tall; many yellow flower heads ½- to ¾-inch broad; leaves divided into 3 to 7 narrow segments, in masses at base of stems and along stems, with tufts of woolly hairs in the leaf axils; phyllaries in 2 series, the inner ones narrow, the outer broader, keeled and united at base. On dry plains and rocky slopes, foothill and montane zones throughout our range.

GAILLARDIA or BLANKETFLOWER, *Gaillardia aristata* (330). Heads large, 2 to 3 inches broad, showy; rays yellow or light orange-yellow, sometimes reddish at base, wedge-shaped and 3-lobed or toothed; disk flowers dark red when open but the central part of disk before these flowers have opened may appear orange; corollas of disk flowers bear hairs. Plants with rays partially or entirely red which are sometimes seen are probably escapes from cultivation. Dry slopes and meadows of the foothill and montane zones throughout our range. The PIN-NATE-LEAF GAILLARDIA, *G. pinnatifida,* occurs in the foothills from southern Colorado southward.

330. GAILLARDIA, ½ ×

331. BLACK-EYED SUSAN, ½ ×

tall, heads with long, drooping yellow rays and cone-shaped dull yellow or greenish disks. Its large, smooth long-petioled leaves are much divided. This grows along streams and on wet ground of the foothill and montane zones from Canada south through the mountains to New Mexico and Arizona. The garden GOLDEN-GLOW was derived from this.

COLORADO RAYLESS CONE-FLOWER, *R. montana,* is similar in habit of growth; its foliage is smooth and grayish and its heads are without ray-flowers, appearing like stout,

332. WILD GOLDENGLOW, ½ ×

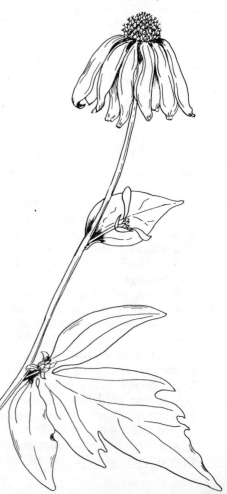

BLACKEYED SUSAN, *Rudbeckia hirta* (331). This plant is sometimes confused with GAILLARDIA but may be distinguished by its pointed, orange rays and mound-shaped dark brown, almost black, disk. Its stems are 1 to 2 feet tall; heads usually one to each stem or long branch; leaves rough-hairy, lanceolate. Widely distributed in North America and on meadows and in aspen groves of the foothills and montane zones of the mountains.

.WILD GOLDEN-GLOW, or TALL CONEFLOWER, *R. laciniata* var. *ampla* (332), has stems up to 6 feet dark greenish thumbs. This is found in the mountains of west central Colorado.

WESTERN RAYLESS CONE-FLOW-ER, *R. occidentalis,* with stems 2 to 6 feet tall has similar rayless heads but its leaves are ovate or ovate-lanceolate with entire or toothed margins. It occurs from Wyoming and Montana westward.

PRAIRIE CONE-FLOWER, *Ratibida columnifera.* A branched plant up to 2 feet tall with leaves pinnately divided into oblong or linear segments; heads with a cylindrical or columnar disk, ½- to 2½-inches high, and more or less reflexed yellow or purplish rays. On dry plains and foothills from Minnesota to British Columbia and south to Tennessee, Colorado and Arizona.

ORANGE SNEEZEWEED, *Helenium hoopsii,* is a stout plant with each stem bearing several orange-yellow flower heads in a rounded or flat-topped inflorescence; heads have a mound-shaped disk nearly an inch broad, and rather drooping rays; lower leaves are oblanceolate or obovate, 5 to 10 inches long, middle and upper ones progressively smaller and sessile. May be distinguished from CURLYHEAD GOLDENWEED (fig. 338) by its clustered heads. Meadows and open areas of the upper foothill, montane and low subalpine zones from Wyoming south to New Mexico. Abundant on the western slope in Colorado, but rare on the eastern slope.

BAHIA or FIELD-CHRYSANTHEMUM, *Bahia dissecta* (333). Stems solitary, between 1 and 3 feet tall from a rosette of dark grayish-green, much divided leaves. Inflorescence a corymb of yellow flower heads each having 12 to 20 short, broad rays; phyllaries in 2 to 3 rows, the outer

ones 3-nerved. Gravelly soil of the foothills and montane zones from Wyoming to Mexico.

333. BAHIA CHRYSANTHEMUM, ½ ✕

334. GOLDEN-ASTER, ½ ✕

335. GUMWEED, ½ ×

ing stems. Leaves, except the uppermost, petioled. The yellow, inch-broad heads which are surrounded by leafy bracts are at the ends of the stem or sometimes on short branches. Dry foothill and lower montane slopes throughout our range.

GUMWEED, *Grindelia subalpina* (335), is still another yellow-flowered member of this big sunflower family. It is easily recognized because its phyllaries have slender recurved tips, like little curls, and the heads are distinctly sticky. In bud the disk has a smooth white, gummy covering. Stems are 8 to 18 inches tall, leaves pinnately lobed or irregularly toothed, heads 1 to 1½-inches broad. On fields and hillsides, foothill and montane zones, especially where soil has been disturbed, Wyoming and Colorado.

GOLDEN-ASTER or GOLDENEYE, *Chrysopsis villosa (Heterotheca villosa)* (334). A grayish-hairy plant usually having several leafy, ascend-

GOLDENWEED or HAPLOPAPPUS, *Haplopappus* (also spelled *Aplopappus).* This genus contains many yellow-flowered species which vary considerably in size and general appearance. About the only characters which they have in common are: alternate leaves, phyllaries imbricated in several rows, rays and disk yellow, and pappus of few or many bristles. The species differ so from each other that some botanists have tried to separate them into several distinct genera. This accounts for the many names given as synonyms.

SPINY GOLDENWEED, *H. spinulosus (Sideranthus spinulosus)* (336). Stems 8 to 30 inches tall, usually several from a woody base; leaves serrate or pinnately divided, teeth or lobes bristle-tipped; head yellow, ½- to 1 inch broad; phyllaries spreading, papery with green midrib, bristle-tipped. Dry ground, plains and foothills along the eastern base of the Rockies.

336. SPINY GOLDENWEED, ½ ×

337. PARRY GOLDENWEED, ½ ×

STAR GOLDENWEED, *H. gracilis (Sideranthus gracilis),* is a much-branched, annual plant rather similar to the last with bristle-tipped leaves and phyllaries and yellow heads. It grows on dry slopes of the foothill and montane zones from western Colorado southward.

MACRONEMA, *H. macronema,* is a small rounded shrub, 6 to 15 inches tall with white-woolly branches and many yellow heads without ray flowers; phyllaries all about the same length. It occurs in sub-alpine and alpine zones from Idaho to Colorado and California.

PARRY GOLDENWEED, *H. parryi (Oreochrysum parryi),* (337). Stems 6 to 18 inches tall; heads clustered, about ½-inch broad with short, light yellow rays and yellow disk flowers. Montane and subalpine zones, often at edge of forest or in open woods, Wyoming to New Mexico and Arizona. Occurs on the North Rim, Grand Canyon National Park.

LANCELEAF GOLDENWEED, *H. lanceolatus,* is a plant with upward-curving stems 8 to 18 inches tall and many yellow heads ½- to 1 inch. broad. The leaves are lance-shaped and most of them have sharp, spine-tipped teeth. There are few leaves on the upper part of the stems. Grows on moist, alkaline soil in the montane zone from Saskatchewan to British Columbia and south to western Nebraska, south-central Colorado and northeastern California.

PLANTAIN GOLDENWEED or GEYSER-DAISY, *H. uniflorus (Pyrrocoma uniflora).* Similar to the last but stems reddish, 4 to 15 inches tall, often with a loose cottony coating; heads usually solitary, *(uniflorus* means one-flowered). On alkaline soil from Montana and Oregon to Colorado and California, especially on geyser formations in Yellowstone National Park.

CURLYHEAD GOLDENWEED, *H. croceus (Pyrrocoma crocea)* (338). A stout plant 10 to 24 inches tall with large alternate leaves and bril-

338. CURLYHEAD   GOLDENWEED, ½ ×

liant, solitary heads about 3 inches broad. The orange rays tend to curl backward as the flower heads age; pappus tawny. Montane and subalpine meadows from Wyoming and Utah to New Mexico and Arizona, in Colorado west of the Front Range. Occasionally seen on the western slope in Rocky Mountain National Park

EVERGREEN GOLDENWEED, *H. acaulis (Stenotus acaulis),* is a matforming plant with a branched, woody base and basal, narrow, 3-nerved leaves ½- to 2 inches long; flower stalks are from 1½- to 4½-inches tall with only a few small leaves or none; head ¾- to 1¼-inch broad with 6 to 15 yellow rays. Found on bad-lands, dry slopes and rocky ridges of the foothill and montane zones from Montana and Idaho to Colorado and California.

ALPINE GOLDENWEED or TONESTUS, *H. lyalii (Tonestus lyalii).* Stems slender, leafy, 2 to 6 inches tall with solitary heads ½- to 1-inch broad; rays more than 15, yellow; phyllaries lanceolate, tapering to a sharp point, glandular. Alpine in the high mountains from Alberta and British Columbia to Colorado and Oregon.

PYGMY TONESTUS, *H. pygmaeus, (Tonestus pygmaeus),* is even more dwarf than the above, forming low cushions of narrow leaves. The bright yellow flowering heads are scarcely raised above the leaves on short, leafy stems; phyllaries are leaf-like and blunt. Alpine, from Wyoming to New Mexico.

ARNICA, *Arnica.* This genus contains about 30 species all of which grow in the northern hemisphere. About half of these occur in the Rocky Mountains and are beautiful wild flowers. Most of them have bright yellow rays. Their stem leaves are opposite; the phyllaries are equal in length see *Plate G, fig. 68,* and the pappus is made up of pure white, cream or brownish bristles which may be either minutely barbed or plumose. To see this character one usually needs a hand lens. ARNICA has long been used in medicine. The species most likely to be found are described in the key and in the text which follows. In the text they are grouped according to habitats but one should remember that sometimes there may be overlapping of one into the habitats of others.

a. Heads with conspicuous ray flowers.
  b. Leaves narrow, at least twice as long as wide.
    c. Tufts of tawny woolly hair in basal leaf axils and between scales on rootstocks; stems usually 1-flowered; rays orange; pappus tawny
                          MEADOW ARNICA, p. 294.
    cc. Tufts of hair in axils white or entirely lacking.
      d. Heads usually 1 to 3; stem leaves 3 to 4 pairs.
        e. Stems usually less than 10 inches tall, often caespitose; long sticky hairs on stalk just below head; phyllaries hairy
                          ALPINE ARNICA, p. 294.
        ee. Stems usually more than 10 inches tall; phyllaries not strongly hairy inside at tips; pappus plumose and tawny
                          SUBALPINE ARNICA, p. 294.
      dd. Heads several to many, usually more than 5; stem leaves more than 5 pairs; pappus barbellate and straw-colored.

  e. Phyllaries blunt, hairy at tip inside
          LEAFY ARNICA, p. 294.
  ee. Phyllaries sharp-pointed, not hairy at tip inside
          LONGLEAF ARNICA, p. 294.
bb. Leaves broad, always less than twice as long as wide, abruptly
    narrowed to a heart-shaped or broad base; basal leaves peti-
    oled; pappus barbellate, white.
  c. Leaves heart-shaped, hairy; stems 8 to 24 inches tall; heads
    solitary, 2 to 3 inches broad
          HEARTLEAF ARNICA, p. 293.
  cc. Leaves ovate or lance-ovate, mostly without hairiness; stems
    6 to 12 inches tall; heads 3 to 9, 1 to 2 inches broad
          SLENDER ARNICA, p. 295.
aa. Heads without ray flowers, nodding; pappus straw-colored or
    tawny
          PARRY ARNICA, p. 293.

The Woodland Arnicas.

HEART-LEAF ARNICA, *A. cordifolia* (339), is the most showy of all species. Its large, bright yellow, usually solitary heads are conspicuous in moist coniferous forests of the montane and subalpine zones in late spring and early summer. Later the seed heads attract attention with tufts of white pappus. The base of the involucre and the stalk just below the head is clothed with long white hairs. This species has a wide distribution occurring on the Keewennaw Peninsula of Michigan and from Alaska down the length of the Rockies to New Mexico and southern California. It is found on the North Rim of the Grand Canyon.

339. HEARTLEAF ARNICA, 2/5 ×

The BROAD-LEAF ARNICA, *A. latifolia*, is very similar and occurs throughout the Rockies. It blooms later, lacks the white hairs at the base of the involucre, and it may have from 1 to 5 heads to a stalk.

PARRY or RAYLESS ARNICA, *A. parryi* (340), is a tall, hairy and slightly sticky plant of moist slopes and open woods throughout our range. The rayless heads which hang down are brownish yellow.

340. PARRY ARNICA, ½ ×

The Meadow Arnicas.

MEADOW or ORANGE ARNICA, *Arnica fulgens.* This strongly scented, sticky-hairy plant is abundant in some montane and subalpine meadows from western Canada south to Colorado and Nevada. It has from 1 to 3 orange heads.

SUBALPINE ARNICA, *A. mollis,* is a plant of moist meadows in the subalpine and alpine zones of our region. It has a very wide distribution and is found from Quebec to the mountains of Maine and New Hampshire and from Alberta and British Columbia to Colorado and California.

LEAFY ARNICA, *A. chamissonis (A. foliosa),* may be recognized by its several, comparatively small heads, 1 to 1½-inches broad, and its more numerous leaves which taper to both ends. Found in meadows of the montane and lower subalpine zones from western Canada to New Mexico and California.

LONG-LEAF ARNICA, *A. longifolia,* is a somewhat glandular-sticky plant with several pairs of leaves. Their bases sheath the stem. It grows in wet meadows of the upper montane and lower subalpine zones from Montana and Idaho to western Colorado and Nevada.

Alpine and Timberline region Arnicas.

ALPINE or RYDBERG ARNICA, *A. rydbergii* (341), has 3-nerved leaves and a spreading rootstock forming patches on rocky slopes and ridges at timberline and above. From Alberta and British Columbia to Colorado.

NORTHERN ALPINE ARNICA, *A. alpina,* extends south into Montana

341. RYDBERG ARNICA, ½ ×

and occurs in Glacier National Park. It has long hairs on its stem and long-pointed leaves.

SLENDER ARNICA, *A. gracilis,* is an alpine species of the northern part of our range and is abundant at and above timberline in Glacier National Park.

SENECIO, *Senecio.* In this large genus there are many attractive wild flowers as well as several weedy species. Leaves are alternate; rays, in our species, yellow, except for one exception, the SAFFRON SENECIO, where they are sometimes orange or orange-red; the involucre is made up of one row of narrow, equal phyllaries with a few smaller ones at base (see *Plate G, fig. 69).* The tips of the phyllaries are often black. In some species this is quite noticeable. A few species are without rays, having heads made up only of disk flowers.

Some have "nodding" heads. The botanist uses this term to describe the position resulting when the stalk is bent just below the head so the head is facing either outward or downward, not upward.

SENECIOS are either quite smooth or cobwebby with white hairs. They are never rough with stiff hairs as are the sunflowers or sticky-hairy as are some of the arnicas. Plants of this group have been given many different common names in different parts of our country or other countries. Some of these are GROUNDSEL, RAGWORT, and BUTTERWORT. The Latin name *Senecio* comes from a word meaning "old man," in reference to the silvery white pappus which is conspicuous as senecios go to seed suggesting white hair. The garden plants called LEOPARD BANE, species of *Doronicum,* are closely related to plants of this group, and the florists' CINERARIAS are of this genus.

```
a. Heads without ray flowers.
  b. Heads nodding, 1/4- to 3/4-inch long, few, in a raceme
                    BIGELOW SENECIO, p. 298.
  bb. Heads erect, 1/4- to 3/8-inch long, numerous in a flat-
      topped cluster
                    TURNIP-LEAF SENECIO, p. 297.
aa. Heads with showy, yellow ray flowers.
  b. Heads nodding, at least in bud, single or few, alpines.
    c. Leaves shaped like those of dandelions and more or
       less whitened with cobwebby hairs
                    DANDELION-LEAF SENECIO, p. 299.
    cc. Leaves smooth, ovate, or oblong to roundish.
      d. Leaves and stalks reddish-purple; rays not over 3/8-inch
         long; basal leaves in tufts
                    ALPINE SENECIO, p. 299.
      dd. Leaves usually bright green; rays 1/2-inch or more in length
                    DAFFODIL SENECIO, p. 299.
  bb. Heads erect.
    c. Plants with leafy stems, 2 to 4 feet tall; leaves 2 to 6 inches
       long.
      d. Leaves triangular, more or less toothed; heads many
                    ARROWLEAF SENECIO, p. 298.
    dd. Leaves linear or lanceolate with long-pointed tips and sharply
```

saw-toothed margins

TOOTHED SENECIO, p. 298.

cc. Plants mostly not over 2 feet tall.

d. Stems 1 to 2 feet tall, much branched; flower heads distributed all over the bushy plant; common along roads and trails.

e. Leaves very narrow with smooth edges

BROOM SENECIO, p. 298.

ee. Leaves 1 to 4 inches long, deeply, pinnately divided into
unequal segments

WESTERN GOLDEN RAGWORT, p. 299.

dd. Stems 8 to 24 inches tall, unbranched except in the inflorescence
which is flat-topped or rounded.

e. Plants white, grayish-, or yellowish-green due to a coating
of cobwebby hairs which may be partially shed as the plant
ages.

f. Leaves grayish, pinnately divided into equal, folded lobes

FENDLER SENECIO, p. 297.

ff. Leaves not pinnately divided into equal folded lobes.

g. Central head larger, on a shorter, stouter stalk than the
others; leaves yellowish-green

COMMON SPRING SENECIO, p. 296.

gg. Heads all alike; leaves silvery gray or whitish.

h. Heads numerous; rays 3 to 5; phyllaries conspicuously
black tipped

BLACK-TIPPED SENECIO, p. 299.

hh. Heads solitary or few; rays 8 to 12

PURSH SENECIO, pp. 297, 299.

ee. Plants green or bluish-green, without cobwebby coating.

f. Leaves more or less toothed or lobed.

g. Stems leafy; plants tufted, growing in alpine and subalpine rock slides or crevices.

h. Stems about 4 inches tall

FREMONT SENECIO, p. 299.

hh. Stems 6 to 20 inches tall

ROCK SENECIO, p. 299.

gg. Stem leaves smaller than basal ones, clasping the stem
with ear-like lobes

SAFFRON SENECIO, p. 298.

ff. Leaves entire or with few, irregularly spaced, small
teeth.

g. Plant bluish-green; heads many

WOOTON SENECIO, p. 299.

gg. Plant green; heads few to several; phyllaries thickened
and having hairy black tips

THICK-BRACTED SENECIO, p. 298.

*1. Senecios found most commonly in open pine woodland of the
foothill and montane zones.*

COMMON SPRING SENECIO, or   *tegerrimus* (342) an early bloom-
LAMBSTONGUE GROUNDSEL, *S. in-*   ing, rather stout plant, somewhat

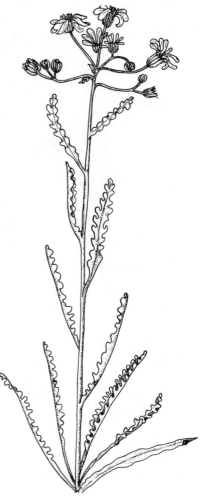

342. COMMON SPRING SENECIO or
LAMBSTONGUE GROUNDSEL,
½ ×

untidy in appearance with its cobwebby pubescence which disappears
as the plant grows older, and its
rather irregularly arranged rays. The
upper leaves clasp the stem and
taper to a slender point. Foothills
slopes and open pine forest from
Minnesota westward and south to
Colorado.

FENDLER SENECIO, S. *fendleri*
(343), is somewhat similar to the
last but usually has more slender
stem and more heads in a more
symmetrical flat-topped cluster. Its
basal leaves are pinnately divided
into folded segments. Dry foothill
slopes and open pine forest from
Wyoming to New Mexico. Sometimes also found in the subalpine
zone.

343. FENDLER SENECIO, ½ ×

TURNIP-LEAF SENECIO, S. *rapi-
folius*, has obovate, sharply-toothed,
petioled basal leaves and numerous,
deep yellow, rayless heads. It occurs
on rocky, wooded canyon slopes and
ridges from South Dakota to Idaho
and south into northern Colorado.
PURSH SENECIO may also be found
in these zones, see under Section 4.

2. Senecios found most commonly in meadows and aspen groves of the montane and subalpine zones and along subalpine stream banks.

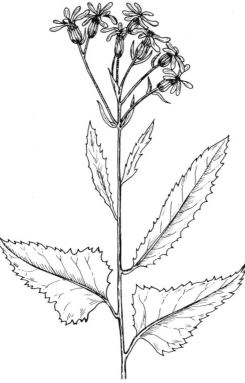

344. ARROWLEAF SENECIO, ½ ×

This may also be found in meadows above timberline. From South Dakota to Idaho and south to New Mexico and Utah.

SAFFRON SENECIO, *S. crocatus* including what has been called *S. dimorphophyllus*. The leaves of this plant are variable, as the name *dimorphophyllus* meaning "leaves of two shapes" indicates. Its basal leaves are oblong or even rounded and petioled with entire or somewhat toothed margins. The stem leaves are pinnately lobed, rays are orange or rarely almost red. Moist meadows, subalpine and alpine, Colorado, Utah, and Wyoming. May be seen in Rocky Mountain and Grand Teton National Parks.

ARROWLEAF SENECIO, *S. triangllaris* (344). A tall, lush plant forming large clumps, especially on very wet ground and along streams. Conspicuous in subalpine meadows in Rocky Mountain National Park. Saskatchewan to Alaska and south to New Mexico and California. [Color Pl. 12b]

BIGELOW or RAYLESS SENECIO, *S. bigelovii*. A rather stout plant 1 to 3 feet tall with top-shaped involucres, yellow disk flowers and purplish phyllaries. Colorado, New Mexico and Arizona.

THICK-BRACTED SENECIO, *S. crassulus,* has stems 9 to 20 inches tall with narrow, tapered leaves 3 to 6 inches long, the upper ones sessile.

TOOTHED SENECIO, *S. serra* var. *admirabilis.* About as tall as the last and with much the same habit but usually with fewer flower heads. May be distinguished by the narrow, long-pointed, toothed leaves. From Montana south to southern Colorado. This forms fields of yellow in Yellowstone National Park in July and August.

3. Senecios found mostly on disturbed soil along roads and trails or on rock-covered slopes.

BROOM SENECIO, *S. spartioides.* The narrow leaves sometimes have 1 or 2 pairs of short, narrow lobes at the base. Usually seen along highways and on roadsides where it is conspicuous when covered with yellow flowers during mid-summer and later when the tufts of white pappus have developed. Nebraska and Wyoming, south to Texas and Arizona.

WESTERN GOLDEN RAGWORT, *S. eremophilus,* is another plant that brightens the roadsides in July and August. It occurs from Wyoming to Idaho and south to New Mexico and Arizona.

BLACK-TIPPED SENECIO, *S. atratus,* with its silvery foliage and numerous small, yellow flower heads, is a handsome plant frequently seen along roads and trails of the subalpine zone, especially along the Trail Ridge Road in Rocky Mountain National Park. Found in Colorado, Utah and New Mexico. [Color Pl. 12f]

WOOTON SENECIO, with bright yellow heads and a cabbage-like sheen to its smooth leaves, is sometimes found in these situations also, see Section 4.

4. Senecios of the timberline region and alpine rock fields and tundra.

PURSH SENECIO, *S. canus (S. purshianus, S. harbourii),* is a silvery gray plant, usually not over 8 inches tall. It may have one or several stems, each with one or few heads. The leaves are obovate to oblanceolate and may be entire or more or less lobed. Widely distributed from the foothills to the alpine zone and from western Canada south through Montana and Wyoming to Nebraska and Colorado.

ROCK SENECIO, *S. fremontii* var. *blitoides (S. carthamoides).* Its bright yellow heads make it easy to see but it is not always easy to reach as it is usually found flourishing among large angular boulders or in rock crevices. Its oval or spatulate leaves are coarsely toothed. Alpine zone in Colorado and New Mexico.

FREMONT SENECIO, *S. fremontii,* is similar in appearance and occurs in similar situations in Montana and Wyoming, and may be seen in Glacier and Yellowstone National Parks. DAFFODIL SENECIO, *S. amplectens,* is a handsome plant with long, light yellow rays and darker disk. Its color and nodding head suggest the name daffodil. In exposed situations it may be only a few inches tall with heads an inch broad but in moist, sheltered, meadowy spots it may be a foot or more in height with larger heads.

ALPINE SENECIO, *S. soldanella,* is a low, tufted plant with many basal, roundish, purplish leaves and yellow heads found on moist gravel in the high mountains of Colorado.

DANDELION-LEAF SENECIO, *S. taraxacoides,* is from 2 to 5 inches tall and its leaves are more or less coated or patched with white cobwebby hairs. It may be distinguished from true dandelions by the presence of two kinds of flowers in the head, both disk and ray are present. Occurs on high alpine ridges and peaks of Colorado and New Mexico.

WOOTON SENECIO, *S. wootoni (S. anacletus)* is a plant of the timberline regions with stems 10 to 20 inches tall, usually several from a stout rootstock. Most of its smooth, glaucous leaves are basal, spatulate or obovate in shape. The combination of bright yellow flowers and bluish-green leaves makes it especially handsome. Found on moist gravel slopes of the subalpine zone in Colorado and New Mexico. E. O. Wooton, for whom this plant was named, was a botanist who spent many years studying the plants of New Mexico and was the senior author of *Flora of New Mexico* published by the United States National Herbarium in 1915.

GOLDENROD, *Solidago*. The individual heads of these plants are very small but each head is made up of separate disk and ray flowers. The heads are clustered and an inflorescence usually contains several clusters. Often they are arranged along one side of the branches which are sometimes arched. The leaves are simple, alternate and entire or slightly toothed. The different kinds look much alike and are difficult to identify.

Goldenrod pollen is comparatively heavy and is distributed by insects, not by the wind. Consequently this plant is not one of the major causes of hay fever as is commonly believed.

SMOOTH GOLDENROD, *S. missouriensis (S. concinna)* (345), is a glabrous plant from 10 to 15 inches tall with an open irregular inflorescence and 3-nerved leaves. Foothill and montane zones throughout our range. *S. multiradiata*, another smooth plant with its head in a narrow panicle but not one-sided, has reddish stems from 8 to 20 inches tall. Each head has about 13 ray flowers. The leaves are obovate, 3-nerved, and have rounded teeth on their upper portions and hairy margins at base. Found throughout our range from the upper foothills to the alpine.

345. SMOOTH GOLDENROD, ½ ×

346. FEW-FLOWERED GOLDENROD, ½ ×

DWARF GOLDENROD, *S. spathulata* var. *nana (S. decumbens)*, is similar but smaller, 4 to 6 inches tall with red stems and rounded clusters of small heads; each head has only about 8 ray flowers and there are no hairs along the margins of the leaf bases. Found on rocky slopes in the subalpine and alpine zones. *S. spathulata*, a closely related, taller plant, occurs in the montane and subalpine regions.

ROUGH GOLDENROD, *S. nana (S. pulcherrima)*, is densely covered with short hairs and its leaves are indistinctly 3-nerved. It grows in clumps in the foothills and the lower montane areas throughout our range.

FEW-FLOWERED GOLDENROD, *S. sparsiflora* (346) has finely pubescent foliage. Its flower heads are arranged in one-sided, elongated clusters and its leaves are distinctly 3-nerved. Foothill and montane zones in Colorado, especially on the western slope.

TALL GOLDENROD, *S. canadensis,* has stems 1½- to 4 feet tall; 3-nerved, distinctly toothed leaves; inflorescence of one-sided branches but more or less flat-topped. Found on wet meadows and along streams of the foothill and montane zones throughout our range.

BROOM SNAKEWEED, *Gutierrezia sarothrae (G. diversifolia),* is a bushy plant somewhat resembling the goldenrods. Its stems grow 8 inches to 2 feet tall from a woody base with very narrow leaves and many very small yellow heads. These are clustered at ends of the branches. A plant of dry ground abundant on the western plains and which may occasionally be seen in dry situations anywhere in our region below the subalpine zone.

Group II. Heads composed entirely of disk (tubular) flowers.

PEARLY EVERLASTING, *Anaphalis margaritacea (A. subalpina)* (347,). The little round heads of this plant appear entirely white because of their white, papery, imbricated phyllaries. Its foliage is whitish or gray from a coating of cobwebby hairs; frequently seen in masses along trails and roads and on rocky slopes of the upper montane and subalpine zones throughout the Rockies.

WESTERN CUDWEED, *Gnaphalium chilense (G. decurrens, G. wrightii)* is somewhat similar but may easily be distinguished on close observation. Its phyllaries are cream-colored or yellowish and very satiny. Its stems and leaves are coated with cottony hairs but are more of a yellowish green rather than grayish as are those of the PEARLY EVER-LASTING. Also the CUDWEED is a sticky plant. It is much less abundant and occurs scatteringly in the foothill and montane zones of the mountains.

PUSSYTOES, *Antennaria.* These are small plants having clusters of heads with papery phyllaries. Most of them have silvery leaves arranged in basal rosettes. They are easily transplanted and make an attractive ground cover in a garden.

347. PEARLY EVERLASTING, ½ ✕

MOUNTAIN PUSSYTOES, *A. parvifolia* (348), is perhaps the commonest one. Its stems are 2 to 6 inches tall and each has a cluster of 3 to 8 heads from ¼- to ½-inch long; basal leaves are obovate or rounded; phyllaries are usually more or less brownish at base and papery-white or pale pink at the tips. This forms silvery mats on dry meadows and open wooded slopes from the foothills to timberline throughout our range.

ALPINE PUSSYTOES, *A. alpina (A.*

348. MOUNTAIN PUSSYTOES, ½ ×,
(left, staminate flowers; right,
pistillate flowers),

umbrinella), is similar but its phyllaries are definitely brown and it
may have even shorter stems.

PINK or MEADOW PUSSYTOES, A.
rosea, is a plant with stems usually
8 to 10 inches tall; sometimes it
may be 15 inches. Its basal leaves

are spatulate with distinct petioles;
its phyllaries are usually bright pink
and its heads less than ¼-inch long.
It occurs in moist meadows and
along stream banks from the foothill to the alpine zones from Alaska
to Montana and south to Colorado
and California.

TALL PUSSYTOES, A. anaphaloides (S. pulcherrima), is a gray or
whitish woodland plant which does
not have the mat-forming habit of
the other species. Its stems are solitary or few together, 10 to 15
inches tall, and it resembles the
PEARLY EVERLASTING, as indicated
by the name anaphaloides which
means "like Anaphalis." Its basal
leaves are 4 to 6 inches long, narrow
and strongly 3-nerved. This leaf
character and its different habit of
growth distinguish it from the EVER-
LASTING. It never forms big beds
but occurs scatteringly in aspen or
open spruce or moist pine forests
from Montana south through Colorado.

THISTLE, Cirsium. All our thistles have toothed- or wavy-margined
leaves and each tooth is tipped by a sharp bristle or spine. Also the
phyllaries are usually spine-tipped. Some thistles have large, showy purple
or pinkish heads but this is a variable character and even the usually
purple-flowered ones may sometimes have pale, dingy heads. The individual flowers making up the heads have deeply and sometimes un-
evenly 5-cleft corollas. The species most frequently seen are described
in the following key.

a. Plants glabrous; leaves green on both sides.
   b. Flower heads erect, less than 1 inch high, several to many in
      clusters at the ends of erect branches
                              CREEPING THISTLE, p. 304.
   bb. Flower heads nodding, 1 to 2 inches high, solitary at the ends
       of leafless branches
                              NODDING THISTLE, p. 304.
aa. Plants more or less grayish or whitish with cottony hairs.
   b. Heads usually pale, whitish, pinkish, or cream.
      c. Spines very numerous, golden; leaves yellow-green; phyllaries
         spine-tipped.

    d. Phyllaries covered with cobwebby hairs; heads in a dense cluster

        HOOKER THISTLE, p. 303.

    dd. Phyllaries glabrous; heads sessile in a large basal rosette of leaves

        ELK THISTLE, p. 303.

  cc. Spines less numerous, not golden; leaves green above, white beneath; phyllaries with fringed tips

        AMERICAN THISTLE, p. 303.

bb. Heads usually purple or rose.

  c. Leaves with clasping bases

        WAVY-LEAF THISTLE, p. 303.

  cc. Leaves with decurrent bases, forming wing-like, spine-edged extensions for 2 or 3 inches along the stem

        BULL THISTLE, p. 304.

WAVY-LEAF THISTLE, *C. undulatum,* (349). Common on the plains and mesas and frequently seen in the foothill and montane zone throughout our range; also on the North Rim of the Grand Canyon.

AMERICAN THISTLE, *C. centaureae (C. americanum)* with pale, dingy or sometimes pink flowers and fringed phyllaries, occurs in ravines of the montane and subalpine zones, often forming colonies. Wyoming, Colorado and Utah.

HOOKER THISTLE, *C. scopulorum (C. hookerianum),* with stems 8 to 24 inches tall, has a dense cluster of pale heads which are overtopped by the excessively spiny leaves. It is a species of rocky slopes in the subalpine and alpine zones from Montana to Colorado and Utah.

ELK THISTLE or DRUMMOND THISTLE, *C. foliosum (S. drummondii),* is somewhat similar but often stemless with the heads sitting in a large basal rosette of very spiny leaves. This is the species which

349. WAVYLEAF THISTLE, 2/5 ×

saved Truman Everts, a lost explorer in Yellowstone National Park in 1870, from starvation. The peeled root and stems are pleasantly flavored and nourishing. The plant is relished by elk and bears. Grows in meadows, on stream banks and around ponds of the montane and subalpine zones throughout the Rockies.

In addition to the four native species named above there are three species, introduced from Europe, which are classed as weeds but are conspicuous and beautiful when in flower.

CREEPING or CANADA THISTLE, *C. arvense,* is one of the most noxious weeds we have. Between its vigorous, deep-seated creeping rootstock and its efficient seed dispersal system, it is able to take over whole meadows in a few years and render them economically useless. It thrives on moist, rich soil and has spread in meadows and along roadsides throughout the northern United States.

NODDING THISTLE, *C. nutans,* is commonly seen on fields and along roadsides in Montana and occasionally in other western states.

BULL THISTLE, *C. vulgare,* is a stout, branched plant, 1 to 6 feet tall, with stiff spines and beautiful purple heads. It is becoming established in pastures and meadows of our region.

GRAY HORSEBRUSH, *Tetradymia canescens.* A little white-felted shrub which grows from 8 to 24 inches tall with narrow leaves and flower heads in small clusters at the ends of the branches. Each head is about ⅜- to ½-inch high, has 4 whitish phyllaries and contains 4 yellow flowers. This grows on dry plains and hillsides of the foothill

and montane zones from Montana south to New Mexico.

SPINY HORSEBRUSH, *T. spinosa,* is a much-branched, very spiny shrub, up to 4 feet tall. Its stems and young leaves are covered with a white coating and the heads, ½- to ⅝-inch high, contain from 5 to 9 flowers and are arranged along the branches. Dry plains and hillsides of the foothill zone from Montana to western Colorado and California.

STICKY-FLOWERED RABBITBRUSH, *Chrysothamnus viscidiflorus (C. pumila)* (350), has many forms. A common one is the shrub with several branches from the base, 10 to 24 inches tall with narrow, usually twisted leaves, and rounded or flat-topped clusters of small yellow flower heads not over ¼-inch high, which occurs on dry hillsides of the foothill and montane zones from Montana to Colorado.

A taller form of this is found farther west. GOLDEN RABBITBRUSH, *C. nauseosus* (351), is also

350. STICKY RABBITBRUSH, ½ ×

352. GOLDEN-SHOWER,   ½ ×

351. GOLDEN RABBITBRUSH, ½ ×

very variable. It is a shrub 2 to 4 feet tall with gray or light green twigs, narrow leaves and large, rounded clusters of golden yellow heads. When this blooms in late summer and fall it is handsome and conspicuous along ditch and stream banks, sometimes on roadsides in the foothill and montane zones throughout our range.

PARRY RABBITBRUSH, *C. parryi,* a shrub not over 2 feet tall, has heads ⅓- to ½-inch high with slender-tipped phyllaries. It occurs in open forests of the montane and subalpine zones from Wyoming to Nevada and south to Colorado and Utah.

GOLDEN SHOWER or TAPERLEAF, *Pericome caudata* (352). A bushy plant from 2 to 5 feet tall with interesting, bright green, opposite, very long-tailed leaves. Its clustered

flower heads are light yellow. Found on rocky slopes and in canyons of the foothills; southern Colorado, New Mexico and Arizona.

TASSELFLOWER or BRICKLEBUSH, *Brickellia grandiflora* (353). Heads pale yellowish in nodding clusters on long stalks from the axils of the

353. TASSELFLOWER, ½ ×

upper leaves. Leaves triangular, toothed, rather strongly veined. Among rocks on dry canyon sides, foothill and montane zones throughout our range.

JOE-PYE WEED, *Eupatorium maculatum,* is a coarse plant with purple-spotted stems 2 to 5 feet tall; leaves whorled, usually 4 or 5 at a node, ovate to lanceolate, short petioled and sharply toothed; heads about ⅜-inch high, pink or purple, in large flat-topped clusters. This plant is widely distributed in North America and is found occasionally in the Rocky Mountain region in foothill meadows.

THOROUGH-WORT, *E. herbaceum,* with stems from 1 to 2½-feet tall, opposite, ovate or triangular leaves and whitish flowers, occurs in foothill canyons and on rocky slopes of southwestern Colorado and in Utah, Arizona, and New Mexico. It occurs in Grand Canyon National Park on the North Rim.

MOUNTAIN-SAGE, SAGEWORT or SAGEBRUSH, *Artemisia.* This group has many representatives in western North America. It includes both woody and herbaceous plants. Most of them are strongly aromatic. Their foliage is usually silvery and their small flower heads, arranged in elongated clusters, have no colorful characters. They bloom in late summer and their wind-blown pollen is a cause of hay fever.

BIG SAGEBRUSH, *A. tridentata* (354). A rigid, much-branched shrub which may be from 6 inches to 10 feet, but is commonly from 1 to 4 feet, tall. Leaves bluish-silvery, wedge-shaped, 3-toothed at apex, strongly aromatic; heads ¼-inch or less in length, numerous, in narrow panicles. Sagebrush usually grows in colonies often covering many acres or square miles on dry,

354. BIG SAGEBRUSH, ½ ×

open valleys, foothills and lower montane slopes, especially where there is deep but dry soil.

ALPINE MOUNTAIN-SAGE, *A. scopulorum,* is a small silvery plant with few or several tufted stems 4 to 10 inches tall and mostly basal leaves divided into narrow segments. Its few heads are ¼- to ⅜-inch broad, arranged as a raceme. It occurs from Montana to New Mexico and Utah.

A. pattersonii (355), ALPINE MOUNTAIN-SAGE, found in Colorado and New Mexico, is similar but has even shorter stems with 1 to 5 heads about ½-inch broad. Both occur on rocky or grassy alpine slopes.

BOREAL MOUNTAIN-SAGE, *A. arctica* ssp. *saxicola,* with clustered,

355. ALPINE MOUNTAIN-SAGE, ½ ×

reddish stems from 4 to 12 inches tall and nodding heads which have dark-margined phyllaries, is another alpine species occurring from Alaska south along the western mountains to Colorado and California.

FRINGED or PASTURE MOUNTAIN-SAGE, *A. frigida* (356), is an attractive plant with finely-divided, silvery leaves in basal tufts and slender clusters of small nodding, yellowish flower heads. Commonly seen on dry slopes of the foothill, montane and subalpine zones throughout the Rockies. This aromatic plant is the one from which early settlers made a very bitter tea which was believed to be a tonic and a remedy for "mountain fever" (typhoid fever). It quickly establishes itself on the disturbed soil of road and trail sides and on overgrazed pasture land.

WESTERN MUGWORT or PRAIRIE SAGEWORT, *A. ludoviciana (A. gnaphalodes)*. This species is a herbaceous plant, very variable. It is covered by a dense tomentum of white cobwebby hairs. It is best recognized by this white coloring, plus the leaf shape. Its leaves vary from narrow and entire to broad and more or less deeply divided into pointed segments. Widely distributed from the Mississippi River westward. Occurring in the mountains on dry open slopes in the foothill and montane zones.

GAYFEATHER, *Liatris*. Clusters of erect, bright rose-purple spikes seen along roadsides and on fields in late summer say that GAYFEATHER is in bloom.

KANSAS GAYFEATHER, *L. punctata* (357), is a beautiful plant with stems from 6 inches to 2 feet tall thickly set along the upper portion with bright purple heads. The stem is covered with narrow, rough-edged leaves which are gradually reduced

356. FRINGED MOUNTAIN-SAGE, ½ ×

357. KANSAS GAYFEATHER, ½ ×

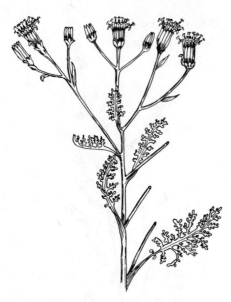

358. DUSTY MAIDEN, ½ ×

ROCKY MOUNTAIN GAYFEATHER, *L. ligulistylis,* is similar but has fewer, broader and shorter heads. It occurs in the same areas but is less common.

DUSTY MAIDEN or BRIDES BOUQUET, *Chaenactis douglasii* (358). A grayish plant with stems 8 to 12 inches tall, leaves pinnately divided with the segments again lobed or divided; heads about ½-inch high, flowers white or pinkish; phyllaries of equal length forming a cylindrical involucre; pappus a crown of 10 narrow, transparent scales, 5 of these shorter than the others. On shady or rocky ground from the foothills to the subalpine zone and from Montana to Colorado and Nevada. The ALPINE DUSTY MAIDEN, *C. alpina,* is similar but has shorter stems and occurs at higher altitudes. A plant with heads very similar to DUSTY MAIDEN but with leaves 2 or 3 times divided into very narrow segments, is *Hymenopappus arenosus.* This occurs on dry, often sandy soil of the foothill and montane zones in Colorado, New Mexico and Arizona.

in length toward the inflorescence. The pistils have 2 thread-like twisted, purple appendages at their tips which give the flower heads a feathery look. Dry situations of the plains, foothills and lower montane zone along the eastern side of the Continental Divide from South Dakota to Texas and New Mexico. In the mountains on the eastern side of the Continental Divide.

Group III, heads composed of only ray flowers having strap-shaped corollas, as in dandelions. All of these have milky juice.

DANDELION,   The   common Dandelion, *Taraxacum officinalis* and the Red-Seeded Dandelion, *T. erythrosperum* are common weeds throughout our area. Tundra dandelion, *T. ceratophorum* (359) a native species, is frequently seen on grassy alpine slopes. It may be distinguished from the others by the hornshaped swellings at the tips of its outer phyllaries.

PALE AGOSERIS or FALSE DANDELION, *Agoseris glauca* (360). This

359. TUNDRA DANDELION, ½ ×

dandelion-like plant may be recognized by its pointed, dark-colored phyllaries which have conspicuous light borders, and its pale green leaves. It usually grows on drier ground than the common dandelion, and is often seen among grasses on open slopes from the foothill to the alpine zone throughout our range.

BURNT-ORANGE AGOSERIS, *A. aurantiaca,* is similar but often smaller and its flowers are a deep orange. It has the same range and also extends into the alpine zone.

SLENDER HAWKWEED, *Hieraceum gracile* (361). Stems usually solitary, 4 to 12 inches tall, with a few, small, dandelion-like yellow heads; involucres densely black-hairy; leaves mostly basal, obovate or oblong-spatulate. Commonly found in moist woods of the montane and subalpine zones and also in the alpine zone.

WHITE HAWKWEED, *H. albiflorum,* has white or creamy flowers, lacks the black hairs on the involucre but has tawny, bristly hairs on the leaves and occurs in similar situations.

DANDELION HAWKSBEARD, *Crepis runcinata,* is somewhat similar to Hawkweed but is usually a stouter plant with several bright yellow heads in a flat-topped cluster. It lacks the hairiness of Hawkweed and its leaves are usually somewhat like dandelion leaves. It is a plant of moist meadows and is found throughout our range.

ALPINE HAWKSBEARD, *C. nana,* is closely related and similar but has very short stems and tufted

360. PALE AGOSERIS, ½ ×

361. SLENDER HAWKWEED, ½ ×

leaves which have an enlarged terminal lobe with smaller teeth below. It occurs in moist rocky situations of the alpine zones.

SALSIFY, *Tragopogon dubius* (362), is an erect plant 1 to 3 feet tall with long, grass-like leaves which clasp the stem, and lemon-yellow flower heads with long pointed phyllaries extending beyond the flowers. The tawny, ball-like seed heads, often 4 inches in diameter, are conspicuous in middle and late summer. This plant is an immigrant from Europe and is closely related to the vegetable known as oyster plant. It has become widely distributed as a weed on roadsides and waste land throughout our range in the foothill and montane zones.

RATTLESNAKE ROOT, *Prenanthes racemosa*. Stems 1 to 3 feet tall with a narrow, elongated inflorescence. Heads ½- to ¾-inch long; flowers pink; phyllaries dark purplish or black, loosely hairy; lower leaves glabrous, oval to oblanceolate on long, winged petioles. Moist ground in ravines and meadows of the foothill and montane zones from Alberta to Colorado.

MILKPINK, *Lygodesmia grandiflora*. Stems 6 to 18 inches tall, leaves linear, 2 to 4 inches long, firm and ascending. Heads at the ends of branches appear like 5- to

362. SALSIFY, ½ ×

10-petaled pink flowers but in reality each "petal" is a separate flower, as in other members of this family. In dry gravelly soil of the foothill and montante zones, from Wyoming to Idaho and south to New Mexico and Arizona. This occurs in Colorado National Monument.

RUSHPINK, or SKELETONWEED, *L. juncea,* is a related plant with bare, green stems. Its lower leaves are not over 2 inches long, narrow and stiff, and the upper ones are reduced to mere scales. Flower heads pink, similar to MILKPINK but smaller. Dry slopes, foothills, Colorado and New Mexico.

WIRE-LETTUCE, *Stephanomeria pauciflora.* Flowers pink, similar to those of MILKPINK, but with feathery pappus wiry green stems and bract-like upper leaves. Dry plains and hillsides.

CHICHORY, *Cichorium intybus,* may be up to 3 feet tall and much branched, branches set with flat, bright blue flower heads. It is a common road side weed below 7,000 ft. WILD LETTUCE, *Lactuca pulchella,* is a somewhat similar but more widely branched and has purplish-blue flowers.

There are a few other plants with dandelion-like flower heads which are often called "false dandelions". Their technical differences are not easily observed but the following few hints may help to distinguish them. *Nothocalais cuspidata* has only basal leaves which have a narrow white hairy margin. *Krigia biflora* has a forking stem which bears 1 to 3 small, sessile leaves and 1 to few heads. *Microseris nutans* has variable leaves, few to several heads, a and a pappus of long, thin scales each ending in a feathery bristle. Its buds are nodding. (It has been called *Ptilocalais nutans.*)

Useful References

Bailey, Virginia Long, and Harold Edwards Bailey
    1949. *Woody Plants of the Western National Parks.* (American Midland Naturalist, Monograph No. 4). The University Press, Notre Dame, Indiana.
Booth, W. E., and J. C. Wright
    1959. *Flora of Montana.* Montana State College, Bozeman, Montana.
Chamberlin, Thomas C., and Rollin D. Salisbury
    1909. *A College Textbook of Geology.* Henry Holt and Co., N.Y.
Clements, Frederic E., and Edith S. Clements
    1928. *Rocky Mountain Flowers.* H. W. Wilson Co., N.Y.
Coulter, John M., revised by Aven Nelson
    1909. *New Manual of Botany of the Central Rocky Mountains.* American Book Co., N.Y.
Craighead, John J., Frank C. Craighead, Jr., and Ray J. Davis
    1963. *A Field Guide to Rocky Mountain Wildflowers.* Peterson Field Guide Series. Houghton Mifflin Co., Boston, Mass.
Davis, Ray J.
    1952. *Flora of Idaho.* Wm. C. Brown Co., Dubuque, Iowa.
Ewan, Joseph A.
    1950. *Rocky Mountain Naturalists.* University of Denver Press, Denver, Colorado.
Harrington, H. D.
    1954. *Manual of the Plants of Colorado.* Sage Books, Denver, Colorado.
    1967. *Edible Plants of the Rocky Mountains,* illustrated by Y. Matsumura. University of New Mexico Press, Albuquerque, N.M.
Harrington, H. D., and L. W. Durrell
    1950. *Colorado Ferns and Fern Allies, Illustrated.* Colorado Agricultural Research Foundation, Colorado A. and M. College (now Colorado State University), Ft. Collins, Colorado.
    1957. *How to Identify Plants.* Sage Books, Denver, Colorado.
Kearney, Thomas H., and others
    1960. *Arizona Flora.* University of California Press, Berkeley.
Long, John C.
    1965. *Native Orchids of Colorado.* Denver Museum of Natural History, Pictorial No. 16.
Marr, John W.
    1961. Ecosystems of the East Slope of the Front Range in Colorado. *University of Colorado Studies in Biology,* No. 8: 1-134.

McDougall, W.B.
    1964, *Grand Canyon Wild Flowers*. Museum of Northern Arizona,
        Flagstaff, Arizona.
McDougall, W.B., and Herma Baggley
    1956. *The Plants of Yellowstone National Park*. Yellowstone Library
        and Museum Association, Wyoming.
McDougall, W.B.
    1973. *Seed Plants of Northern Arizona*. Museum of Northern Arizona,
        Flagstaff, Arizona.
Matsumara, Yoshiharu, and H. D. Harrington
    1955. *The True Aquatic Vascular Plants of Colorado*. Colorado
        Agricultural and Mechanical College Technical Bulletin 57,
        Ft. Collins, Colorado.
McKean, William T. (ed.)
    1956. *Winter Guide to Native Shrubs of the Central Rocky Moun-
        tains with Summer Key*. State of Colorado, Department of
        Game and Fish, Denver.
Nelson, Aven (see also under Coulter)
    1909. *Revision of the New Manual of Botany of the Central Rocky
        Mountains,* by John M. Coulter. American Book Co., N.Y.
Nelson, Ruth Ashton
    1953. *Plants of Rocky Mountain National Park*. Government Print-
        ing Office, Washington, D.C. (New revised edition by the
        Rocky Mountain Nature Association, Estes Park, Colorado,
        1970.)
Nelson, Ruth Ashton
    1976. *Plants of Zion National Park*. Zion Natural History Association,
        Springdale, Utah, 84767
Oosting, Henry J.
    1958. *The Study of Plant Communities*. 2nd Ed. W. H. Freeman
        and Co., San Francisco.
Pesman, M. Walter
    1966. *Meet the Natives,* 7th Ed. Botanic Gardens House, Denver.
        Colorado.
Porter, C. L.
    A. *Flora of Wyoming*. In preparation. Parts I through VI
        available as separates from the Agricultural Experiment Sta-
        tion, University of Wyoming, Laramie.
Preston, Richard J.
    1940. *Rocky Mountain Trees; A Handbook of the Native Species with
        Plates and Distributional Maps*. Iowa State College Press,
        Ames.
Ramaley, Francis
    1927. *Colorado Plant Life*. University of Colorao Semicentennial
        Publications, Boulder.
Roberts, Harold D. and Rhoda Roberts
    1953. *Some Common Colorado Wild Flowers*. Denver Museum of
        Natural History, Pictorial No.8.
Roberts, Rhoda, and Ruth Ashton Nelson
    1957. *Mountain Wild Flowers of Colorado*. Denver Museum of
        Natural History, Pictorial No. 13.

Rydberg, P. A.
  1906. *Flora of Colorado.* Bulletin 100, Colorado Agricultural Experiment Station, Ft. Collins.
Rydberg, P. A., (cont.)
  1922. *Flora of the Rocky Mountain and Adjacent Plains.* Published by the author, N.Y.
Standley, P. C.
  1921. *Flora of Glacier National Park, Montana.* Contributions of the U.S. National Herbarium, Vol. 22, No. 5. Washington, D.C.
  1926. *Plants of Glacier National Park.* Government Printing Office, Washington, D.C.
Weaver, John E. and Frederic E. Clements
  1938. *Plant Ecology.* 2nd Ed. McGraw Hill Book Co., N.Y.
Weber, William A.
  1967. *Rocky Mountain Flora.* University of Colorado Press, Boulder. 5th edition, revised, 1976.
Willard, Bettie E. and C. H. Harris
  1963. *Alpine Wild Flowers of Rocky Mountain National Park.* Rocky Mountain Nature Association, Estes Park, Colorado. Revised, 1975.

Glossary

Achene. A small, hard, one-seeded, dry fruit.

Acuminate. Taper pointed. *Pl. C 27, p.* 42.

Acute. Sharp-pointed or ending in a point which is less than a right angle. *Pl. C 26,* p. 42.

Alternate. (Used of leaves, buds or branches.) Occurring singly at the nodes. *Plate A 3,* p. 40.

Ament. Same as catkin.

Anther. The essential part of the stamen, often yellow. It contains the pollen.

Appressed. Lying flat against another part.

Awl-shaped. Sharp-pointed from a broader base.

Axil. The upper angle between a leaf and the stem. *Pl. A 3,* p. 40.

Axillary. Occurring in the axils.

Axis. The central line of any body; the organ around which others are attached.

Awn. A stiff, bristlelike appendage.

Blade. The flat, expanded portion of a leaf or petal.

Bract. A much reduced leaf without a petiole and usually close below (subtending) a flower.

Bulb. A round, underground bud of fleshy, overlapping scales (leaf bases) attached to a short, flattened stem, as in onions.

Caespitose. Growing in a compact mat or tuft.

Calyx. The outer circle of perianth segments made up of sepals which may be either separate or joined, p. 44.

Capsule. A dry fruit composed of more than one carpel which splits open when ripe.

Carpel. The unit of structure of the pistil which may consist of one or more carpels.

Caudex. The persistent, woody base of an otherwise herbaceous stem.

Catkin. A scaly spike of inconspicuous flowers, as in willows. Also called an *ament.*

Ciliate. With a fringe of hairs on the margin.

Compound. Made up of from 2 to many similar parts—as a compound ovary or a compound leaf.

Conifer. A cone-bearing tree, a member of the PINE family.

Corm. The enlarged, fleshy base of a stem, bulblike but solid.

Corolla. The inner circle of perianth segments, a collective name for the petals. Commonly used when the petals are united.

Corymb. A flat or convex flower cluster, with branches arising from different levels. P. 45.

315

Cotyledon. The first or seed leaves of a plant, usually differing from the later leaves.

Crenate. (Used of margins of leaves or petals.) With rounded teeth.

Deciduous. Used of leaves which fall off at the end of one season of growth, or of petals or sepals which fall early.

Decumbent. Bent at the base of the stem and more or less leaning or lying on the ground, the tip tending to rise.

Dentate. Toothed. Having sharp teeth pointing straight out.

Dioecious. Unisexual, with two kinds of flowers on different plants.

Disk. The face of any flat body, especially the central region of a head of flowers as in the Composite Family.

Dissected. Cut deeply into many lobes or divisions.

Ecology. The study of plants in relation to other living organisms and to their environment.

Elliptical. Oval in outline.

Entire. Having the margin not at all toothed, notched or divided. P. 42.

Exserted. Protruding from, as the stamens may protrude from the corolla.

Fertile. Capable of producing seed, pollen, or sporangia.

Filament. The stalk of a stamen, or any slender, threadlike structure. P. 43.

Floret. A small flower, especially applied to the individual flowers of grasses or composites.

Frond. The leaf of a fern.

Genus. (plural, *genera.*) A group of plants made up of closely related species.

Glabrous. Completely smooth, without any kind of hairs or bristles.

Glumes. (Used in describing grasses). The outer husks or bracts of each spikelet.

Glaucous. Covered with a fine, white powder which gives foliage a bluish color.

Habitat. The situation in which a plant grows in its wild state.

Head. A short, compact inflorescence. Pp. 45-6.

Herbaceous. Applied to plants of soft texture. Used of plants whose stems die back to the ground at the end of the growing season.

Imbricated. Applied to leaves or flower parts arranged in an overlapping pattern as shingles on a roof.

Imperfect. Used in reference to flowers which lack either stamens or pistils.

Indusium. (plural, *indusia*). The very small covering over the *sorus* (fruit "dot") on many ferns.

Inferior. Applied to the ovary or seedpod when the calyx and corolla are placed on top of it. P. 43.

Inflorescence. The flowering part of a plant and especially its arrangement.

Insectivorous. Used of plants which have organs developed to digest insects.

Involucre. A whorl or set of bracts surrounding a flower, umbel or head.

Irregular. Used to describe a calyx or corolla in which the parts are not all alike, i.e. the calyx or corolla is not radially symmetrical.

Keel. Used especially to describe the boatlike structure formed by the fusing of the two lower petals in flowers of the pea family; or any projecting ridge on a surface.

Lanceolate. Lance-shaped. P. 42.

Leaflet. A segment of a compound lead.

Legume. The fruit (pod) of a member of the pea family, also a member of that family.

Lemma. The outer bract of the grass floret.

Lenticels. Wartlike, usually light-colored spots on the bark of tree or shrubs.

Lenticular. Lentil-shaped (convex on both sides).

Ligulate. Tongue or strap-shaped.

Linear. Narrow and flat, the margins parallel. P. 42.

Lobe. A division of a leaf, especially a rounded one; also divisions of a united corolla.

-merous. Refers to the number of flower parts, i.e., a flower having 5 sepals, 5 petals, 5 carpels, and 5 stamens is 5-merous. P. 48.

Monocotyledonous. Used of plants having only one seed leaf.

Node. A point on a stem from which one or more leaves arise. P. 40.

Nodding. Used of flowers or buds that hang down.

Obovate. The broad end upward; reversed egg-shaped. P. 42.

Opposite. Applied to leaves and branches when an opposing pair occurs at each node. P. 40.

Ovary. The part of the pistil that contains the ovules and ripens into the "seedpod." P. 43.

Ovate. Shaped like a section through a hen's egg with the broader end downwards. P. 42.

Palmate. Applied to a leaf whose leaflets, divisions, or main ribs all spread from the apex of the petiole, like a hand with outspread fingers. P. 41.

Panicle. A type of repeatedly branched inflorescence with flowers on pedicels. P. 45.

Papilionaceous. Butterfly, flowers as in the pea family with standard, wings and keel.

Parasitic. An organism which depends on living tissue of another living organism for a source of food.

Pedicel. The stalk of each individual flower of a cluster. P. 43.

Peduncle. A flower stalk, whether of a single flower or of a cluster.

Perfect. Used of flowers which have both pistils and stamens. The calyx and corolla are not necessarily present.

Perianth. A collective name for the sepals and petals, especially when the two sets are not easily distinguished.

Petal. One of the inner perianth segments, usually colored and more or less showy. *Pl. D 29.* P. 43.

Petaloid. Petallike, resembling or colored like petals.

Petiole. The stalk of an individual leaf. P. 41.

Phyllaries. Bracts, especially those making up the involucre of composites. *Pl. G,* P. 46, 268.

Pinna (plural, *pinnae*). A primary division of a fern frond. P. 41.

Pinnate. Used of leaves having leaflets disposed along the main axis of the leaf; also a type of leaf veining where the secondary veins arise from a midrib (like a feather). P. 41.

Pinnatifid. Cut into lobes or divisions that are pinnately arranged.

Pistil. The female, or seed-bearing organ of the flower, made up of *ovary, style,* and *stigma.* P. 43.

Pistillate. Having pistils but no functional stamens; female.

Pollen. The grains or *spores* in the anther which contain the male element. These must reach the *stigma* in order for pollination and fertilization to take place.

Plumose. Plumed or feathery.

Pubescence. A covering of fine soft hairs.

Pubescent. Covered with short hairs.

Raceme. A type of elongated inflorescence in which the stalked *(pedicelled),* flowers are arranged singly along a central axis. P. 45.

Rachis. The axis (to which other parts are attached), of a compound leaf or of the inflorescence; the stalk of a fern frond.

Radiate. Used of composites which have *ray* flowers.

Ray. The marginal flower of a head or cluster when different from the rest, especially when *ligulate.*

Receptacle. The more or less enlarged top of the stalk to which other parts are attached. *Pl. D 29.* P. 43.

Regular. Radially symmetrical, used to describe a calyx or corolla in which all the parts are similar. p. 44.

Rhizome. Underground stem.

Rootstalk. Underground stem, rhizome.

Rotate. Wheel-shaped, applied to flat, open corollas. P. 44.

Salverform. A type of corolla with a slender tube and an abruptly expanded *limb.* P. 44.

Saprophytic. Used to describe plants which live on decayed vegetable matter such as rotted wood or leaf mold. They have small or no green parts.

Seed. A ripened ovule; it contains an embryo.

Sepal. One of the separate parts of the *calyx,* usually green but may be petallike. P. 43-4.

Serrate. With margin cut into teeth pointing forward; like teeth on a saw. *Pl. C 21.* P. 42.

Sessile. Without any stalk, as a leaf without a petiole, a flower without a pedicel, or an anther without a filament. P. 40.

Simple. Said of a leaf when not compound, of a stem when not branched. P. 41.

Sorus (plural *sori*). The fruit dots usually found on the under side of fruiting fern fronds.

Spatulate. Gradually narrowed downwards from a rounded summit. p. 42.

Spathe. The bract or leaf surrounding or subtending a flower cluster.

Species. A group containing all the individuals of a particular kind of plant.

Spike. An inflorescence in which the flowers are *sessile* on a more or less elongated common axis. P. 45.

Spikelet. (in grasses and sedges) the smallest flower cluster in an inflorescence, usually forming a distinct and compact unit.

Spore. A simple reproductive body, usually nearly microscopic in size.

Sporangia. The structure which contains spores.

Stamen. The pollen bearing organ, made up of the *filament* and *anther*. P. 43.

Staminode. A sterile stamen.

Staminate. Having stamens but no pistil.

Sterile. Lacking functional sex organs.

Stigma. The part of the pistil that receives the pollen. P. 43.

Stipe. A stalk.

Stipitate. Having a *stipe*.

Stipules. Appendages at the base of the petiole of a leaf. P. 41.

Style. If the stigma is raised above the ovary the connecting portion is the style. P. 43.

Submersed. Said of plants or their parts when growing under water.

Subtend. To occur below.

Succulent. Used of plants or their parts which are fleshy and juicy, usually thickened.

Tendril. A slender, clasping or twining outgrowth of stems or leaves.

Tuber. A short, thickened structure, usually part of a stem and usually underground.

Tundra. The vegetation type found above timberline either in the arctic or on high mountains.

Umbel. A type of inflorescence in which all the rays (branches) originate at the same point, umbrellalike. P. 45.

Unisexual. Having only either female or male flowers.

Venation. The type of arrangement of veins, usually used in referring to leaves. P. 41.

Whorl. A circle or ring of organs, especially a leaf arrangement where three or more arise from the same node. *Pl. A 6.* P. 40.

Wing. A thin, usually dry extension of an organ or structure; the lateral petals of a flower of the pea family.

Woody. Of firm texture; applied to plant parts above ground which remain alive from season to season.

Index

320

NOTES

NOTES

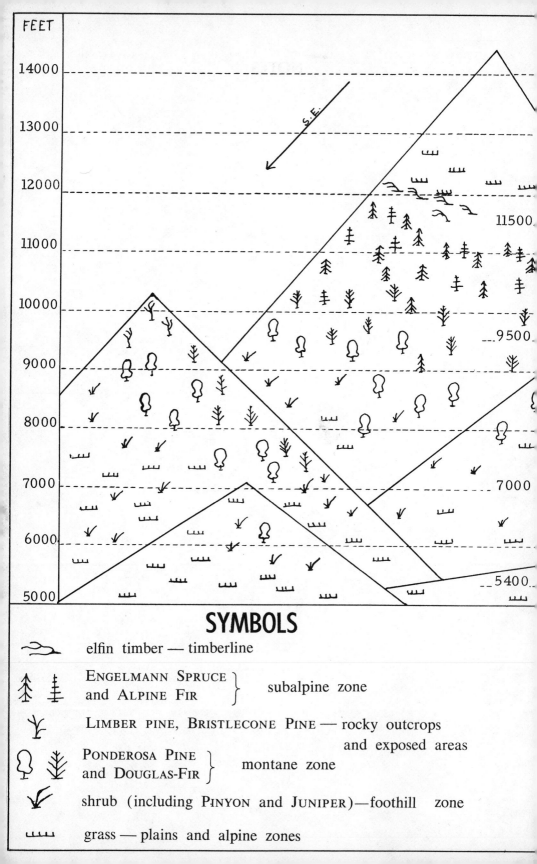

FEET

14000

13000

S.E.

12000

11500

11000

10000

9500

9000

8000

7000

7000

6000

5400

5000

SYMBOLS

elfin timber — timberline

ENGELMANN SPRUCE and ALPINE FIR } subalpine zone

LIMBER PINE, BRISTLECONE PINE — rocky outcrops and exposed areas

PONDEROSA PINE and DOUGLAS-FIR } montane zone

shrub (including PINYON and JUNIPER) — foothill zone

grass — plains and alpine zones